...you make my head spin

On her wrist gleams the new Longines PrimaLuna.
A study in curvaceous allure, her watch salutes the
new moon, symbol of renewal. Elegant to its soul,
contemporary in style, the Longines PrimaLuna collection
opens its bewitching universe to women everywhere.

LONG

HUBLOT

GENEVE

KING POWER

Full 18K King Gold and Rubber Case
with Skeleton Tourbillon Chronograph.

WATCHES INTERNATIONAL®

THE ORIGINAL ANNUAL OF THE WORLD'S FINEST WRISTWATCHES

First published in the United States in 2010 by

TOURBILLON INTERNATIONAL
A MODERN LUXURY MEDIA, LLC COMPANY
11 West 25th Street, 8th Floor
New York, NY 10010
Tel: +1 (212) 627-7732   Fax +1 (312) 274-8418
www.modernluxury.com/watches

CHIEF EXECUTIVE OFFICER
Bill Cobert

CHIEF OPERATING OFFICER
Michael Lipson

PUBLISHER
Caroline Childers

EDITOR IN CHIEF
Michel Jeannot

SENIOR VICE PRESIDENT OF FINANCE
John Pietrolungo

In association with **RIZZOLI**
INTERNATIONAL PUBLICATIONS, INC.

300 Park Avenue South, New York, NY 10010

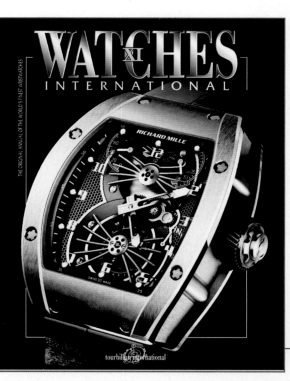

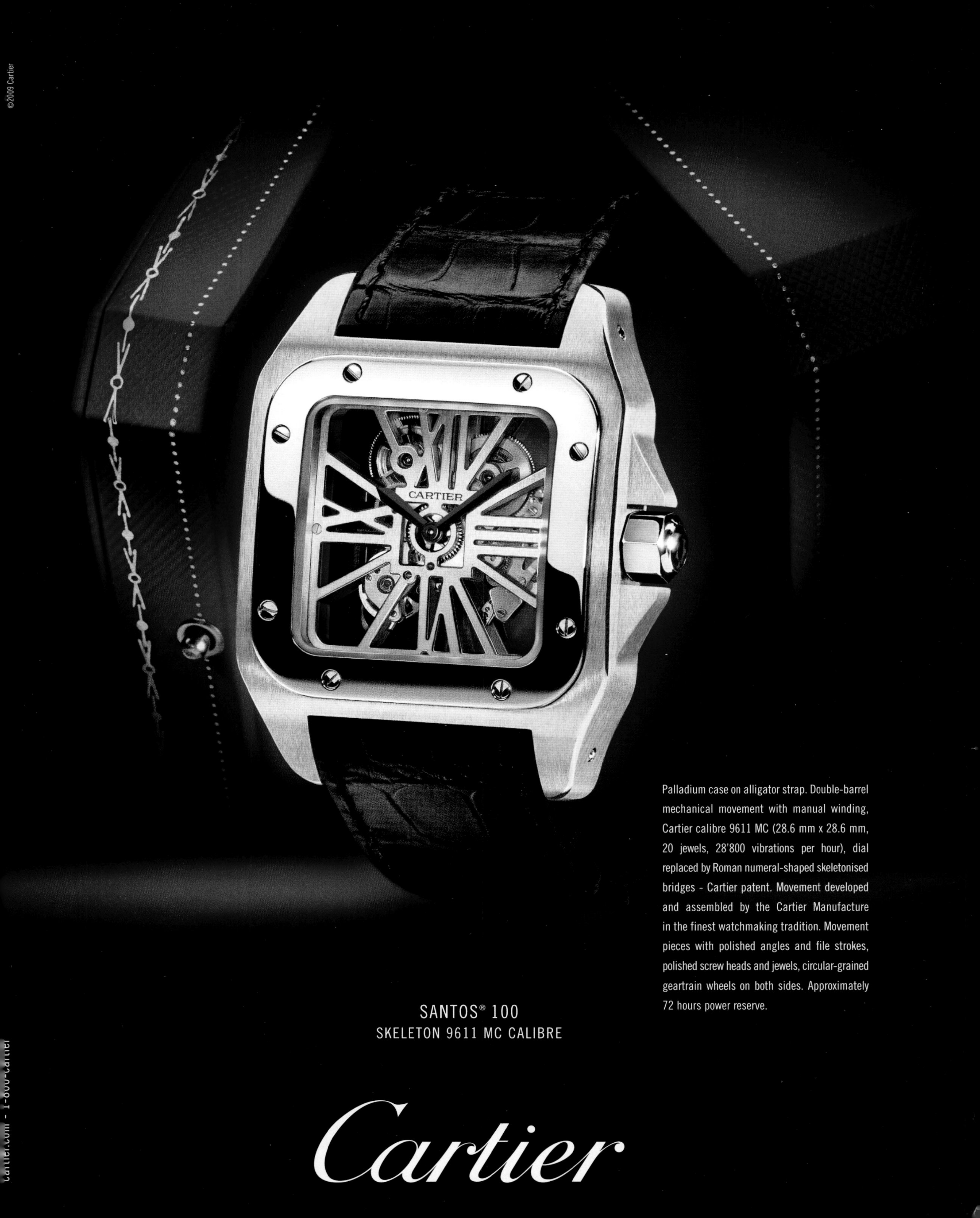

©2009 Cartier
Palladium case on alligator strap. Double-barrel mechanical movement with manual winding, Cartier calibre 9611 MC (28.6 mm x 28.6 mm, 20 jewels, 28'800 vibrations per hour), dial replaced by Roman numeral-shaped skeletonised bridges - Cartier patent. Movement developed and assembled by the Cartier Manufacture in the finest watchmaking tradition. Movement pieces with polished angles and file strokes, polished screw heads and jewels, circular-grained geartrain wheels on both sides. Approximately 72 hours power reserve.
SANTOS® 100
SKELETON 9611 MC CALIBRE
cartier.com - 1-800-Cartier
Cartier

Watch in black high-tech ceramic and 18K yellow gold. Self-winding mechanical movement custom-made by AUDEMARS PIGUET
exclusively for CHANEL: CHANEL - AP3125 (40 jewels, 21'600 vibrations/hour).
Rotor in black high-tech ceramic with a segment in rhodium-plated 22K yellow gold mounted on high-tech ceramic ball bearings.
Balance with 8 giromax regulating weights. 60-hour power reserve.

CHANEL

J 12

CALIBRE
3125

The Power of Seduction
Endures

by Michel Jeannot

Despite these troubled times, which have shaken the global economy to the core over the last several months, certain economic sectors are still vibrant, one of them being horology. Though the industry definitely has been affected by the bleak situation, it has managed to hold on to its power of seduction. The unique attraction exercised by luxury watchmaking and its exceptional products is interesting in several ways, as it reveals the distinctive nature of this industry that so skillfully combines tradition and innovation, hand-crafted artisanship and the latest technologies. This subtle alchemy allows the most prestigious brands to attain the highest reaches of art while using the most sophisticated machines to make that everyday object, the watch, ever more reliable.

The artistic dimension of horology, which goes far beyond the simple notion of telling time, is a rare phenomenon in the luxury industry. But with the dissemination of information to more and more people in all regions of the world—and *Watches International* is proud to have contributed to this trend for more than a decade—the artistic element of horology has moved to the forefront, touching traditional art and artistic expression. Watch lovers now regard the purchase of a watch in much the same way they would the acquisition of a painting. Continuing down this path, horology prepares for a brilliant future in which it will always have the power to make us dream...

The Limited Edition Ralph Lauren Stirrup Watch

950 PLATINUM. LARGE MODEL WITH ENAMEL DIAL. 67 PIECES INDIVIDUALLY ENGRAVED. MANUFACTURE MOVEMENT.
SELF-WINDING CHRONOGRAPH. 261 COMPONENTS, 41 JEWELS, 48-HOUR POWER RESERVE. SWISS MADE.

NEW YORK   LONDON   PARIS   MILAN   TOKYO   GREENWICH   CANNES   ST MORITZ   GSTAAD   MACAU

RALPHLAURENWATCHES.COM

cellini

When Cellini Jewelers opened in the lobby of the Waldorf-Astoria in 1977, it arrived at a time when Americans were rediscovering the art of watchmaking. More than a fashion statement, for some the survival of mechanical watches signified a gentle pushback against the rapid proliferation of quartz clocks and a longing for handmade authenticity amid a mass-production society.

Many of those early collectors found a kindred spirit in Cellini's president Leon Adams, whose appreciation for rare timepieces and demanding standards echoed their own. Early on, his showcases were home to rare editions from venerable firms and inventions from exclusive ateliers.

Guests who frequented Cellini in those early years witnessed the mechanical watch industry undergo a rapid renaissance. Advances in computer-aided design and production redefined what was possible in the realms of mechanics and aesthetics, from fine-tuning performance to expanding imaginations.

The next generation of timepieces resonated among collectors, whose ranks grew steadily in the '80s. To keep apace of the growing thirst for fine watchmaking, Cellini added a boutique on New York's Madison Avenue in 1987. Today, the two locations combine to form one of the world's largest and most prestigious collections of timepieces from Europe's historic manufactures and independent watchmakers.

**Chapter Two
(Maîtres du Temps)**

Blue Blazes: Sapphires and diamonds artfully set in platinum.

RAISING THE BAR

That well-edited selection has elevated Cellini's reputation among the industry's cognoscenti, making it an influential arbiter of style and an important proving ground for rising watch brands. In fact, a number of successful brands first found a home in the U.S. at Cellini, where collectors were introduced to A. Lange & Söhne, Guy Ellia, H. Moser & Cie., Maîtres du Temps, and of course Audemars Piguet, which was part of Cellini's collection from the start.

Through the years, watchmakers have recognized Cellini's influence and created limited editions exclusively for the independent jeweler. Companies like Panerai, Jaeger-LeCoultre and IWC are among the most recent brands to honor Cellini with special timepieces.

Today, these watchmakers are cornerstones of a collection dominated by watch brands with strong and varied personalities. "One of our biggest strengths is that our collection never stops changing and growing," Adams says. "We'll always make room for a brand that has a fresh look or is technically advanced. I'm not afraid to take a chance on a new brand if it's one I believe in."

Adams's attention to the smallest detail extends to the service provided by the watch experts at Cellini. Welcoming and fluent in the eccentricities of high horology, they are available to answer questions about both the art and value of mechanical timepieces.

"Most people ask: 'Am I going to love this watch two years from now?' and 'Will this watch be an asset in the future?' It's our responsibility to help them find the right answers," says Abe Azaria, a Cellini watch specialist. "To do that, we ask questions to get a sense of the person and offer them guidance based on their answers and our own experiences. That honest approach is why clients trust our opinions and keep coming back."

Perpetual Calendar
Chronograph
(Vacheron Constantin)

CELLINI JEWELERS

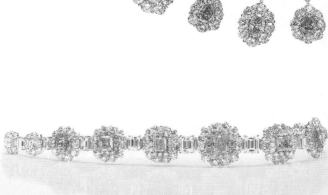

Symphony of Color: These one-of-a-kind pieces highlight Cellini's vast assortment of natural color diamonds with an extraordinary array of pink, blue, green, orange, and yellow stones.

GOTHAM GLAMOUR

For those who prefer haute couture to haute horlogerie, sparkling scintillation beckons from Cellini's windows, tempting passers-by with a breathtaking array of jewelry that ranks among New York City's best.

Adams maintains the jewelry collection's reputation for excellence by personally choosing each gemstone featured in Cellini's one-of-a-kind pieces. "We've earned people's trust and I take that responsibility very seriously. Clients expect an impeccably high standard and I make sure we exceed their expectations."

From elegant understatement to over-the-top glitz, imagination is the only limit when it comes to creating custom jewelry, says Lauren Goldsmith, the company's certified gemologist. "Starting with a simple drawing or an idea, we can design something tailored to the individual's unique style. Another advantage of custom jewelry is that it's properly proportioned to fit the client's features. That personalized sizing is what makes a piece truly look and feel one-of-a-kind."

Skilled at restoring everything from family heirlooms to sentimental favorites, Cellini's workshop can also redesign an existing piece. "People still enjoy handing down jewelry to their children, but that tradition has changed," Goldsmith explains. "One woman wanted to give her mother's ring to her daughter, but she knew her daughter wouldn't like the antique setting. We suggested she use the ring's three diamonds to make a necklace for herself and earrings for her daughter. What's old is new again."

After just one visit, it's easy to see why any conversation about the world's finest jewelry and best watches would be incomplete without Cellini.

STORE LOCATIONS

Hotel Waldorf-Astoria • 301 Park Avenue at 50th Street • New York, NY 10022
tel: 212-751-9824

509 Madison Avenue at 53rd Street • New York, NY 10022
tel: 212-888-0505

800-CELLINI • www.CelliniJewelers.com

BRANDS CARRIED

A. Lange & Söhne	H. Moser & Cie.
Audemars Piguet	Hublot
Bell & Ross	IWC
Cartier	Jaeger-LeCoultre
Chopard	Jean Dunand
Daniel Roth	Maîtres du Temps
De Bethune	Panerai
DeWitt	Parmigiani Fleurier
F.P. Journe	Piaget
Franck Muller	Richard Mille
Gérald Genta	Ulysse Nardin
Girard-Perregaux	Vacheron Constantin
Guy Ellia	

RICHARD MILLE
A RACING MACHINE ON THE WRIST

**Grand Prix d'Horlogerie
de Genève**

Prix de la Montre Sport · 2009

GPdH Asia

Best ladies watch 2009

GPHG Asia

Traiblazer award 2008

RICHARD MILLE

CALIBER RM 025
CHRONOGRAPH DIVER'S WATCH

Manual winding tourbillon movement
Carbon nanofiber baseplate
Chronograph (Column wheel in titanium)
Power reserve : circa 50 hours
Torque indicator
Power reserve indicator
Function indicator
Variable inertia, free sprung balance with overcoil
New in-line escapement design
Fast rotating barrel
(6 hours per revolution instead of 7.5 hours)
Winding barrel teeth and third-wheel pinion
with central involute profile
Barrel pawl with progressive recoil
Modular time setting mechanism fitted against the case back
Torque limiting crown
Wheel based time setting system (back of the movement)
Closure of the barrel cover using excentric screws
Spline screws in grade 5 titanium for the bridges and case
Bezel turning unidirectionally following ISO 6425 norm
300 meter water resistant case in titanium and red gold

Letter from the Publisher

Do you know what time it is?

At the end of 2008, watchmakers' hearts skipped a beat—or several—and many wondered if it was just passing indigestion or the start of something more serious. Since the turn of the millennium, horology had been undergoing an unprecedented expansion, eventually being faced with just one problem: how to produce and deliver all the watches that were being ordered. The shortage of manpower stretched delays ever longer, and the industry's biggest names were worried only by the thought of missing out on sales…What a lucky industry to face just one challenge: running fast enough to meet demand! Let's remember that very few sectors are confronted with the same challenges.

Eighteen months later, the times have changed, and naturally many are longing for the "difficulties" of yesteryear. In that time, the global economic crisis hit horology with sudden overwhelming force and everyone—clients, retailers and brands—has returned to more reasoned behavior. So, after a slightly tarnished 2009, the global situation has improved on the horological front. The first big salons of the year have shown that, even though no one is expecting the industry to take off again at full speed, the hardest part is most surely over. Now is the time for reconstruction, for a new confidence and for cautious optimism.

In Asia, the frenzy for the most beautiful timepieces has begun to simmer again, allowing the quickest companies to produce respectable results. Of course Asia alone has not compensated for the many other weak regions around the globe, but it has greatly softened the blow to the industry. Many believe that this positive trend, especially in China, will remain a source of growth for horology. After a difficult 2009, Europe seems to be regaining its footing slowly, though the situation is quite different from one country to the next. In Eastern Europe, countries that had achieved an impressive leap forward suffered through an equally dramatic slamming of the brakes. But even there, the forecast seems to be looking up. As for the United States—long the most important market for high-end watchmaking—the recession that affected absolutely everyone in 2009 seems to be lifting. At the same time, watchmakers' hearts seem to be beating at a steadier rhythm once again and haute horology's EKG is looking healthier and healthier to the great happiness of all passionate watch lovers.

Caroline Childers

eau" chrono watch,
matic movement,
• in Barénia calf.

HERMÈS
PARIS

HERMÈS, LiFE AS A TALE

INFORMATION:
00-441-4488

CONCORD

OTHERS WILL FOLLOW

MOVADO

THE ART OF DESIGN

introducing movado master™. stainless steel with black sapphire bezel, rubber strap. automatic movement with
exhibition case-back. at movado boutiques and select fine retailers nationwide. visit movado.com for locations.

Letter from the Editor in Chief

True Values

Haute horology underwent one of the nastiest shocks in its history in 2009. After a string of very successful years, the setback was even harder to deal with because no one thought such a reversal of fortune was even possible. At this point, when the situation seems to have stabilized and the sun seems to be shining once again on the horological front, what lessons can we (or should we) draw from this crisis? The oblivious will say that we should just carry on as before, and the crisis now in the history books won't happen again. We'll see. The risk of another crisis will only grow if we learn nothing from the last one.

Globally, the overheated growth in the years leading up to mid-2008 led to all kinds of excess. When virtually anything could easily find a taker, established brands sometimes got caught up in the insanity. At the same time, many new arrivals saw watchmaking as the next El Dorado, and some dove into the business completely ignorant of what it entailed. Some of the newcomers managed to carve out a spot for themselves, but others were quickly disenchanted. Watchmaking is not an easy business; the production processes are often extremely complex, involving several different agents and just as many (or more) obstacles to overcome, as any recently established watchmaker can tell you—that is, if the company is still in business. This leads to the question raised at this point, as we emerge from the crisis: who is no longer with us?

The list of defunct retailers is a long one, and many of the survivors have had to reduce their offerings drastically due to insufficient liquidity. For the watchmaking brands, the view is often uneven, but cash still dictates the terms of business. Some companies, with a comfortable cushion of savings, can stick it out, waiting for better times to return, while others, short on money, haven't been so fortunate. The most striking trend of the crisis has been bearing down on the industry with uncontestable logic: the weakest have gotten weaker and the strongest have gotten stronger. This is rather reassuring for the true watch lovers, who have used their knowledge and discernment to concentrate on true values, whether it is the traditional and well-established houses, or one of the rare younger brands that has truly brought a fresh outlook to haute horology.

Michel Jeannot

CHIFFRE ROUGE D02 MODEL
BLACK AUTOMATIC WATCH. DIVING FUNCTIONS.
BLACK SUNBRUSHED DIAL WITH LUMINESCENT INDEXES AND NUMBERS. SCREW-
IN-CROWN AND ARM PROTECTING CROWN. TURNING BEZEL. 300M WATERPROOF.
CALIBRE ETA 2824. FREQUENCY OF BALANCE WHEEL: 28 800 VIBRATIONS PER HOUR.
POWER RESERVE: 42 HOURS. 42MM CASE AND BRACELET IN 316L STAINLESS STEEL
SHEATHED IN RUBBER. RED TINTED SAPPHIRE CRYSTAL.   WWW.DIOR.COM

1860 —————————————————— 1916 ——————

PIONEERING SWISS WATCHMAKING
FOR 150 YEARS

1860   Edouard Heuer founded his workshop in the Swiss Jura.
1916   First mechanical stopwatch accurate to 1/100th of a second.
1969   First automatic chronograph.
2010   TAG Heuer CARRERA Calibre 16 Day Date.

1969 —————————————————— 2010 ——————

SWISS AVANT-GARDE SINCE 1860

INTERNATIONAL®

THE ORIGINAL ANNUAL OF THE WORLD'S FINEST WRISTWATCHES

TOURBILLON INTERNATIONAL
A MODERN LUXURY MEDIA, LLC COMPANY
ADMINISTRATION, ADVERTISING SALES, EDITORIAL, BOOK SALES

11 West 25th Street, 8th Floor
New York, NY 10010
Tel: +1 (212) 627-7732   Fax: +1 (312) 274-8418

CHIEF EXECUTIVE OFFICER
Bill Cobert

CHIEF OPERATING OFFICER
Michael Lipson

PUBLISHER
Caroline Childers

EDITOR IN CHIEF
Michel Jeannot

EDITOR
Elizabeth Kindt

ASSOCIATE EDITOR
Claire Loeb

CONTRIBUTING EDITORS
Fabrice Eschmann
Scott Hickey
Elise Nussbaum

TRANSLATIONS
Susan Jacquet

ART DIRECTOR
Mutsumi Hyuga

INTERNATIONAL ART DIRECTOR OF PRE-PRESS AND PRODUCTION
Franca Vitali - Grafica Effe

COORDINATION
Caroline Pita

VICE PRESIDENT OF PRODUCTION
Meg Eulberg

VICE PRESIDENT OF MANUFACTURING
Sean Bertram

SENIOR VICE PRESIDENT OF FINANCE
John Pietrolungo

VICE PRESIDENT OF AUDIENCE DEVELOPMENT
Eric Holden

WEBMASTER
Jade Chang

WEB DISTRIBUTION
www.modernluxury.com/watches

PHOTOGRAPHERS
Photographic Archives
Property of Tourbillon International,
a Modern Luxury Media, LLC company

FOUNDED IN 1755, ON AN ISLAND IN LAKE GENEVA. AND STILL THERE.

17th of September 1755. In the offices of the solicitor Mr. Choisy, a young Master Watchmaker from Geneva named Jean-Marc Vacheron is about to hire his first apprentice. This agreement is the first known reference to the founding watchmaker of a prestigious dynasty and it represents the establishment of Vacheron Constantin, the oldest watchmaking manufacturer in the world in continuous operation.

Ever since this agreement, and true to the history that built its reputation, Vacheron Constantin has been committed to passing on its knowledge to each of its Master Watchmakers in order to guarantee the excellence and durability of its craftsmanship and of its timepieces.

Patrimony Traditionnelle Calibre 2755
Hallmark of Geneva, Pink gold case, Hand-wound mechanical movement, Minute-repeater, Tourbillon, Perpetual calendar
Réf. 80172/000R-9300

VACHERON CONSTANTIN
Manufacture Horlogère, Genève, depuis 1755.

INSTRUMENTO
Nº UNO

de GRISOGONO
GENEVE

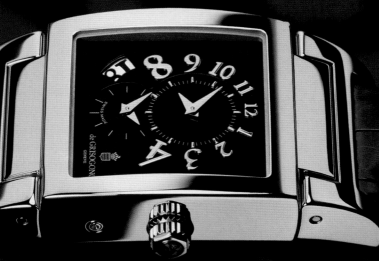

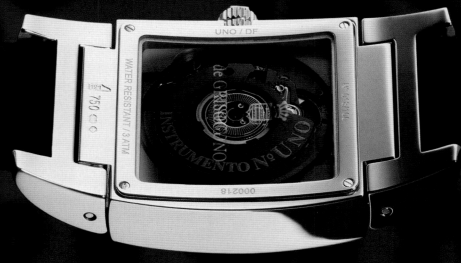

⊙Westime

For two decades, Westime has distinguished itself as the ultimate retail destination for finding extraordinary watches. Throughout those 20 years, Westime has earned the return business of discriminating clients from around the globe who value Westime's extraordinary service as well as its watch selection.

Westime's two elegant boutiques create the perfect settings for watch shopping. At its original location, a 6,000-square-foot showroom at Los Angeles's Westside Pavilion, Westime features a wide range of brands at every price point. Within the boutique are expansive showcases, comfortable seating arrangements and two specialty boutiques. Two full-time master watchmakers are on site at all times and utilize state-of-the-art equipment for service and repairs. In Beverly Hills, Westime's intimate, multilevel boutique resides at the heart of the city's most glamorous shopping district. Here, connoisseurs and fashionistas alike will find the most sought-after timepieces in the world.

Westime prides itself on offering highly regarded and rare watches. Limited editions, unique pieces, and even custom models created exclusively for Westime take pride of place in the boutiques' showcases. Westime is frequently selected by brands to carry their most complicated timepieces on an exclusive basis.

From day one, Westime has also dedicated itself to seeking the new guard in haute horology by presenting the finest creations of contemporary watchmakers. Three brands stand powerfully for the new watchmaking vanguard. Richard Mille is regarded as the master of materials that are redefining the vocabulary of luxury; Greubel Forsey hails as a tourbillon revolutionary; and URWERK has emerged as the master of kinetic sculpture.

THIS PAGE
UR-202 (URWERK)

FACING PAGE
Westime boutique on Rodeo Drive in Beverly Hills.

Westime boutique on West
Pico Boulevard, Los Angeles

BRANDS CARRIED

A. Lange & Söhne	Hautlence
Alain Silberstein	HD3
Audemars Piguet	Hermès
Baume & Mercier	Hublot
Bell & Ross	Ikepod
Blancpain	IWC
Bovet	Longines
Breguet	MB&F
Breitling	MCT
Chanel	Milus
Chopard	Nubeo
Concord	Omega
Corum	Richard Mille
DeWitt	Roland Iten
Dimier	Mechanical Luxury
Dior Phones	Romain Jerome
Ebel	TAG Heuer
F.P. Journe	TAG Heuer Meridiist
Franck Muller	Tissot
Gérald Genta	URWERK
Girard-Perregaux	Vacheron Constantin
Glashütte Original	Vertu
Greubel Forsey	Vincent Bérard
Guy Ellia	Wyler Genève
Hamilton	Zenith
Harry Winston	

Westime hosts unique customer events to introduce preferred clients to the newest watches, or to meet the owners, presidents and even master watchmakers of some of the key brands.

Founded 20 years ago, Westime is owned by a third-generation watch connoisseur with a passion for mechanical timepieces and a true love of the business; now, the fourth generation is taking an instrumental role in Westime's future. Every member of Westime's affable, multi-lingual staff is dedicated to providing exceptional service—from explaining the specifics of complications, to hand-delivering a watch across the country.

The purchase of a watch from Westime marks only the beginning of a relationship. "We believe fine timepieces should be a source of pleasure, not frustration, to our clients. Should a watch require service, we strive to ensure that it is done as expeditiously as possible and with the highest level of skill," says Barbara Simonian, co-founder of Westime. "Of course, our close relationship with the unique and sophisticated brands, whom it is our privilege to represent, helps ensure the quality communication and impeccable service our clients have come to expect."

STORE LOCATIONS

10800 West Pico Blvd., #197 • Los Angeles, CA 90064
tel: 310-470-1388 • fax: 310-475-0628

254 North Rodeo Drive • Beverly Hills, CA 90210
tel: 310-271-0000 • fax: 310-271-3091

www.westime.com

RM 028
(Richard Mille)

Chopard

Time, incomparably crafted

L.U.C Tourbillon Titanium SL. Chopard provides spectacular new proof of both its technical know-how and its undeniable flair for design. This super-light (SL) model features a case made in titanium that is remarkably sturdy, corrosion-resistant and biocompatible. Meanwhile, the filigree-worked tourbillon carriage, crafted from aluminium using cutting-edge expertise, weighs two and a half times less than its steel equivalent. Composed of 222 parts in all, of which 62 for the tourbillon alone, the resulting ultra-precise COSC-certified movement is powered by Chopard's famous "L.U.C Quattro" four-barrel technology. The exhibition case-back, the delicate applique carrying the hour, minute and seconds markers, as well as the tourbillon bridge itself, are all crafted from transparent sapphire crystal serving to highlight the beauty of the intricate mechanism within. Meanwhile, exquisite blued steel hands set the stunningly pure and infinitely expressive finishing touch to the face of this miniature marvel.

L.U.C
MANUFACTURE DE HAUTE HORLOGERIE
LOUIS-ULYSSE CHOPARD

L.U.C Tourbillon Titanium SL: available in a limited numbered series of 100, ref. 168502-3001.

Summary

PIAGET POLO
FortyFive

Piaget Manufacture movement 880P

Mechanical self-winding chronograph

Flyback, dual time

100 meter water resistant

Titanium, sapphire case-back

Rubber strap

www.piagetpolo.com

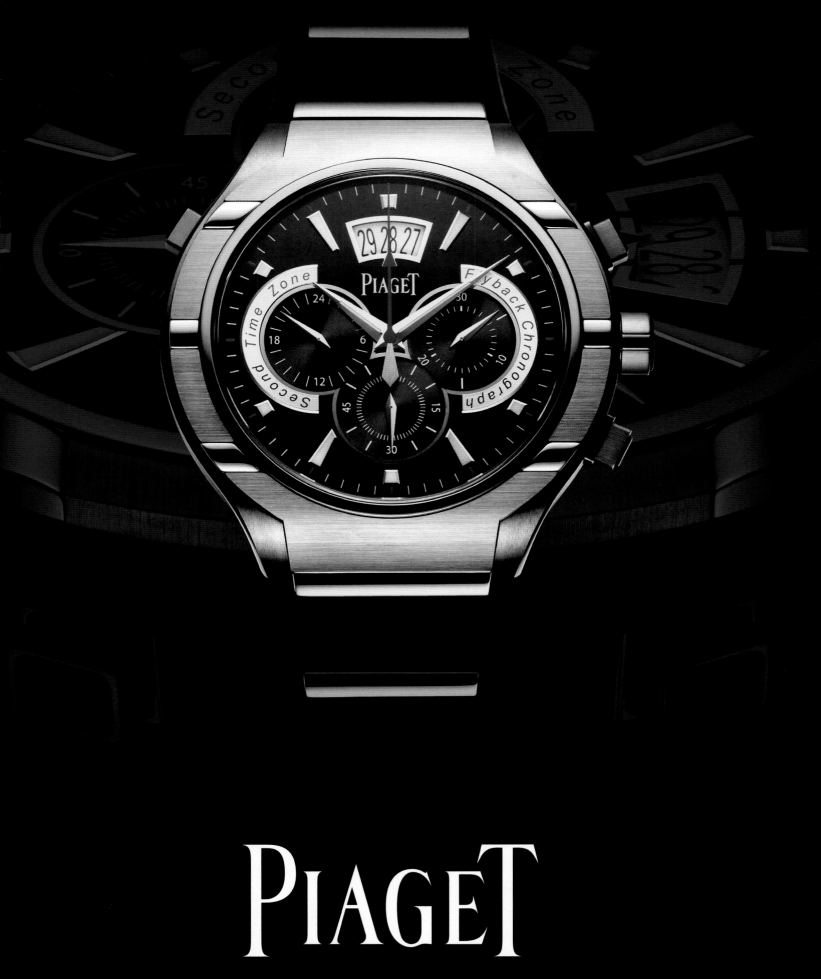

Web Site Directory

A. LANGE & SÖHNE	www.alange-soehne.com
ALAIN SILBERSTEIN	www.a-silberstein.fr
ALPINA	www.alpina-watches.com
AUDEMARS PIGUET	www.audemarspiguet.com
B.R.M	www.brm-manufacture.com
BELL & ROSS	www.bellross.com
BERTOLUCCI	www.bertolucci-watches.com
BLANCPAIN	www.blancpain.com
BOUCHERON	www.boucheron.com
BOVET	www.bovet.com
BREGUET	www.breguet.com
CARL F. BUCHERER	www.carl-f-bucherer.com
CARTIER	www.cartier.com
CHANEL	www.chanel.com
CHOPARD	www.chopard.com
CLERC	www.clercwatches.com
CONCORD	www.concord.ch
CORUM	www.corum.ch
CUERVO Y SOBRINOS	www.cuervoysobrinos.com
DE GRISOGONO	www.degrisogono.com
DIOR HORLOGERIE	www.diorhorlogerie.com
EBEL	www.ebel.com
ETERNA	www.eterna.ch
FRANC VILA	www.francvila.com
FRÉDÉRIQUE CONSTANT	www.frederique-constant.com
GREUBEL FORSEY	www.greubelforsey.com
GUY ELLIA	www.guyellia.com
H. MOSER & CIE.	www.h-moser.com
HERMÈS	www.hermes.com
HUBLOT	www.hublot.com
IWC	www.iwc.com
JACOB & CO.	www.jacobandco.com
LEVIEV	www.leviev.com
LONGINES	www.longines.com
LOUIS MOINET	www.louismoinet.com
MCT	www.mctwatches.com
MONTBLANC	www.montblanc.com

MOVADO	www.movado.com
PANERAI	www.panerai.com
PATEK PHILIPPE	www.patek.com
PIAGET	www.piaget.com
PORSCHE DESIGN	www.porsche-design.com
RALPH LAUREN	www.ralphlauren.com
RAYMOND WEIL	www.raymond-weil.com
RICHARD MILLE	www.richardmille.com
ROLEX	www.rolex.com
SALVATORE FERRAGAMO	www.ferragamo.com
TAG HEUER	www.tagheuer.com
ULYSSE NARDIN	www.ulysse-nardin.com
URWERK	www.urwerk.com
VACHERON CONSTANTIN	www.vacheron-constantin.com
VALENTINO	www.valentino.com
VERSACE	www.versace.com
VINCENT BÉRARD	www.vincentberard.ch
ZANNETTI	www.zannettiwatches.it
ZENITH	www.zenith-watches.com

RELATED SITES

BASELWORLD	www.baselworld.com
SIHH	www.sihh.ch
BULGARI GROUP	ir.bulgari.com
GUCCI GROUP	www.guccigroup.com
LVMH GROUP	www.lvmh.fr
MOVADO GROUP, INC.	www.movadogroup.com
PPR GROUP	www.ppr.com
RICHEMONT GROUP	www.richemont.com
SWATCH GROUP	www.swatchgroup.com
TIMEX GROUP	www.timexgroup.com

AUCTION HOUSES

CHRISTIE'S	www.christies.com
SOTHEBY'S	www.sothebys.com

"Reflet XL" Watch

BOUCHERON
PARIS

POWER
in Numbers

by Michel Jeannot

Following watchmaking's quartz crisis, the 1990s' wave of consolidation in the industry gave rise to a few dominant giants of the industry. Over the last few years, however, it has been the specialized subcontractors that have interested the leading lights of the industry—which is entirely understandable, given their mastery of the field.

TOP   Monaco 4 (TAG Heuer)

ABOVE   Double Tourbillon (Breguet)

LEFT   Lange Zeitwerk (A. Lange & Söhne)

For Stéphane Marchand, author of *Les guerres du luxe* (The Luxury Wars), the key date in this universe was the day before the tragedy of September 11, 2001, "the day peace was signed between Moët Hennessy Louis Vuitton (LVMH) and Pinault-Printemps-Redoute (PPR), ending their war over the conquest of Gucci. Since 1999, this struggle for dominance had led to a frenzy of mergers, acquisitions, and purchases of brands at completely insane prices. The peace between LVMH and PPR put an end to this unique period in the history of luxury."

As background, remember that these transactions culminated in 2000 with Richemont's purchase from Mannesmann-VDO of Les Manufactures Horlogères (IWC, A. Lange & Söhne, Jaeger-LeCoultre) for 3.2 billion Swiss francs. LVMH had been extremely interested in this acquisition, since the most prominent luxury group in the world had joined the ranks of haute horology after entering the sector with its 1999 purchases of TAG Heuer and Zenith, as well as Ebel—a company that was later sold to Movado Group, Inc.

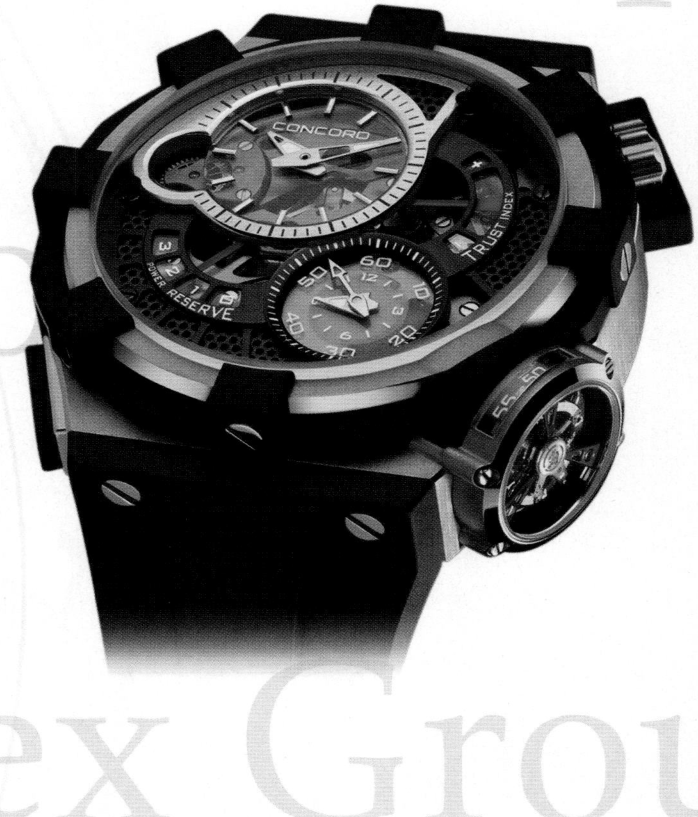

TOP   ChronoMaster Open Grande Date Sun and Moonphase (Zenith)

RIGHT   C1 Tourbillon Gravity (Concord)

The CFB A1000 automatic caliber with peripheral rotor. Leaves conventional movements behind.

R 38,415

37,965

CARL F

CDAS - BEAT ERROR

CDAS - RATE

A1000

The CFB A1000 caliber, developed and produced by Carl F. Bucherer, writes watchmaking history. Innovative use of traditional watchmaking expertise transforms this unique micro-mechanical device into the movement of the future. The ingenious self-winding system with its peripheral rotor provides an unimpeded view of the detail inside. This is craftsmanship at its finest, expressed through state-of-the-art technology and, in the Patravi EvoTec DayDate, set off to its best advantage. Its unmistakable design, with the large date and day-of-the-week display, places it firmly in the Carl F. Bucherer tradition of only making watches as unique as the people who wear them.

www.carl-f-bucherer.com   info@cfbnorthamerica.com

To locate an authorized retailer nearest you, please call 800 395 4306

CARL F. BUCHERER

FOR PEOPLE WHO DO NOT GO WITH THE TIMES.

CONSOLIDATING POSITIONS

This unique period, marked by the voracious appetites of the sector's largest companies, concluded with the emergence of a handful of big groups that were for the most part publicly traded on the stock market, such as Swatch, Richemont, LVMH, Timex Group Company, Bulgari, PPR or Movado. These players joined the large independent houses such as Rolex, Patek Philippe, Chopard, Girard-Perregaux, Audemars Piguet, and Franck Muller, as well as a multitude of smaller players. From that point on, the biggest names in the industry would concentrate on the integration of their brands, the efficiency of their means of production, and the coherence of their distribution networks.

EPIC II

JACOB & CO

Vertical integration is now the order of the day in the industry, expressed through the use of subcontractors and no longer through the top-dollar acquisition of prestigious brands, as it was a decade ago. The only transactions of note occurred when the larger companies acquired (usually) minority holdings in smaller, up-and-coming businesses: for example, Richemont bought 20% of Greubel Forsey (Prix Gaïa 2009), and Audemars Piguet bought a 10% share in Richard Mille. Even more significant was the purchase of the Minerva Villeret manufacture by Richemont—mostly to bolster its high-end Montblanc line—or the majority stake acquired by Franck Muller in the German brand Martin Braun (not to mention the 25% share in Vaucher Manufacture owned by Hermès, the 23% stake in Sowind Group (Girard-Perregaux) owned by PPR, Timex Group's purchase of Vincent Bérard, and the purchase of the industrial capabilities and then the brand name of Roger Dubuis, again by Richemont).

ABOVE RM 017 (Richard Mille)

LEFT Quadruple Tourbillon à Différentiel (Greubel Forsey)

HE ENGINEERS OF
IME

Dashboard. A classic. Redesigned.

Dashboard chronograph is the perfect expression of
puristic, function-oriented character of Porsche Design.
ect materials and ingenious technical details – such as the
rgy-optimised rotor – guarantee superior performance.

PORSCHE DESIGN
DASHBOARD
P'6612

ZENITH

SWISS WATCH MANUFACTURE
SINCE 1865

EL PRIMERO

NEW VINTAGE 1969

For almost one and a half centuries, the Manufacture ZENITH has been shaping the destiny of time through its tireless pursuit of absolute perfection. This passion gave rise in 1969 to the legendary El Primero, which 40 years later is still the only high-frequency (36'000 vph) mechanical self-winding chronograph movement able to measure tenths of a second. ZENITH and El Primero have made their mark on watch-making history and are continuing to write new chapters of its present and indeed its future. All watches crafted by ZENITH are equipped with mechanical ZENITH movements.

THE BENCHMARK.

HUBLOT: THE LAST BIG ACQUISITION

The only important transactions of the last few years have been Aber Diamond's purchase of the remaining 47% of Harry Winston for $157 million and 100% ownership; the acquisition of STM Holding, an important movement producer, first by Chinese investors, then by Festina; Bovet's purchase of three manufacturing businesses (tourbillons, movements and spirals) joined under STT Holding to create Dimier 1738; and finally LVMH's acquisition of Hublot for an amount estimated at 500 million Swiss francs.

The Swiss watch subcontracting subculture has lately become the most desirable aspect of the industry, which comes as no surprise given the robust health of a sector that has piled up record upon record since 2003. The financial crisis that first showed up in the world's markets in 2007 before spreading to the global economy certainly put the brakes on the ardor of the watchmaking industry and has resulted in widespread layoffs. Nonetheless, the major groups have consolidated their grips on the industry, and they are well placed to hang in there and wait for better days.

LEFT   Tourbillon Jumping Hours (Bovet)

BELOW   The Bovet ateliers at the Château de Môtiers

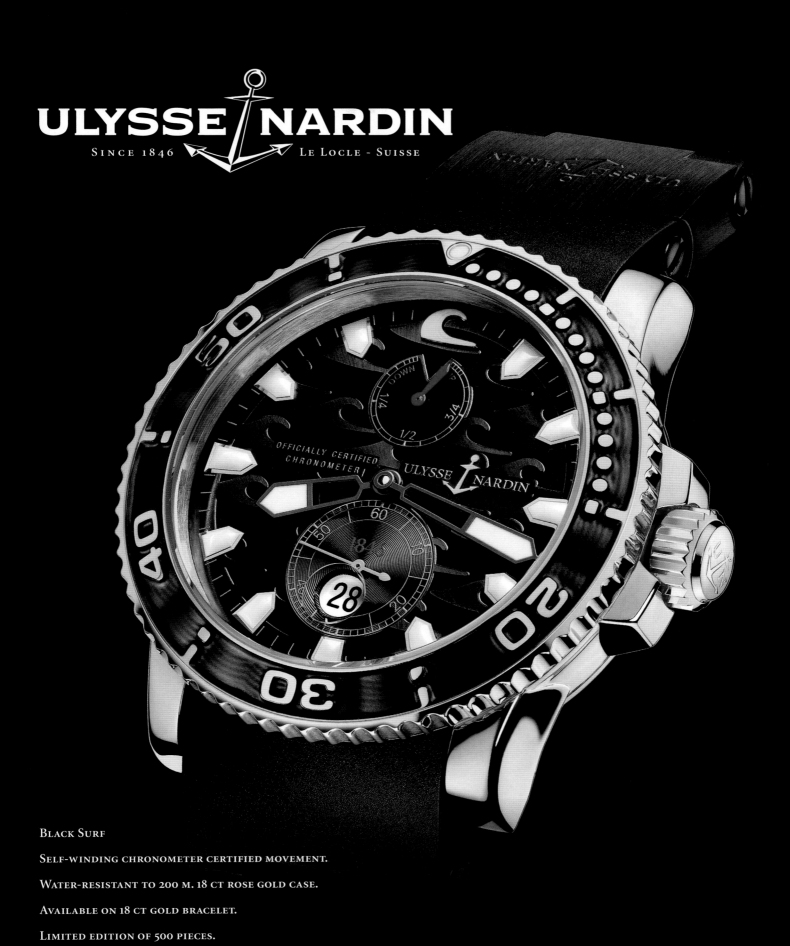

ULYSSE NARDIN

SINCE 1846 · LE LOCLE - SUISSE

BLACK SURF

SELF-WINDING CHRONOMETER CERTIFIED MOVEMENT.

WATER-RESISTANT TO 200 M. 18 CT ROSE GOLD CASE.

AVAILABLE ON 18 CT GOLD BRACELET.

LIMITED EDITION OF 500 PIECES.

THE GLOBAL HEGEMONY OF THE SWATCH GROUP

At more than 80 years old, Nicolas G. Hayek is a self-styled living legend who doesn't conceal his opinion that "modesty is hypocrisy for those who have succeeded." Hayek definitely belongs to the category, since he is widely regarded as the savior of Swiss watchmaking. However, his success was by no means a sure bet. At the end of the 1970s, the world of Swiss horology was stagnating, having completely missed the boat on the quartz craze. It wasn't that the Swiss watchmakers had not mastered the technology—the Centre Electronique at Neuchâtel had actually produced the world's first quartz wristwatch in 1967. But the ranks of watchmaking professionals, taken by surprise by quartz's sudden popularity, were decimated by the invasion of Japanese watches and mechanical watches and found themselves relegated to the status of historical curiosities. The two giants of the field, Société Suisse pour l'Industrie Horlogère (SSIH, founded in 1930 in the merger between Tissot and Omega) and Allgemeine Schweizerische Uhrenindustrie AG (ASUAG, founded in 1931 and owner of Rado, Longines and Ebauches), were well on their way to being left to their fates by the banks, who were horrified by annual losses running to almost a half-billion Swiss francs.

Nicolas G. Hayek, president of the Swatch Group, is at the head of the largest watch group in the world.

WIRZ
THE PASSIONS OF THE MOSERS
131
One power plant every 200 years.
Even a Moser can't do better.
In 1850, when watchmaking entrepreneur Heinrich Moser gifted his home town of Schaffhausen a hydro-mechanical power plant, and with it lasting economic prosperity, he must have guessed his entrepreneurial spirit would catch on. Today, his descendants have brought the full weight of his legacy – at 90.17 g not dauntingly heavy – to bear on the Mayu, a watch testifying to Moser-style ingenuity in the 21st century. And boasting a full eighty hours of power in reserve, even without a power plant.
H. Moser & Cie.
MAYU, ref.325.503-010, Palladium. Handwound cal. HMC 321.503 with bevel wheels. At least three days power reserve. Power reserve indication on movement side. Hacking seconds. Moser interchangeable escapement module. Straumann Double Hairspring. Pallet fork and escapement wheel made of white gold. See-through back. PASSIONATELY DIFFERENT.
For further information please contact Milestone Distribution,
1 678 827 7900 or www.h-moser.com
H. Moser & Cie.

SWATCH, ONCE UPON A TIME

Hayek, an adoptive Swiss born in Beirut in 1928 and owner of his own consulting company, was called to the rescue. His prescription, however, was so iconoclastic that the bankers could not find anyone who could—or would—implement it. His idea involved merging the two companies that deserved to thrive (namely SSIH and ASUAG), but he also focused on going after the bottom of the market, to block the path of the Japanese companies then flooding the market. Nobody really believed in the plan except Hayek himself, who agreed to lead the charge in exchange for control of operations via a shareholders' agreement.

The rest of the story is widely known, as it is intimately entwined with the success of the Swatch watch brand, the production/manufacturing cost of which still hovers around eight Swiss francs per watch after more than 20 years of existence and more than 350 million watches sold. These exceptional watches, comprising just 51 components each, chose to ignore the classic division of timepieces and were instead designed on plastic bases that served as both case and bottom plate, housing movements mounted from their tops and featuring ultrasonically soldered protective glass. The immediate success of the first "disposable" timepiece, which completely revolutionized watch wearing, has been maintained over the years through the marketing genius of the charismatic industrialist. Building on this breakthrough that remains unmatched within the watch industry to this day, Hayek accomplished the remarkable feat of restarting the company that now stands head and shoulders above the global watchmaking industry.

A legendary brand that gave its name to the group, Swatch is releasing a new model with mechanical movement: the Swatch Chrono Automatic.

Walter von Känel, *President of Longines, Swatch Group*

How does your brand benefit from belonging to a group?

The Longines brand benefits considerably from belonging to Swatch Group, which is the largest producer of watch products in the world. That provides a lot of advantages—we can take advantage of its international structure, its distribution and supply networks, and a close collaboration among the businesses of Swatch Group. Their legal service also supports our struggle against counterfeit Longines watches.

Do you think increasing consolidation in the watch industry is inevitable, why or why not?

It's already happened.

What advantages would there be to independence?

I don't think the brand would be at the level it is today had it remained independent.

In two or three words, how would you describe the group to which your brand belongs?

Stability, vision, structure and emotion.

In two or three words, how would you describe your brand?

Elegance, tradition, timelessness and consistency.

What will be the defining moments for your brand in 2010?

There's a big surprise in store for BaselWorld…and later in the year we are organizing a big event for the launch of a new collection. We are also continuing our activities as timekeeper in tennis—notably at the French Open—alpine skiing, equitation and gymnastics.

A COLOSSAL MANUFACTURE

There are no two ways about it: Swatch Group—with 22,000 employees in 50 countries, 160 factories and more than 100 affiliated companies accounting for six billion Swiss francs in sales in 2008 (almost the entire value of 2008 watch imports to Hong Kong)—is surely the only watchmaker in the world to enjoy such dominance and control over its industrial capacities. This tentacular production network allows Swatch to produce all of the components of a timepiece, assemble them and market them through 19 different brands. Essentially, the company is a huge stand-alone watch manufacturer, not just for Swatch and Flik Flak watches, but also for the prestigious brands Omega, Breguet, Blanpain, Jaquet Droz and Glashütte Original, all members of the high-end watch industry that has performed so impressively over the last few years, as well as Tissot, Longines, Rado, Certina, Hamilton, Balmain, CK, Tiffany & Co, and Swatch's private label, Endura watches. In short, Swatch Group is the only company to cover the entire spectrum of horology—and now jewelry—with truly inimitable success.

Longines Lindbergh's Atlantic Voyage Watch

FREDERIQUE CONSTANT
GENEVE

Live your passion

Innovation and uncompromising quality are the hallmarks of Frédérique Constant. Driven by an un-paralleled passion for precision and craftsmanship, our watchmakers manufacture Geneva timepieces of contemporary, classic design and exceptional value.

Maxime
Manufacture
Automatic

Without a doubt, Hayek has several masterstrokes under his belt. In buying Blancpain and Breguet in the 1990s, Swatch not only acquired two prestigious brands at reasonable prices, but also snapped up two movement manufacturers considered to be genuine gems within the industry, namely Frédéric Piguet and Nouvelle Lémania. These two ateliers complemented the production capacities of Valjoux and ETA—a central piece of the puzzle with its annual production rate of 90 million movements. According to watch industry estimates, Swatch Group represents between 20% and 30% of global production of movements and watch components.

ABOVE Tradition 7027 (Breguet)

RIGHT The L-evolution Moon Phase 8 Jours (Blancpain)

CLERC
GENEVE

1874

HYDROSCAPH

CREATED BY GERALD CLERC
ACCORDING TO A NEW
CONSTRUCTION TYPE EMBODYING
STATE-OF-THE-ART
TECHNOLOGY. PATENTED CASE
IN 18 KT ROSE GOLD AND
BLACK TITANIUM COMPOSED
OF OVER 75 ELEMENTS AND
EQUIPPED WITH AN AUTOMATIC
HELIUM ESCAPEMENT VALVE
ENSURING WATER RESISTANCE
TO 1000 METERS. EXCLUSIVE
CROWN-ACTIVATED ROTATING
BEZEL MECHANISM AND
ADAPTABLE LUGS. AUTOMATIC
MOVEMENT WITH BIG DATE AND
POWER-RESERVE INDICATOR,
VULCANIZED RUBBER STRAP.
HAND-CRAFTED IN
SWITZERLAND, THREE-YEAR
INTERNATIONAL WARRANTY

THE MOST SOPHISTICATED
DIVING INSTRUMENT

HY-PR
312

COLLECTION: *Hydroscaph*
MODEL: *#hy.1pr 312 Gold*
CREATED BY: *Gerald Clerc*

FOR INFORMATION PLEASE CALL
+41 22 716 25 50
VISIT CLERCWATCHES.COM

*Specifications may be subject
to change without notice.
Internationally registered
trademarks and models.*
© *Clerc 2009*

Marc A. Hayek, *President and CEO of Blancpain, Swatch Group*

How does your brand benefit from belonging to a group?

Blancpain benefits from global strength and mastery of distribution, as well as exceptional technical support and methods of development.

Do you think increasing consolidation in the watch industry is inevitable, and why or why not?

Rather than speak of this "inevitable" trend, the consolidation you're referring to actually makes up some of the charm of our industry. There are so many different segments of the market that it becomes a stimulating factor.

What advantages would there be to independence?

Since it's something of a chore to manage a brand as an entrepreneur, there are no advantages to independence.

In two or three words, how would you describe the group to which your brand belongs?

High technology, emotions and family.

In two or three words, how would you describe your brand?

Innovative yet traditional, timeless, emotions, high technology.

What will be the defining moments for your brand in 2010?

Blancpain will be celebrating its 275th anniversary; we'll have surprises at BaselWorld and throughout the year.

THE HAYEK DYNASTY

These days, it is almost impossible to produce a Swiss watch without going through the group controlled by the Hayek family. A few examples: Universo, which belongs to Swatch, accounts for half the global production of watch hands; Nouvelle Lémania built its reputation on complicated movements, especially tourbillons, for which competition is still rare; as for the famous balance-springs (which regulate mechanical watches along with the balance), there are not many alternatives to Nivarox-FAR, another Swatch Group subsidiary. Swatch Group is also the most active in terms of diversification. In the late 1980s, it tried to fill a gap in medical technologies by developing a system of disposable mobile pumps that could be worn on the wrist like a watch. The project's failure did not prevent Swatch from exploring other fields via EM Microelectronic, producer of ultra low-power integrated circuits; Oscilloquartz, noted specialist in synchronization systems for satellite positioning; and Asulab, the group's center of research of development in microtechnology, microelectronics, telecommunications, liquid crystal screens and sensors. The portrait would not be complete without mentioning the group's excursions into the world of automobiles. After its hybrid car project, which was handed over to Mercedes a few years ago, Swatch recently signed a partnership agreement with the Swiss Paul Scherrer Institute for Nuclear Physics, which is working on the development of a hydrogen motor.

Georges Nicolas Hayek, son of Nicolas G. Hayek who goes by the nickname "Nick," has been the CEO of Swatch Group since 2003.

Hayek's family has not hesitated to get involved in running the company, and observers describe the family as a new watchmaking dynasty. Running the company with Nicolas G., Board Chairman, is his son Nick, who has been Managing Director since the beginning of 2003. His daughter Nayla also sits on the administrative board and manages Tiffany & Co's watch division, and his grandson Marc-Alexandre is the President of Blancpain. In less than two decades, Hayek has created an extremely healthy watchmaking group from scratch. Its own funds make up more than 75% of the balance sheet. The company also generates a solid cash flow, allowing massive stock buybacks to the tune of 587 million Swiss francs in 2008, including distribution of dividends, which still leaves more than a half-billion francs of available liquidity. One could say that the sun never sets on the Hayek Empire.

Innovation on the move.

Eterna · Spherodrive
Another landmark Eterna innovation.

ETERNA
Nothing but Watchmaking.
Since 1856.

The Richemont Group (with headquarters in Bellevue, Geneva) cultivates autonomy among its brands.

RICHEMONT: AN ESSENTIAL PLAYER IN THE WORLD OF LUXURY

Though Swatch Group and Richemont dominate the watch world, their business models could not be more different, as evidenced by the brands in the groups' portfolios. Swatch, born from the fusion of two tottering giants at the height of the quartz crisis, focuses on centralizing the management of its different companies. Richemont, which grew with successive purchases of the most prestigious brands over the last 20 years, cultivates autonomy. "Each house has its own identity, born from its heritage and its culture," the group explains. "So it is critical that each of them can take advantage of good strategies and the necessary resources to reinforce that identity. The houses' independence within the group is essential to our strategy for continued growth."

THE SIMPLICITY OF INNOVATION.

LUMINOR 1950 8 DAYS GMT
Hand-wound mechanical movement
P.2002 calibre, three spring barrels,
second time zone with 12/24 h
indicator, 8-day power reserve with
linear indicator, seconds reset.
Steel case 44 mm Ø. Steel buckle.

PANERAI
LABORATORIO DI IDEE.

www.panerai.com

ABOVE LEFT   South African Johann Rupert is chairman of Richemont, head-quartered in Geneva.

ABOVE RIGHT   Le Cirque Animalier Panther Decor (Cartier)

BELOW   Da Vinci Perpetual Calendar Digital Date-Month (IWC)

That growth, for the time being, shows no signs of stopping. At the end of March 2009, Richemont had recorded a 2% rise in its sales, bringing them to 5.4 billion euros, despite the financial crisis that began in the autumn of 2008. Its profits were at 1.07 billion euros. At the end of that period, Richemont had net liquidity of 822 million euros. For many years, the company was a notable shareholder in British American Tobacco with 19.3% of the capital, which meant significant dividend distribution. Those days are no more. To clearly mark its identity as an active company in the luxury world, Richemont commenced a separation from its other interests. From that point on, a newly created company known as Reinet Investments would trade in Luxembourg and South Africa, handling all of the group's investments not related to luxury.

Success is a journey.
Bring back a souvenir.

IWC
SCHAFFHAUSEN
SINCE 1868

A DECADE OF ACQUISITION

In 1988, the South African group Rembrandt, founded in the 1940s by Anton Rupert, began to spin off its international activities (luxury and tobacco), holding on to only its investments within the country (financial services, wines, spirits, gold and diamonds). The goal was to avoid the sanctions that were being leveled against the apartheid regime. This new entity took the name of Richemont. Already enjoying a minority stake in Cartier Monde and interests in Alfred Dunhill, Montblanc and Chloé, Richemont acquired Piaget and Baume & Mercier the same year. A new schism between the tobacco and luxury branches would come about five years later, with the creation of Vendôme in 1993 allowing Richemont to group all of its luxury companies under the same umbrella.

TOP   Métiers d'Arts Les Masques (Vacheron Constantin)

RIGHT   Lange 1 (A. Lange & Söhne)

GREUBEL FORSEY
INVENTEURS HORLOGERS

ART *of* INVENTION

No 11

Grand Prix
Horlogerie
Genève»
ntre Haute
mplication 2009

DOUBLE TOURBILLON TECHNIQUE   1st **Fundamental Invention**

TOP Luminor 1950 GMT (Panerai)

BOTTOM Star Eternal White Gold Diamonds (Montblanc)

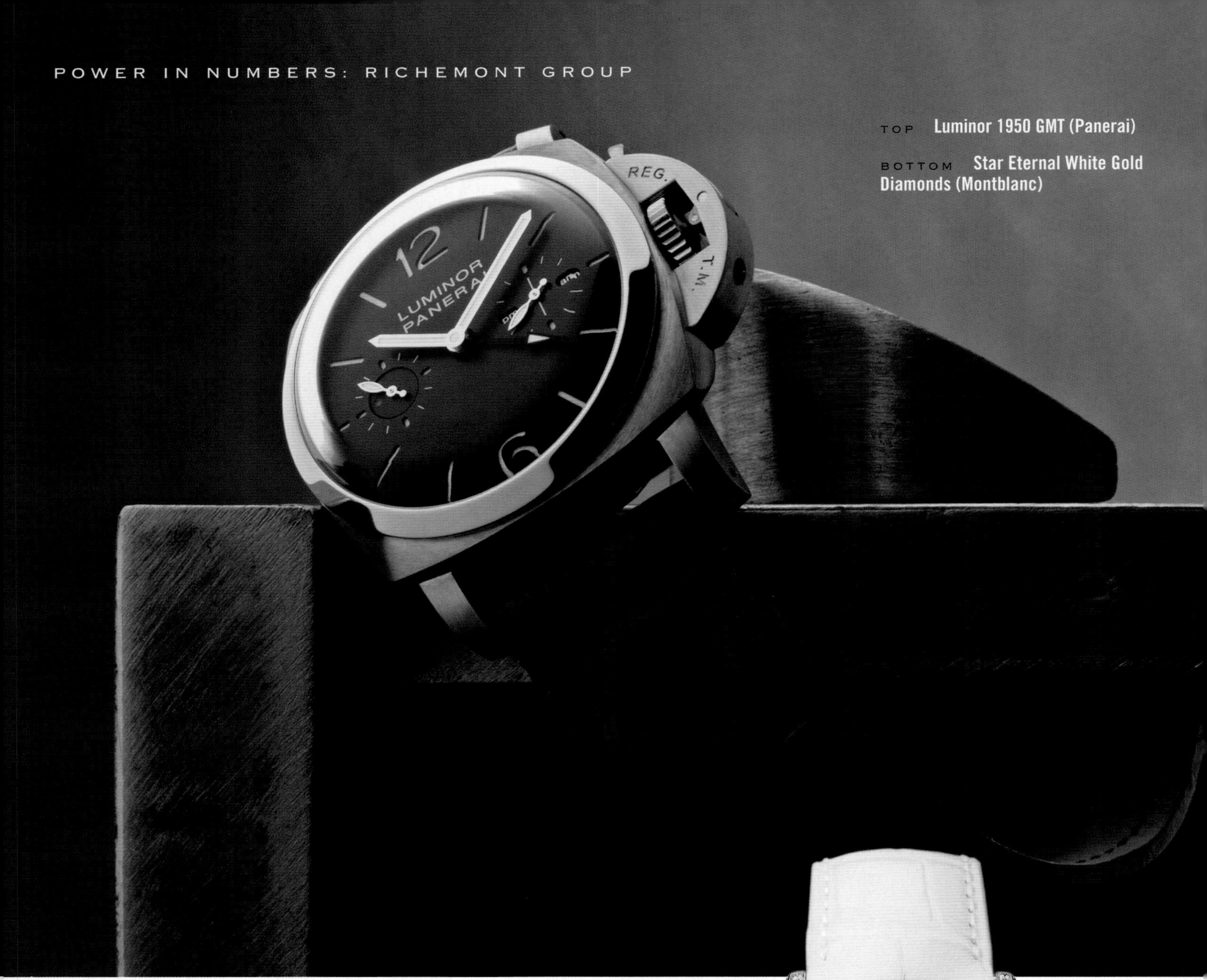

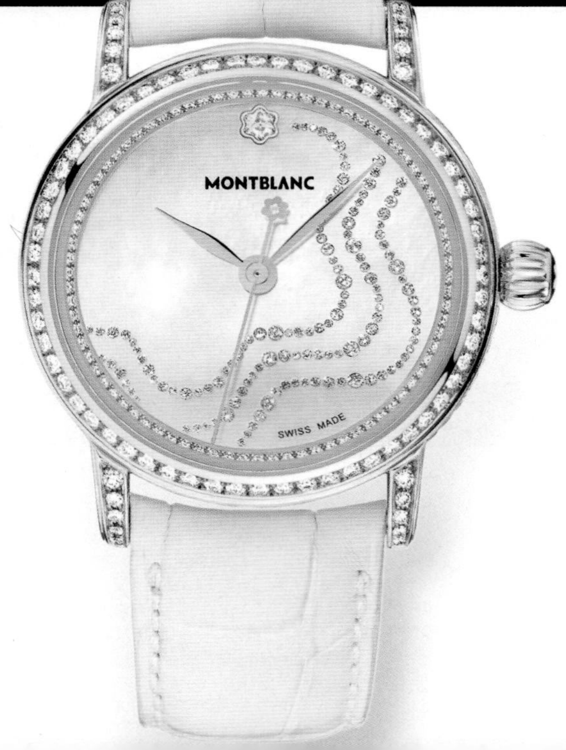

Over the last 15 years, Vendôme, which would be completely bought back by Richemont in 1998, kept adding new notches to its belt: all of Cartier in 1993, Vacheron Constantin in 1996, Panerai and Lancel in 1997, Van Cleef & Arpels in 1999, Stern Group, IWC, A. Lange & Söhne and Jaeger-LeCoultre in 2000, Minerva in 2006 (for Montblanc), and the factory and then the brand of Roger Dubuis between 2007 and 2008. This is in addition to the recent agreement with Ralph Lauren for the development of a jewelry and watch line with the couturier's name. With some 16,000 employees involved in horology and jewelry as well as writing instruments (Montblanc and Montegrappa, which is to be resold), hunting weapons (Purdey), leather goods (Alfred Dunhill, Lancel) and fashion (Chloé, Alaïa, Shanghai Tang), Richemont and its 17 brands clearly occupy second place in the luxury universe, just behind LVMH.

TIMEWRITER. | In 1821 Nicolas Rieussec invented the first chronograph, a revolutionary device with two rotating discs beneath an index with an ink-filled tip that left a mark on the dials to indicate the time. Taking the essence of his invention, Montblanc has created a time-keeping masterpiece incorporating the rotating disc technique: the Montblanc Nicolas Rieussec.

Monopusher chronograph, MB R100 *manual-winding manufacture movement. 13 3/4 lines, large screw-balance of 9.7 mm, 4 Hz. Off-centre hour, minute and date display. 30 min. and 60 sec. counters with rotating discs fixed on the counter bridge. Column wheel control, vertical disc clutch running virtually friction-free. Special toothing for more efficient power transmission. 72-hour power reserve display, sapphire glass back. 18 K red gold 43 mm case and clasp, alligator-skin strap. Limited edition of 125 pieces. Crafted in the Montblanc Manufacture in Le Locle, Switzerland.* MONTBLANC. A STORY TO TELL.

MONT BLANC

How does your brand benefit from belonging to a group?

As strong as the brand personality of Roger Dubuis is, it does need solid logistical support and particularly the distribution network that Richemont provides. Those are major benefits.

Do you think increasing consolidation in the watch industry is inevitable, and why or why not?

No, certain brands are very successful independently from any group. That said, in any time of upheaval, a larger group has the resources to resist.

What advantages would there be to independence?

None, really, especially since our brand can freely express its characteristics and specificities while still benefiting from the support, experience and infrastructures that a group can provide.

In two or three words, how would you describe the group to which your brand belongs?

Dynamic, structured and efficient.

In two or three words, how would you describe your brand?

Very personalized, exuberant and manufacturing refinement.

What will be the defining moments for your brand in 2010?

We headed into SIHH with a particular focus on the redesigned Excali through highly exclusive events.

Richemont has also carved out an essential place for itself in the watch universe, with a portfolio of manufacturers whose roots stem from the watchmaking ferment of the 19th century, and even, in the case of Vacheron Constantin, the 18th century. The "youngest" brands of the group, Van Cleef & Arpels and Montblanc, can boast only of a history stretching back to...1906. Building on their time-honored heritages, these prestigious houses have consistently upheld their longstanding traditions of excellence, studded with exceptional pieces and technological breakthroughs in the realms of ultra-thin watches, jewelry, timing and grand complications. This is even more noticeable in that Richemont, unlike Swatch Group, focuses on the ultra high-end of the market, with the one exception being Baume & Mercier.

Some examples drawn from the last few years: the Master Compressor Extreme LAB from Jaeger-LeCoultre, the first watch to operate entirely lubricant-free; the Piaget Diamond Emperador Temple, a pyramid of diamonds hiding a quartz movement and a mechanical one, and revealing a tourbillon in the in-house 602P caliber; the Métiers d'Art Les Masques collection from Vacheron Constantin, a blend of art and exceptional artisanship; the Panerai Luminor 1950 GMT whose tourbillon cage rotates on an axis parallel to the movement's bottom plate; or even A. Lange & Söhne's Pour le Mérite, with its fusée and chain transmission. These few examples are sufficient to show the level at which the group's houses have chosen to position their products. Watch lovers, of course, never stop clamoring for more.

TOP   The Piaget Diamond Emperador Temple

RIGHT   Master Compressor Extreme LAB (Jaeger-LeCoultre)

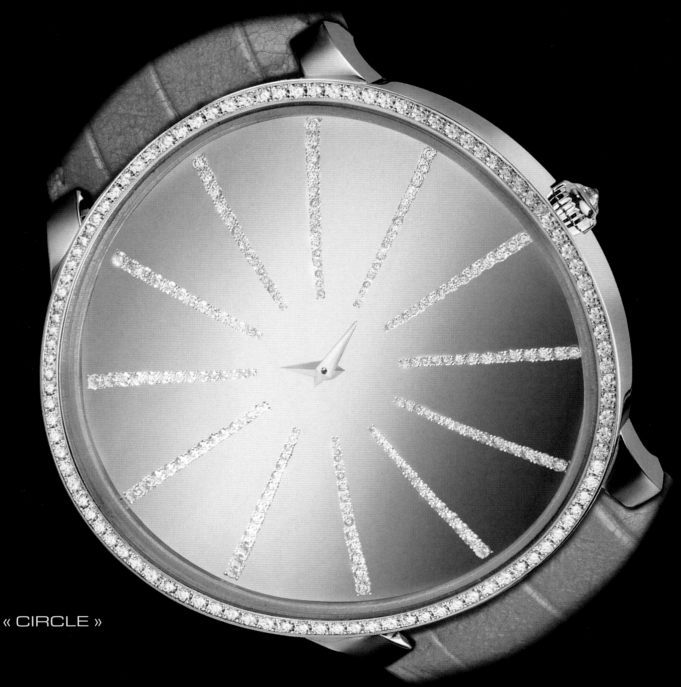

GE | GUY ELLI.

« CIRCLE »

Arije Paris

Doux Joaillier Courchevel   Zegg & Cerlati Monaco   Doux Joaillier Saint Tropez

Carat & Time Saint Barthelemy   Piantelli London   Avakian Geneva

Hubner Vienna   Diamond Time Athens   Steltman Den Haag   Lydion Mucevher Antalya

Azal Dubaï   Harvey Nichols Dubaï   Louvre Moscow   Crystal Kiev   Sincere Kuala Lumpur

Sincere Singapore   Cellini New York   Westime Los Angeles

www.guyellia.com

WITH ZENITH, TAG HEUER AND HUBLOT, LVMH TAKES ITS PLACE IN THE WATCH WORLD

In 1999, when the giant LVMH broke out the heavy artillery to become a new center of activity in the jewelry and watch markets, few onlookers were totally convinced. Criticisms focused on the relative paucity of brands, their elevated prices and low profitability—some were even losing money—but were somewhat quieted by the 2003 sale of Ebel, a brand that had led to heavy losses for the group.

The El Primero movement was released in 1969 as one of the first automatic-winding chronographs. It has been, and continues to be, one of Zenith's crowning glories.

FRANC VILA
— *esprit unique* —

A very contemporary return to traditional high-end standards

FV EVOS 8 "Cobra" Chronograph Grand Date Automatic

Limited Edition 88 pieces

18kt Red Gold and Carbon Fiber $58,000

Due to the very limited production of these timepieces, there may be slight variances in the details of each watch

RIGHT   Bernard Arnault, owner of LVMH
and the wealthiest individual in France.

BELOW   Chiffre Rouge 102 (Dior Watches)

About six years later, these criticisms have completely disappeared. Of course, the Watch and Jewelry sector of LVMH, which consists of TAG Heuer, Zenith, Montres Dior, Chaumet, Fred, De Beers LV, OMAS, and Hublot (acquired in 2008), represents only 4.5% of the sales of the world's most important luxury company, but those numbers represent remarkable growth. Between 2006 and 2008, sales actually increased by almost 20% to 879 million euros, for 118 million euros in profit. Though this striking performance did not repeat in 2009, due to the sudden fall of the markets, LVMH is not abandoning its ambitions in this sector.

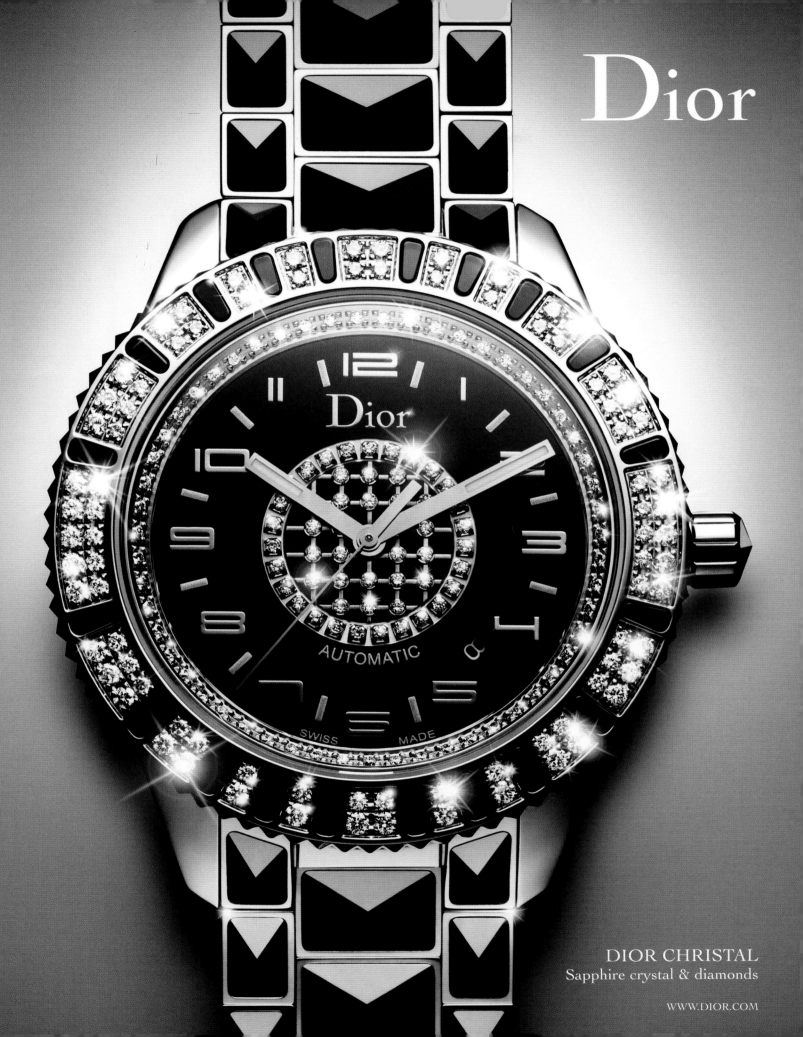

Elegance is an attitude

Aishwarya Rai

Aishwarya Rai

Longines Primal una

THE RETURN OF ZENITH

Zenith, which had often been considered a "sleeping beauty" before its acquisition by LVMH, has woken up and regained its former glory. With Thierry Nataf in charge, the brand succeeded in returning to center-stage and making important investments, especially in its production capacities. Research and development also has been key, as shown by the launch of the Defy collection, Zenithium, and the famous Tourbillon Zero-G presented in the Academy collection in 2009. Research has been largely oriented towards "motorization." When Zenith was acquired, the manufacture, founded in 1865, had developed 12 movements from the noted El Primero and Elite bases. Six years later, the company has added ten more, spread out over five collections that run the gamut of the horological spectrum, from the haute horology Academy to more classic models (ChronoMaster), and everything in between: timepieces that are distinguished (Port-Royal), elegant (Class) and sporty (Defy Classic and Xtreme). The profusion of new models, however, does not seem to have had the desired effect. In April 2009, Nataf handed over the reins to Jean-Frédéric Dufour, defector from Chopard.

Defy Tourbillon Zero-G (Zenith)

Jean-Frédéric Dufour, *President and CEO of Zenith, LVMH Group*

How does your brand benefit from belonging to a group?

By belonging to the largest luxury group in the world (one and a half times the Swiss watch industry), we benefit from very strong support with respect to distribution, finances and expertise in luxury.

Do you think increasing consolidation in the watch industry is inevitable, and why or why not?

It's not inevitable, because there will always be new entrepreneurs and creators joining the adventure. That is the beautiful thing about our profession: it is "easier" to start a watch company than a car company. And it's the same thing at the industrial level: if one knows about micromechanics and loves horology, one might go into the fabrication of watch components.

What advantages would there be to independence?

None, because the way that LVMH functions, the brands are really independent when it comes to running our businesses. You also have to define "independence"—if Zenith belonged to me, that would be perfect, but if there would just be other shareholders, I don't really see the upside.

In two or three words, how would you describe the group to which your brand belongs?

Creative, dynamic and entrepreneurial.

In two or three words, how would you describe your brand?

Authentic (145 years of continuous history), avant-garde (El Primero and 40 years of leadership in the field of high-frequency movements), precise (1,546 prizes for timekeeping), inventive (176 patents), but also reliable and determined!

What will be the defining moments for your brand in 2010?

BaselWorld 2010 saw the launch of our new El Primero collection, with the only mechanical chronograph that displays 1/10 of a second (patented by Zenith). The collection has a neo-retro inspiration and a direct lineage from the first El Primero collection, launched in 1969 for the release of the first high-frequency automatic chronograph

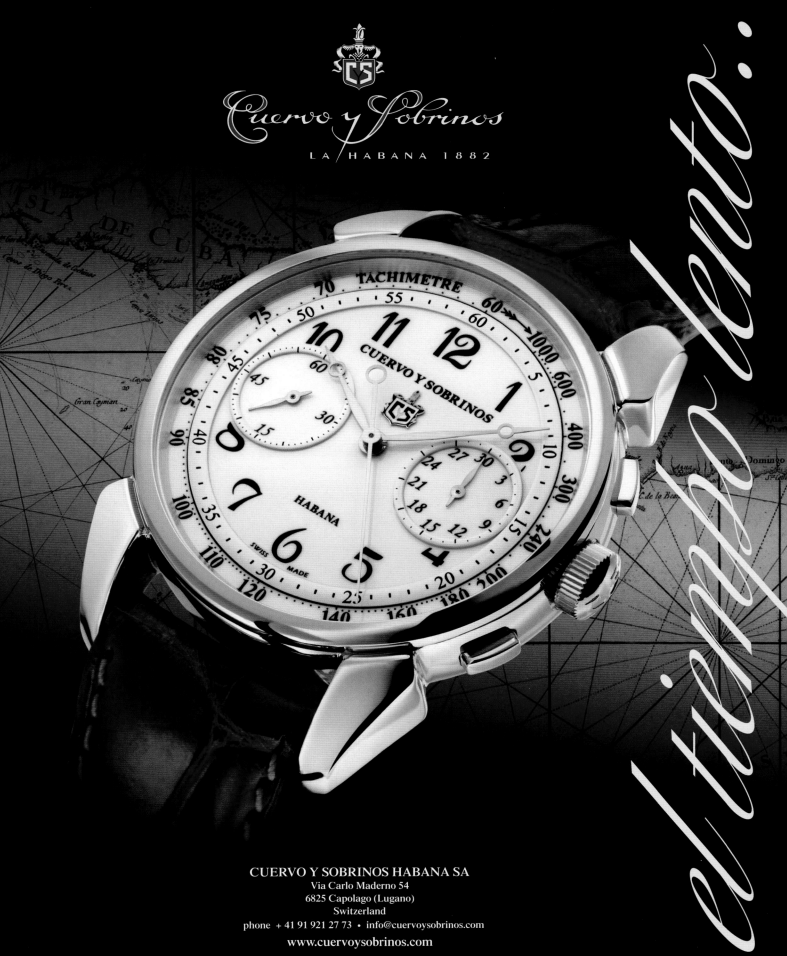

TAG HEUER: INVENTOR OF "CONCEPT WATCHES"

From the first patent for a chronograph mechanism in 1882 to the patent for the oscillating gearwheel in 1887, from the first chronograph capable of measuring 1/100 of a second in 1916 (the Micrograph) to the first electronic Micro-timer with precision up to 1/1,000 of a second in 1966, Heuer has surely written some of the greatest chapters in horology. However, this reputation has not always been accompanied by commercial success. In 1982, the brand was bought by Piaget, which held onto it for just three years before selling it to the TAG (Technique d'Avant-Garde) group, then in charge of the Formula 1 McLaren stable. TAG Heuer was then placed under the leadership of Christian Viros, who would orchestrate the globalization of the brand. In a few years its sales figures grew sixfold to reach almost 400 million francs by the middle of the 1990s, with a production that had almost doubled to 700,000 pieces. However, when LVMH came along to acquire it, TAG Heuer was again losing speed. A course was set for the innovation that had forged Heuer's reputation. This strategy led to explosively original pieces, true concept watches such as the Monaco 69 (a watch with two movements, quartz and mechanical, joined in a unique reversible case), the 360 movement (the only mechanical chronograph movement accurate to 1/100 of a second) and even the Monaco V4 (with a mechanical movement that operates with transmission belts). For TAG Heuer, the future is a sport again.

THIS PAGE
In 2009, TAG Heuer re-released the famous Monaco 69 under the name Monaco Sixty Nine. The timepiece combines two movements (mechanical and quartz) in one reversible case.

FACING PAGE
TOP LEFT   The Heuer brand was bought in 1982 by the TAG group, then in charge of the F1 McLaren stable. Today, TAG Heuer belongs to LVMH and is based in La Chaux-de-Fonds.

TOP RIGHT   After five years of development, TAG Heuer has lifted the veil from the Monaco V4 with its belt-driven movement.

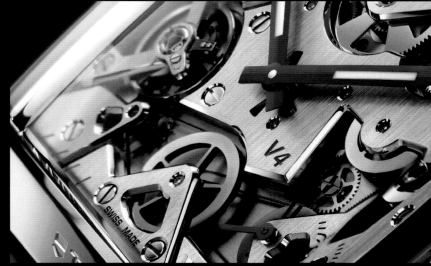

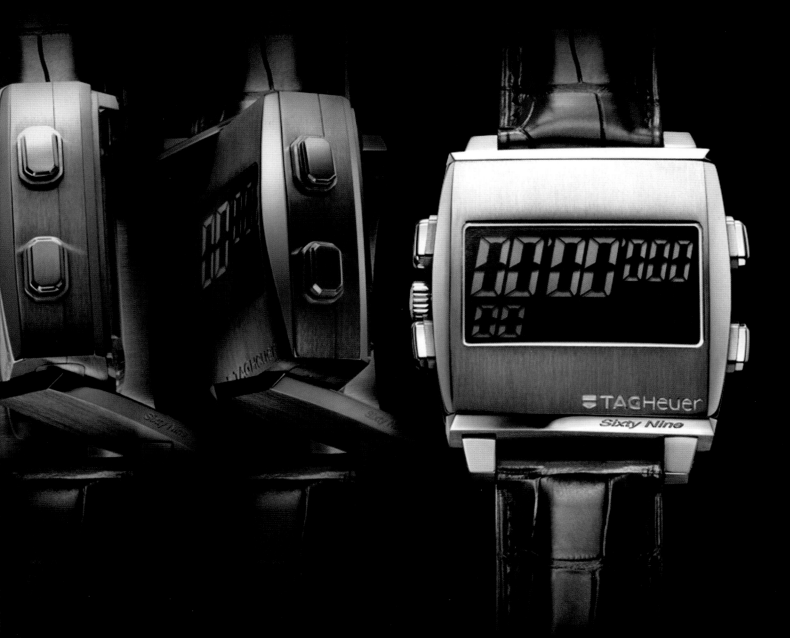

Jean-Claude Biver, *CEO and Managing Director of Hublot, LVMH Group*

How does your brand benefit from belonging to a group?

Job security, better resistance to crises, distribution synergies, administrative support, ease of investment and long-term policy are all topics that spring to mind.

Do you think increasing consolidation in the watch industry is inevitable, and why or why not?

Inevitable, yes, because it's a global process that is affecting all industrial sectors, including the world of luxury.

What advantages would there be to independence?

Very few—we are very autonomous in the way we run the brand and we behave just like responsible independent entrepreneurs.

In two or three words, how would you describe the group to which your brand belongs?

Entrepreneurial spirit, open-minded, long-term vision and harmoniously dynamic.

In two or three words, how would you describe your brand?

Innovative, creative, unique and different.

What will be the defining moments for your brand in 2010?

We will be releasing Unico, the first completely in-house movement, as well as continuing partnerships with Alinghi and Usain Bolt.

HUBLOT STAYS THE COURSE

The appetite of LVMH has not been sated, as show by the purchase of Hublot in 2008 for an amoun estimated at 500 million Swiss francs. Once mor the brilliant Jean-Claude Biver, who righted Blancpai and Omega, was involved. "Tradition, as far as it i legitimate, is certainly a very good thing, but it must b projected into the future. That is exactly what Hublot i doing," he recently declared. This concept, first applie by Biver in 2004, has worked rather well up until nov producing a sixfold increase in sales over the las four years, with sales in 2008 reaching almost 20 million Swiss francs. This growth also reflects Hublot specialized research on materials of the future, i accordance with the brand's signature concept "fusion." With Hublot, LVMH has acquired a house wit marvelous resilience.

THIS PAGE
Hublot is the latest acquisition of LVMH, purchased in 2008. The brand recently moved into its new building in Nyon, in Canton Vaud.

FACING PAGE
Hublot has only one collection, the Big Bang, released in multip versions such as this Big Bang Apple.

PPR'S SPECTACULAR ENTRY INTO THE LUXURY WORLD

PPR did not enter into the world of luxury until 1999, a year that marked the beginning of its merciless fight with LVMH for control of Gucci Group. Founded in 1963 by François Pinault, the group that would eventually be called PPR started by dealing in wood and construction materials. In the mid-1980s, the group rapidly became one of the most important players in the retail sector. Following the acquisition of the department stores Au Printemps and La Redoute, the group continued to grow over the years, acquiring Conforama, Fnac and Puma, among other brands.

In 1999, Bernard Arnault, CEO of LVMH, snapped up 34% of Gucci on the stock market. Domenico De Sole, then head of Gucci, was furious that the number one luxury group in the world had made inroads into his group. In March 1999, François Pinault was called in to play the white knight. He bought back 42% of Gucci in a seasoned equity offering, reducing the participation of LVMH to 20%. This kicked off a financial battle that would last two years, finally ending in victory for PPR, who would achieve the status of majority shareholder by buying at an elevated price the shares of Gucci still held by LVMH. In 2004, following a takeover bid, PPR would come to control 99.4% of Gucci and take its place as the third biggest luxury company in the world.

Jean-Christophe Bédos, *CEO of Boucheron, PPR Group*

How does your brand benefit from belonging to a group?

Being connected to a larger group is definitely a real financial advantage, to be sure. Beyond that, Gucci Group is very valuable for Boucheron, because we share a lot of information on the fashion business and trends in consumption by women, who are our most important clients.

Do you think increasing consolidation in the watch industry is inevitable, and why or why not?

Yes, that is the way history is going, as watchmakers need financial backing in order to develop. Not to mention that in terms of distribution, the strongest brands are often those that act in groups.

What advantages would there be to independence?

Boucheron already enjoys a lot of independence within Gucci Group, because "freedom without a framework" is the philosophy of our group. I don't see any advantage to being any more independent than we are already.

In two or three words, how would you describe the group to which your brand belongs?

Entrepreneurial, daring and creative.

In two or three words, how would you describe your brand?

The ultimate in luxury, passionately creative and completely devoted to our clients.

What will be the defining moments for your brand in 2010?

I can promise you a great year in creative haute jewelry. We're moving toward watches that are more and more feminine, with a return to jeweled watches and temps précieux, "precious time." Boucheron boutiques are opening everywhere in Asia and the Middle East, where the brand is more and more popular.

Before Pinault's arrival, Gucci owned Bottega Veneta, Balenciaga and Bédat & Co, in addition to its own brand. Over the following years, Yves Saint Laurent (ready-to-wear), YSL Beauté (cosmetics), Sergio Rossi (shoes) and Boucheron (watches and jewelry) wound up in Gucci's pocket. Since then, YSL Beauté and Bédat & Co have gone elsewhere. Gucci has also entered into partnership agreements with Stella McCartney and Alexander McQueen. Finally, in 2008, PPR made a capital investment in the Sowind Group (Girard-Perregaux and JeanRichard), buying up 23% of the group.

On the horology side, Gucci moved its production from Bern to Neuchâtel. In 2001 it created the new entity Gucci Group Watches, based in Neuchâtel, which directs the horological activities of the group. PPR's share in the Sowind Group now allows for a technical collaboration between Girard-Perregaux and PPR'S watch brands, one fruit of which is Boucheron Reflet XL, which is equipped with an automatic movement created by Girard-Perregaux's workshops in La Chaux-de-Fonds.

Boucheron Reflet XL (in collaboration with Girard-Perregaux)

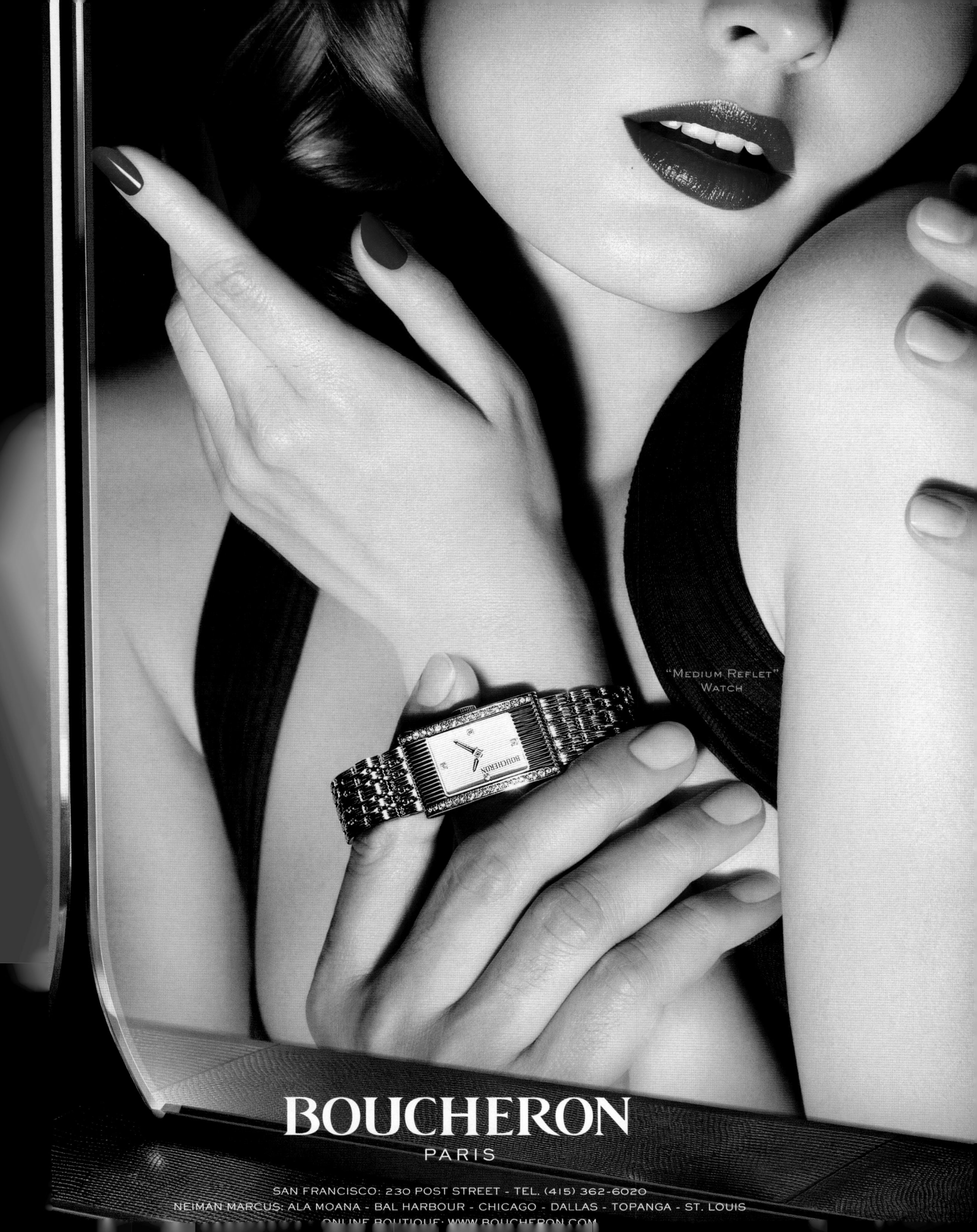

"Medium Reflet"
Watch

BOUCHERON

PARIS

MOVADO NOW COVERS THE ENTIRE HOROLOGICAL PALETTE

"Movado's goal is to become recognized as a forward-looking company in the watch industry, with exceptional products and quality customer service. Up until now, we have not been considered as one of the sector's leaders, but we plan to grow, in sales as well as in profits." With these words, Movado announced its latest significant purchase, that, of "The Architects of Time" Ebel from LVMH in 2004, for 61.5 million Swiss francs.

THIS PAGE
1947 Horwitt Museum Watch (Movado)

FACING PAGE
C1 Tourbillon Gravity (Concord)

FROM "FASHION" WATCHES TO HAUTE HOROLOGY

With this acquisition, Movado, which boasts annual US sales of $500 million, has clearly become a major player. The company now owns nine brands that cover the gamut of the watch world in terms of price and positioning. The Tommy Hilfiger line was first launched in the US in 2001 (with five collections per year) and then in Europe, which secured the group a place on the lower end of the scale with less expensive watches that are in touch with the latest trends. ESQ aims at the sporty, affordable segment of the watch market, followed by Coach, a licensed line from the American leather goods manufacturer that targets a more selective audience.

Then come the company's two historic brands: Movado (active in affordable luxury and best known for its Museum Watch, the first watch chosen by New York's Museum of Modern Art to be in its permanent collection) and Concord (which has now won a place in haute horology with a completely revamped collection, including the stunning C1 Tourbillon Gravity). On the strength of that first contract with Tommy Hilfiger, Movado has also made a name for itself in the field of licensed watch collections in fashion lines such as Hugo Boss, Juicy Couture and recently Lacoste, a group of fashionable watch lines that strengthen the group's distribution network, which includes 30 stores under their own names.

EBEL AND MOVADO

Though Movado's headquarters moved to the United States after the brand's purchase in 1983, there was never any question that its watches would continue to be Swiss made. The Grinberg family—which owns a majority share in the company and introduced Movado first to NASDAQ in 1993 and then to the New York Stock Exchange in 2001—holds as tightly to the company's Swiss foundation as it does to its own roots. The purchase of Ebel in 2004, which had been passed to Investcorp in 1994 then LVMH five years later, fits in perfectly with this logic. However, it was not easy to rehabilitate the brand. Though it enjoyed an excellent reputation, Ebel had not been able to counteract the slow erosion of sales, and had lost 40 million Swiss francs by the time of its acquisition. Two years later, Movado lived up to its word, bringing Ebel back into the black. The brand now projects sales of 100,000 pieces in the medium term, most of them equipped with in-house movements. With Ebel's turnaround coming just before the financial crisis, Movado had proved itself. However, it is clear that the group is suffering as a result of the particularly abrupt slowdown that has affected all of the brands in the American market.

TOP   Ebel 1911 Tekton Ajax

LEFT   Ebel Classic

FRANCK MULLER: A GROUP WITH RAPID GROWTH

The adventure of Franck Muller and Vartan Sirmakes (maker of cases and diamond settings) began in 1991 with the creation of the Franck Muller Techno Watch company. A few years later, on the strength of the brand's phenomenal success, the holding company Franck Muller Watchland took up the baton. But the house makes no secret of its intention to beef up its portfolio in order to become a true horological group. In 2001, the group acquired Pierre Kunz and European Company Watch (ECW). In March of 2005, the company snapped up Rodolphe, a watch designer whose logo shows up on six or seven million watches produced by third parties such as Esprit or Breil, as well as Rodolphe Montres et Bijoux, the company's atelier. Two months later, Franck Muller Watchland set its cap for Alexis Barthelay, a French company that was founded in Paris in the 1930s and had grown since to reach sales of seven to eight million Swiss francs per year.

BELOW LEFT   Franck Muller

BELOW RIGHT   Vartan Sirmakes, CEO of Franck Muller Group

VERTICAL INTEGRATION

Over the years, Franck Muller has also invested massively in its production capacities in order to enter fully into the universe of horological manufactures. This continual quest for complete industrial autonomy has led to the creation of companies such as FM Technocase (for cases and sapphire crystals), and Neo (research and development) at Neuchâtel. It has also motivated the company to acquire subcontractors in the Jura region such as GecoH (crowns, hands and straps), Linder (dials), Poli-Indus (polishing) and Pignon Juracie (pinions and gears).

The acquisition of new brands continues apace. In 2007, after Backes & Strauss, Franck Muller bought back Martin Braun. Specializing in astronomical watches, Martin Braun powers all of its complicated watches with internally manufactured movements. In fewer than 15 years, Franck Muller Watchland had gone from a single brand to nine, its ample success evidenced by its nearly 1,100 employees and annual production of 60,000 watches.

The company's latest project is the launch of a new brand under the signature of master watchmaker Pierre-Michel Golay, who has been responsible for the group's research and development since 2002. The first six original movements are ready but will probably have to wait for better days. Facing enormous difficulties, the group was forced to make massive layoffs in 2009.

ABOVE   The main office of the Franck Muller Group is in Genthod, Geneva

RIGHT   Ronde Freedom Chronograph (Franck Muller)

ZANNETTI
HANDMADE WATCHES

Full Sky
automatic · steel
full hand-engraved
and enamelled dial

Frog Cuff
sterling silver
and white jade

ZANNETTI - 00186 Rome/ITALY - Via di Monte d'Oro, 23A - Tel. +39/06.6819.2566 Fax +39/06.6875.027
www.zannettiwatches.com - mail: info@zannettiwatches.it

Francesco Trapani,
CEO of Bulgari Group.

TEN YEARS OF EFFORT

"There are two essential reasons why we bought the company," explained Francesco Trapani at the time of the acquisition. "Firstly, it had two brands with good growth potential, which we will fully realize with Bulgari's expertise and organization. And secondly, we wanted to obtain a recognized savoir-faire in the production of grand complications, a field in which Bulgari has very little experience."

Everything took a little longer to come together. As was recently explained by Gérald Roden, who orchestrated the renaissance of the brands and left the group at the end of last year. "There were of course certain industrial foundations," he said, " but no one really thought we could resurrect the brands, given the product-quality issues we were experiencing. So we ended up with a small boutique, which had international ambitions but not really the methods to realize them." To reposition these brands, a total reworking would have to be done, especially with the watch movements that have historically included perpetual calendars, tourbillons and especially sonneries.

BULGARI WITH MECHANICAL TOUCHES

For Bulgari, an active group in the luxury world with sales over a billion euros, it was far from a sure thing. Little by little, the synergies began to come together, and Daniel Roth and Gérald Genta began to produce mechanical watches for Bulgari, which the group positioned at the very high end. While he was at it, Roden also reduced the output of both brands by almost 12,000 units, to 4,000 for both brands, while focusing efforts on the production of proprietary complicated movements. The entire process involved considerable investments, including in terms of personnel. However, Bulgari recently announced the closure of the brands' headquarters in Meyrin and Daniel Roth and Gérald Genta are completely under the aegis of the Bulgari Group. As for the production workshops in Sentier, which include a brand new 3,000-meter-square building, their futures are uncertain.

In the early 1980s, Bulgari Time, the department in charge of the creation and production of all Bulgari watches, moved to Neuchâtel, Switzerland.

ABOVE Donatella Versace is head designer and Creative Director for all of Gianni Versace SpA's ventures, from its signature clothing, accessories, watches and jewelry lines to Versace Home Couture for New York City's Plaza Hotel residences and Versace Design, an interior design service for private jets and helicopters.

RIGHT Destiny Spirit (Versace)

THE AMERICAN AMBITION OF TIMEX GROUP COMPANY

The history of Timex Group Company is as intimately linked with the United States as Swatch's is with Switzerland. Founded in 1854 in Waterbury, Connecticut, Timex was originally called Waterbury Clock Company. In 1900, it was the first company to market a $1 pocket watch. Called the "Yankee," the timepiece appealed to the huge market of newly arrived immigrants.

Watch provider to the U.S. Army, Waterbury Clock Company became known in Europe by equipping American doughboys in World War I with wristwatches. But it was with its Ingersoll model, whose dial featured a picture of Mickey Mouse, that the brand would leave a lasting impression on the Old World.

The first Timex watch was created in 1949, combining high-quality mechanics and a low price. The launch of this watch inspired the company to abandon old habits and sell its products in general stores. Just thirteen years later, one out of every three watches sold in the US was a Timex.

Timex Group Company would become known in Europe in the 1970s when it licensed several brands, including Kelton watches with the famous slogan: "If you change, change your watch…Only Kelton prices give you that luxury." Today, Timex Group brands include Timex, Times Ironman, Marc Ecko, Nautica, Opex Paris and TX.

F-80 Chronograph
(Salvatore Ferragamo)

SALVATORE
166 DIAMONDS AND STAINLESS STEEL, ALLIGATOR STRAP

Salvatore Ferragamo
TIMEPIECES

Having easily weathered the quartz storm of the 1970s, Timex Group began to draw closer to the Old World by making luxury a new focus of development. In 2004, the company created the Vertime division, based in the Netherlands with branches in Switzerland, in order to better direct its newly acquired Versace and Versus brands. In 2006, Timex bought the high-end Swiss line Vincent Bérard, which has just opened a brand new manufacture in the mountains of Neuchâtel. In 2007, the company welcomed Valentino Timeless and Salvatore Ferragamo Timepieces in to its fold under the Timex Group Luxury Watches division. And last but not least, the same year saw the creation of Sequel, a Swiss arm of the company, which produces Guess and Gc Watches. Today, some 5,000 people in 80 countries work for Timex Group, which earned $800 million in 2008.

Liaison (Valentino Timeless)

A. LANGE & SÖHNE

GLASHÜTTE I/SA

When A. Lange & Söhne resumed watch production after a 50-year hiatus in 1995, the Lange 1 was the first model it introduced. Since then, its instantly recognizable off-center dial configuration and patented date display have become the face of the Glashütte-based company.

The model's runaway popularity and growing list of critical accolades have inspired the company to expand the Lange 1 family, which now includes six different members, each equipped with a manual movement. This year, the brand welcomes the first automatic model to its iconic collection with the Lange 1 Daymatic.

To power its latest creation, A. Lange & Söhne developed caliber L021.1 entirely at its manufactory. Like all of the company's movements, it exhibits a high level of craftsmanship, including a hand-engraved balance cock over the brand's manufacture balance spring.

The Daymatic shares another trait with its Lange 1 brethren, a solid silver dial, but the similarities end there. The new model's dial represents a mirror image of the layout found on the manual versions, moving the time to the right side and the date to the left. When worn on the left wrist, the arrangement ensures the time will be revealed first when the sleeve is raised. To balance the design, the Daymatic includes a retrograde day-of-the-week display in place of the power-reserve indicator.

A. Lange & Söhne presents the Daymatic in a 39.5mm case offered in a choice of yellow gold, pink gold or platinum.

Just as the Lange 1 marked A. Lange & Söhne's entrée into the modern age, the 2009 Lange Zeitwerk symbolizes the dawn of the next era in the watchmaker's legendary history.

The Lange Zeitwerk's progressive mechanics and unique aesthetics join eloquently on the dial where a time bridge—made of German silver—encompasses the watch's distinctive jumping hour and minute windows separated by the small seconds display. A dip at the top of the bridge follows the arc of the power-reserve indicator at 12:00, giving the dial a harmonious visual balance.

The proprietary movement that resides below the dial's fresh design is specially designed to provide the substantial amount of power necessary to animate the rotating discs used for the jumping display. At the center of this innovative mechanism is a patented mainspring that supplies the requisite torque to advance all three discs simultaneously at the turn of every hour. Another patented creation integrated into the movement is a constant-force escapement devised to distribute the mainspring's energy evenly through its 36-hour supply.

While the previous two models stake claim to A. Lange & Söhne's present and future, the 1815 evokes the company's past, commemorating the year that founder Ferdinand Adolph Lange was born.

Originally released in 1995, the dimensions of the latest 1815 expand to 40mm in diameter. The sleek outline frames a solid-silver dial where the hours, minutes and small seconds are arranged to reflect the timeless elegance of a classic pocket watch.

With this tasteful triumvirate, A. Lange & Söhne explores its past, present and future with timepieces that are emblematic of the watchmaker's dedication to both tradition and innovation.

This year, A. Lange & Söhne welcomes **the first automatic model to its iconic Lange 1 collection** with the Daymatic.

FACING PAGE

The Daymatic is the first Lange 1 model to feature automatic winding. Instead of a power-reserve indicator, the watch offers a retrograde day-of-the-week indicator opposite the time display.

THIS PAGE

ABOVE   Lange Zeitwerk distinguishes itself from other timepieces thanks to a unique time bridge that spotlights a jumping hour and minute indication that is both technically advanced and easy to read.

LEFT   Named for the birth year of A. Lange & Söhne's founder, the 1815's understated style takes its visual cues from traditional pocket watches.

1815   REF. 233.032

Movement: manually wound Lange manufacture Caliber L051.1; 55-hour power reserve; 21,600 vph; 21 jewels; 188 parts; decorated and assembled by hand; precision-adjusted in five positions; three-quarter plate made of untreated German silver; balance cock engraved by hand; five screwed gold chatons; shock-resistant Glucydur screw balance; Nivarox balance spring; whiplash precision index adjuster with patented beat adjustment mechanism.

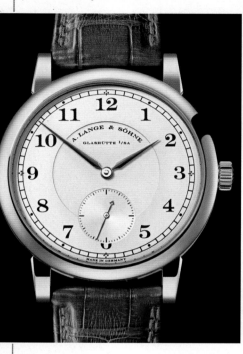

Functions: hours, minutes; small seconds.
Case: pink gold; 40x8.9mm; crown for winding the watch and setting the time; sapphire crystal caseback.
Dial: solid silver; blued steel hands.
Strap: crocodile; Lange prong buckle in solid gold.
Also available: other dial and case combinations.

DATOGRAPH   REF. 403.035

Movement: manually wound Lange manufacture Caliber L951.1; 36-hour power reserve; 18,000 vph; 40 jewels; 405 parts; decorated and assembled by hand; precision-adjusted in five positions; plates and bridges made of untreated German silver; balance cock engraved by hand; four screwed gold chatons; shock-resistant Glucydur screw balance; Nivarox 1 hairspring; whiplash precision index adjuster with patented beat adjustment mechanism.

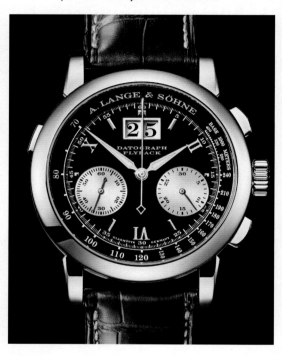

Functions: hours, minutes; small seconds with stop seconds; outsize date; chronograph: 30-minute counter, flyback and precisely jumping minute counter.
Case: platinum; Ø 39mm; crown for winding the watch and setting the time; two pushpieces for chronograph; one pushpiece for rapid correction of the outsize date; antireflective sapphire crystal caseback.
Dial: solid silver and black; platinum hands.
Strap: hand-stitched crocodile; Lange prong buckle in solid platinum.
Also available: other dial and case combinations.

LANGE 1   REF. 101.021

Movement: manually wound Lange manufacture Caliber L901.0; 72-hour power reserve; 21,600 vph; 53 jewels; 365 parts; decorated and assembled by hand; precision-adjusted in five positions; twin mainspring barrels; patented two-disc outsize date mechanism; stop seconds mechanism; three-quarter plate made of cross-laminated untreated German silver, damascened with Glashütte ribbing; hand-engraved balance cock; shock-resistant screw balance; Nivarox 1 balance spring; screwed gold chatons; whiplash precision index adjuster with patented beat adjustment mechanism.

Functions: hours, minutes; small seconds with stop seconds.
Case: 18K yellow gold; Ø 38.5mm, thickness: 10mm; antireflective sapphire crystal caseback.
Dial: solid silver and champagne; yellow-gold hands.
Strap: hand-stitched crocodile; Lange prong buckle in 18K yellow gold.
Also available: other dial and case combinations.

LANGE 1 DAYMATIC   REF. 320.032

Movement: automatic Lange manufacture Caliber L021.1; 50-hour power reserve; 21,600 vph; 67 jewels; 426 parts; decorated and assembled by hand; precision-adjusted in five positions; central rotor with centrifugal mass in platinum; balance cock engraved by hand; seven screwed gold chatons; shock-resistant Glucydur balance with eccentric poising weights; superior quality balance spring manufactured in-house; whiplash precision index adjuster with patented beat adjustment mechanism.

Functions: hours, minutes; small seconds with stop seconds; patented outsize date; retrograde day-of-week display.
Case: pink gold; Ø 39.5mm, thickness: 10.4mm; crown for winding the watch and setting the time; pushpieces for correcting the date and day-of-week displays; sapphire crystal caseback.
Dial: solid silver and argenté; pink gold hands.
Strap: hand-stitched crocodile; Lange prong buckle in solid pink gold.
Also available: other dial and case combinations.

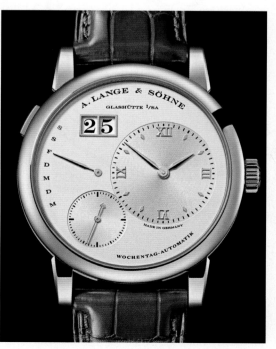

LANGE 1 TIME ZONE   REF. 116.025

Movement: manually wound Lange manufacture Caliber L031.1; 72-hour power reserve; 21,600 vph; 54 jewels; 417 parts; decorated and assembled by hand; precision-adjusted in five positions; twin mainspring barrel; plates and bridges made of untreated German silver; balance cock and intermediate-wheel cock engraved by hand; four screwed gold chatons; shock-resistant Glucydur screw balance; Nivarox balance; whiplash precision index adjuster with patented beat adjustment mechanism.

Functions: hours, minutes, small seconds with stop seconds; outsize date for home time; separate day and night indicators for main and second time zones with city ring.

Case: platinum; 41.9x11mm; crown for winding the watch and setting the time; pushpiece for switching the outsize date; pushpiece for advancing the city ring; synchronized with the hour hand of the time-zone display and the day/night indicator for time zone; antireflective sapphire crystal caseback.

Dial: solid silver and rhodié; blued steel hands.

Strap: hand-stitched crocodile; Lange prong buckle in platinum.

Also available: other dial and case combinations.

SAXONIA   REF. 215.032

Movement: manually wound Lange manufacture Caliber L941.1; 45-hour power reserve; 21,600 vph; 21 jewels; 164 parts; decorated and assembled by hand; precision adjusted in five positions; plates and bridges made of untreated German silver; balance cock engraved by hand; four screwed gold chatons; shock-resistant Glucydur screw balance; Nivarox hairspring balance; whiplash precision index adjuster with patented beat adjustment mechanism.

Functions: hours, minutes; small seconds with stop seconds.

Case: 18K pink gold; Ø 37mm, thickness: 7.3mm; crown for winding movement and setting the time; sapphire crystal caseback.

Dial: solid silver and argenté; pink-gold hands.

Strap: crocodile; Lange prong buckle in solid pink gold.

Also available: other dial and case combinations.

SAXONIA ANNUAL CALENDAR   REF. 330.026

Movement: automatic Lange manufacture Caliber L085.1 SAX-0-MAT; 46-hour power reserve; 21,600 vph; 43 jewels; 476 parts; decorated and assembled by hand; precision-adjusted in five positions; three-quarter plate made of untreated German silver with integrated three-quarter rotor in 21K gold and centrifugal mass in platinum; reversing and reduction gear with four ball bearings; balance cock engraved by hand; shock-resistant Glucydur screw balance; Nivarox balance spring; whiplash precision index adjuster with patented beat adjustment mechanism.

Functions: hours, minutes; small seconds with stop seconds and zero-reset function; annual calendar with patented outsize date, day-of-week, month, and moonphase displays.

Case: white gold; Ø 38.5mm, thickness: 9.8mm; crown for winding the watch and setting the time; sapphire crystal caseback.

Dial: solid silver and argenté; blued steel hands.

Strap: hand-stitched crocodile; Lange prong buckle in solid white gold.

Also available: other dial and case combinations.

LANGE ZEITWERK   REF. 140.029

Movement: manually wound Lange manufacture Caliber L043.1; 36-hour power reserve; 18,000 vph; 66 jewels; 388 parts; decorated and assembled by hand; precision-adjusted in five positions; three-quarter plate made of untreated German silver; balance cock engraved by hand; jumping minutes; constant-force escapement; shock-resistant Glucydur balance with eccentric poising weights; superior-quality balance spring manufactured in-house with patent-pending attachment system (balance spring clamp); whiplash precision index adjuster with patented beat adjustment mechanism.

Functions: jumping hours and minutes; small seconds with stop seconds.

Case: white gold; Ø 41.9mm, thickness: 12.6mm; crown for winding the watch and setting the time; sapphire crystal caseback.

Dial: solid silver and black; rhodium gold hands; German silver and rhodium time bridge.

Strap: hand-stitched crocodile; Lange prong buckle in solid white gold.

Also available: other dial and case combinations.

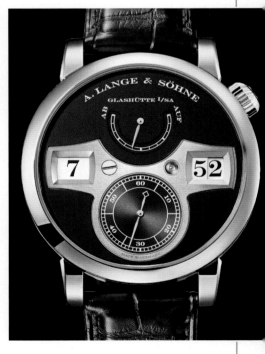

ARCHITECTE HORLOGER

Some watch designers are born into the profession, the next in line to carry on the horological tradition often passed from generation to generation. Like Alain Silberstein, however, some start out as interior designers and architects. It is only within the strict aesthetic confines of horology that they find, paradoxically, their ultimate freedom of expression.

Silberstein hung out a shingle as a watchmaker in the late 1980s in Besançon, center of the French watch world. This was still in the days of the quartz crisis, a phrase that still makes haute horologists shudder with dread. The mechanical watch had been pronounced all but dead—not an auspicious time to begin a company based on centuries-old tradition! But Alain Silberstein paid no heed to the naysayers and was soon showing his collection at the Basel Fair and winning fans all over the world with his distinctive designs and superbly executed complications.

Like all Alain Silberstein models, the Krono Bauhaus II (KT 608) was produced in a limited edition—the quantity for this particular design was 999 numbered pieces. The automatic Valjoux 7751 movement powers several functions, including a chronograph and moonphase display. The 40mm-diameter steel case boasts an alligator-skin veneer that matches the cheerful yet elegant strap. The case also shows off the three color-coded pushbuttons—a yellow circle, red triangle and blue square—that form part of the Alain Silberstein aesthetic.

This famous motif has become Alain Silberstein's most recognizable—and beloved—characteristic, and it lends itself to the Blue Sea Tourbillon (MTA-005). Modern art has always had a huge influence on the French designer, particularly the bold use of primary colors and simple shapes of De Stijl. The bright underwater scene depicted on the Blue Sea Tourbillon's dial incorporates both the tourbillon at 6:00 and a date display indicated by a yellow starfish's red-tipped arm.

Modern art has always had a huge influence on the French designer, particularly the bold use of primary colors and simple shapes of De Stijl.

FACING PAGE   The steel case of the Krono Bauhaus II houses a Valjoux 7751 automatic chronograph movement and is water resistant to 3 bar.

THIS PAGE   The iKrono "Blue Ring" with its blue-toned tachymetric scale around the dial is fitted with an ETA Valjoux 7750 automatic chronograph movement.

Released in a numbered and limited edition of 100 watches, the Marine 20 beats to the ETA 2892-J, an automatic movement with power reserve.

The White Night Tourbillon is powered by an exclusive manual movement inside a steel case that is water resistant to 10 bar.

The Marine 20 (MV 301 B) adds a new twist to Silberstein's iconic design philosophy. The classic blue minute hand and red triangular hour hand sweep across the dial as usual, joined by the playful second hand, a squiggle of yellow. A fourth hand, relatively restrained, indicates the date. As part of the Rondo collection, however, the Marine 20 features an intense emphasis on the circular form, adding a dotted circle to the tip of the hour hand and enclosing the signature triangular crown within a slightly convex circle.

This "circular reasoning" also influences the White Night Tourbillon (TS 504), whose exposed tourbillon at 6:00 mirrors a date subdial at 12:00. A cloisonné lacquer finish enhances the 40mm-diameter steel case, and the design includes all the quirky touches that watch lovers have come to expect from Alain Silberstein, including a crown that superimposes one triangle atop another. As with all Alain Silberstein timepieces, the movement can be seen through a transparent caseback—yet another proud but playful tradition.

Alpina
GENEVE

For a century, the Swiss watch brand Alpina has inspired a dedicated following of collectors who call themselves Alpinists. Its membership has grown since 2002, when Peter and Aletta Stas assumed the company's reins, reviving it as a manufacture specializing in complicated timepieces designed to fit active lifestyles.

As new owners, the Stases marshaled the talents of designers, engineers and watchmakers, focusing their wherewithal on the creation of a line of sports watches and reestablishing Alpina as a manufacture.

They succeeded in 2008, celebrating the company's 125th anniversary with the introduction of automatic caliber AL-950, a movement designed entirely at Alpina's workshops. AL-950 debuted in Alpina's Manufacture Regulator, a stainless steel timepiece whose dial is arranged with separate scales for the hours, minutes and date.

The company took an important step in its ongoing revival a year later, unveiling its first proprietary tourbillon movement. "Our team took on the challenge of creating this dazzling invention," says Peter Stas, company CEO. "The result is a watch that combines one of the highest technical achievements in watchmaking with the exceptional, iconic Alpina design language, in which form follows function."

The Manufacture Extreme Tourbillon is equipped with AL-980, a movement that was developed in Alpina's Geneva workshop and features a high-performance silicon escapement wheel and lever.

The Extreme 12 Hours of Sebring's black dial and strap recall the **carbon-fiber material used to construct the racecars** that roar around the corners at Sebring.

From one extreme to another, the company switches gears from high horology to high speeds for a special timepiece dedicated to the 12-hour endurance race at Sebring, Florida. Last year, Alpina not only served as the race's official timekeeper, but also took the occasion to unveil the Extreme 12 Hours of Sebring.

The watch is a classic three-hand with a date window between 4:00 and 5:00. Sporting a brushed finish, the stainless steel case lives up to its "extreme" billing with its large 48mm size. A black PVD-coated bezel with luminous numerals is attached to the case by six of Alpina's signature triangular screws.

The Extreme 12 Hours of Sebring's black dial and strap share a hatch pattern that recalls the carbon-fiber material used to construct the racecars roaring around the corners at Sebring.

Alpina softens that masculine edge with the feminine charms of its latest addition to the Extreme collection, one of its most emblematic collections.

For a crisp look in white, the new Regulator combines a white ceramic case and rubber strap with a bezel set with 48 diamonds. For a dynamic dash of color, Alpina uses its trademark red triangle to punctuate the white enamel on the end of the watch's screw-down crown.

Despite occupying opposite ends of the spectrum, the white Regulator and black Sebring do share one common bond: the creativity and expertise of Alpina's workshops made them possible.

FACING PAGE

LEFT   The Manufacture Extreme Tourbillon's Ø 48mm rose-gold case is topped with a black ceramic bezel. Alpina will make only 18 pieces for this limited edition.

RIGHT   Launched in 2008 to celebrate Alpina's 125th anniversary, Manufacture Regulator boasts the company's first manufacture movement since its 2002 revival.

THIS PAGE

TOP   Alpina honors the 57th edition of Florida's popular endurance race with the Extreme 12 Hours of Sebring. Only 257 pieces will be made.

RIGHT   This diamond-set version of the Extreme Regulator includes a white ceramic case on a rubber strap. Skilled artisans decorated and finished its automatic movement by hand.

EXTREME AUTOMATIC   REF. AL-525BB5FBAE6

Movement: automatic-winding AL-525 caliber; 42-hour power reserve; bridges decorated with perlage; black rotor decorated with Côtes de Genève.
Functions: hours, minutes, seconds; date at 3.
Case: steel; Ø 48mm; three-part case secured by six triangular stainless steel screws; black PVD bezel and caseback; ABS-coated screw-down crown with red Alpina triangle pattern; transparent sapphire crystal caseback; water resistant to 20atm.

Dial: black with trademark Alpina triangle pattern in center; silver applied steel indexes; fine-brushed steel hands with white luminescence in the center.
Strap: black rubber; optional deployment buckle.
Suggested price: $2,190

SPECIAL LTD EDITION FOR THE 12 HOURS OF SEBRING 2009   REF. AL-525BR5AES6

Movement: automatic-winding AL-525 caliber; 42-hour power reserve; 28,800 vph; 26 jewels; bridges decorated with perlage; anglage finishing; black Alpina rotor decorated with Côtes de Genève.
Functions: hours, minutes, seconds; date between 4 and 5.
Case: brushed stainless steel; Ø 48mm; three-part case secured by six triangular stainless steel Alpina screws; fixed black PVD-coated bezel with luminescent digits; sapphire crystal; ABS-coated screw-down crown with red Alpina triangle; exhibition caseback with red engraving; water resistant to 20atm.
Dial: matte black with carbon in center; applied white and red luminescent Arabic numerals; white luminescent painted hands; exclusive 12 Hours of Sebring logo at 6.
Strap: carbon; red lining and stitching; black PVD Alpina deployment buckle.
Suggested price: $2,350
Note: exclusive gift box in black lacquered wood: black leather cover with famous Sebring Raceway-track printed on the top, red leather interior and special engravings on aluminum plaques, numbered in correspondence with the watch from 001/257 through 257/257.

EXTREME DIVER   REF. AL-525LFB5FBAEV6

Movement: automatic-winding AL-525 caliber; 42-hour power reserve; 28,800 vph; 26 jewels; bridges decorated with perlage; anglage finishing; black rotor decorated with Côtes de Genève.
Functions: hours, minutes, seconds; date at 3.
Case: black PVD steel; Ø 48mm; three-part case secured by six triangular stainless steel screws; unidirectional turning bezel with luminescent indexes and numerals; ABS-coated screw-down crown with red Alpina triangle pattern; transparent sapphire crystal caseback; water resistant to 100atm.
Dial: black with trademark Alpina triangle pattern in center; applied black luminescent indexes and Arabic numerals; black luminescent painted hands.
Strap: black rubber; optional deployment buckle.
Suggested price: $3,190

EXTREME REGULATOR   REF. AL-650BB5AE4

Movement: manual-winding proprietary AL-650 caliber; 42-hour power reserve; bridges decorated with Côtes de Genève; matte-black ratchet and winding wheels.
Functions: hours (regulator at 10), minutes, seconds.
Case: rose gold; Ø 48mm; three-part case secured by six triangular stainless steel screws; black PVD bezel and caseback; ABS-coated screw-down crown with red Alpina triangle pattern; transparent sapphire crystal caseback; water resistant to 10atm.
Dial: black regulator with trademark Alpina triangle pattern in center; rose-gold applied indexes in steel; fine-brushed rose-gold hands with white luminescence in the center.
Strap: black rubber; optional deployment buckle.
Suggested price: $2,790

MANUFACTURE REGULATOR   REF. AL-950BB4FBAE6

Movement: new regulator; automatic-winding proprietary AL-950 caliber; 48-hour power reserve; Incabloc anti-shock system; 28,800 vph; 25 jewels; Glucydur balance; Nivarox No.1 balance spring; bridges decorated with perlage and Côtes de Genève; anglage finishing; black rotor decorated with Côtes de Genève.
Functions: hours (regulator at 10), minutes, date at 6.
Case: black PVD; Ø 46mm; three-part case secured by six triangular stainless steel screws; black PVD bezel and caseback; individually numbered; ABS-coated screw-down crown with red enameled Alpina triangle; transparent sapphire crystal caseback; water resistant to 20atm.
Dial: matte black; black fine-brushed applied steel indexes; skeleton in brushed and black steel.
Strap: black rubber; optional deployment buckle.
Suggested price: $3,750

EXTREME TOURBILLON REGULATOR MANUFACTURE   REF. AL-980BC5AE9

Movement: tourbillon regulator; automatic-winding proprietary AL-980 caliber; 48-hour power reserve; Silicium escapement wheel and Silicium lever; one-minute tourbillon; openworked cage bridges; 28,800 vph; 33 jewels; Incabloc anti-shock system; Glucydur balance; Nivarox No. 1 balance spring; bridges decorated with perlage and Côtes de Genève; anglage finishing; black PVD-plated rotor decorated with Côtes de Genève; 188 components; each movement individually numbered.
Functions: hours (regulator at 10), minutes, seconds.
Case: rose gold; Ø 48mm; three-part case secured by six triangular stainless steel screws; black ceramic bezel and caseback; ABS-coated screw-down crown with red Alpina triangle pattern; transparent sapphire crystal caseback; each case is individually numbered; water resistant to 10atm.
Dial: matte black; fine-brushed applied steel indexes; skeleton in brushed and black steel.
Strap: black rubber; optional deployment buckle.
Suggested price: $52,500
Note: limited edition of 18 pieces.

EXTREME REGULATOR   REF. AL-650LSSS3AEDC4

Movement: automatic-winding AL-650 caliber ETA 2895 base; 42-hours power reserve; Incabloc anti-shock system; 28,800 vph; 25 jewels; Glucydur balance; Nivarox No.1 balance spring; bridges decorated with perlage; black rotor decorated with Côtes de Genève; anglage finishing.
Functions: hours, minutes, seconds.
Case: ceramic and surgical steel; Ø 42mm; three-part case secured by six triangular stainless steel screws; rose-gold-plated bezel set with 48 VS Top Wesselton diamonds; ABS-coated screw-down crown with enameled Alpina triangle; transparent sapphire crystal caseback; individually numbered; water resistant to 10atm.
Dial: white coated with trademark Alpina triangle pattern in center; applied polished indexes; luminescent rose-gold-plated hands.
Strap: rubber; optional deployment buckle.
Suggested price: $5,250

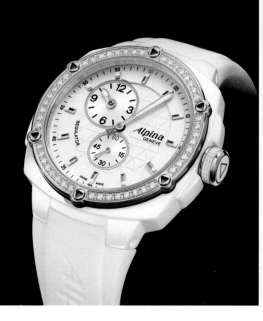

EXTREME CHRONO DOUBLE DIGIT   REF. AL-850BR4FBAE6

Movement: automatic-winding AL-850 caliber; 28,800 vph; 37 jewels; Alpina black PVD-plated rotor.
Functions: hours, minutes, seconds; date indicator at 6; chronograph: seconds counter, 30-minute counter.
Case: black PVD; Ø 46mm; three-part case secured by six triangular stainless steel screws; black PVD bezel and caseback; ABS-coated screw-down crown with red Alpina triangle pattern; two pushbuttons for the chronograph; transparent sapphire crystal caseback; water resistant to 10atm.
Dial: matte black; red counters; silver applied steel indexes; skeleton in fine-brushed steel.
Strap: black rubber; optional deployment buckle.
Suggested price: $3,990

AUDEMARS PIGUET

Le maître de l'horlogerie depuis 1875

With its Royal Oak Offshore Grand Prix, Audemars Piguet sets collectors' hearts racing with three limited edition chronographs whose technical and aesthetic characteristics reflect the power and precision of high-performance automobiles. In fact, each shares a sophisticated design that references the assertive aerodynamics, cutting-edge materials and powerful engines found in the world of racing.

The Royal Oak Offshore Grand Prix quickly establishes its dynamic look with a black ceramic ring topped by a forged carbon bezel, both with open channels that evoke air scoops found on the hoods of turbocharged cars. The meticulous detailing extends to the side of the case with a crown whose notches call to mind a gear and its teeth.

The auto-inspired look continues on the dial, where the intuitive layout of the chronograph subsidiary dials, small seconds and date aperture looks like a stylized dashboard. The Grand Prix's dial also offers a clever visual twist on the Royal Oak Offshore by inverting the watch's signature Méga Tapisserie motif. The decoration not only adds a multi-dimensional aspect, but also echoes the bezel's air-scoop design.

For the Royal Oak Offshore Grand Prix collection, the company pairs different colored dials and case metals: red with forged carbon, black with rose gold, and blue with platinum. All three share the same forged carbon bezel. The lightweight material—exclusive to Audemars Piguet—is also used to form the guards that protect the chronograph pushers on the rose-gold and platinum models.

While stylistic variations establish the unique personality exhibited by each watch, all three share the same automatic movement, a chronograph envisioned and assembled entirely by Audemars Piguet at its Le Brassus workshop.

The Grand Prix's dial inverts the Royal Oak Offshore's multi-dimensional Méga Tapisserie motif, echoing the bezel's air-scoop design in tribute to racecars.

For the Grand Prix's engine, the company modified its Caliber 3126 with the 3840 chronograph to create an integrated mechanism that offers a high level of precision. An important factor contributing to the movement's constancy is its resistance to shocks and knocks. The robust design is achieved, in part, by a cross-through balance-bridge and variable-inertia balance equipped with eight inertia blocks.

A crystal caseback allows a peek beneath the Grand Prix's hood, revealing the painstaking attention to detail lavished on the movement by Audemars Piguet's dedicated artisans. To illustrate the point, the edge of the bridges are chamfered and polished to gleaming perfection while the top and bottom are covered with Côtes de Genève. Perhaps the most noticeable detail is the 22-karat gold rotor. Exclusive to this limited edition, the special oscillating weight is partially blackened and hollowed to reinforce the Grand Prix's scoop leitmotif.

Just as the proprietary movement underscores Audemars Piguet's technical accomplishments, so too does the forged carbon—which uses exclusive technology to create parts of the case, including the bezel. According to the brand, the bezel's signature octagonal form is created by compressing carbon filaments at high temperatures. The result is a bezel that is exceptionally hard yet ultra-light. In fact, the forged carbon version of the watch weighs just 120 grams.

With its Royal Oak Offshore Grand Prix, Audemars Piguet thrills with a sophisticated design that leads the pack with innovation and style.

FACING PAGE
LEFT   The bezel and 44mm case of this Royal Oak Offshore Grand Prix are made of forged carbon, a lightweight and sturdy material developed exclusively by Audemars Piguet. The bronze-colored tachymeter flange is reminiscent of a racecar's magnesium-alloy rims. The red eloxed aluminum dial presents a "negative-printed" variation of the Méga Tapisserie motif common among Audemars Piguet's other Royal Oak Offshore models. Only 1,750 pieces will be produced.

RIGHT   The ultra-rare platinum version of the Royal Oak Offshore Grand Prix is released in a limited edition of 75 pieces. Along with the blue dial, the design also features a splash of red on the tachymeter scale and 30-minute counter. The watch is powered by Audemars Piguet's proprietary chronograph movement, which combines reliable accuracy, beautiful hand finishing and a 60-hour power reserve.

THIS PAGE
Audemars Piguet will produce only 650 pieces of the Royal Oak Offshore Grand Prix with the case, crown and chronograph pushers in pink gold. The black dial includes a small seconds at 12:00 along with the 30-minute and 12-hour chronograph counters at 9:00 and 6:00, respectively.

AUDEMARS PIGUET ROYAL OAK   REF.153000R.00.D002CR.01

Movement: automatic Caliber 3120; up to 60-hour power reserve; 21,600 vph; 40 jewels; 278 parts; variable inertia balance with eight inertia blocks and flat balance-spring; Geneva-type mobile balance-spring stud holder; three-position winding stem; all parts decorated by hand; circular graining on the plate; diamond polishing on the countersinks, the bevels and the recesses; beveling, snailing, Côtes de Genève on the bridges; AP engraving and Audemars and Piguet family crests on 22K gold oscillating weight.

Functions: hours, minutes; direct-drive center seconds; date window with rapid correction via the crown; balance stop mechanism during time setting.
Case: 18K pink gold; Ø 39mm; transparent sapphire caseback; water resistant to 50 meters.
Dial: black; Grande Tapisserie motif; luminescent hour-markers, appliques and facetted hands in 18K pink gold.
Strap: full-grain crocodile leather; 18K pink-gold AP folding clasp.
Suggested price: $22,500
Also available: in steel with AP triple-blade double-safety folding clasp.

ROYAL OAK CHRONOGRAPH   REF. 26300ST.00.1110ST.06

Movement: mechanical automatic Audemars Piguet Caliber 2385 with chronograph; up to 40-hour power reserve; 21,600 vph; 37 jewels; Côtes de Genève decorative pattern and circular graining; all parts decorated by hand.
Functions: hours, minutes; small seconds; chronograph with central seconds hand, 30-minute and 12-hour counters; date.
Case: stainless steel; Ø 39mm; caseback engraved with Royal Oak logo; water resistant to 50 meters.

Dial: silvered; Grande Tapisserie motif; bi-color counters; applied luminescent white-gold indexes; luminescent white-gold hour and minute hands; red central chronograph seconds hand.
Bracelet: stainless steel; AP folding clasp.
Suggested price: $16,600
Also available: with dark blue or brown dial.

ROYAL OAK CHRONOGRAPH   REF. 260220R.00.D098CR.01

Movement: mechanical automatic Audemars Piguet Caliber 2385 with chronograph; up to 40-hour power reserve; 21,600 vph; 37 jewels; Côtes de Genève decorative pattern and circular graining; all parts decorated by hand.
Functions: hours, minutes; small seconds; chronograph with central seconds hand, 30-minute and 12-hour counters; date.
Case: 18K pink gold; Ø 39mm; caseback engraved with the Royal Oak logo; water resistant to 50 meters.

Dial: silvered with Grande Tapisserie pattern; bi-color counters; applied luminescent pink-gold indexes; luminescent pink-gold hour and minute hands; pink-gold central chronograph seconds hand.
Strap: brown crocodile leather; 18K pink-gold AP folding clasp.
Suggested price: $30,800
Also available: with brown dial.

ROYAL OAK SKELETON SELFWINDING PERPETUAL CALENDAR   REF. 25829ST.00.0944ST.01

Movement: automatic Caliber 2120/2802SQ, openworked; 21K gold rotor segment; up to 40-hour power reserve; 19,800 vph; 38 jewels; 355 parts; 22K gold oscillating weight; Geneva-type mobile balance-spring stud holder; all parts decorated by hand.
Functions: hours, minutes; perpetual calendar: month, day and date, leap years, moonphases.
Case: stainless steel; Ø 39mm; 18K gold assembly screws; sapphire crystal and caseback; water resistant to 20 meters.

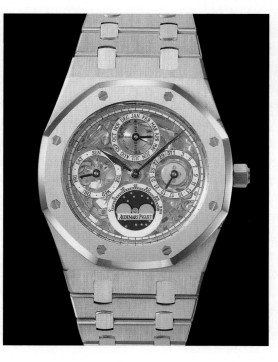

Dial: transparent sapphire dial revealing the engraving work on the movement.
Bracelet: stainless steel; AP folding clasp.
Note: model delivered in a rotating presentation box.
Suggested price: $67,500

ROYAL OAK OFFSHORE GRAND PRIX   REF. 26290IO.00.A001VE.01

Movement: automatic Caliber 3126/3840; up to 60-hour power reserve; 21,600 vph; 59 jewels; 365 parts; variable inertia balance with eight inertia blocks and flat balance-spring; Geneva-type mobile balance-spring stud holder; three-position winding crown; all parts meticulously decorated; circular-grained mainplate; bridges rhodium-plated, chamfered, snailed and adorned with Côtes de Genève; diamond-polished jewel sinks; wheels featuring chamfered arms and diamond-polished sinks; chamfered screw slots; 22K gold oscillating weight partially blackened and decorated with two scoops. **Functions:** hours, minutes, small seconds at 12; date; chronograph with central seconds hand, 30-minute and 12-hour counters at 9 and 6; tachymetric scale.

Case: forged carbon; Ø 44mm, thickness: 15.65mm; forged carbon and black ceramic bezel; flange with tachymetric scale; blackened titanium crown; black ceramic and titanium pushpieces; titanium push-piece guards; titanium exhibition case-back fitted with a sapphire crystal and engraved with inscription Royal Oak Offshore Grand Prix–Limited Edition; water resistant to 100 meters.
Dial: black; red center with exclusive negative-printed Méga Tapisserie motif in eloxed aluminum; anthracite small seconds counter at 12; silvered and yellow 30-minute counter at 9; silvered and black 12-hour counter at 6; yellow eloxed aluminum flange; white-gold hour-markers with luminescent coating; openworked and luminescent hour and minute hands in white or pink gold.
Strap: black calfskin and Alcantara; hand-sewn with Alcantara inserts and edges; pin buckle in bead-blasted titanium, 18K pink gold or 950 platinum.
Note: limited edition of 1,750 pieces.
Suggested price: $34,500

ROYAL OAK OFFSHORE CHRONOGRAPH   REF. 26170TI.00.1000TI.01

Movement: exclusive automatic Audemars Piguet Caliber 3126/3840; up to 60-hour power reserve; 21,600 vph; all parts decorated by hand.
Functions: hours, minutes, small seconds; date; chronograph with central seconds hand, 30-minute and 12-hour counters; tachymeter.
Case: titanium; Ø 42mm; caseback engraved with the Royal Oak Offshore logo; water resistant to 100 meters.
Dial: anthracite; exclusive Méga Tapisserie motif; black numerals.
Bracelet: titanium; AP triple-blade folding clasp.
Also available: in stainless steel; silvered dial.
Suggested price: $20,300

ROYAL OAK OFFSHORE DIVER   REF. 15703ST.00.A002CA.01

Movement: automatic proprietary Caliber 3120; up to 60-hour power reserve; 21,600 vph; 40 jewels; 278 parts; variable inertia balance with eight inertia blocks and flat balance-spring; Geneva-type mobile balance-spring stud holder; three-position winding stem; all parts finely decorated; circular-grained mainplate; bridges rhodium-plated, chamfered, snailed and adorned with Côtes de Genève; diamond-polished jewel sinks; wheels with chamfered spokes and diamond-polished jewel sinks; chamfered screw rims and slots; 22K gold oscillating weight engraved with the AP monogram and the Audemars and Piguet family crests.
Functions: hours, minutes; date; dive-time measurement.

Case: stainless steel; Ø 42mm, thickness: 13.75mm; black rubber crowns; caseback with medallion inscribed with Royal Oak Offshore; water resistant to 300 meters.
Dial: black; exclusive Méga Tapisserie motif; inner rotating ring with diving scale; applied gray hour-markers with luminescent coating; facetted white-gold hour and minute hands with luminescent coating.
Strap: black rubber; oversized stainless steel pin buckle.
Suggested price: $15,200

ROYAL OAK OFFSHORE CHRONOGRAPH   REF. 26176FO.00.D101CR.01

Movement: automatic Caliber 3126/3840; up to 60-hour power reserve; 21,600 vph; 59 jewels; 365 parts; variable inertia balance with eight inertia blocks and flat balance-spring; Geneva-type mobile balance-spring stud holder; three-position winding crown; all parts decorated by hand; mainplate rhodium-plated, beveled and circular-grained; bridges adorned with Côtes de Genève.
Functions: hours, minutes, small seconds; date; chronograph function with central seconds hand, 30-minute and 12-hour counters at 9 and 6, respectively; tachymeter.
Case: forged carbon strong-box-type case with anti-magnetic system; Ø 42mm, thickness: 14.7mm; ceramic bezel; steel screws; vulcanized rubber-clad crown and pushpieces; blackened steel caseback featuring a medallion engraved with Royal Oak Offshore logo; water resistant to 100 meters.
Dial: black; exclusive Méga Tapisserie motif; luminescent hour and minute hands; black counters with yellow numerals and hands; yellow central chronograph seconds hand; yellow tachymetric scale.
Strap: black Hornback saddle-cut crocodile leather; yellow hand-sewn seams and lined with Alcantara; bead-blasted titanium AP folding clasp with blackened cover.
Suggested price: $25,800

JULES AUDEMARS SELFWINDING CHRONOGRAPH   REF. 261000R.00.D088CR.01

Movement: exclusive automatic Caliber AP 3124/3841; over 60-hour power reserve; 21,600 vph; 59 jewels; 400 parts; variable inertia balance with eight inertia blocks and flat balance-spring; Geneva-type mobile balance-spring stud holder; two-position winding crown; all parts decorated by hand; rhodium-plated, beveled, circular-grained mainplate; bridges adorned with Côtes de Genève.
Functions: hours, minutes, small seconds; chronograph with central seconds hand, 30-minute counter, tachymetric scale.

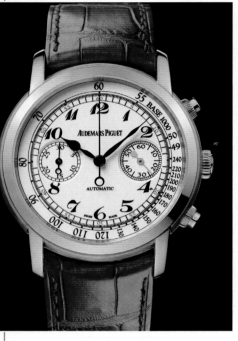

Case: 18K pink gold; Ø 41mm, thickness: 12.6mm; sapphire crystal caseback; water resistant to 20 meters.
Dial: off-white lacquer; black transferred Arabic numerals; black leaf-shaped hands.
Strap: large-square-scale hand-sewn brown crocodile leather; 18K pink-gold AP folding clasp.
Suggested price: $28,600
Also available: white lacquer dial; in 18K white gold on black crocodile leather strap with 18K white-gold AP folding clasp.

JULES AUDEMARS WITH AUDEMARS PIGUET ESCAPEMENT   REF. 26153PT.00.D028CR.01

Movement: manually wound Caliber 2908 with Audemars Piguet escapement; up to 56-hour power reserve; 43,200 vph; 34 jewels; 267 parts; all parts decorated by hand: beveling, polishing, frosting and guilloché work.
Functions; hours, minutes; small seconds; power-reserve indicator.
Case: 950 platinum; Ø 46mm, thickness: 12.64mm; sapphire crystal caseback; water resistant to 20 meters.

Dial: white enamel hour and minute subdial; black painted Roman numerals; silver-colored small seconds subdial with satin-brushed center and outer zone; polished ornamental fillet; blued steel hands.
Strap: large-square-scaled hand-sewn rolled-edge alligator leather; platinum AP folding clasp.
Suggested price: $239,600

JULES AUDEMARS EQUATION OF TIME   REF. 26003BC.00.D002CR.01

Movement: automatic Calibre 2120/2808; up to 40-hour power reserve; 19,800 vph; 41 jewels; 423 parts; all parts meticulously finished: mainplate chamfered and circular grained; bridges adorned with Côtes de Genève; customizable oscillating weight.
Functions: hours, minutes; date, days and leap-year indication; (astronomical) moonphase display; sunrise and sunset times for a given location; equation of time.
Note: on request, the equation of time may be customized for 250 cities or for most other locations.

Case: stainless steel; Ø 42mm, thickness: 10.45mm; sapphire crystal; flange with equation-of-time graduation and the time of the sun's zenith adjusted to the reference city chosen by the owner.
Dial: silvered; Grande Tapisserie motif; silvered counters; applied gold hour-markers with luminescent coating; gold hour and minute hands with luminescent coating; blued steel pointers for the counters and the equation-of-time display.
Strap: large-square-scaled black alligator leather; stainless steel AP folding clasp.
Suggested price: $84,200
Also available: 18K pink gold; on brown strap.

JULES AUDEMARS PERPETUAL CALENDAR   REF. 263900R.00.D088CR.02

Movement: automatic ultra-thin Caliber 2120/2802; up to 40-hour power reserve; 19,800 vph; 38 jewels; 355 parts; all parts decorated by hand; mainplate chamfered and circular grained; bridges adorned with Côtes de Genève.
Functions: hours, minutes; day, date, month, leap year-cycle indication; moonphase.
Case: 18K pink gold; Ø 41mm, thickness: 9.15mm; sapphire crystal exhibition caseback; water resistant to 20 meters.

Dial: brown; applied pink-gold hour-markers; pink-gold hour and minute hands.
Strap: large-square-scaled hand-sewn brown alligator leather; 18K pink-gold AP folding clasp.
Suggested price: $58,700
Also available: silvered dial.

MILLENARY QUINCY JONES WATCH REF. 15161SN.OO.D002CR.01

Movement: automatic Caliber 3120; up to 60-hour power reserve; 21,600 vph; 40 jewels; 278 parts; variable inertia balance with eight inertia blocks and flat balance-spring; Geneva-type mobile balance-spring stud holder; three-position winding stem; all parts finely decorated: circular-grained mainplate, bridges rhodium-plated, chamfered, snailed and adorned with Côtes de Genève; diamond-polished jewel sinks; wheels with chamfered arms and diamond-polished; chamfered screw rims and slots; 22K gold oscillating weight engraved with the AP monogram and the Audemars and Piguet family crests.

Functions: hours, minutes, central seconds; date.
Case: blackened steel; 45x40mm; inscription Millenary Quincy Jones - Limited Edition on caseback; water resistant to 20 meters.
Dial: black dial with two zones; off-centered hour zone with applied white-gold Roman numeral; minute circle with black piano-key motif; openworked white-gold hour and minute hands; central seconds hand.
Strap: hand-sewn black leather; blackened steel AP folding clasp.
Note: limited edition of 500 pieces.
Suggested price: $17,300

MILLENARY CARBON ONE TOURBILLON CHRONOGRAPH REF. 26152AU.OO.D002CR.01

Movement: manually wound Caliber 2884; tourbillon and twin barrel; up to 240-hour power reserve; 21,600 vph; 30 jewels; 336 parts; all parts decorated by hand; carbon mainplate; bridges in eloxed aluminum and blackened steel.
Functions: hours, minutes; chronograph; power-reserve indicator.
Case: forged carbon with black ceramic bezel, crown and pushbuttons; 47x42mm; cambered antireflective sapphire crystal; blackened titanium caseback fitted with sapphire crystal; water resistant to 20 meters.
Dial: openworked to reveal the movement; white hour-markers with luminescent coating; blackened luminescent hands.
Strap: large-square-scaled hand-sewn crocodile leather; blackened titanium AP folding clasp.
Note: limited edition of 120 pieces.
Suggested price: $268,100

MILLENARY BLACK & WHITE LADIES' WATCH COLLECTION REF. 77301ST.ZZ.D002CR.01

Movement: automatic Caliber 2325; up to 40-hour power reserve; 28,800 vph; 32 jewels; rotor mounted on a ball-bearing mechanism with a 21K gold segment; adjustable inertia balance; all parts decorated by hand; circular-grained plate; diamond-polished countersinks, angles and sinks; bridges beveled, snailed and adorned with Côtes de Genève. **Function:** hours, minutes, central seconds. **Case:** satin-brushed and polished stainless steel; 39.5x35.5mm, thickness: 8.1mm; bezel set with 66 brilliant-cut diamonds (0.62 carat); polished stainless steel crown set with a translucent sapphire cabochon (0.25 carat); caseback engraved with Millenary logo; water resistant to 20 meters.
Dial: two zones; light silvery base adorned with a flinqué motif bearing black Roman numerals and a snailed light silvery offset disc with black Arabic numerals. **Strap:** matte white crocodile leather with tone-on-tone stitching; polished steel double-blade AP folding clasp.
Note: the diamonds used to set Audemars Piguet watches are of Top Wesselton IF (Internally Flawless) quality; sapphires are natural. Each watch is delivered with a certificate guaranteeing the number, quality and weight of the precious stones.
Suggested price: $12,200
Also available: matte black strap; dial with black base adorned with a flinqué motif bearing white Roman numerals; black satin-brushed sunburst offset disc with white Arabic numerals.

MILLENARY PRÉCIEUSE COLLECTION REF. 77227OR.ZZ.A012SU.01

Movement: manually wound Calibre 2046; 21,600 vph (3 Hz); 18 jewels; rhodium plating, circular graining and Côtes de Genève.
Functions: hours, minutes.
Cases: 18K pink gold; 28x25.2mm, thickness: 7.6mm; set with 187 brilliant-cut diamonds (2.35 carats); 18K pink-gold crown set with a translucent cabochon; caseback engraved with Millenary logo; water resistant to 20 meters.
Dial: white mother-of-pearl dial; Arabic numerals; applied gold cabochons; inserts set with diamonds; pink-gold hands.
Suggested price: $35,100
Also available: 18K white-gold case and crown set with a blue cabochon; white mother-of-pearl dial with Arabic numerals, applied gold cabochons, inserts set with diamonds and blued hands; silvered dial with flinqué motif, blue applied Arabic numerals, five diamond hour-markers, gray transferred Roman numerals and blued hands; silvered dial with flinqué motif, pink-gold applied Arabic numerals, five diamond hour-markers, gray transferred Roman numerals and pink-gold hands.

B.R.M
Bernard Richards Manufacture

The French company B.R.M (Bernard Richards Manufacture) builds luxury watches as it would a racecar: with outstanding mechanics under the hood and intentionally "imperfect" finishings such as crude brushing and polishing on the body.

The brand fuses founder Bernard Richards's lifelong adulation for motor sports and precision engineering into every detail of every high-end watch that it produces. The brand's watchmakers work with the same high-tech materials used in racecar construction, checkered flags are evoked on the straps and piston-shaped modular cases, and engine parts inspire even the models' names.

In 2008, B.R.M teamed up with U.S.-based Ecosse Moto Works to design and build the ultimate gift set: a titanium Ecosse Heretic motorcycle and matching Ecosse watch.

The collaboration with Ecosse Moto Works seemed a natural one—both companies are imbued with a competitive spirit, a unique character and a flair for distinctive designs—and the ten resulting motorcycle/watch sets are superb fruits of those qualities and their flawless meshing with high technology.

RIGHT The Ø 52mm TR-Tourbillon (TR1) is shown here in a titanium case with stainless steel crown and lugs, and on an alligator leather strap. It is also available in rose gold (TR3 OR), or black PVD-coated titanium with rose-gold lugs, crown, crown protection, rotor weights and screws (TR2 TN OR).

FAR RIGHT Crafted in stainless steel and titanium with black PVD, CT-48 is also available with orange or yellow accents on its skeletonized carbon-fiber dial and strap. The watch's mechanics are visible through a sapphire crystal caseback.

BOTTOM The V12-44 is manufactured with a superfine 18/8 stainless steel piston-shaped case.

B.R.M teamed up with Ecosse Moto Works to design and build the ultimate package: an Ecosse Heretic motorcycle and matching watch.

The ultra-precise accessory for an ultra-precise machine, Ecosse's 48mm titanium case is fitted on a reversible strap: one side is black rubber, the other is black leather with orange stitching matching the Ecosse Heretic's seat. The automatic chronograph's brushed titanium bezel recalls the motorcycle's brushed titanium chassis, both watch and bike expose their inner mechanics, and both are engraved with a shared serial number.

A new addition to B.R.M's fleet is the CT-48 chronograph. This striking timepiece is based on the same engineering principles as the R50 and Birotor models and is also powered by the proprietary Precitime movement with Isolastic System® shock absorption. The 48mm case is water resistant to 100 meters and features the brand's offset horns and a carbon-fiber dial bearing a tachymeter.

Also unveiled recently is the TR-Tourbillon. Available in titanium, rose gold, or black PVD-coated titanium with rose-gold elements, the watch's dial is completely skeletonized and fitted between two sapphire crystals. Its Precitime movement is suspended on carbon-fiber triangle bridges and equipped an automatic tourbillon with a 1.45-minute rotation and Isolastic System® shock absorbers.

B.R.M's racing watches can be personalized on request, both in color and materials.

TOP AND BOTTOM The matching titanium Ecosse chronograph and Ecosse Heretic motorcycle were created as special sets for ten privileged collectors.

ABOVE Developed in-house, the Precitime caliber is visible through sapphire crystal slats in the Birotor's caseside.

TR - TOURBILLON REF. TR1

Movement: Precitime; suspended on triangle bridges in carbon fiber; shock absorbers with cone-shaped spring, Isolastic System® (certified); differential automatic tourbillon, rotation: 1.45 minutes; tourbillon bar in carbon fiber set on Isolastic System; protection bush of the escapement axis set on Isolastic System; titanium tourbillon cage; ARCAP plate and bridges assembled movement with bolts; B.R.M balance with ruby gyroscopic effect; double ceramic rotor bearings; aluminum Fortale HR rotors; tantalum rotor weights.

Case: titanium; Ø 52mm; polished stainless steel lugs; stainless steel crown moved to 2 for better comfort; double-face scratchproof sapphire crystal; water resistant to 10atm.
Dial: skeleton.
Strap: alligator.
Also available: 48mm; red or orange hands.

BIROTOR REF. BRT3N

Movement: Precitime; suspended on triangles in carbon fiber; shock absorbers with cone-shaped spring, Isolastic System® (certified); differential automatic Birotor mechanics; ARCAP plate and bridges; six-sided bolts; lightened motor structure; B.R.M pendulum with gyroscopic effect; double ceramic rotor bearings; Fortale HR rotor hubs; tantalum rotor bob weights.
Functions: bipolar time system with double crowns (certified).

Case: titanium with black PVD; 40x48mm; 18K rose-gold, ergonomic lugs with three adjustable positions (certified); 18K rose-gold crown transfer for better comfort; curvilinear double-face scratchproof sapphire crystal; water resistant to 3atm.
Dial: skeleton.
Strap: alligator leather.
Also available: titanium and steel; rose gold; on leather Winner checkerboard strap.

CT 48 REF. CT48

Movement: Precitime based on ETA Valjoux 7753; suspended on triangles in carbon fiber; shock absorber with cone-shaped spring, Isolastic System® (certified); Fortale HR rotor hubs; tantalum rotor bob weight.
Functions: chronograph; tachymeter.
Case: polished stainless steel, titanium with black PVD; Ø 48; double-face scratchproof sapphire crystal; water resistant to 10atm.

Dial: carbon-fiber skeleton.
Strap: black leather with red stitching.
Also available: yellow, orange and white hands.

R50T REF. R50TN

Movement: automatic Precitime A07161 engine caliber; 48-hour power reserve; 28,800 vph; 24 rubies.
Functions: hours, minutes, seconds; power reserve at 6.
Case: titanium and black PVD-treated; Ø 50mm; stainless steel lugs and crown; double-face scratchproof sapphire crystal.
Dial: skeleton; orange ultra-light hands.

Strap: black leather with orange and white stitching.
Also available: rose-gold case; rose-gold and black PVD-treated case; red or yellow hands.
Note: 3-year warranty.

V18 — REF. V18

Movement: automatic Swiss chronograph 7753 ETA Valjoux; 46-hour power reserve; 28,800 vph; 27 rubies; ultra-slim stainless steel specific screws.
Functions: 60-second chronograph function; 30-minute and 12-hour registers; calendar in window.
Case: gray and black checkered grade-2 titanium case; Ø 48mm; extra-hard black PVD case protection; ultra-slim stainless steel lugs 18/8; start/stop chronograph button at 2; chronograph reset button at 4; date corrector at 10; double-face scratchproof sapphire crystal; water resistant to 10atm.
Dial: applied carbon-aluminum; super light, red and black hands.
Strap: black rubber.
Also available: leather strap.
Note: 3-year warranty.

V12 — REF. V12-44-BN

Movement: automatic 7753 ETA Valjoux chronograph; 46-hour power reserve; 28,800 vph; 27 rubies.
Functions: 12-hour and 30-minute countdown registers; 60-second chronograph function; calendar window.
Case: brushed black; Ø 44mm; start/stop button at 2; chronograph reset button at 4; date corrector at 10; double-face scratchproof sapphire crystal; extra-hard PVD-treatment protection; water resistant to 10atm.
Dial: black; white ultra-light hands.
Strap: black rubber.
Also available: brushed or polished case: gray, black, red or yellow hands; carbon or fiberglass dial with various designs.
Note: customizable through company web site; 3-year warranty.

GP44 — REF. GP-44-109

Movement: automatic 7753 ETA Valjoux chronograph; 28,800 vph; 27 rubies.
Functions: 12-hour and 30-minute countdown registers; 60-second chronograph function; calendar window.
Case: gray; grade-2 titanium; Ø 44mm; ultra-slim 18/8 stainless steel lugs; start/stop button at 2; chronograph reset button at 4; date corrector at 10; double-face scratchproof sapphire crystal; extra-hard PVD-treatment protection; water resistant to 10atm.
Dial: black; ultra-light hands.
Strap: black genuine rubber.
Also available: gray case and dial; black case and dial.
Note: 3-year warranty.

V8 COMPETITION — REF. V8

Movement: automatic 7753 ETA Valjoux chronograph; 28,800 vph; 27 rubies.
Functions: 12-hour and 30-minute countdown registers; calendar window.
Case: black PVD-treated titanium; Ø 44mm; engraved with V8 COMPETITION; brushed ultra-slim 18/8 stainless steel or titanium lugs; start/stop button at 2; chronograph reset button at 4; date corrector at 10; double-face scratchproof sapphire crystal; water resistant to 10atm.
Dial: carbon with white tracings; yellow ultra-light hands.
Strap: leather Winner checkerboard strap.
Also available: gray, white, red, or orange hands.
Note: 3-year warranty.

TIME INSTRUMENTS

In the early 1990s, a team of designers and specialists of aircraft controls joined forces to work on the same project: to be part of the great Swiss watch making tradition while meeting the demands of professionals facing extreme situations.

THE SEARCH FOR THE EXTREME

There are trades that require one to bear extreme temperatures, undergo violent accelerations, or resist dangerous pressures. Bell & Ross studies these extreme situations with those who experience them: pilots, divers, astronauts and bomb disposal experts—professionals for whom a watch must not only be a tool to serve them in their missions, but an ally at all moments.

To ensure that a watch perfectly meets the expectations of its users, Bell & Ross gathers men with complementary know-how. United around a unique project—to create a utility watch—master watchmakers, engineers, designers and professional users have combined their expertise and experience. Their sole motto: The essential is never compromised by the superfluous.

Over the years and with each new success, Bell & Ross has built a selective network of 500 points of sale in 50 countries worldwide. Bell & Ross has thus become a point of reference in the exclusive world of professionals, collectors and fine Swiss watchmaking.

Designed for professionals who demand tools with optimum reliability, Bell & Ross watches correspond to four fundamental principles: Legibility, Functionality, Precision, and Reliability.

Since 1996, Bell & Ross has manufactured in its own production unit in La Chaux-de-Fonds, Switzerland. It is there that all the master watchmakers develop, assemble and carry out the ultimate adjustments to Bell & Ross watches.

Regardless of the watch's mechanical complexity, the art is revealed in the precision of the measurements, the rigor of the controls, and the care given to each work stage.

WATCHMAKING REFERENCES

BR 01 TOURBILLON The Instrument watch Grande Complication: a tourbillon, a regulator, a power-reserve indicator, and a precision indicator. Bell & Ross joined forces with leading Swiss master watchmakers to create an exceptional movement in a state-of-the-art timepiece.

VINTAGE JUMPING HOUR The first watch with a jumping hour and power reserve. A masterpiece of ingenuity, this watch is the fruit of the collaboration between Bell & Ross and Swiss master watchmaker Vincent Calabrese. It combines the complexity of a mechanical movement with the simplicity of a new reading system.

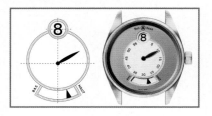

HYDROMAX 11 100 M Holds the world's water-resistance record. By introducing a liquid into the case, this watch possesses perfect water resistance and masters incomparable readability. It can withstand a pressure of 1,110 bar, or a depth of 11,100 meters.

Bell & Ross's watches are designed with the help of men who dare to risk and demand the best in professional-grade timepieces.

FRENCH AIR FORCE

FRENCH MARINE

Bell & Ross takes flight with the BR 01 Instrument collection for pilots. In their search for the ideal professional watch and armed with their experience in the aeronautic and military fields, in-house engineers, master watchmakers, designers, and professional users pooled their knowledge to create a unique, revolutionary concept: the BR 01 Instrument. Aeronautic instrumentation is the absolute reference for readability, reliability and performance. Bell & Ross replicates a plane's clock as accurately as possible in a size proportionate to the wrist.

The new BR 02 Instrument collection is to divers as the BR 01 series is to pilots. Extreme resistance to crushing underwater pressure, precision and easy legibility are all very important features provided to divers via helium release valves, precisely rotating internal unidirectional bezels, and bold, highly luminous dials to aid them in their missions. BR 02 Instruments are available in stainless steel, 18-karat pink gold, or a combination of carbon-coated steel and pink gold.

RIGHT   A professional user tests the water resistance and functions of this new BR 02 Instrument for divers.

BOTTOM LEFT   A mechanical automatic movement powers the BR 02 Instrument Chronograph from within a 44mm case of vacuum carbon- finished 316L steel. The dial features photo-luminescent numerals, indexes and hands, and is framed by a unidirectional, cranted interior bezel with a photoluminescent reference point for the graduating minutes. Water resistant to 500 meters and equipped with a decompression valve for deep-sea diving and secured on a black rubber strap and steel buckle.

BOTTOM RIGHT   The 44mm BR 02 Instrument Steel houses a mechanical automatic movement beneath a black dial with numerals, hands and indexes treated with white photo-luminescence to optimize nighttime reading. Fitted on a rubber or heavy-duty synthetic fabric strap, the stainless steel case features a unidirectional, cranted interior bezel with screw-in crown at 2:00, and is water resistant to 1,000 meters.

VINTAGE 123 JUMPING HOUR PLATINUM DOUBLE SUBDIAL

Movement: mechanical automatic; quality finishing; 28,800 vph; 30 jewels; high-precision setting in five positions; rhodium-treated, decorated and engraved plates, oscillating weight and bridges; bluish screws; 40-hour power reserve.
Functions: hours, minutes; power reserve.
Case: satin-finished 950 platinum; screw-in crown; antireflective sapphire crystal; screw-on, flat caseback in sapphire crystal; water resistant to 10atm.

Dial: gray; double subdial: hour subdial at top of dial, power-reserve subdial in an arc at bottom of dial.
Strap: full-skin alligator.
Suggested price: $30,000
Note: limited edition of 99 pieces.

VINTAGE 123 JUMPING HOUR PLATINUM

Movement: mechanical automatic; quality finishing; 28,800 vph; 30 jewels; high-precision setting in five positions; rhodium-treated, decorated and engraved plates, oscillating weight and bridges; bluish screws; 40-hour power reserve.
Functions: hours, minutes; power reserve.
Case: satin-finished 950 platinum; screw-in crown; antireflective sapphire crystal; screw-on, flat caseback in sapphire crystal; water resistant to 10atm.

Dial: hand-chased 18K gold.
Strap: full-skin alligator.
Suggested price: $30,000
Note: limited edition of 99 pieces.

VINTAGE 126XL EDICION LIMITADA

Movement: mechanical automatic; Côtes de Genève decoration; 40-hour power reserve.
Functions: hours, minutes, seconds; big date for 1 calendar year; indication of day and month; two-counter chronograph: 60-second and 30-minute accumulators.
Case: Ø 42.5mm; polished, satin-finished 18K pink gold; antireflective sapphire crystal; flat sapphire caseback; screw-in crown and caseback; water resistant to 20atm.

Dial: brown; gold-plated counters; gold-plated hands and indexes with photoluminescent coating to optimize nighttime reading.
Strap: leather.
Suggested price: $19,900
Note: limited edition of 99 pieces.

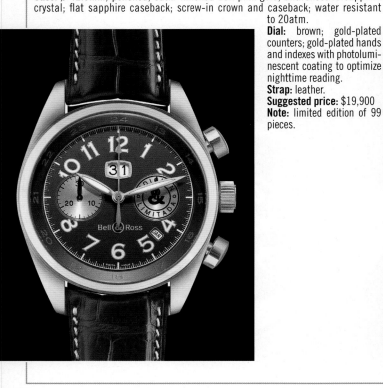

VINTAGE 126 YELLOW-GOLD PEARL

Movement: mechanical automatic ETA 2894; high-quality finish; rhodium-plated or gold movement with Côtes de Genève engraved winding rotor; 28,800 vph; 28 rubies; pearled plate and bridge; hardened steel screws; high-precision settings; approx. 42-hour power reserve.
Functions: hours, minutes, seconds; two-counter chronograph: 60-second and 30-minute accumulators; date with rapid date correction; second hand stops when time is set.
Case: polished 18K yellow gold; curved, antireflective sapphire crystal; sapphire crystal caseback; crown and back are screwed on in order to ensure perfect water resistance of 20atm.
Dial: pearl with antireflective with anti-UV treatment; hands and indexes with photoluminescent coating to optimize nighttime reading.
Strap: crocodile leather.
Suggested price: $9,600

BR 01-92 HERITAGE

Movement: mechanical automatic ETA 2892.
Functions: hours, minutes, seconds.
Case: Ø 46x46mm; carbon-powder coating; screw-in crown; antireflective sapphire crystal; water resistant to 10atm.
Dial: black; numerals, hands and indexes with photoluminescent coating to optimize nighttime reading.
Strap: printed natural leather.
Suggested price: $4,200
Also available: steel glass bead-blasted with black finishing; heavy-duty synthetic fabric strap.

BR 01-93 GMT

Movement: mechanical automatic; 28,800 vph; 21 jewels; high-precision setting in four positions (tolerance of 0/+10 seconds a day); 40-hour power reserve.
Functions: hours, minutes, seconds; second time zone in a 24-hour scale; fast date correction; time setting with second stop.
Case: 46x46mm; steel; screw-in crown; antireflective sapphire crystal; water resistant to 10atm.
Dial: black; numerals, hands and indexes with photoluminescent coating to optimize nighttime reading.
Strap: rubber.
Suggested price: $4,500
Also available: black powder coating with glass bead-blasted; ultra-strong synthetic fabric

BR 01-96 COMMANDO BIG DATE

Movement: mechanical automatic; 22 jewels; 40-hour power reserve.
Functions: hours, minutes, seconds; large date with two independent discs (units + tens).
Case: 46x46mm; shot-peened stainless steel; screw-in crown; antireflective sapphire crystal; water resistant to 10atm.
Dial: painted gray; hands and indexes with photoluminescent coating to optimize nighttime reading.
Strap: rubber.
Suggested price: $5,000
Also available: vacuum carbon black finish; black dial; ultra-strong synthetic fabric strap.

BR 01-94 PRO TITANIUM

Movement: mechanical automatic ETA 2894.
Functions: hours, minutes, seconds; 3-counter chronograph: 12-hour, 30-minute and 60-second; date.
Case: XL Ø 46mm; satin-finished grade-2 titanium; screw-in crown; antireflective sapphire crystal; water resistant to 10atm.
Dial: gray; numerals and hands coated with white photoluminescent coating to optimize nighttime reading.
Strap: rubber.
Suggested price: $8,000

BR 02 CHRONOGRAPH CARBON FINISH

Movement: mechanical automatic.
Functions: hours, minutes, seconds; date; two-counter chronograph: 30-minute and 60-second totalizers.
Case: Ø 44mm; satin-polished stainless steel; unidirectional cranted interior bezel graduated to 60 minutes; antireflective sapphire crystal; screw-in pushpiece, crowns and caseback; decompression valve for deep sea diving; water resistant to 50atm.

Dial: black; hands and indexes with photolmines-cent coating to optimize nighttime reading.
Strap: rubber.
Suggested price: $7,500
Also available: 316L steel with black glass bead-blasted vacuum carbon black finish; heavy-duty synthetic fabric strap.

BR 02 CHRONOGRAPH STEEL FINISH

Movement: mechanical automatic.
Functions: hours, minutes, seconds; date; two-counter chronograph: 30-minute and 60-second totalizers.
Case: Ø 44mm; satin-polished stainless steel; unidirectional, cranted interior bezel graduated to 60 minute with photoluminescent reference point; screw-in pushpiece, crowns and caseback; antireflective sapphire crystal; decompression valve for deep-sea diving; water resistant to 50atm.

Dial: black; numerals, indexes and hands with photo-luminescent coating to optimize nighttime reading.
Strap: rubber.
Suggested price: $6,500
Also available: 316L steel with black glass bead-blasted vacuum carbon finish; heavy-duty synthetic fabric strap.

BR 02 PINK GOLD

Movement: mechanical automatic.
Functions: hours, minutes, seconds; date.
Case: Ø 44mm; brushed solid 18K 5N pink gold; unidirectional, toothed interior bezel graduated to 60 minutes with photoluminescent reference point; point screw-in crowns; antireflective sapphire crystal; decompression valve for deep sea diving; water resistant to 30atm.

Dial: carbon fiber; numerals, gold indexes and hands with photoluminescent coating to optimize nighttime reading.
Strap: rubber.
Suggested price: $22,000

BR 02 PINK GOLD CARBON FINISH

Movement: mechanical automatic.
Functions: hours, minutes, seconds; date.
Case: Ø 44mm; pink gold; unidirectional, toothed interior bezel graduated to 60 minutes with photoluminescent reference point; screw-in crowns; antireflective sapphire crystal; decompression valve for deep sea diving; water resistant to 100atm.

Dial: carbon fiber; numerals, gold indexes and hands with photoluminescent coating to optimize nighttime reading.
Strap: rubber.
Suggested price: $9,900
Also available: steel with vacuum carbon black finish.

BR 01 TOURBILLON

Movement: mechanical automatic BR 01 Tourbillon with carbon-fiber mainplates and black-gold tourbillon carriage; 120-hour power reserve.
Functions: hour counter at 12, central minutes; power-reserve indicator at 9; trust index at 3.
Case: XXL Ø 46x46mm; screw-in crown; antireflective sapphire crystal caseback; virtually non-scratchable coating (4,000 Vickers); water resistant to 10atm.
Dial: black carbon fiber; hands and indexes with photoluminescent coating to optimize nighttime reading.
Strap: black rubber.
Suggested price: $131,000
Also available: titanium glass bead-blasted with DLC (Diamond Like Carbon).

BR 01 TOURBILLON PHANTOM

Movement: tourbillon movement with carbon-fiber mainplates and black-gold tourbillon carriage associated to three additional complications; 120-hour power reserve.
Functions: regulator at 12 (dissociating hour counter at 12 and main central hand for the minutes); trust index at 3; power-reserve indicator at 9.
Case: virtually non-scratchable titanium with DLC (Diamond Like Carbon); water resistant to 10atm.
Dial: black carbon fiber; numerals, hands and indexes with photoluminescent coating to optimize nighttime reading.
Strap: rubber.
Suggested price: $148,000

BR 01 TOURBILLON PINK GOLD

Movement: mechanical automatic BR 01 Tourbillon with carbon-fiber mainplates and black-gold tourbillon carriage; 120-hour power reserve.
Functions: hour counter at 12, central minutes; power-reserve indicator at 9; trust index at 3.
Case: XXL Ø 46x46mm; pink gold; screw-in crown; antireflective sapphire crystal caseback; water resistant to 10atm.
Dial: black carbon fiber; hands and indexes with photoluminescent coating to optimize nighttime reading.
Strap: black alligator leather.
Suggested price: $184,000

BR 01 GRAND MINUTEUR TOURBILLON

Movement: mechanical automatic; pink-gold anodized aluminum bridges; 3-day power reserve.
Functions: hours, minutes, small second counter; minuteur with flyback function (back to zero and fast boosting of the measure of time, two graduations of 60 minutes and ten 10th's of an hour segment); power-reserve indicator.
Case: XXL 44x50mm; satin-polished pink gold; screw-in crown; antireflective sapphire crystal caseback; water resistant to 10atm.
Dial: black; hands and indexes with photoluminescent coating to optimize nighttime reading.
Strap: rubber.
Suggested price: $250,000
Also available: alligator leather strap.

BERTOLUCCI

Mediterranean inspiration, Swiss craftsmanship

Bertolucci watches exist at the crossroads of emotion and reason, where passion is tempered by restraint to create a graceful symmetry of style and substance. Italian and Swiss cultures unite in a rich confluence of creativity and craftsmanship to define the company's collection of luxurious timepieces.

That duality emerges elegantly in the Giro, a chic men's chronograph presented in 5N rose gold. Measuring 42mm, the round case plays host to a white-silvered opaline dial, embossed with decorative patterns and enhanced with gold hour-markers.

A sense of balance informs the case design, starting physically with the way it rests comfortably on the wrist, continuing visually on the dial where its intuitive arrangement makes reading the time or measuring a moment a treat for the eyes.

A circle at 6:00 interrupts the smooth trajectory of Giro's bezel. The loop surrounds a rotating gold disc numbered 1 to 12 that registers the chronograph's hours.

The Giro's bezel seems to ripple outward, evoking a pool into which a smooth pebble has been toseed. This striking design element meshes perfectly with the Bertolucci philosophy of exclusive creations realized by following an exacting but original vision. The company's unique history, distinctive viewpoint and thorough savoir-faire combine to build on the Bertolucci legacy of crafting elegant, beautiful timepieces.

With its common thread which has always been a mixture of Swiss sense and Italian sensibility, Bertolucci turns its attention to women with two versions of the Serena that channel feminine charisma.

The first is Serena garbo Lady, a classically styled two-hand watch that mixes stainless steel and 5N rose-gold elements. Its round 36.5mm case includes a rose-gold bezel that flares up at the sides to create a subtle dished effect that draws attention to the lively design. Beneath its curved crystal, Bertolucci decorates the center of the Serena garbo Lady's mother-of-pearl dial with a sunray guilloché. The final stylish touch is a ribbon of diamond pavé around the bezel, incorporating 180 diamonds for a total of 2.02 carats.

Offered in 5N rose gold, the Giro's 42mm case includes a loop at 6:00 that frames the chronograph's rotating hour disc. A skeleton caseback provides a view of the watch's automatic movement.

A unique history, distinctive viewpoint and savoir-faire combine to build on Bertolucci's legacy.

The Serena offers a contemporary look that is elevated with a touch of glamour thanks to a sleek oval-shaped bezel. Its gentle curves echo throughout the piece, from the oval at the center of the dial and the oval date window to the arched elements of the bracelet or the rounded stitching of the calfskin strap on which the watch is also available.

With the Volta, the company lets its imagination flow, weaving black opaline across the dial like a stream that's buffered on both sides by sparkling banks made up of 92 diamonds, weighing approximately 0.28 carat. Bertolucci crafts a version of the Volta in pink, replacing the black stream with a cascading torrent of pink sapphires. Caught in the surging waves are two round displays: one for the home time and the other attuned to a second time zone. The displays are powered by separate Swiss-made quartz movements, each expected to operate for at least three years between battery changes.

The Mediterranean theme carries over to the Stria's case, instantly recognizable for its shell guilloché. In between the guilloché stripes gleam rays of diamond pavé, radiating out from a slightly off-center point like the ridges in a clam's shell. Ten 0.03-carat diamonds share space on the dial with golden dots in a sequence that evokes nature's perfect golden spiral.

With watches for men and women, Bertolucci presents a wide-ranging collection anchored by the brand's guiding principles of creativity, curvaceousness, comfort and construction.

ABOVE   A trio of ovals defines the Serena's rounded look, from the curved white-silvered opaline dial and three-row bracelet in stainless steel to the date window at 6:00. The case measures 29x40mm and is water resistant to 100 feet.

BOTTOM LEFT   Hour and minute hands with black lacquer inlays and black Roman numerals provide vivid contrast against the 36.5mm Serena garbo Lady's iridescent mother-of-pearl dial.

BOTTOM CENTER   Waves of white diamonds and pink sapphires buffet the Volta's dial, which includes mother-of-pearl subsidiary dials for the main and second time-zone displays. Presented in a 42mm case, the Volta uses two ETA movements to power the time displays.

BOTTOM RIGHT   Stria's 40mm case is paved with 274 diamonds (1.26 carats) whereas its back opaline dial is decorated with ten diamond hour-markers and golden dots.

BELLA COSTA   REF. 1093.51.42.1033.901

Movement: Swiss quartz chronograph; caliber ETA 13¼ G10.711; 36-month battery life.
Functions: hours, minutes, seconds; calendar date at 4; time- and date-setting crown at 3; chronograph: minute, second and 1/10 second; pushbuttons start/stop at 2; reset at 4.
Case: stainless steel; Ø 41mm, thickness: 12.1mm; black PVD coated; BERTOLUCCI engraved on the caseside at 9; domed sapphire crystal with antireflective treatment; caseback screwed on with four screws; water resistant to 5atm.
Dial: black; vertical pattern; three azuré subcounters; black inner flange with 11 luminescent indexes; Côtes de Genève decor; magnifying lens; BERTOLUCCI printed in white above the 6-hour subcounter; rhodium-plated symbol Bertolucci "B" applied at 12; polished, rhodium-plated, leaf-shaped hour and minute hands with luminescent SuperLumiNova inlays; polished, rhodium-plated, baton-shaped second hand; three polished, rhodium-plated, drop-shaped subcounters with luminescent SuperLumiNova inlays.
Strap: black rubber; stainless steel triple-folding clasp.

GIRO   REF. 1144.51.67.31D.501

Movement: Swiss automatic; caliber ETA 11½ 2824-2.
Functions: hours, minutes, seconds; calendar date at 6; time- and date-setting crown at 3.
Case: 18K 5N rose gold; Ø 42mm, thickness: 11.6mm; mirror-polished finish; sapphire crystal with antireflective treatment; skeleton with sapphire crystal revealing the movement; caseback screwed on with four screws; water resistant to 5atm.
Dial: black opaline; shell pattern; plain center; BERTOLUCCI at 12; AUTOMATIC at 6; minute track on a vertical flange printed in gold; seven point indexes (4 long + 3 short); center and date metallic ring with three Arabic numerals; Bertolucci "B" applied at 12; rose-gold plated, polished, leaf-shaped hour and minute with luminescent SuperLumiNova inlays; polished, rose gold-plated, baton-shaped second hand.
Strap: black alligator leather on stainless steel and 18K 5N rose-gold folding clasp (solid gold cover with stainless steel clasp).

SERENA GARBO LADY   REF. 303.55.47P.3B1

Movement: Swiss quartz; caliber ETA 5½ x 6¾ 976.001; 50-month battery life.
Functions: hours, minutes; time-setting crown at 3.
Case: stainless steel; Ø 36.5mm, thickness: 9mm; 18K 5N rose-gold bezel with plated crown; mirror-polished finish; curved sapphire crystal with antireflective treatment; caseback screwed on with four screws; water resistant to 3atm.
Dial: curved white natural mother-of-pearl; sunray guilloché center; twelve printed anthracite Bertolucci Roman numerals; rose-gold plated Bertolucci "B"; anthracite BERTOLUCCI printed at 12; polished, rose gold-plated, leaf-shaped hands with anthracite lacquer inlays.
Bracelet: stainless steel and 18K 5N rose gold (first three central links on each side); triple-folding clasp; fitted and secured with a four-screw ring (back bezel) allowing interchangeability.

SERENA GARBO GENT   REF. 344.51.41.30D.311

Movement: Swiss automatic; caliber Soprod 11½ TT651.
Functions: hours, minutes, seconds; second time zone; big date; time- and date-setting crown at 3.
Case: stainless steel; Ø 41mm, thickness: 12mm; mirror-polished finishing; curved sapphire crystal with antireflective treatment; caseback screwed on with four screws; water resistant to 3atm.
Dial: curved black opaline; circular pattern hour-track framed by a metallic coppered contour; double calendar date at 12; azure subdial at 6 with white printed hour track; BERTOLUCCI printed in black at 6; eight rhodium-plated trapezoid indexes with a central groove; rhodium-plated Bertolucci "B" applied at 12; subdial with coppered adornment at 6 with two rhodium-plated screws; pendule second hands; polished, rhodium-plated, baton-shaped subdial hands; Dauphine-style skeleton hour and minute hands.
Strap: black alligator and calf leather; orange stitching; stainless steel triple-folding clasp; fitted and secured with a four-screw ring (back bezel) allowing interchangeability.

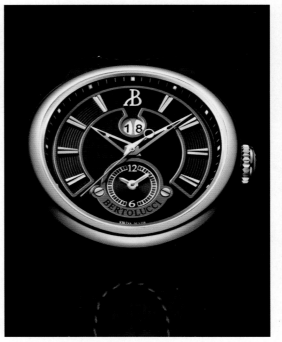

SERENA — REF. 323.51.41.12E.233

Movement: Swiss quartz; caliber ETA 8¼ 256.041; 52-month battery life.
Functions: hours, minutes; calendar date at 6; time- and date-setting crown at 3.
Case: stainless steel; 29.1x40mm, thickness; 8.3mm; curved sapphire crystal with antireflective treatment; caseback screwed on with four screws; water resistant to 3atm.
Dial: curved white silvered opaline; white natural; BERTOLUCCI at 12; center metalic ring; eight marker indexes; four Roman numerals; Bertolucci "B" applied at 12; polished with engraved double line pattern; rhodum-plated Dauphine-style hands.
Strap: natural calf leather; ivory stitching; stainless steel double-folding clasp; fitted and secured with a four-screw ring (back bezel) allowing interchangeability.

VOLTA — REF. 1213.50.41.107D.501

Movements: Swiss quartz; caliber ETA 5½ x 6¾ 976.001 and 4⅞ E01.701; 50- and 42-month battery life. **Functions:** hours, minutes; time-setting crown at 10; setting of second time zone by a corrector on the caseback. **Case:** stainless steel; Ø 42mm, thickness; 8.2mm; mirror-polished finishing; antireflective sapphire crystal; caseback screwed on with four screws; water resistant to 3atm. **Dial:** black opaline; wave pattern set at 2 and 8 with 92 diamonds (0.28 carat); single-cut diamonds in FGH color and VVS clarity; BERTOLUCCI at 6 printed in silver; principal subdial at 10, silvered with a concentric pattern and eleven applied rhodium-plated flame indexes; second subdial at 4 in black mother-of-pearl, rhodium-plated metallic ring; eight point indexes and four rhodium-plated Arabic numerals applied on the second subdial; 1 diamond (0.01 carat) set on the principal subdial; full-cut diamond in FGH color and VVS clarity; rhodium-plated Bertolucci "B" applied at 6; polished, rhodium-plated Dauphine-style hands.
Strap: black alligator leather strap with interchangeable spring bar; stainless steel pin buckle.
Also available: white technological satin strap with steel pin buckle.

STRIA — REF. 723.50.67.3.301.R00

Movement: Swiss quartz; caliber ETA 4⅞ E01.701; 42-month battery life.
Functions: hours, minutes; time setting by a corrector on the caseback.
Case: 18K 5N red gold; Ø 39.7mm, thickness; 7.8mm; full-cut diamonds in FGH color and VVS clarity; shell guilloché set with 162 diamonds (0.7 carat); domed sapphire crystal with antireflective treatment; caseback screwed on with four screws; water resistant to 3atm.
Dial: white natural mother-of-pearl sunray guilloché; BERTOLUCCI printed in gold at 12; four applied lozenge indexes and symbol; rhodium-plated Bertolucci "B" applied at 12; polished, rhodium-plated, fine-brushed Dauphine-style hands.
Strap: 18K white-gold technological satin; rosegold steel pin buckle.

GIOCO — REF. HJ153.50.69.88.171.101

Movement: Swiss quartz; caliber ETA 4⅞ E01.701; 42-month battery life.
Functions: hours, minutes; time setting by a corrector on the caseback.
Case: 18K white gold; 41.7x49.2mm, thickness; 10.15mm; paved with 362 diamonds (4.9 carats); full-cut diamonds in FG (Top Wesselton) color and IF-VVS clarity; black metallization BERTOLUCCI at 6; sapphire crystal with antireflective treatment; caseback screwed on with four screws; water resistant to 3atm.
Dial: paved with 66 diamonds (0.17 carat); full-cut diamonds in FG (Top Wesselton) color and IF-VVS clarity; polished, rhodium-plated, Dauphine-style hands.
Strap: black kid leather; 18K white-gold pin buckle set with 99 diamonds (0.41 carat); full-cut diamonds in FG (Top Wesselton) color and IF-VVS clarity.
Also available: various colored straps are available upon request.

As Blancpain continues its inexorable pursuit of innovation in the realm of haute horlogerie, **the watchmaker has trained its extensive expertise on writing a new chapter in its storied history: it's titled L-evolution.**

The manufacture based in Le Brassus, Switzerland, inaugurated the L-evolution with a quartet of complementing timepieces: the Tourbillon, Automatique 8 Jours, Moon Phase 8 Jours, and Alarm GMT. In addition to the family name, they also share family resemblances within their sleek 43.5mm cases.

The Automatique 8 Jours provides an appropriate introduction to the L-evolution collection. It contains a newly developed movement (Calibre 13R5) that delivers eight days (192 hours) of reserve power. To heighten the movement's precision, Blancpain adds tiny screws to its balance rim, which can be finely tuned.

For the Moon Phase 8 Jours, Blancpain includes a lunar indicator, a complication that's earned the brand acclaim and legitimacy for three decades. This new version pairs the movement's mechanical beauty with a multi-level dial decorated with Côtes de Genève. The dial also features a pair of beveled openings that are used to frame the day of the week and the month.

Blancpain tempts modern travelers with the Alarm GMT, an elegant timepiece that combines a second time-zone display with an alarm. More than practical, the watch highlights the movement's groundbreaking winding system. Unlike similar models that require the alarm to be wound separately, Alarm GMT's automatic-winding mechanism powers the movement and alarm simultaneously—a first in alarm watches.

LEFT Available in red gold or stainless steel, the Ø 43.5mm L-evolution Alarm GMT combines a second time zone with an alarm.

CENTER The L-evolution Automatique 8 Jours features a new proprietary movement from Blancpain that includes three barrels delivering eight days of reserve power.

BELOW The L-evolution Moon Phase 8 Jours' dial combines oversized Roman numerals with beveled cutaways that reveal the day of the week, month and moonphase.

More than 50 years after it first surfaced, **the Fifty Fathoms rises from the deep** in a 50-piece limited edition.

With this next timepiece, Blancpain calls to mind one of its biggest triumphs, the Fifty Fathoms. Introduced in 1953, it is widely considered to be the first diving watch of the modern era. Originally designed for military purposes, the watch has always been accustomed to meeting rigorous performance standards, including its water resistance to 50 fathoms (more than 90 meters).

More than 50 years after it first surfaced, the Fifty Fathoms rises from the deep in a 50-piece limited edition.

Its 45mm white-gold case is fitted with a unidirectional rotating bezel and a crown guard. Beneath the gently arched sapphire crystal, the hands and markers feature a luminescent coating that contrasts brightly against the cobalt-blue dial, whether under the sun or under the sea.

Blancpain dives even deeper for its 500 Fathoms Automatic, a diving watch that is water resistant to 1,000 meters and equipped with an automatic helium decompression valve.

Unveiled last year, the round watch's 48mm brushed titanium case houses an automatic movement created in Blancpain's Le Brassus workshops. Finished by hand, the movement is decorated with circular graining and circular satin brushing and includes an oscillating weight engraved with the image of a boat propeller.

Not only is the 500 Fathoms' design tough enough to handle the intense pressures of diving, its sporty aesthetics translate effortlessly when back on land and swimming with a different breed of sharks.

These latest entries into the Blancpain canon magnificently honor the watchmaker's respect for the past and hope for the future with a diving duo that celebrates one of the company's high-water marks and an "evolutionary" collection that maps its destiny.

TOP   A diving mask is engraved on the rotor that powers the automatic movement inside the limited edition Fifty Fathoms, a progeny of the first modern diving watch.

BOTTOM   The 500 Fathom Automatic's black dial is coated with a luminescent material that makes it easy to read in low-light conditions.

FIFTY FATHOMS REF. 5015-1540-52

Movement: automatic Blancpain Calibre 1315; 5-day power reserve; oscillating weight with engraved diving mask;
Functions: diver with final 15-minute graduation.
Case: white gold; Ø 45mm; crown guard; unidirectional rotating bezel with notched, raised pattern and luminescent markings; slightly cambered sapphire crystal; sapphire exhibition caseback revealing the movement; water resistant to 300 meters.

Dial: cobalt blue; hour-markers and hands coated in luminescent substance;
Strap: rubber-lined blue sail canvas; white-gold pin buckle.
Note: limited edition of 50 pieces; accompanied by book of art photographs of the subaquatic world, which reflects the qualities of the watch.
Suggested price: $37,400

500 FATHOMS GMT REF. 50021-12B30-52B

Movement: automatic Blancpain Calibre 5215; 5-day power reserve via three series-coupled barrels; unique system of micrometrical balance-regulating screws; delicately engraved oscillating weight shaped like a boat propeller; côtes paraboliques, beveling and circular graining finishes.
Functions: date at 3; GMT dual time zone; diver with automatic decompression valve inside case at 10.

Case: brushed titanium; Ø 48mm; ratcheted, slightly convex, unidirectional rotating bezel in titanium and scratch-resistant sapphire; water resistant to 1,000 meters.
Dial: large trapeze-shaped hour-markers; a fourth red-tipped central hand for 24-hour second time zone.
Strap: rubber-lined black canvas; triple-blade folding system.
Note: delivered in ultra-rugged water-resistant box designed to withstand extreme conditions.
Suggested price: $25,900

500 FATHOMS AUTOMATIC REF. 50015-12B30-52B

Movement: Calibre 1315; 5-day power reserve via three series of coupled barrels; balance with micrometric regulating screws; calendar mechanism enables fast date adjustments in either direction even at midnight.
Functions: date at 4; diver with automatic decompression valve inside case at 10.
Case: brushed titanium; Ø 48mm; ratcheted, slightly convex, unidirectional rotating bezel in titanium and scratch-resistant sapphire; water resistant to 1,000 meters.

Dial: large phosphorescent Arabic numerals hollowed into the sunray-brushed metal appliqués; luminescent coating on the hour-markers, bezel markings and hands; sweep seconds hand with red tip.
Strap: rubber-lined black canvas strap; triple-blade folding system.
Suggested price: $22,100
Note: delivered in an ultra-rugged water-resistant box designed to withstand extreme conditions.

SUPER TROFEO CHRONOGRAPH REF. 560ST-11D30-52B

Movement: automatic Calibre F185 coated by NAC; 40-hour power reserve; 37 jewels; 308 components.
Functions: hour, minute; small seconds and date display at 6; flyback chronograph with central sweep seconds hand, 30-minute counter at 3, 12-hour counter at 9.
Case: DLC (Diamond Like Carbon) steel; Ø 43.5mm; sapphire crystal; water resistant to 100 meters.

Dial: black dial with red and white 9 and 12 numerals stylized to evoke the numbers painted on the 30 Lamborghini Gallardo LP560-4 racing cars.
Strap: alcantara strap; steel folding clasp.
Suggested price: $17,300
Note: limited edition of 300 pieces; presentation box inspired by the lines of the ultra-dynamic Lamborghini Gallardo.

L-EVOLUTION ALARM GMT
REF. 8841-1134-53B

Movement: automatic Calibre 1241H; 40-hour power reserve; 38 jewels; 407 components; twin barrels: one for the rate, one for the alarm.
Functions: small seconds at 6; GMT dual time zone; date at 8 (indexed to second time zone; mechanical alarm (reserve indicator between 10 and 12); power-reserve indicator at 1.
Case: steel; Ø 43.5mm, thickness: 13.75mm; sapphire crystal; water resistant to 100 meters.
Dial: black; multi-level; Côtes de Genève pattern; cut-out design; a red-tipped central hand for 24-hour second time zone.
Strap: rubber-lined black alligator leather; triple-blade folding clasp.
Suggested price: $23,000
Also available: red-gold case; rubber-lined brown alligator leather strap.

L-EVOLUTION TOURBILLON GMT
REF. 8841-3630-53B

Movement: automatic Calibre 5025; 8-day power reserve; 33 jewels; 304 components.
Functions: double-hand date display at 9; flying tourbillon at 12; GMT dual time zone.
Case: red gold; Ø 43.5mm, thickness: 13.45mm; sapphire crystal exhibition caseback; water resistant to 100 meters.
Dial: center provides distinct view of the dial baseplate adorned with Côtes de Genève; oversized 3 and 6 numerals.
Strap: rubber-lined brown alligator leather.
Suggested price: $129,500
Also available: white gold.

L-EVOLUTION AUTOMATIQUE 8 JOURS
REF. 8805-1134-53B

Movement: automatic Calibre 13R5; 8-day power reserve via three barrels; 36 jewels; 243 components; unique system of micrometrical balance-regulating screws; high-density gold rotor; baseplate with Côtes de Genève.
Functions: center seconds; date at 6 (can be changed at any time, in either direction, without damaging mechanism); power-reserve indicator at 12.
Case: steel; Ø 43.5mm, thickness: 13.4mm; sapphire crystal exhibition caseback; water resistant to 100 meters.
Dial: black; cut-out design reveals baseplate.
Strap: rubber-lined black alligator leather.
Suggested price: $17,300
Also available: red-gold case; rubber-lined brown alligator leather strap; steel bracelet, changeable via detachable lugs.

L-EVOLUTION MOON PHASE 8 JOURS
REF. 8866-3630-53B

Movement: automatic Calibre 66R9; 8-day power reserve; 36 jewels; 325 components; flat balance spring; titanium balance with micrometric adjustment screws; high-density gold oscillating weight; finely circular-grained mainplate; beveled and polished parts; côtes paraboliques motif; beveled bridges.
Functions: small seconds and moonphase at 6; day and month at 12; date ring; original date-correction system; power-reserve indicator at 12.
Case: red gold; Ø 43.5mm, thickness: 15.55mm; sapphire crystal caseback; water resistant to 100 meters.
Dial: black; three levels; Côtes de Genève pattern on mainplate; beveled cut-out design.
Strap: rubber-lined brown alligator leather strap.
Suggested price: $37,400
Also available: steel version.

BOUCHERON
PARIS

Founded by Frédéric Boucheron in 1858, the house that bears his name is now one of the most prestigious Parisian jewelers—it is a member of the elite club of jewelers on the Place Vendôme whose numbers can be counted on one hand. More than 150 years of history have allowed Boucheron to cater to a number of legendary clients: maharajas, movie stars, kings, queens, courtesans and the like. Continually drawing on its unique heritage, Boucheron carries on an expertise and creativity that never cease to amaze in both jewelry and horology.

Creating watches had been a project for Frédéric Boucheron ever since he founded the company. In the rich archives of the house are a number of extraordinary pieces, such as a chatelaine described as "intriguing and fantastic," and a watch that got him noticed by the jury of the 1867 Exposition Universelle in Paris and earned him the nickname, "the jeweler of time." The daring that animates Boucheron's horological creations is largely inspired by the unbridled imagination at work in his jewelry collection. This domain is packed with creations, each one more incredible than the last: scarf necklaces, plume brooches, secret rings or even imperial crowns brush up against a multicolored menagerie of snakes, felines and chameleons, all crafted in the most precious materials—gold, platinum, diamonds, and such—but also the most unusual ones—silk, lions' teeth and claws, tortoiseshell, or snakewood. Gold was reinvented: pleated and woven, manipulated to imitate lace, scales, cloth, and even feathers. Engraved diamonds! Such techniques were brand new. It was this eclecticism in the choice of materials and this unique way of transforming them that distinguished Boucheron so in the French world of haute jewelry. Faced with so much talent, Boucheron's clients knew exactly what they had at their disposal. One such client was the Maharaja of Patiala, who, on August 1, 1928, sent more than 1,432 emeralds and 7,571 diamonds with which to make ceremonial jewelry. In 1930, the Shah of Iran counted on the expertise of Boucheron to appraise the entirety of the Persian imperial treasure, a titanic job that took months to complete.

THIS PAGE
Jean-Christophe Bédos holds the reins at Boucheron.

FACING PAGE
26, Place Vendôme is the historic address of Boucheron.

Boucheron's domain is **packed with creations,** each one more incredible than the last.

TOP This Reflet Medium in polished 18-karat 3N yellow gold is set with 36 diamonds.

The design on the dial of the Reflet Medium in polished stainless steel continues the pattern of the vertical gadroons on its case.

The Reflet XL is shown here in a steel case with an interchangeable watch strap.

The Reflet XL Automatic is available in a steel and pink-gold case with silver dial.

BOTTOM The bejeweled Ava Deco line is inspired by Boucheron's jewelry creations.

A TOUCH OF MADNESS

The watch collections from Boucheron today are the reflection of the founder's creative talent, still touched with whimsy. All the models, even the most classic ones, bear this touch of madness, a twist reminding us that this is, after all, a Boucheron watch. For example, take the Reflet model, created in 1947. Its sober rectangular form and the gadroons that refine its surface have made it an icon of horology and French discretion and elegance. However, each of its incarnations contains an original detail: the marking of "Place Vendôme" at 6:00; the boutique's address engraved on the crown; the Reflet XL Seconde Folle (crazy second) hand that seems to change length; the off-center oval aperture revealing the movement on the automatic XL model; Boucheron's name written vertically on the dial…these details transform the Reflet into much more than just a watch like any other, and lend it a latter-day classicism. These collections are no exception to this rule. All of the men's models are equipped with the GP4000 automatic mechanical movement, exclusively provided by the Girard-Perregaux; its artistic finishing, its rotor decorated with the Boucheron hallmark, and, of course, its Swiss origin all place this watch securely within the exclusive world of haute horology. The Ladies' Reflet models proudly bear diamonds on the dial and case for elegant occasions, on both steel and gold versions. Naturally, all of the emblematic Reflect models are equipped with Boucheron's exclusive interchangeable-strap system that allows a woman to match her watch to her outfit with the greatest of ease.

EXTRAORDINARY TABLEAUX

Boucheron's savoir-faire often leads us to places we don't expect. These models are perfect examples of the tricky art of covering one's tracks. Indeed, some models become homes for an entire improbable and good-natured menagerie, such as the Bestiaire Ronde Seconde Folle collection. Here is a ravenous chameleon after a fly, a genial frog that seems to wink at us, and an owl with a squint. It is a cabinet of beastly curiosities that can almost make us forget the incredible talent and effort that the jewelers bestow upon each gem-set piece. Each one of these tableaux vivants is actually the result of an assemblage of several elements. Some are located under the crystal, such as the gem-set dial and its interactions with beautiful stones like aventurine, chalcedony, or mother-of-pearl, as well as the mobile seconds disc. Some are affixed to the bezel, covering the crystal. All compose an ensemble whose technical sophistication leaves no room for "almost." The choice of stones also tells a tale of unrivaled jewelry expertise: rubies, tsavorites, colored sapphires and diamonds are assembled to create bright, almost cartoonish colors. Each stone has been carefully selected to enhance a certain shade of color and the compiled setting of each watch takes hours to perfect. The watches' animation is activated by the GP4000 movement, whose seconde folle complication breathes life into the animals.

The year 2010 brings the excellence and imagination we have come to expect from Boucheron. The new Paname line celebrated 2009 in a chronograph model permeated with very Parisian elegance and classicism. In 2010, Boucheron is adding women's versions of the Paname, set with diamonds. Another reason for rejoicing on the part of Boucheron's feminine fans: at BaselWorld 2010, the brand presented the Ava Deco line, sensual jeweled watches for women, inspired by the company's jewelry collection. In the proud tradition of Boucheron's jewelry, the Ava Deco line is consummately feminine and precious. Its elegant lines evoke a return to 1950s style that seduces any woman who gazes upon it.

Crazy Jungle collection, shown here in its chameleon, owl and frog versions, summons all of the extravagance of Boucheron's haute jewelry.

PANAME AUTOMATIC CHRONOGRAPH · REF. WA010212

Movement: mechanical automatic movement.
Functions: hours, minutes, seconds; date at 6; chronograph.
Case: polished stainless steel; Ø 42mm, thickness 12.2mm; polished bezel set with 52 diamonds (1.7 carats); fluted crown engraved with "26 Place Vendôme Paris"; polished middle case with "Pointe de diamant" pattern; rectangular pushbuttons; sapphire crystal with antireflective treatment on the inner side; brushed caseback with elliptical sapphire crystal; water resistant to 5atm.

Dial: silver; rhodium Arabic numerals; anthracite minute-scale; two horizontal counters set with 72 diamonds; rhodium-plated hands; horizontal Boucheron mark at 12; "26 Place Vendôme" at 6.
Strap: white varanus; steel folding buckle with "Pointe de diamant" pattern and Boucheron mark.
Also available: steel anthracite dial and black galuchat strap.

PANAME AUTOMATIC CHRONOGRAPH · REF. WA010207

Movement: mechanical automatic movement.
Functions: hours, minutes, seconds; date at 6; chronograph.
Case: polished stainless steel; Ø 42mm, thickness: 12.2mm; polished bezel with gadroons; fluted crown engraved with "26 Place Vendôme Paris"; sapphire crystal with antireflective treatment on the inner side; polished middle case with "Pointe de diamant" pattern; rectangular pushbuttons; brushed caseback with elliptical sapphire crystal; water resistant to 5atm.

Dial: anthracite; rhodium Arabic numerals; white minute-scale; two horizontal counters with rhodium outline and white graduation; rhodium-plated hands; horizontal Boucheron mark at 12; "26 Place Vendôme" at 6.
Strap: black alligator; steel folding buckle with "Pointe de diamant" pattern and Boucheron mark.
Also available: steel: silver dial with black alligator strap, or silver dial with white brushed-satin strap; pink gold: silver dial with brown alligator strap.

RONDE AUTOMATIC WATCH PINK GOLD · REF. WA010304

Movement: mechanical automatic Girard-Perregaux GP4000 caliber.
Functions: hours, minutes, seconds; date at 1.
Case: 18K 5N pink gold; Ø 39mm, thickness: 8.9mm; fluted crown engraved with "26 Place Vendôme Paris"; polished "Pointe de diamant" pattern on the caseback with six screws; sapphire crystal with antireflective treatment on the inner side; water resistant to 3atm.

Dial: silver gadroons with sunray effect; Roman numerals indexes; 3N gold-plated hour and minute hands; vertical BOUCHERON mark at 7; "26 Place Vendôme" at 6; special Automatique mark between 4 and 5.
Strap: black alligator strap with black alligator lining; 18K 5N pink-gold buckle with "Pointe de diamant" pattern.
Also available: steel case with silver dial.

REFLET XL AUTOMATIC WATCH · REF. WA009204

Movement: mechanical automatic movement.
Functions: hours, minutes, seconds; date at 1.
Case: polished 18K 5N pink gold; polished bezel with vertical gadroons; 45x31.5mm, thickness: 9.75mm, fine brushed middle case; fine brushed caseback with polished angles, elliptic sapphire crystal opening, BOUCHERON mark; serial number and BOUCHERON historical stamp engraving; 5N pink-gold crown engraved with "26 Place Vendôme Paris"; sapphire crystal with antireflective treatment on the inner side; water resistant to 5atm.

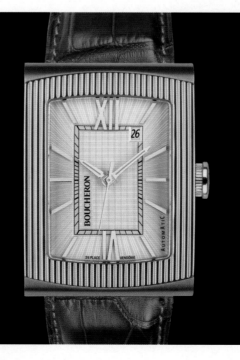

Dial: stamped silver dial with 4N pink-gold Roman numerals and applied indexes; 4N pink-gold hour and minute hands; vertical BOUCHERON mark at 7; anthracite minute scale; "26 Place Vendôme" at 6; special Automatique mark between 4 and 5.
Strap: sold with two straps chosen in the assortment.
Also available: steel case with silver dial; steel case with black dial; steel and pink-gold case with silver dial.

REFLET MEDIUM WATCH — REF. WA009405

Movement: quartz movement.
Functions: hours, minutes.
Case: polished 18K 3N yellow gold; vertical gadroons; 34x21mm, thickness: 6.5mm; bezel set with 36 diamonds (total 0.57 carat); caseback with "Pointe de diamant" pattern, specific cartouches with BOUCHERON signature, serial number and BOUCHERON historical stamp; fluted crown engraved with "26 Place Vendôme Paris"; sapphire crystal with antireflective treatment on the inner side; water resistant to 3atm.
Dial: silver dial with vertical gadroons pattern; vertically set with 30 diamonds (total 0.13 carat); 18K 3N yellow-gold hour and minute hands; vertical BOUCHERON mark at 7.
Strap: sold with two straps chosen in the assortment.
Also available: yellow-gold bracelet.

REFLET SMALL WATCH IN STEEL — REF. WA009502

Movement: quartz movement.
Functions: hours, minutes.
Case: polished stainless steel; vertical gadroons; 29.5x18mm, thickness: 6.4mm; caseback with "Pointe de diamant" pattern, specific cartouches with BOUCHERON signature; serial number and BOUCHERON historical stamp; crown engraved with "26 Place Vendôme Paris"; sapphire crystal with antireflective treatment on the inner side; water resistant to 3atm.
Dial: silver dial with vertical gadroons pattern; four diamond indexes (total 0.04 carat); nickel-plated hour and minute hands; vertical BOUCHERON mark at 7.
Strap: sold with two straps chosen in the assortment.
Also available: diamond-set case and in medium size; steel bracelet.

RONDE — REF. WA010321

Movement: quartz movement.
Functions: hours, minutes.
Case: polished stainless steel; Ø 38mm, thickness: 5.5mm; polished bezel and case with "Pointe de diamant" pattern; fluted crown engraved with "26 Place Vendôme Paris"; sapphire crystal with antireflective treatment on the inner side; water resistant to 3atm.
Dial: blue-gray mother-of-pearl; blue Roman numerals; vertical Boucheron mark at 7; "26 Place Vendôme" at 6; rhodium-plated hands.
Strap: dark blue technological satin; steel pin buckle with "Pointe de diamant" pattern and Boucheron mark.
Also available: steel; pink mother-of-pearl dial and pink satin strap.

RONDE AUTOMATIC — REF. WA010323

Movement: mechanical automatic movement.
Functions: hours, minutes, seconds; date at 1.
Case: polished stainless steel; Ø 39mm, thickness: 8.9mm; polished bezel with gadroons; fluted crown engraved with "26 Place Vendôme Paris"; sapphire crystal with antireflective treatment on the inner side; polished case with "Pointe de diamant" pattern; brushed caseback with elliptical sapphire crystal; water resistant to 3atm.
Dial: white mother-of-pearl; applied XII and VI indexes set with 35 diamonds; white Roman numerals; vertical Boucheron mark at 7; "26 Place Vendôme" at 6; rhodium-plated hands.
Strap: white brushed satin; steel pin buckle with "Pointe de diamant" pattern and Boucheron mark.
Also Available: 18K 5N pink gold; white mother-of-pearl dial and pink satin strap.

BOVET
1822

CREATING ARTFUL TIMEPIECES

The *Mona Lisa* has probably been the cause of more ink spilled by art historians than any other painting in the history of art. It is also probably the cause of the most blood, sweat and tears spilled by artists trying to reproduce the subject's enigmatic smile. Pascal Raffy, owner of Bovet, was not intimidated by these considerations. For Monaco's ONLY WATCH '09 (an auction of one-of-a-kind watches whose proceeds go to Duchenne Muscular Dystrophy research), the manufacture donated the first model from the Amadeo collection. It was a jumping-hours model, one of Bovet's specialties, whose dial depicted a reproduction of the *Mona Lisa*. This masterpiece of miniaturization, which required more than a month of work to complete, was purchased by an American collector for $136,000.

POCKET WATCHES FOR THE WRIST

Immediately recognizable by the silhouette of its timepieces—the aesthetics of a pocket watch but designed to be worn on the wrist—Bovet decided to go a step further, creating a timepiece that could seamlessly switch between one mode of use and the other. After seven years of development, the Amadeo collection realizes this goal: all pieces in the collection incorporate a device allowing the wearer to transform the wristwatch into a pocket watch—or even a table clock—without the need for any extra support. This innovation, which the house describes as a "turning point in the history of Bovet," was officially presented at Geneva in January 2010 at the eighth Bovet Salon. This innovative conceptual grace note of interchangeability from wristwatch to pocket watch to table clock will eventually join all of Bovet's collections.

But Amadeo has not been the only surprise up Bovet's sleeve these last few months. At the beginning of autumn 2009, the company also enriched its Sport*ster* line with a red-gold/black-titanium Saguaro Tourbillon released in two 100-piece limited editions: one sized at 45mm and the other at 51mm. The painstaking attention to detail on the Saguaro Tourbillon is typical of Bovet, from the case, which is water resistant to 300 meters and evokes the Art Deco style of a Bovet pocket watch from 1930, to the finishing of the movement and the exterior. The rotor and the dial plate, for example, have been engraved by hand in the "bris de verre" (broken glass) style, to contrast with the matte of the blackened bridges.

With its new Amadeo collection, Bovet exercises its bent for innovation while still scrupulously adhering to the brand's traditions. In fact, the entire production grows out of the technical perfection of the movements and the originality of the watches' geometry, two Bovet characteristics interpreted through the brand's perfect mastery of the horological art.

This innovative conceptual grace note of **interchangeability from wristwatch to pocket watch to table clock** will eventually join all of Bovet's collections.

IN-HOUSE MOVEMENT 13BA05

The Sport*ster* Saguaro is powered by the 13BA05, an in-house movement designed to incorporate functions that are useful and practical in the day-to-day wearing of the watch. Using this as a base, Bovet was recently able to give free rein to ambitions already clearly displayed in its complicated watches. The Orbis Mundi from both Bovet and Dimier (the second brand resuscitated by Raffy) illustrates this beautifully. Orbis Mundi takes the base of the 13BA05 and adds a tourbillon, whose cage (adorned with a lotus flower decoration) bears the second hand, linked to a second time zone with day/night indication and a power-reserve indicator. Bovet had previously set the bar quite high with its Cathedral Chime Minute Repeater Tourbillon Triple Time Zone Automaton, a watch equipped with a movement that comprised more than 600 components!

Bovet, a company that devotes almost half of its nearly 2,000-piece annual production to custom-made pieces for clients, has enough feathers in its cap to fascinate true watch lovers, especially those devoted to a veritable cult of exceptional timepieces in which the horological art finds its full flower of expression. More than one third of Bovet's pieces are decorated with miniature paintings, engravings and enamel decorations, and are set with diamonds. The brand has evolved significantly since its establishment in 1822. Edouard Bovet, a Frenchman living in London and creator of the "Chinese watch," a high-quality, humidity-resistant timepiece with a reasonable price, had quickly understood China's market potential in the 19th century and secured an almost absolute monopoly on horological imports to China. Other houses rushed to follow suit; Vaucher Frères, Edouard Juvet, and Dimier Frères would all put Chinese watches into production.

SUCCESSFUL VERTICAL INTEGRATION

Competition for Chinese watches from Besançon, France, and the United States at the turn of the 20th century, counterfeiters, the worldwide depression of the 1930s, and finally the upheaval of the quartz crisis of the 1970s and '80s would all get the best of Bovet. Devotees had to wait until 1989 for the brand to rise from the ashes, and another ten or so years until Raffy purchased it and began to restore its historic luster by adapting pocket watches for use as wristwatches.

Following the difficult path of vertical integration, Bovet bought three subcontractors that produced, respectively, tourbillons, movements and balance springs, uniting them under the name Dimier 1738. This foundation was completed by the purchase of Aigat (stamping) and a share in Aubert Complications. At this point, Bovet could now launch into the quest for the horological Holy Grail: a proprietary movement designed and built entirely in-house (in Bovet's case, the 13BA05). Finally, to clearly signify its foundation in the city that witnessed its beginnings, the company acquired the Château de Môtiers, former property of the Bovet family where Edouard Bovet had established the roots of the brand, and the place that would become its nerve center.

Nearly 190 years after the start of a business that placed the small village of Fleurier in the center of the horological map, Bovet is a full participant in the revival of this region alongside Chopard, Parmigiani Fleurier, and Vaucher Manufacture—each of which raises the measuring of time to an art form.

FACING PAGE

TOP   One of Bovet's newest additions: The Sport*ster* Saguaro Tourbillon.

BOTTOM   An exceptional piece, the Orbis Mundi tourbillon displays two time zones.

THIS PAGE
Bovet watches are prized for their superb blend of art and horology, such as the Tourbillon Jumping Hours, which combines a tourbillon, seven days of power reserve, and a jumping hour.

Breguet

Depuis 1775

More than two centuries after Abraham-Louis Breguet started his company, the Swiss inventor's creations remain a vital part of modern horology and Breguet's influences can be seen today in everything from cases and complications to decorations and dials.

Nicolas G. Hayek, the brand's director since 1999, aims to protect and maintain Breguet's historic legacy with timepieces that refine the 18th-century watchmaker's mechanical and aesthetic achievements.

"The company was created by one of the greatest geniuses of the watch business, Abraham-Louis Breguet, who practically invented every type of watch known today," Hayek said in a recent interview. "Many of the political and cultural figures who have influenced Europe since the 18th century—Napoleon, Churchill, Balzac, Hugo—had the pleasure of wearing Breguet. The culture of Breguet is the history of Europe."

The company evokes a pivotal moment from its past with the Double Tourbillon, a grand complication that provides a stage for Breguet's most iconic invention, the tourbillon. Patented in 1801, the mechanism compensates for errors in a watch's rate that are caused by gravity's effect on the watch's moving parts.

More than two hundred years later, the Double Tourbillon beguiles with its complexity. To achieve its signature look, the tourbillons and guilloché dial are mounted together on a platform that propels them both around the dial, rotating fully every 12 hours.

This animated arrangement conceals the technical flourishes beneath that bequeath the watch its high level of accuracy. Working independently, the tourbillons are connected by differential gears that average their rates, effectively doubling the precision of single-tourbillon watches.

Beyond the mechanical, the Double Tourbillon's movement provides an exquisite reminder of Breguet's dedication to the handcrafted art of traditional watchmaking with an intricately detailed engraving of the solar system in relief.

ABOVE   Breguet's craftsmen engrave the solar system onto the Double Tourbillon's movement, which is visible through a transparent caseback.

RIGHT   The Double Tourbillon's hour hand, twin-tourbillon assembly and dial are connected, rotating once every 12 hours. Breguet introduced this Ø 44mm pink-gold model last year.

The Tradition 7027 exposes the inner workings of its celebrated Calibre 507DR.

In 1783, Breguet improved the sound of striking watches, replacing their bells with a gong spring. This metal strip encircles the movement, resonating when struck by tiny, mechanized hammers. Even now, nearly 230 years after its debut, the gong spring's tuneful song continues to delight.

The Classic Grand Complication is one of the latest members to join Breguet's remarkable choir of repeaters. Its patented design incorporates the latest materials and includes a precision striking system reengineered in 2008.

The company now offers a high jewelry version paved entirely with diamonds. More than an extravagance, the company says the stone's hardness helps reduce the loss of sound vibrations, enhancing the minute repeater's sonorous voice.

The watch's expert engineering is matched by the artful gem-setting skills required to create this objet d'art. Diamond baguettes weighing more than 11 carats cover the watch's surface, while the dial provides a dazzling exhibition of Breguet's mastery of the invisible setting. It encompasses nearly 400 princess-cut diamonds, set upside down, to create a pattern similar to Clous de Paris.

Breguet enhances the charm of its Tradition 7027 collection—launched in 2005—by pairing a new anthracite-gray version of its 507DR movement with a pink- or white-gold case. The two-tone combination provides a striking visual contrast that highlights the exposed inner workings of the celebrated caliber, which includes a "pare-chute" escapement invented by the company's namesake. The Tradition 7027 displays the time on an off-centered dial at 12:00 alongside an engraved power-reserve indicator.

All of these remarkable timepieces confirm that, like its founder, Breguet is well ahead of its time.

TOP The Tradition 7027's movement features a new anthracite-gray treatment achieved with an advanced electroplating technique applied to metals in the platinum family.

BOTTOM LEFT Every surface of the High Jewelry Grand Complication is set with more than 450 diamonds. In addition to their beauty, the gemstones are well suited for transmitting the minute repeater's sound.

BOTTOM RIGHT The hand-engraved image on the diamond-set minute repeater's movement reflects a musical motif.

TRADITION 7027   REF. 7027BB/G9/9V6

Movement: mechanical manual-winding Calibre 507DR in an anthracite gray alloy of platinum-group metals; 50-hour power-reserve indicator engraved on front and back of movement; 3Hz frequency; 34 jewels; straight-line lever escapement; monometallic balance wheel; BREGUET overcoil; adjusted in five positions; numbered and signed BREGUET.
Case: 18K white gold; Ø 37mm; finely fluted caseband; rounded horns welded to case; sapphire crystal caseback; water resistant to 3atm.
Dial: black electroplated 18K gold; hand engraved on rose engine; polished steel open-tipped BREGUET hands; individually numbered and signed BREGUET.
Strap: leather; screw-in pin connection to case.
Suggested price: $24,850
Also available: in pink gold.

TRADITION 7027   REF. 7027BR/R9/9V6

Movement: mechanical manual-winding Calibre 507DR plated in rose gold; 50-hour power-reserve indicator engraved on front and back of movement; 3Hz frequency; 34 jewels; straight-line lever escapement; monometallic balance wheel; BREGUET overcoil; adjusted in five positions; numbered and signed BREGUET.
Case: 18K pink gold; Ø 37mm; finely fluted caseband; rounded horns welded to case; sapphire crystal caseback; water resistant to 3atm.
Dial: black electroplated 18K gold; hand engraved on rose engine; polished steel open-tipped BREGUET hands; individually numbered and signed BREGUET.
Strap: leather; screw-in pin connection to case.
Suggested price: $24,100

CLASSIQUE GRANDE COMPLICATION – TWIN ROTATING TOURBILLONS   REF. 5347BR/11/9ZU

Movement: mechanical manual-winding Calibre 588; twin tourbillon regulators mounted on manually engine-turned rotating center plate; 50-hour power reserve; 2.5Hz frequency; 85 jewels; monometallic BREGUET balance wheels with four gold regulating screws; BREGUET overcoil; adjusted in six positions; hand-engraved representation of the solar system on back; numbered and signed BREGUET.
Functions: two 60-second tourbillons rotating independently as well as in tandem around center axis once per 12-hour period.
Case: 18K pink gold; Ø 44mm; finely fluted caseband; rounded horns welded to case; sapphire crystal caseback; water resistant to 3atm.
Dial: ring shaped, forming a flange in silvered 18K gold; manually engine-turned center plate featuring apertures for the two tourbillons and rotating in step with the hours; rose-gilt open-tipped BREGUET minute hand; hour hand an extension of bridge supporting the two tourbillon carriages; individually numbered and signed BREGUET.
Strap: leather; screw-in pin connection to case.
Suggested price: $374,900

CLASSIQUE GRANDE COMPLICATION – MINUTE REPEATER   REF. 7637BB/12/9ZU

Movement: manual-winding Calibre 567/2; 40-hour power reserve; 31 jewels; 2.5Hz balance wheel with load screws; straight-line lever escapement; BREGUET overcoil; adjusted in five positions; entirely engraved by hand; numbered and signed BREGUET.
Functions: minute repeater; 24-hour indication at 3; running seconds at 9.
Case: 18K white gold; Ø 42mm; finely fluted caseband; horns welded to case; sapphire crystal caseback.
Dial: silvered 18K gold; hand engraved on rose engine; blued steel open-tipped BREGUET hands; individually numbered and signed BREGUET.
Strap: leather; screw-in pin connection to case.
Suggested price: $214,900
Also available: in 18K rose gold.

CLASSIQUE — REF. 7337BA/1E/9V6

Movement: mechanical automatic-winding Calibre 502.3 QSE1; 45-hour power reserve; 35 jewels; 3Hz BREGUET balance wheel with load screws; adjusted in six positions; numbered and signed BREGUET.
Functions: date at 2; running seconds at 5; day of the week at 10; age and phase of moon at 12.
Case: 18K yellow gold; Ø 39mm; finely fluted caseband; rounded horns welded to case; sapphire crystal caseback; water resistant to 3atm.
Dial: silvered 18K gold; hand engraved on rose engine; engine-turned basket pattern; blued steel open-tipped BREGUET hands; individually numbered and signed BREGUET.
Strap: leather; screw-in pin connection to case.
Suggested price: $35,200
Also available: in 18K white gold.

CLASSIQUE — REF. 5967BA/11/9W6

Movement: mechanical manual-winding Calibre 506.2; 20 jewels; 3Hz balance wheel with poising screws; adjustable in five positions; numbered and signed BREGUET.
Case: 18K yellow gold; Ø 41mm; finely fluted caseback; rounded horns welded to case; sapphire crystal caseback; water resistant to 3atm.
Dial: silvered 18K gold; engine-turned by hand; Art Deco Checkerboard pattern by BREGUET; blued steel open-tipped BREGUET hands.
Strap: leather; screw-in pin connection to case.
Suggested price: $16,400
Also available: in 18K white gold.

CLASSIQUE GRANDE COMPLICATION – HIGH JEWELLERY   REF. 7639BB/6D/9XV DD0D

Movement: manual-winding Calibre 567/2; 40-hour power reserve; 31 jewels; 2.5Hz balance wheel with load screws; straight-line lever escapement; BREGUET overcoil; adjusted in five positions; entirely hand-engraved with musical decoration; numbered and signed BREGUET.
Functions: minute repeater.
Case: 18K white gold; Ø 44.5mm; rounded horns welded to case; fully set with 178 baguette-cut diamonds totaling approx. 11.18 carats; crown set with diamond (approx. 0.46 carat); sapphire crystal caseback.
Dial: 18K gold; full-pavé with 392 princess-cut diamonds "invisibly set" upside down; blued steel open-tipped BREGUET hands; individually numbered and signed BREGUET.
Strap: leather; screw-in pin connection to case.
Price: available upon request.

MARINE ROYALE – ALARM WATCH   REF. 5847BR/32/5ZU

Movement: mechanical automatic-winding Calibre 519R; 45-hour power reserve; 4Hz frequency; 36 jewels; engine-turned 18K rose-gold rotor; straight-line lever escapement; balance wheel with regulating screws; adjusted in five positions; individually numbered and signed BREGUET. **Functions:** date at 6; alarm and power-reserve indication between 9 and 11; alarm on/off indicator at 12.
Case: 18K rose gold; Ø 45mm; finely fluted caseband; rounded horns welded to case; screw-locked crowns; wave-shaped ratchet at 3 to ensure the bezel's unidirectional rotation; rubber-covered alarm-setting pushpiece at 4; rubber-covered alarm on/off pushpiece at 8; engine-turned caseback fitted with sapphire crystal; water resistant to 30atm.
Dial: 18K pink gold; wave pattern manually engraved on rose engine; chapter ring with applied Roman numerals and luminescent dots; facetted, open-tipped BREGUET hands in 18K blued gold and covered with a luminescent compound; triangular center hand for setting the alarm time.
Strap: rubber.
Suggested price: $42,000
Also available: in 18K white gold with rhodium dial; on leather strap.

CARL F. BUCHERER

FINE SWISS WATCHMAKING

From a small watch and jewelry shop in Lucerne in 1888 to an independent stalwart of the Swiss watch industry to a full-fledged manufacture with unquestionable technical prowess, Carl F. Bucherer has grown organically and on its own terms since Carl Friedrich Bucherer presented his first collection in 1919.

Every serious watchmaker eventually becomes dissatisfied with the trappings of horology and hungers for the ultimate accomplishment: creating a movement that crosses boundaries and wins accolades from demanding watch connoisseurs. Carl F. Bucherer crossed this threshold with its CFB A1000 automatic movement. The peripherally mounted rotor revolves around the movement—instead of over, as is usually the case—and delivers a steady stream of energy while turning in either direction. The movement marries the practical utility of an automatic movement and the aesthetic fascination of a manual movement, revealing an unobstructed view of its workings. The patented peripheral rotor is joined by a dynamic shock-absorption system and the central dual adjusting system.

The first timepiece to take advantage of the new movement's incredible technique is the Patravi EvoTec DayDate. The timepiece's cushion-shaped case provides the perfect framework for the various complications and functions provided by the new CFB A1001 (based on the CFB A1000). A small seconds display at 6:00 cleverly echoes the rounded sides of the iconic case, and the day display at 9:00 reveals in the elegant simplicity inherent to the Patravi aesthetic. The large date display sprawls across the upper left quadrant of the dial in a form that also pays sly tribute to the case's shape.

Released at BaselWorld 2008, the CFB A1000 caliber won the Goldene Unruh (Golden Balance) 2009 prize from the German publication *Uhren-Magazin* for its technical and aesthetic innovation.

The name of the Patravi T-ChronoGrade is a portmanteau, referring to the unique combination of a chronograph function with a retrograde hour display. After the central chronograph hand has completed a revolution, the minute counter at 9:00 jumps to the next mark on the scale. This mechanism is in turn connected to an hour counter with its own flyback system between 7:00 and 8:00. The retrograde hour counter and chronograph are just two of the useful functions of the CFB 1902 caliber that powers the Patravi T-Chronograde, featuring as it does a large date display, power-reserve indication and annual calendar.

The ergonomic tonneau case of the Patravi T-24 features a 24-hour display that can be adjusted independently of the hour and minute hands. When Carl F. Bucherer decided to make a feminine version of the Patravi T-24, aesthetics were an important consideration. Echoing the hour-markers along the edge are twelve segments along the bezel, featuring four diamonds gleaming out from each. The 24-hour scale now operates in a chic oval, and the power reserve stands out in more pronounced contrast from its background. The Patravi T-24 Ladies holds true to its strongest principles while adding the feminine grace that make it irresistible.

The CFB A1000 caliber won the Goldene Unruh 2009 prize from the German publication *Uhren-Magazin.*

TOP LEFT   The Patravi EvoTec DayDate's indexes insistently echo the geometric sparseness and refined modern power of its design.

TOP RIGHT   The Patravi T-ChronoGrade melds a chronograph function with a retrograde hour display. The chronograph hour hand moves downwards across its arc; when it reaches the end of its semicircular scale, it flies back to the starting position and begins again.

RIGHT   The Patravi T-24 Ladies boasts a 24-hour display that resides conveniently at 12:00, across the dial from the power-reserve indicator at 6:00.

PATRAVI EVOTEC DAYDATE   REF. 00.10625.13.33.01

Movement: automatic CFB A1001 caliber; 33 jewels; 55-hour power reserve.
Functions: small seconds; big date; weekend display.
Case: stainless steel; 44x44.5mm; rubber bezel; screwed crown; sapphire crystal; water resistant to 5atm.
Dial: black.
Strap: calf leather; stainless steel folding clasp.

Suggested price: $15,500
Also available: 18K rose gold: $37,500.

PATRAVI T-CHRONOGRADE   REF. 00.10626.08.63.21

Movement: automatic CFB 1902 caliber; 51 jewels; 42-hour power reserve.
Functions: chronograph; big date; retrograde hours; flyback; annual calendar; power-reserve indicator.
Case: stainless steel; 43x46mm; tonneau shaped; screwed crown; sapphire crystal; water resistant to 5atm.
Dial: rhodium.

Bracelet: stainless steel.
Suggested price: $15,300
Also available: black dial with strap: $14,700.

PATRAVI CHRONODATE   REF. 00.10624.08.53.21

Movement: automatic CFB 1956 caliber; 49 jewels; 42-hour power reserve.
Functions: chronograph; big date.
Case: stainless steel; Ø 44.6mm; screwed crown; sapphire crystal; water resistant to 5atm.
Dial: blue.
Bracelet: stainless steel.

Suggested price: $6,900
Also available: 18K rose gold; with strap: $6,300; various dial color combinations.

PATRAVI TRAVELTEC   REF. 00.10620.03.33.01

Movement: automatic CFB 1901.1 caliber; 39 jewels; COSC certified; 42-hour power reserve.
Functions: chronograph; date; third time zone.
Case: 18K rose gold; Ø 46.6mm; screwed crown; sapphire crystal; water resistant to 5atm.
Dial: black.

Strap: calf leather; 18K rose-gold pin buckle.
Suggested price: $44,000
Also available: stainless steel; rose-gold bracelet: $63,500; various dial color combinations.

PATRAVI T-GRAPH
REF. 00.10615.03.93.01

Movement: automatic CFB 1960.1 caliber; 47 jewels; COSC certified; 42-hour power reserve.
Functions: chronograph; big date; power-reserve indicator.
Case: 18K rose gold; screwed crown; sapphire crystal; water resistant to 5atm.
Dial: brown.
Strap: Louisiana alligator leather; 18K rose-gold pin buckle.
Suggested price: $25,900
Also available: stainless steel; rose-gold bracelet: $43,500; various dial color combinations.

PATRAVI CHRONOGRADE
REF. 00.10623.03.13.01

Movement: automatic CFB 1902.1 caliber; 39 jewels; COSC certified; 42-hour power reserve.
Functions: chronograph; big date; retrograde hours; flyback; annual calendar; power-reserve indicator.
Case: 18K rose gold; Ø 44.6mm; screwed crown; sapphire crystal; water resistant to 5atm.
Dial: rhodium.
Strap: calf leather; 18K rose-gold pin buckle.
Suggested price: $33,900
Also available: stainless steel; rose-gold bracelet: $51,000; various dial color combinations.

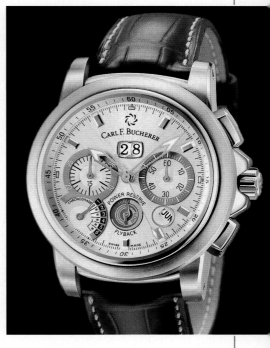

ALACRIA DIVA WILDCAT
REF. 00.10706.01.99.12

Movement: quartz movement.
Case: 18K yellow gold; 181 sapphires (3.6 carats); sapphire crystal; water resistant to 3atm.
Dial: 150 sapphires (2 carats).
Strap: Galuchat leather; 18K yellow-gold pin buckle.
Suggested price: $75,500
Note: limited to 25 pieces.

PATRAVI T-24 LADIES
REF. 00.10612.08.23.11

Movement: automatic CFB 1953 caliber; 28 jewels; 42-hour power reserve.
Functions: date; second time zone; power-reserve indicator.
Case: stainless steel; 48 diamonds FC TW (0.60 carat); screwed crown; sapphire crystal; water resistant to 5atm.
Dial: white.
Strap: alligator leather; folding clasp.
Suggested price: $10,700
Also available: 18K rose gold; without diamond bezel; stainless steel bracelet: $11,300.

Cartier

When Cartier introduced its Fine Watchmaking Collection two years ago, it launched an ambiguous initiative to prototype, develop and produce its own unique calibers in-house. As proof of both Cartier's resolve and competence, its proprietary collection grew substantially in just a few short months; today, it encompasses many of its classic models.

The push for independence began in 2007 when Cartier acquired Roger Dubuis's manufacturing facility in Geneva along with more than two dozen of its movements. Today, this location works in concert with Cartier's watchmaking facility in La Chaux-de-Fonds, Switzerland, to create the manufacture movements featured in the Cartier Fine Watchmaking Collection.

One key aspect of the move is that it allows Cartier to produce watches marked with the Geneva Seal. First used in 1886, the hallmark is earned by mechanical movements that are assembled and adjusted in the canton of Geneva and that meet strict criteria in the areas of precision, reliability and finishing. Impartial experts from the Watchmaking School of Geneva perform the quality control testing required for the Geneva Seal.

The first caliber to receive this exalted honor was Cartier's 9452 MC, a tourbillon movement that debuted in 2008's Ballon bleu de Cartier. The same caliber can now be found in two famous models as well as a new white-gold version of the Ballon bleu de Cartier.

Cartier recently welcomed the 9452 MC into the Santos 100 and the Tank Américaine.

The roots of the former stretch back more than a century to 1904, when Louis Cartier invented the Santos wristwatch for his friend Alberto Santos-Dumont, a pioneering aviator from Brazil. Larger than its ancestor, the latest Santos 100 features a white-gold case that measures 46.5x54.9mm.

Introduced in 1978, the Tank Américaine's history is shorter, yet its position in the Cartier watchmaking canon is no less important. Indeed, its rectangular case is instantly recognizable as Cartier and the pink-gold version featured in the Fine Watchmaking Collection offers modern dimensions that measure 35.8x52mm.

Despite the different case shapes that define the Santos 100, Tank Américaine and the round Ballon bleu de Cartier, all three easily accommodate the 9452 MC, which includes 142 elements and is 4.5mm thick. The painstaking decoration lavished on the movement reflects the Geneva Seal's strict parameters with respects to traditional craftsmanship, a defining characteristic of Genevan watchmaking.

To ensure timekeeping precision, the movement uses a one-minute flying tourbillon positioned at 6:00. Cartier tops the mechanism with a rotating C-shaped carriage that indicates the seconds on a rail-track scale that surrounds the tourbillon aperture.

While the mechanical aspect showcased in these three models is exceptional, it is equaled by the dial's beauty. The design consists of two layers, guilloché on the bottom layer, covered by a plate intricately skeletonized to highlight the indexes' Roman numerals.

The 9452 MC, debuted in the **Ballon bleu de Cartier in 2008** and has recently joined the Santos 100 and Tank Américaine.

The 9611 MC movement in the Santos 100 skeleton is shaped to look like Roman numerals, eliminating the need for a traditional dial.

Cartier reduces the openworked-dial concept to its barest essentials for the Santos 100 skeleton. Produced exclusively by Cartier, the dial is actually a movement whose brushed bridges are shaped into Roman numerals. In fact, Cartier recently submitted the 9611 MC caliber's unconventional design for a patent.

The movement's airy design says more with less in a generously portioned 46.5x54.9mm palladium case. Its circular-grained wheels store three days of power, which is used to drive the blued minute and hour hands.

When the watch is not on the wrist, a crystal caseback illuminates the interior, highlighting the satin-brushed bridges and a C-shaped adjustor used to fine-tune the balance wheel vibrating below.

The Santos 100 skeleton's brushed palladium case echoes the movement's finish, while its polished bezel matches the sides of the mainplate. The design harmony extends to the crown, its octagonal shape a sharp rendering of the Santos's smooth profile. As a final luxurious touch, Cartier tops the palladium crown with a faceted sapphire.

BELOW LEFT The pink-gold Rotonde de Cartier central chronograph measures elapsed time on the upper level of the dial, which features a small seconds and a 30-minute arc.

BELOW RIGHT Released in a 50-piece limited edition, the platinum Rotonde de Cartier single-pusher chronograph tourbillon is the first watch to include a single-pusher chronograph and tourbillon.

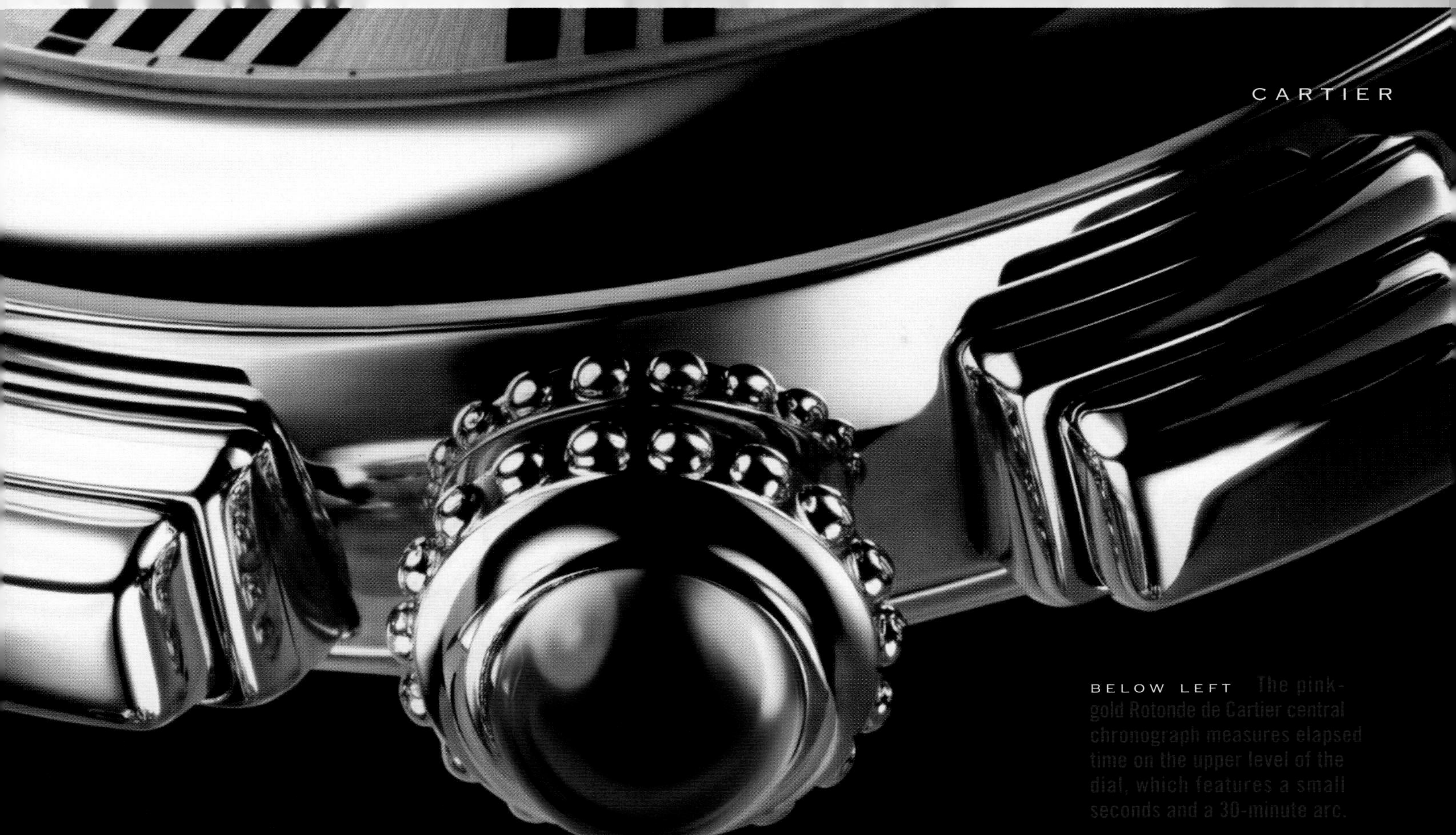

The watchmaker shows off its in-house capabilities and vast creativity with a superb Rotonde de Cartier central chronograph.

Fitted with Cartier's exclusive 9907 MC movement, the watch is easily identifiable thanks to a chronograph display that appears to float above the center of the round dial. The circular chronograph section—decorated with a handsome guilloché—combines a centered hand for the seconds with an arc for measuring times up to 30 minutes. Beyond its originality, the display ensures that the blued hour and minute hands that rotate below will never obscure the chronograph timers. In fact, Cartier has submitted a patent application for this innovative display.

Among the 9907 MC's technical advantages is its chronograph's vertical coupling system. The construction represents a break from the past, replacing the chronograph's traditional gear trains with an efficient system that uses friction, much like a clutch found in an automobile. This system reduces the amount of energy used by the chronograph while preserving precision.

Two pushers located on the side of the round, 42mm pink-gold case control the chronograph. The buttons flank a beaded crown, which is topped with a blue sapphire cabochon, a signature Cartier flourish.

In just a few short years, the company has established its credentials as an inventive manufacture. At this pace, Cartier is on track to quickly expand its royal moniker as the "King of Jewelers" to include the "King of Horology."

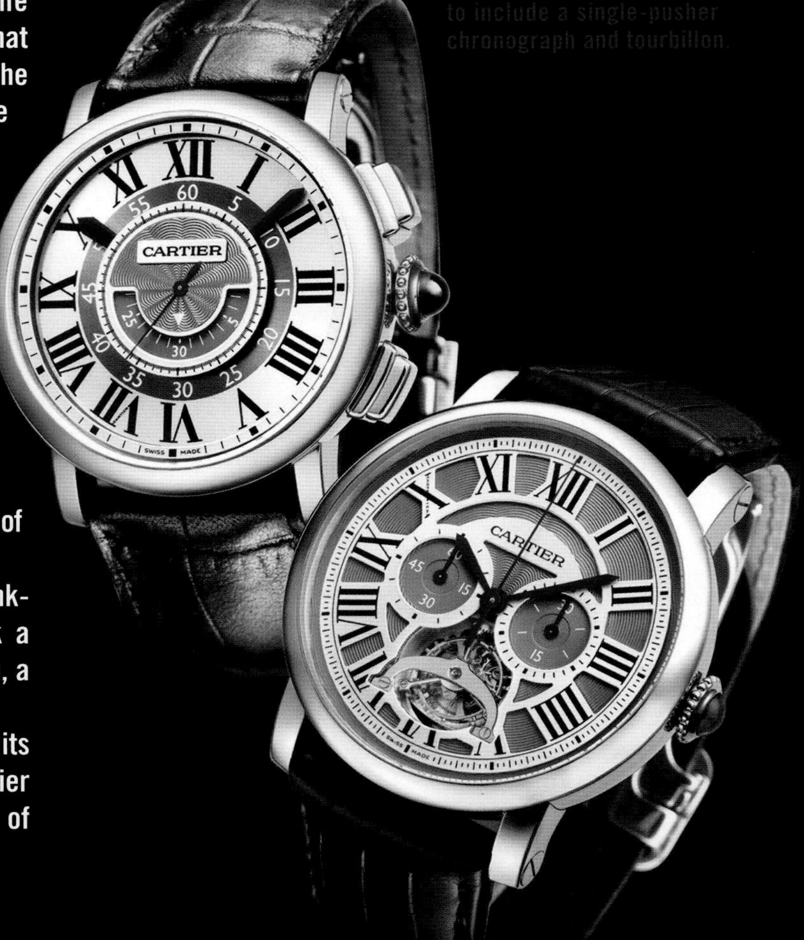

ROTONDE DE CARTIER ASTROTOURBILLON — REF. W1556204

Movement: mechanical manual-winding 9451 MC caliber; Cartier workshop-crafted; Astrotourbillon (central tourbillon with off-centered balance-wheel and hairspring).
Functions: hours, minutes, seconds indicated by the tourbillon carriage.
Case: 18K white gold; 47mm; 18K white-gold circular-grained crown set with sapphire cabochon; sapphire crystal; water resistant to 3atm.
Dial: guilloché; silver-colored upper and lower dial; Roman numerals section displaying a satin finish sunburst motif with black transfer Roman numerals; two-tone flange, silver-colored and slate-colored with a satin finish; blued steel sword-shaped hands.
Strap: alligator leather with 18K gold double adjustable deployant buckle.
Also available: 18K rose-gold case.

ROTONDE DE CARTIER TOURBILLON SKELETON — REF. W1580031

Movement: mechanical manual-winding 9455 MC caliber; Cartier workshop-crafted with the Geneva Seal.
Functions: hours, minutes; flying tourbillon with seconds indicated by the C-shaped index assembly; skeleton bridges shaped as Roman numerals.
Case: rhodiumized 18K white gold; 45mm; 18K rhodiumized white-gold circular-grained crown set with sapphire cabochon; sapphire crystal; water resistant to 3atm.
Dial: patented skeleton bridges of the movement shaped as Roman numerals; sword-shaped blued steel hands.
Strap: alligator leather with 18K gold double adjustable deployant buckle.

ROTONDE DE CARTIER CENTRAL CHRONOGRAPH — REF. W1555951

Movement: mechanical manual-winding 9907 MC caliber; Cartier workshop-crafted.
Functions: hours, minutes, seconds; chronograph with central display functions.
Case: 18K rose gold; 42mm; 18K rose-gold circular-grained crown set with sapphire cabochon; sapphire crystal; open back with a sapphire crystal; water resistant to 3atm.
Dial: guilloché; metal- and slate-colored upper dial; satin-finish sunray effect; silver- and slate-colored lower dial; 12 black Roman numerals; blued steel sword-shaped hands.
Strap: alligator leather; 18K rose-gold adjustable deployant buckle.
Also available: 18K white-gold case.

BALLON BLEU DE CARTIER CHRONOGRAPH — REF. W6920009

Movement: mechanical automatic-winding 8101 MC caliber; Cartier workshop-crafted.
Functions: hours, minutes, seconds; date; chronograph with two counters.
Case: 18K rose gold; 44mm; 18K rose-gold fluted crown set with a blue cabochon sapphire; water resistant to 3atm.
Dial: silvered opaline; guilloché and lacquered; 12 black Roman numerals; calendar with aperture at 9; sword-shaped blued steel hands.

Strap: alligator leather with adjustable buckle.
Suggested price: $22,325
Also available: 18K yellow gold or 18K white gold; on bracelet.

SANTOS 100 CARBON — REF. W2020009

Movement: mechanical automatic-winding Cartier caliber 049.
Functions: hours, minutes, seconds.
Case: ADLC coated steel; 51x38mm; 18K rose-gold bezel; ADLC coated steel crews; 18K rose-gold octagonal crown set with a blued faceted spinal; sapphire crystal; water resistant to 10atm.
Dial: 12 Roman numerals; sword-shaped metal hands.
Strap: black fabric; double adjustable deployant buckle.
Suggested price: $9,200
Also available: ADLC-coated steel and steel bezel.

ROADSTER S — REF. W6206018

Movement: mechanical automatic-winding Cartier caliber 3110.
Functions: hours, minutes, seconds; date at 3.
Case: stainless steel; 34.6x38.9mm; ADLC bezel; steel fluted crown; sapphire crystal; water resistant to 10atm.
Dial: silvered opaline; 12 black Roman numerals; rhodiumized steel sword-shaped hands.
Strap: rubber, interchangeable.
Suggested price: $4,200
Also available: on bracelet.

TANK AMÉRICAINE XL — REF. W2609956

Movement: mechanical automatic-winding Cartier caliber 191; workshop-crafted.
Functions: hours, minutes, seconds; date at 6.
Case: rhodiumized 18K white gold; 52x31.4mm; 18K rhodiumized white-gold octagonal crown set with a blue faceted sapphire; sapphire crystal and caseback; water resistant to 3atm.
Dial: silvered opaline; guilloché; 12 black Roman numerals; sword-shaped blued steel hands.
Strap: alligator leather; 18K white-gold adjustable deployant buckle.
Suggested price: $19,260
Also available: 18K rose gold.

BALLON BLEU DE CARTIER LM — REF. W69005Z2

Movement: mechanical automatic-winding Cartier caliber 049.
Functions: hours, minutes, seconds; date at 3.
Case: 18K yellow gold; 42mm; 18K yellow-gold fluted crown set with a blue cabochon sapphire; sapphire crystal; water resistant to 3atm.
Dial: silvered opaline; guilloché and lacquered; 12 black Roman numerals; sword-shaped blued steel hands.
Bracelet: 18K yellow gold; triple deployant clasp.
Suggested price: $30,100
Also available: 18K white gold or 18K rose gold; on strap.

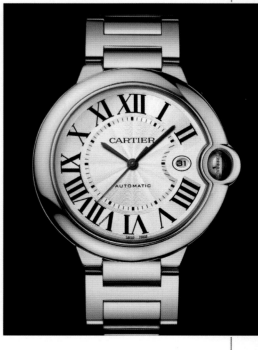

LE CIRQUE ANIMALIER PANTHER DECOR REF. HPI00338

Movement: mechanical manual-winding 437 MC caliber; workshop-crafted.
Functions: hours, minutes.
Case: 18K rhodiumized white gold set with round diamonds; 43mm; rhodiumized 18K white-gold grid with an openwork design set with round diamonds; circular-grained crown set with a diamond; two emerald eyes, enamel nose; opening pushbutton at 4; sapphire crystal; water resistant to 3atm.

Dial: 18K rhodiumized white gold set with round diamonds and mother-of-pearl; black enamel; 18K rhodiumized white-gold sword-shaped hands.
Strap: toile brossée; 18K rhodiumized white-gold ardillon buckle set with round diamonds.
Total carats: 6.22 carats.
Note: limited and numbered edition of 100 pieces.

CAPTIVE XL REF. WG600004

Movement: quartz Cartier caliber 056.
Functions: hours, minutes.
Case: rhodiumized 18K white gold; 18K rhodiumized white-gold bezel; attachment set with round diamonds; 50mm; sapphire crystal; water resistant to 3atm.
Dial: 18K rhodiumized white gold; sun-like finish; 12 indexes set with round diamonds; sword-shaped blued steel hands.

Strap: toile brossée; 18K rhodiumized white-gold ardillon buckle set with round diamonds.
Also available: 18K rose gold and paved case version; in 27mm and 35mm.

TANK ENLACÉE-CARTIER LIBRE COLLECTION REF. WJ306014

Movement: quartz Cartier caliber 056.
Functions: hours, minutes.
Case: rhodiumized 18K white gold; 18K rhodiumized white-gold bezel set with round diamonds; sapphire crystal; water resistant to 3atm.
Dial: silvered; sun-like finish and lacquer; two dark gray Roman numerals; sword-shaped blued steel hands.

Strap: toile brossée; 18K rhodiumized white-gold ardillon buckle set with round diamonds.

BAIGNOIRE LM REF. WB520005

Movement: mechanical manual-winding 430 caliber; Cartier workshop-crafted.
Functions: hours, minutes.
Case: 18K rose gold set with round diamonds; 44x32mm; 18K rose-gold octagonal crown set with a diamond; sapphire crystal; water resistant to 3atm.
Dial: silvered opaline; guilloché and lacquered; 12 black Roman numerals; sword-shaped blued steel hands.

Strap: toile brossée; 18K rose-gold ardillon buckle.
Suggested price: $32,800
Also available: 18K yellow gold or 18K white gold; on bracelet; in smaller size.

BALLON BLEU DE CARTIER MM   REF. WE9004Z3

Movement: mechanical automatic-winding Cartier caliber 076.
Functions: hours, minutes, seconds.
Case: 18K yellow gold set with round diamonds; 36.5mm; 18K yellow-gold fluted crown set with a blue cabochon sapphire; water resistant to 3atm.
Dial: silvered opaline; guilloché and lacquered; 12 black Roman numerals; sword-shaped blued steel hands.
Bracelet: 18K yellow gold; triple deployant clasp.
Suggested price: $39,175
Also available: in steel, steel and 18K yellow gold, 18K white gold, 18K rose gold; on strap; without diamonds; in 28mm and 42mm.

BALLON BLEU DE CARTIER MM   REF. W6920046

Movement: mechanical automatic-winding Cartier caliber 076.
Functions: hours, minutes, seconds.
Case: stainless steel; 36.5mm; stainless steel fluted crown set with a blue spinel cabochon; sapphire crystal; water resistant to 3atm.
Dial: silvered opaline; guilloché and lacquered; 12 black Roman numerals; sword-shaped blued steel hands.
Bracelet: stainless steel; steel security clasp.
Suggested price: $5,100
Also available: in steel and 18K yellow gold, 18K yellow gold, 18K rose gold; on strap; with diamonds; in 28mm and 42mm.

TANK SOLO LM   REF. W5200014

Movement: quartz Cartier caliber 690.
Functions: hours, minutes.
Case: stainless steel; 30.3x34.8mm; stainless steel fluted crown set with a blue spinel cabochon; sapphire crystal; water resistant to 3atm.
Dial: pale silvered opaline; 12 black Roman numerals; sword-shaped polished blued steel hands.
Bracelet: stainless steel.
Suggested price: $2,550
Also available: on strap.

MISS PASHA   REF. W3140008

Movement: quartz Cartier caliber 157.
Functions: hours, minutes.
Case: stainless steel; 27mm; stainless steel fluted crown set with a pink spinel cabochon; sapphire crystal; water resistant to 3atm.
Dial: pink; sword-shaped polished blued steel hands.
Bracelet: stainless steel.
Suggested price: $2,950
Also available: pale-silvered opaline dial.

CHANEL

A Unique Universe of Fine Jewelry and Watches

Inspired by Mademoiselle Chanel's creations, the brand's watches bring a new dimension to luxury watchmaking.

Gabrielle Chanel once said, "Fashion goes out of fashion, but style never." Simply inimitable, the CHANEL style was born from a subtle alchemy of highly original materials and colors rich with emotion. It became established through an extraordinary, avant-garde vision and endures thanks to its constant reinvention.

Naturally, the spirit of Gabrielle Chanel is found in the watches' designs—eliminating the superfluous, going straight for the essentials and aiming for simplicity while observing the CHANEL design codes. As for technology, CHANEL always champions the quality of its products.

WATCHMAKER EXPERTISE

La Chaux-de-Fonds in Switzerland, located at an altitude of 1,000 meters above sea level, has 37,000 inhabitants and the highest concentration of fine watchmakers and related activities worldwide. It was quite natural that the watchmaking facility of CHANEL was set up at La Chaux-de-Fonds, ideally situated among fir trees, mountain pastures and in close proximity to the neighboring watch manufacturers and workshops, which serve the world's most prestigious watchmaking brands. From conception to the final assembly process, CHANEL teams conceive, design, shape, mold, polish, assemble and fit all watch parts, including some components of the mechanical movements housed in the famous J12 watchcases of high-tech ceramic.

THE MASTERY OF CERAMIC

The production of high-tech ceramic requires a demanding level of know-how that unites earth, water, air and fire. Earth provides the natural materials combined to form the "powder" of which an exclusive mix is used to produce high-tech ceramic. Water is used for binding, forming and filtering these natural components. Air is used for drying and giving them form and structure. Fire is used for amalgamating them, lending the material its immutable resistance and beauty, which has built the reputation of the J12 collection's watchcases and bracelets today. This chain of events would not be complete without the metal necessary for sculpting, piercing, grinding and beautifying the high-tech ceramic, nor without the secrets behind its polishing process. These production processes—held in confidence to protect the exclusivity of CHANEL watches—are unique in Switzerland and probably in the world.

THE PASSION FOR PRECIOUS STONES

To adorn the famous black or white ceramic J12 watches with precious stones—diamonds, rubies, emeralds and sapphires—CHANEL's master watchmakers called on its master jewelers. To emphasize the J12's trademark elegance, the shape of its links and the beauty of its stones, they chose to use different cuts: brilliant-cut stones on the dial, the crown and the pushbuttons of the chronograph, and baguette-cut stones on the bezel and bracelet. A prestigious jeweler and watchmaker, CHANEL combines boldness, watchmaking expertise and High Jewelry mastery to perfection.

TOP J12 Haute Joaillerie, numbered and limited to 12 pieces, 18K white gold and black high-tech ceramic, 578 baguette-cut diamonds and 84 baguette-cut black high-tech ceramic.

BOTTOM CHANEL workshops in La Chaux-de-Fonds, Switzerland.

J12

One material, two colors: black high-tech ceramic and white high-tech ceramic, with gold, steel or rubber necessary to equip each model. Then a few handfuls of diamonds, rubies, and sapphires add the final precious touch. The same watchcase in four different sizes and thicknesses, simple or more complex movements, with some coming from the most prestigious and specialized manufacturers, and some variations in dials which play with the codes of CHANEL, without ever losing their identities: the J12 is a simple idea charged with emotion.

The J12 is a sober piece of elegance on the wrist. It has become a manifesto of CHANEL style and one of the iconic objects of the 21st century. J12: a class from yacht racing, the graphic codes from automobiles, it is inspired by sports, a watchmaking vocation, and a strong taste for exquisite jewelry and mechanical one-upmanship. One must not forget the role of dreams in all CHANEL creations, a particular idea of style and an audacious approach to modernity.

CAMÉLIA

A flower without perfume, of moving simplicity, seemingly obeying the subtle rules of a rigorous internal logic…so many graphic qualities quickly made the camellia one of the most symbolic flowers of the CHANEL tradition since Gabrielle Chanel made it her emblem. This symbol of purity, worn by La Traviata as well as the "elegants" of the Belle Epoque, in the CHANEL collections—white petals on a little black dress; worn in a model's hair for a fashion show, plume-like on a haute couture creation; and of course, set with diamonds, precious gemstones or onyx on a gold flower-watch, a flower that will never wilt. Camélia is a promise of purity and a guarantee of eternity, to tick away the hours that escape time.

PREMIÈRE

Getting straight to the essential is one of the keys to the "code" of CHANEL. It is not surprising that the first watch launched by CHANEL in 1987 was baptized the "Première": it was both logical and fundamental for a new tradition. This Première had been carefully thought out by Jacques Helleu, who immediately shaped it as a heritage and a message—a reminder of the very characteristic geometry of Place Vendôme. A resemblance can be found between the octagonal shape of the Première watchcase and the shape of the bottle stopper Gabrielle Chanel had chosen for her N° 5 perfume. The message: this heritage can flourish in the watchmaking world with a timelessly precious watch capable of bridging the gap between traditional women's timepieces and the new generation of contemporary watch designs.

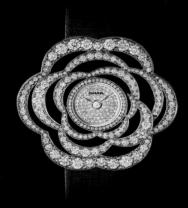

TOP   J12 Mother-of-Pearl dial, white high-tech ceramic and steel, mother-of-pearl dial set with 8 diamond indicators.

CENTER   Première, black ceramic, 18K white gold, case set with 52 diamonds, bracelet set with 216 diamonds.

BOTTOM   Fil de Camélia, 18K white gold, case set with 197 diamonds, dial paved with 86 diamonds.

J12 HAUTE JOAILLERIE   REF. H2140

Movement: self-winding mechanical movement.
Functions: hours, minutes, seconds.
Case: 18K white gold; 38mm; set with 74 baguette-cut diamonds (4.95 carats, F/G VVS1); 18K white-gold bezel set with 46 baguette-cut diamonds (4.4 carats, F/G VVS1); water resistant to 5atm.
Dial: 84 black baguette-cut ceramic accents; 57 baguette-cut diamonds (1.81 carats, F/G VVS1).

Bracelet: 18K white gold set with 400 baguette-cut diamonds (19.7 carats, F/G VVS1); 18K white-gold triple-folding buckle; adjustable standard size.
Suggested price: upon request.
Note: limited edition of 12 pieces.
Also available: 33mm (high-precision quartz movement); 42mm (self-winding mechanical movement).

J12 CALIBRE 3125   REF. H2129

Movement: self-winding CHANEL manufactured AP 3125 movement; black ceramic and 22K rhodium-plated yellow-gold rotor mounted on ceramic ball bearings; 60-hour power reserve.
Functions: hours, minutes, seconds; date.
Case: black ceramic; 42mm; 18K yellow gold and black ceramic unidirectional bezel; sapphire crystal caseback; water resistant to 5atm.

Dial: 18K yellow-gold numerals; SuperLumiNova indexes (luminous in the dark).
Bracelet: black ceramic; 18K yellow-gold triple-folding buckle patented CHANEL; adjustable standard size.
Suggested price: $25,000
Also available: black alligator strap as an accessory.

J12 JOAILLERIE   REF. H2029

Movement: self-winding mechanical movement.
Functions: hours, minutes, seconds.
Case: white ceramic and 18K white gold; 38mm; bezel set with 46 baguette-cut diamonds (4.4 carats, F/G VVS1); water resistant to 10atm.
Dial: white ceramic center; 84 baguette-cut diamonds (2 carats, F/G VVS1) and 12 black baguette-cut ceramic indicators.

Bracelet: white ceramic; 18K white-gold triple-folding buckle; adjustable standard size.
Suggested price: $99,500
Also available: 33mm (self-winding mechanical movement); 42mm (self-winding mechanical movement).

J12 JOAILLERIE   REF. H2311

Movement: self-winding mechanical movement.
Functions: hours, minutes, seconds; date.
Case: white ceramic and 18K pink gold; 38mm; bezel set with 46 baguette-cut diamonds (4.4 carats, F/G VVS1); water resistant to 10atm.
Dial: white lacquered; 8 diamond indicators.
Bracelet: white ceramic; 18K pink-gold triple-folding buckle; adjustable standard size.
Suggested price: $64,500
Note: limited edition of 100 pieces.
Also available: 33mm (high-precision quartz movement); black ceramic.

J12 DIAMONDS   REF. H2428

Movement: high-precision quartz movement.
Functions: hours, minutes; date.
Case: black ceramic and steel; 38mm; bezel set with 24 brilliant-cut diamonds (1.7 carats, F/G VVS); water resistant to 20atm.
Dial: 11 diamond indicators.
Bracelet: black ceramic; steel triple-folding buckle; adjustable standard size.
Suggested price: $14,250
Also available: 33mm (high-precision quartz movement); white ceramic.

J12 DIAMOND DIAL   REF. H1757

Movement: self-winding mechanical movement.
Functions: hours, minutes, seconds; date.
Case: black ceramic and steel; 38mm; water resistant to 20atm.
Dial: center paved with 110 diamonds (0.27 carat, F/G VVS); 12 diamond indicators.
Bracelet: black ceramic; steel triple-folding buckle; adjustable standard size.
Suggested price: $9,250
Also available: 33mm (high-precision quartz movement); white ceramic.

J12 DIAMONDS   REF. H0969

Movement: self-winding mechanical movement.
Functions: hours, minutes, seconds; date.
Case: white ceramic and steel; 38mm; steel bezel set with 118 brilliant-cut diamonds (1.6 carats, F/G VVS); water resistant to 20atm.
Bracelet: white ceramic; triple-folding buckle; adjustable standard size.
Suggested price: $12,900
Also available: 33mm (high-precision quartz movement); black ceramic.

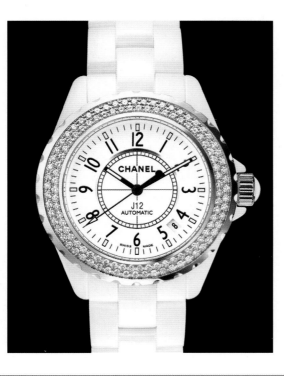

J12 MOTHER-OF-PEARL DIAL   REF. H2423

Movement: self-winding mechanical movement.
Functions: hours, minutes, seconds.
Case: white ceramic and steel; 38mm; water resistant to 20atm.
Dial: mother-of-pearl; 8 diamond indicators.
Bracelet: white ceramic; steel triple-folding buckle; adjustable standard size.
Suggested price: $5,800
Also available: 33mm (high-precision quartz movement).

J12 GMT REF. H2012

Movement: self-winding mechanical movement.
Functions: hours, minutes, seconds; date; second time zone read from the engraved 24-hour bezel.
Case: black ceramic and steel; 42mm; water resistant to 10atm.
Dial: black lacquered.
Bracelet: black ceramic; steel triple-folding buckle; adjustable standard size.
Suggested price: $5,800
Also available: white ceramic (limited edition).

J12 REF. H0685

Movement: self-winding mechanical movement.
Functions: hours, minutes, seconds; date.
Case: black ceramic and steel; 38mm; water resistant to 20atm.
Dial: black lacquered.
Bracelet: black ceramic; steel triple-folding buckle; adjustable standard size.
Suggested price: $4,500

Also available: 33mm (self-winding mechanical movement); white ceramic.

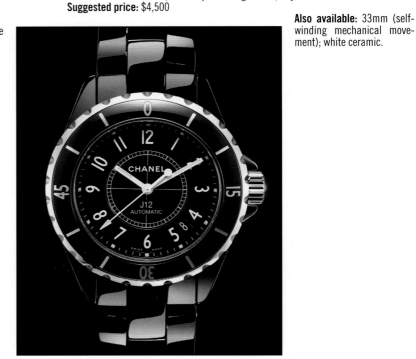

J12 CHRONOGRAPH REF. H1007

Movement: self-winding mechanical chronograph movement; COSC certified.
Functions: hours, minutes, seconds; date; chronograph (three counters: 12 hours, 30 minutes, 60 seconds).
Case: white ceramic and steel; 41mm; water resistant to 20atm.
Dial: white lacquered.
Bracelet: white ceramic; steel triple-folding buckle; adjustable standard size.
Suggested price: $6,750
Also available: black ceramic.

J12 REF. H0970

Movement: self-winding mechanical movement.
Functions: hours, minutes, seconds; date.
Case: white ceramic and steel; 38mm; water resistant to 20atm.
Dial: white lacquered.
Bracelet: white ceramic; steel triple-folding buckle; adjustable standard size.
Suggested price: $4,500

Also available: 33mm (self-winding mechanical movement); black ceramic.

PREMIERE
REF. H2147

Movement: high-precision quartz movement; 11mm.
Functions: hours, minutes.
Case: 18K white gold set with 52 diamonds (0.26 carat, F/G VVS); water resistant to 3atm.
Dial: black lacquered.
Bracelet: 18K white gold and black ceramic set with 216 diamonds (1.55 carats, F/G VVS); spring clasp; adjustable size.
Suggested price: $24,850
Also available: 18K white gold and white ceramic set with white diamonds; steel version.

PREMIERE PEARLS
REF. H2032

Movement: high-precision quartz movement; 11mm.
Functions: hours, minutes.
Case: 18K white gold; caseback set with 136 diamonds (0.7 carat, F/G VVS); water resistant to 3atm.
Dial: set with 34 baguette-cut diamonds (1.25 carats, F/G VVS).
Bracelet: 194 Akoya cultured pearls mounted on 18K white-gold threads; detachable 18K white-gold buckle set with 110 diamonds (0.55 carat, F/G VVS); bracelet ends set with 38 diamonds (0.2 carat, F/G VVS); adjustable size.
Suggested price: $50,000

PREMIERE
REF. H2132

Movement: high-precision quartz movement; 11mm.
Functions: hours, minutes.
Case: steel set with 52 diamonds (0.26 carat, F/G VVS); water resistant to 3atm.
Dial: white lacquered.
Bracelet: steel and white ceramic; spring clasp.
Suggested price: $5,600
Also available: steel and black ceramic.

PREMIERE
REF. H2433

Movement: high-precision quartz movement; 11mm.
Functions: hours, minutes.
Case: steel set with 52 diamonds (0.26 carat, F/G VVS); water resistant to 3atm.
Dial: white mother-of-pearl dial; 4 diamond indicators.
Bracelet: white rubber strap; ardillon buckle.
Suggested price: $3,850
Also available: black rubber strap.

Chopard

150th
ANNIVERSARY
1860|2010

From the creation of a small horological manufacture founded in Sonvilier in the Swiss Jura to the Genevan watch and jewelry brand with international reach that we know today, Chopard's has been quite the journey—one strewn with timepiece collections that are now legendary in the world of jewelry as well as complicated watches.

Though Chopard's history began in 1860 with the founding of its manufacture by Louis-Ulysse Chopard, it was under the direction of the Scheufele family, who bought the brand from Chopard's heirs in 1963, that the company truly took flight. The Scheufele family was not new to the industry, as it had operated a watch and jewelry business in Pforzheim, Germany, for three generations. This heritage clearly shone through: one of the family's most memorable moves at the helm of Chopard was a pure stroke of genius. In 1976, the brand unveiled what would become its bestseller, and an icon of both jewelry and horology: the Happy Diamonds watch. A concept such as this had never been seen before: diamonds moved freely around the dial beneath the crystal! The collection met with immense success, and the Happy Diamonds motif was incorporated into new watch models, as well as jewelry.

In 1988, Chopard embarked on an important new leg of its journey with the launch of its Mille Miglia collection. The creation of this sporty and masculine watch celebrates the partnership between Chopard and the eponymous Italian rally that annually showcases the finest vintage racecars.

ABOVE   Mille Miglia GMT Chronograph in stainless steel.

RIGHT   A Happy Amore pendant and Happy Sport ladies' watch in rose gold.

182

Chopard celebrates 150 years of watchmaking.

AN INDEPENDENT FAMILY MANUFACTURE

In the early 1990s, the brand took a new turn when the younger generation of Scheufeles, Karl-Friedrich and his sister Caroline, took its destiny in hand. The autonomy granted by the brand's complete independence gives free rein to their creativity and enterprising ideas. In 1993, the brand launched the Happy Sport watch, a casual version of the Happy Diamonds concept. It was 1996, however, that marked a major stage in the house's history: the creation of the Chopard Manufacture. Based in Fleurier in the Swiss Jura, it signifies not only a return to the company's Jura roots, but also the company's ascent to the envied status of "manufacture." Thanks to its new production capacities, Chopard would once more be able to create and produce its own movements, which the brand dubbed L.U.C in honor of Louis-Ulysse Chopard. This strategy paid off the following year when the watch containing the manufacture's first movement won the coveted Watch of the Year title from the Swiss magazine *Montre Passion/Uhrenwelt*. Chopard has produced several movements since then, including the L.U.C Quattro 1.98 with four barrels and nine days' power reserve in 2000, and the L.U.C 1.02 Tourbillon in 2003. These remarkable horological creations bear witness to Chopard's savoir-faire, enhance the brand's reputation, and confirm its place among the ranks of the most prestigious in Swiss watchmaking.

TOP L.U.C Tourbillon Classic: This model with an artfully curved bearing bridge above its tourbillon completes the L.U.C Steel Wings collection. Within the white-gold case beats the mechanical hand-wound tourbillon movement L.U.C 4T with the poinçon de Genève hallmark.

CENTER Watchmaking production departments at the Chopard Manufacture in Fleurier.

RIGHT L.U.C Tourbillon Tech Twist Palladium: The first L.U.C watch equipped with a silicon escapement. Encased in palladium, the mechanical hand-wound tourbillon caliber was developed, built and assembled by Chopard Manufacture.

L.U.C TWIN — REF. 161880-0001

Movement: automatic L.U.C 4.96 movement; COSC-certified chronometer; 65-hour power reserve; L.U.C Twin technology (two stacked barrels).
Functions: hours, minutes, seconds; date at 6.
Case: yellow gold; glare- and scratch-proof sapphire crystal; sapphire crystal caseback; water resistant to 3atm.
Dial: white guilloché dial.

Strap: leather; yellow-gold buckle.
Also available: white gold.

L.U.C LUNAR ONE — REF. 161894-5001

Movement: mechanical automatic L.U.C 96QP caliber; 65-hour power reserve; bridges decorated with straight-line Côtes de Genève pattern; COSC-certified chronometer; hallmarked with the Geneva Seal.
Functions: hour, minute, small seconds; 24 hour; perpetual calendar (date, day, month, year, moonphase).
Case: rose gold; glare- and scratch-proof sapphire crystal; sapphire crystal caseback; water resistant to 3atm.
Dial: solid gold, argenté; guilloché by hand with a wave pattern at the center; brushed hour ring; guilloché subdials; printed minute track with luminescent dots; applied faceted pink-gold markers and Roman numerals; luminescent pink-gold dauphine-style hour and minute hands.
Indications: month and 4-year cycle at 3; moonphase and small seconds at 6; day of the week and 24-hour at 9; large date display with a double window at 12.
Strap: hand-stitched crocodile leather; pink-gold fold-over clasp.
Note: limited edition of 250 numbered pieces.
Also available: white gold.

L.U.C CHRONO ONE — REF. 161916-1002

Movement: automatic L.U.C 11 CF movement; COSC certified chronometer; 60-hour power reserve; 28,800 vph; "Variner" balance.
Functions: hours, minutes; 30-minute counter at 3, small seconds at 6, 12-hour counter at 9; flyback chronograph; stop seconds; chrono; date at 4:30.
Case: white gold; glare- and scratch-proof sapphire crystal; sapphire crystal caseback; water resistant to 3atm.

Dial: black dial.
Strap: leather; white-gold folding clasp.
Also available: rose gold.

L.U.C EXTRA PLATE — REF. 161902-1001

Movement: mechanical automatic L.U.C 96HM caliber; equipped with two barrels; 65- to 70-hour power reserve; bridges decorated with Côtes de Genève pattern.
Functions: central hour, minute.
Case: white gold; antireflective sapphire crystal; water resistant to 3atm.
Dial: black dial with four Arabic numerals and applied baton hands; dauphine-style hour and minute hands.

Strap: crocodile leather; gold buckle.
Also available: yellow gold with white dial.

L.U.C TOURBILLON SL REF. 168502-3001

Movement: manual-winding L.U.C 4TSL movement; COSC-certified chronometer; approx. 216-hour power reserve (9 days); 28,800 vph; L.U.C Quattro technology (4 barrels – 2 sets of 2 stacked barrels); "Variner" balance.
Functions: hours, minutes, small second; power-reserve indicator at 12; tourbillon at 6.
Case: titanium; glare- and scratch-proof sapphire crystal; sapphire crystal caseback; water resistant to 3atm.
Dial: black dial; contemporary dauphine-style hour and minute hands.
Strap: leather; titanium buckle.
Note: limited edition of 100 pieces.

GRAND PRIX DE MONACO HISTORIQUE TIME ATTACK MF REF. 158518-3001

Movement: quartz movement; COSC-certified chronometer.
Functions: date; timer; UTC time; chronograph; alarm; second time zone; alarm in the second time zone.
Case: stainless steel; cambered, glare- and scratch-proof sapphire crystal; water resistant to 5atm.
Dial: black dial; luminescent hands, numerals and indicators.
Bracelet: stainless steel.

L.U.C PRO ONE GMT REF. 168959-3001

Movement: mechanical automatic L.U.C 4.96 Pro One caliber; two stacked barrels (L.U.C Twin® Technology); 65-hour power reserve; COSC-certified chronometer.
Functions: hour, minute, center seconds; date window; fixed second time-zone hand.
Case: steel; antireflective sapphire crystal; screw-lock crown and screw-in caseback; water resistant to 30atm.
Dial: black dial; SuperLumiNova-coated arrow-style hands and hour markers for excellent nighttime readability.
Strap: hand-stitched crocodile leather strap; steel folding clasp.

MILLE MIGLIA GTXL CHRONO REF. 168459-3001

Movement: self-winding movement; COSC-certified chronometer; 46-hour power reserve.
Functions: hours, minutes; 30-minute and 12-hour counters, small seconds; chrono; tachometer; date at 3.
Case: stainless steel; screw-down crown; glare- and scratch-proof sapphire crystal; sapphire crystal caseback; water resistant to 10atm.
Dial: black dial; luminescent numerals and hands with SuperLumiNova.
Strap: rubber.
Also available: rose gold.

CLERC
GENEVE
1874

Hydroscaph, Odyssey—these are names that beckon for escape and adventure. Clerc watches, highly technical yet impeccably distinguished, cultivate their unique characteristics to thrill their fans with new surprises. Women are a major part of Clerc's base, and there are delights in store for them as well.

History has meaning only when we use it to interpret the present and to clarify the future. This universal concept is particularly pertinent in the world of haute horology; however, history alone is not enough to plan out the contours of a global success. Electricity was not discovered by someone trying to improve the candle! Understanding this, Gérald Clerc, CEO of Clerc, founded in 1874, has made a place for himself in the limited circle of watch designers. His timepieces could find no better realization than through his ancestral savoir-faire, but Clerc has chosen to use that expertise in the service of out-of-this-world design. Not waiting for time to catch up with the brand, Clerc has already populated its collections with watches seamlessly integrated into the most advanced space and aquatic research, like archaeological remains from an invented future.

THE ERA OF MECHANICAL TECHNO-LUXURY

Creator of "futuristic haute horology," as he likes to call it, Clerc is a cosmopolite and a student of architecture. Fascinated by the 1960s, a period colored with optimism and confidence, during which humanity threw itself headlong into the quest for progress, Clerc considers the exploration of space to be the greatest adventure of all time. When this fourth-generation watchmaker took over the business in 1997, he inherited both horological expertise and a passion for the art. This legacy is an inexhaustible vector of exceptional horology and technical innovations; it is a heritage from which Clerc draws his inspiration, and which allows him to take his place as a pioneer of an emerging movement—the watchmaking of tomorrow.

Ruptures with the past, Clerc's creations obey just one rule: inventiveness. Each one is designed as a unique piece of art, and Clerc makes no concessions but those that will improve its quality. "I create watches the same way I love them," Clerc likes to say, "without any compromise." This liberty is an indisputable passport to exclusivity, a quality that Clerc values extremely highly. Despite commercial demands, this independent creator has long preferred to follow his heart, placing aesthetics and technique above industrial production. He does all of this, of course, without breaking with the Swiss luxury watch world's highest standards of production and finishing.

THIS PAGE
Creator of "futuristic haute horology," as he calls it, Gérald Clerc is a cosmopolite and an admirer of architecture.

FACING PAGE
Distinguished, sophisticated, and in a case so complex that it required totally new methods of construction, the Hydroscaph offers a novel vision of haute horology.

'I create watches the same way I love them,' says Clerc, 'without any compromise.'

PURE SOPHISTICATION

The Hydroscaph, one of Clerc's latest creations, perfectly illustrates this philosophy. Distinguished and sophisticated in a case so complex that it required a totally new method of construction, the Hydrograph proposes an unusual vision for haute horology. Water resistant to 1,000 meters, this exceptional piece is equipped with a lateral valve and lateral reinforcements. Its exclusive automatic Swiss-made movement offers hours, minutes, seconds and power reserve as well as a large date or a second time zone, depending on the model. But the most notable innovation of the cutting-edge Hydroscaph lies in its rotating bezel mechanism: at 10:00, a knob allows the wearer to turn the bezel to the desired position. Once it is retracted, the knob is protected by unique lateral protectors, thus avoiding any risk of accidentally changing the settings during a dive. One of the brand's signature is the watch's grade-5 titanium case, an octagonal shape born from the overlap of a circle and a square. With a diameter of 49.6mm and lugs that conform perfectly to any wrist, the Hydrograph is one of the world's most perfect diving watches.

TOP The strap of the Hydroscaph—shown here in the rose-gold and titanium version of HY-GMT-312b—adjusts easily to be worn with a diving suit.

RIGHT The Hydroscaph—shown here is the model HY-PR-212 in titanium and carbon fiber—is equipped with a rotating bezel that is controlled by an adjusting knob at 10:00. Once retracted, it is protected by unique lateral elements, avoiding the risk of accidentally changing the settings during a dive.

A PRECIOUS VERSION

The Hydroscaph Limited Edition Gold Tourbillon is even more spectacular. Invaluable and timeless, this piece of technical haute horology is a ticket to serious thrills. Besides the technical aspects involved, the Hydroscaph Limited Edition Gold Tourbillon is precious in more than one way. For example, its exclusive manual-winding tourbillon caliber possesses two barrels for a power reserve of 120 hours. This remarkable power reserve is exceptional in a diving watch, and means, significantly, that the wearer will never have to adjust the crown underwater.

This Hydroscaph's exclusive 60-Second Clerc Tourbillon movement, which lives up to the highest standards of Swiss haute horology, offers the functions of hours, minutes, retro-grade date at 1:30, and power-reserve indicator at 5:00. The modern, skeletonized dial hides nothing of this high-precision mechanism. The vertical S-shaped skeletonized tourbillon bridge recalls the hour and minute hands, which are also skeletonized. The numerals and the indexes are engraved on the inside of the antireflective sapphire crystal, ensuring perfect readability.

The exterior of the Hydroscaph Limited Edition Gold Tourbillon is just as precious. The imposing 18-karat rose-gold and black titanium case is so complex that it required 75 components and an entirely new method of construction. Water resistant to 500 meters, the watch features adaptable lugs to fit over a diving suit or on any wrist.

The new Hydroscaph Limited Edition Gold Tourbillon is equipped with an exclusive manual-winding tourbillon movement that possesses two barrels for a power reserve of 120 hours.

Another new model is the Odyssey Lady. The 2008 release of the men's Odyssey caused a huge stir. Inspired by space research for its materials—black titanium, ceramic, carbon fiber, and palladium—the Odyssey was designed for exploration and adventure. A bridge covers the crown, pushers and the mechanism that rotates the bezel; this unique device prevents any involuntary manipulation. The exclusive manual-winding movement, powered by two barrels for an exceptional power reserve of 120 hours, offers the functions of hours, minutes, seconds, retrograde date at 2:00, and power reserve at 6:00. "In designing the Odyssey, I was seeking purity," emphasizes Clerc.

SPEAKING TO WOMEN

A watch designer must also know how to appeal to women. The Odyssey Lady Skeleton is an open invitation to all women who wish to join the adventure. Not just a watch but a piece of haute jewelry, it offers an exclusive automatic movement in a ceramic or 18-karat rose-gold case, delicately set with diamonds. The Arabic numerals at 6:00 and 12:00, also set with diamonds, lend a particular depth to the transparent face, which offers a penetrating view of the movement. Gears and bridges decorated with Côtes de Genève are also visible through a transparent dial, skillfully fixed to a skeletonized bottom plate, pushing this test of horological savoir-faire to an extreme.

SWISS EXPERTISE

Clerc watches are produced entirely in Switzerland according to the industry's strictest standards with respect to the fabrication of the case, the artisanal finishing of movements, and the details of the dial. Famed brands such as Rolex, Vacheron Constantin, and Jaeger-LeCoultre were associated with the manufacture of a number of watches for Clerc until the 1970s.

Clerc boasts an impressively prestigious list of celebrities that have for generations chosen to wear a Clerc model because they desired one-of-a-kind pieces made to order. The list includes members of royalty like Princess Grace Kelly of Monaco, chiefs of state like Nikita Khrushchev, and artists like Maurice Chevalier, Salvador Dalí and Paco Rabanne. More recently, actors such as Michael Douglas, Jack Scalia and Goldie Hawn have chosen Clerc. For the former French President Charles de Gaulle, Clerc crafted a clock in the form of a globe. A small dial adorned with a sapphire shone from the location of Paris, while another dial, this one decorated with a ruby, indicated the time in Moscow. The French president gave the timepiece to Khrushchev.

Available in the United States, Japan, Hong Kong, the Middle East and Europe through a network of carefully selected distributors, Clerc's creations carry three-year international guarantees.

FACING PAGE
Launched in 2008, the Odyssey (311) in
titanium and rose gold is equipped with a
device that protects the crown, the pushers
and the system of the interior rotating bezel.

THIS PAGE
Not just a watch, this haute jewelry Odyssey
Lady Skeleton offers an exclusive automatic
movement in a diamond-set case crafted
in ceramic or 18-karat rose gold.

CONCORD

In 2008, Concord launched C Lab Series—a research and development group within the company—and charged it with the task of exploring beyond the boundaries of watchmaking to create revolutionary timepieces. The team launched the second futuristic fruit of its labor last year, defying the norm with the C1 Quantum-Gravity.

The deconstructionist design fills the massive titanium and white-gold case—48.5mm in diameter and 22mm thick—with carefully arranged negative space. Its industrial aesthetic produces an otherworldly, three-dimensional setting. The minimalist spirit focuses attention on a series of remarkable inventions that contravene watchmaking tradition.

The first is a bi-axial tourbillon, dangling visibly from a suspension-bridge-inspired structure complete with tension cables for support. Like a Ferris wheel gone mad, the tourbillon cage rotates in its traditional clockwise direction as the entire mechanism spins perpendicularly to the movement in a manner that is as mesmerizing as it is unorthodox. A sapphire crystal window positioned at 9:00 on the case middle provides a clear view of the tourbillon in action.

The C1 QuantumGravity puts another spin on convention with its liquid-filled power-reserve indicator. Dubbed the "energy tank" and filled with an acid-green fluid, a clear cylinder rises and falls in relation to the amount of power remaining in the watch's three-day reserve. A trio of lines on the inner case displays the remaining power.

Adding further technical flourish to the design, the C Lab Series engineers devised a deployable crown that remains hidden at 2:00 on the side of the case when not in use. To wind the movement, the wearer pushes a button that ejects the crown. When finished, the assembly stows away neatly.

Even the C1 QuantumGravity's basic time-telling function gets a cutting-edge makeover. A round scale—open to the movement below—places the hour and minute hands on the dial. The seconds, however, have broken free and taken up residence on the side of the case where they can be read through a small window.

Concord first introduced this avant-garde small seconds display in 2008 on the C1 Tourbillon Gravity, the first creation from C Lab Series. The ground-breaking timepiece earned 2008's Watch Design Of The Year award at the prestigious Grand Prix d'Horlogerie de Genève. The C1 QuantumGravity followed in its predecessor's footsteps in 2009, earning a nomination in the competition's complicated watch category.

In fact, the C1 QuantumGravity owes a great deal of its style to the C1 Tourbillon Gravity, the world's first watch to relocate the tourbillon to the outside of the case. Mounted perpendicularly to the movement, the mechanism is visible through a crystal aperture.

RETURNING CHAMPIONS

Concord continues its Champions program, mixing high horology with high-profile watch aficionados. Each year, the watchmaker selects an ambassador who embodies the company's uncompromising dedication to performance and creates a limited edition timepiece in his or her honor.

Concord's latest Champion is Ronny Turiaf, an NBA forward and charity founder. Shortly after the Los Angeles Lakers drafted him in 2005, team doctors discovered Turiaf had an enlarged aortic root that required surgery to correct. Just six months after open-heart surgery, Turiaf rejoined the Lakers. Soon after, he initiated the Ronny Turiaf Heart to Heart Foundation, a charity dedicated to providing treatment and testing for underprivileged patients—especially children—who suffer from heart disease. A portion of the proceeds from sales of the C1 Heart2Heart Chronograph will benefit Turiaf's foundation.

Having celebrated its 100th anniversary in 2008, Concord rocketed into its second century with brilliant cutting-edge innovation. Two years later, the company's acclaimed designs declare that the future is now.

Concord's designs declare that the future is now.

C1 CHRONOGRAPH   REF. 0320072

Movement: mechanical self-winding Caliber A07.211 Valgranges; 16 1/2 '''; Ø 37.2mm; thickness: 7.9mm; official COSC-certified chronometer; 25 jewels; 28,800 vph; 48-hour power reserve; black PVD treatment; snailed bevel; vertical Côtes de Genève; "C1" engraved in center. **Functions:** hours, minutes, central sweep seconds; small seconds on permanent turning disc at 9; 30-minute counter at 12; 12-hour counter at 6; date window at 3. **Case:** PVD-treated stainless steel; Ø 44mm, thickness:

16.7mm; 53 elements; metal protective ring coated in black rubber and fixed laterally by 7 self-blocking screws; screw-down crown with embossed C1 logo; 3.3mm-thick sapphire crystal, anti-reflective on both sides; exhibition caseback embossed "Audace—Savoir Faire—Avant-Garde"; water resistant to 20atm.
Dial: three layers; black carbon fiber; rhodium-plated polished hour-markers with SuperLumiNova SLN C1; dauphine hands, asymmetrically hollowed out, rhodium, lacquered, SuperLumiNova SLN C1; chronograph seconds hand in blue Pantone 287 U.
Strap: black vulcanized rubber; PVD-treated stainless steel deployment buckle with embossed CONCORD cover.
Suggested price: $13,300

C1 CHRONOGRAPH   REF. 0320076

Movement: mechanical self-winding Caliber A07.211 (ETA Valgranges); 16 1/2 '''; Ø 37.2mm, thickness: 7.9mm; official COSC-certified chronograph; 25 jewels; 28,800 vph; 48-hour power reserve; black PVD treatment; snailed bevel; vertical Côtes de Genève; "C1" engraved in center.
Functions: hours, minutes, central sweep seconds; small seconds on turning disc at 9; 30-minute counter at 12; 12-hour counter at 6; date window at 3.

Case: 18K 5N rose gold; Ø 44mm, thickness: 16.7mm; 53 elements; metal protective ring coated in black rubber and fixed laterally by 7 self-blocking screws; screw-down crown with embossed C1 logo; 3.3mm-thick sapphire crystal, antireflective on both sides; exhibition caseback embossed "Audace—Savoir Faire—Avant-Garde"; water resistant to 20atm.
Dial: three layers; black carbon fiber; rhodium-plated polished hour-markers; chronograph seconds hand in bright blue Pantone 293 C; dauphine hands, asymmetrically hollowed out, lacquered, SuperLumiNova SLN C1.
Strap: brown alligator leather.
Suggested price: $34,500

C1 PURE   REF. 0320028

Movement: mechanical self-winding Caliber A07.211 (ETA Valgranges); 16 ½'''; Ø 37.2mm, thickness: 7.9mm; height: 2.39mm; official COSC-certified chronograph; 132 components; 25 jewels; 28,800 vph; 48-hour power reserve; rhodium treatment; snailed bevel; vertical Côtes de Genève; "C1" engraved in center. **Functions:** hours, minutes, central sweep seconds; small seconds on turning disc at 9; 30-minute counter at 12; 12-hour counter at 6; date window at 3. **Case:** stainless steel; Ø 44mm, thickness: 16.7mm; diamond-set bezel;

protective ring with 8 blocks in white rubber-coated stainless steel; screw-down crown with embossed C1 logo; 80 VVS diamonds (52 x 1.6; 12 x 1.4; 16 x 0.8; TCW=0.99) set on the bezel and the case; 3.3mm-thick sapphire crystal, antireflective on both sides; exhibition caseback embossed "Audace—Savoir Faire—Avant-Garde"; water resistant to 20atm.
Dial: three layers; white; fiberglass texture; rhodium-plated polished hour-markers with SuperLumiNova SLN C1; chronograph seconds hand in bright blue Pantone 293 C; dauphine hands, asymmetrically hollowed out, in gray Pantone 430 U, lacquered, with SuperLumiNova SLN C1.
Strap: white vulcanized rubber; stainless steel deployment buckle with embossed CONCORD cover.
Suggested price: $17,700

C1 RETROGRADE   REF. 0320054

Movement: mechanical self-winding movement Caliber 9094 Soprod; 11 1/2'''; Ø 25.6mm, thickness: 5.25mm, height: 13.15mm; 150 components; 30 jewels; 28,800 vph; 42-hour power reserve; black PVD treatment; snailed bevel; vertical Côtes de Genève; "C1" engraved in center.
Functions: hours, minutes, and seconds; retrograde date at 3; day at 9; power reserve at 6. **Case:** titanium; Ø 44mm, thickness: 13.15mm; protective ring coated in black

rubber and fixed by 7 self-blocking screws; screw-down crown with C1 logo; 3.3mm-thick sapphire crystal, antireflective on both sides; exhibition caseback embossed "Audace—Savoir Faire—Avant-Garde"; water resistant to 20atm.
Dial: black ribbed; guilloché; dark gray date disc, lacquered and sandblasted; rhodium-plated polished hour-markers with SuperLumiNova SLN C1; dauphine hands, asymmetrically hollowed out, lacquered, sandblasted, SuperLumiNova SLN C1.
Strap: black vulcanized rubber; DLC-coated stainless steel deployment buckle with embossed CONCORD cover.
Suggested price: $14,290

C1 WORLDTIMER   REF. 0320048

Movement: mechanical self-winding GMT Worldtimer 201 Dubois-Dépraz (ETA 2892-A2, 11 1/2'''); Ø 26.2m, thickness: 5mm; 256 components; 21 jewels; 42-hour power reserve; black PVD treatment; snailed bevel; vertical Côtes de Genève; "C1" engraved in center.
Functions: hours, minutes, seconds; 24 time zones with cities at 9; date window with magnifying glass at 3.
Case: black DLC-coated stainless steel; Ø 47mm, thickness: 13.55mm; 53 elements; metal protective ring coated in black rubber and fixed by 7 self-blocking screws; screw-down crown with embossed C1 logo; 3.3mm-thick sapphire crystal, anti-reflective on both sides; exhibition caseback embossed "Audace—SavoirFaire—Avant-Garde"; water resistant to 20atm.
Dial: black; engine turned; wide opening for second time zone; rhodium-plated polished hour-markers with SuperLumiNova SLN C1; dauphine hands, asymmetrically hollowed out, lacquered, sandblasted, SuperLumiNova SLN C1.
Strap: black vulcanized rubber; DLC-coated stainless steel deployment buckle with embossed CONCORD cover.
Suggested price: $16,900

C1 CHRONOGRAPH   REF. 0320074

Movement: mechanical self-winding Caliber A07.211 (ETA Valgranges); 16 1/2 '''; Ø 37.2mm, thickness: 7.9mm; official COSC-certified chronograph; 25 jewels; 28,800 vph; 48-hour power reserve; black PVD treatment; snailed bevel; vertical Côtes de Genève; "C1" engraved in center.
Functions: hours, minutes, central sweep seconds; small seconds on turning disc at 9; 30-minute counter at 12; 12-hour counter at 6; date window at 3.
Case: stainless steel; Ø 44mm, thickness: 16.7mm; 53 elements; metal protective ring coated in black rubber and fixed laterally by 7 self-blocking screws; screw-down crown with embossed C1 logo; 3.3mm-thick sapphire crystal, antireflective on both sides; exhibition caseback embossed "Audace—Savoir Faire—Avant-Garde"; water resistant to 20atm.
Dial: orange; three layers orange hour-markers and chronograph seconds hand; dauphine hands, asymmetrically hollowed out, lacquered, SuperLumiNova SLN C1.
Strap: orange rubber-coated alligator leather.
Suggested price: $12,800
Also available: on black rubber strap.

C1 CHRONOGRAPH   REF. 0320083

Movement: mechanical self-winding Caliber A07.211 (ETA Valgranges); 16 1/2 '''; Ø 37.2mm, thickness: 7.9mm; official COSC-certified chronograph; 25 jewels; 28,800 vph; 48-hour power reserve; black PVD treatment; snailed bevel; vertical Côtes de Genève; "C1" engraved in center.
Functions: hours, minutes, central sweep seconds; small seconds on turning disc at 9; 30-minute counter at 12; 12-hour counter at 6; date window at 3.
Case: 18K white-gold diamond-set case and full-set bezel, crown and pushers (142 baguette-cut diamonds, 13.7 carats); water resistant to 3atm.
Dial: full-pavé dial set with 32 baguette-cut diamonds, 2.7 carats.
Strap: black vulcanized rubber; 18K white-gold deployment buckle with embossed CONCORD cover.
Suggested price: $430,000

C1 BIRETROGRADE   REF. 0320045

Movement: mechanical self-winding Caliber 3535 La Joux-Perret 13 1/4''' (ETA 2892-A2, 11 1/2'''); 89 components; 29 jewels; 28,800 vph; 42-hour power reserve; skeletonized plate, pallet bridge, module plate and module bridge; circluar graining; black PVD treatment; snailed bevel; vertical Côtes de Genève; "C1" engraved in center.
Functions: hours, minutes; retrograde date between 3 and 6; retrograde day between 6 and 9.
Case: 18K 5N rose gold; Ø 44mm, thickness: 14.6mm; protective ring with 8 rubber-coated rose-gold blocks; 3.3mm-thick sapphire crystal with antireflective treatment on both sides; rose-gold exhibition caseback, embossed "Audace—Savoir Faire Avant-Garde"; black rubber and composite screw-down crown with embossed C1 logo; water resistant to 5atm.
Dial: black skeletized dial; 5N polished hour-markers; dauphine hands, assymmetrically hollowed out, lacquered, sandblasted, SuperLumiNova SLN C1.
Strap: black vulcanized rubber strap; 18K 5N rose-gold deployment buckle with embossed CONCORD cover.
Suggested price: $52,500

As Corum honors the rich heritage of its legendary Admiral's Cup collection this year, the Swiss watchmaker charts a new course with a 50th anniversary model that is more about riding a wave into the future than taking a cruise through the past.

The Admiral's Cup Minute Repeater Tourbillon 45 honors half a century of innovation with a limited edition (10 pieces) anniversary model that combines a tourbillon with a minute repeater.

Corum uses gray-tinted sapphire glass for the dial, which is surrounded by nautical flags on the bezel's flange. The 45mm 5N red-gold case is fitted with a 12-sided bezel that rotates clockwise 27 degrees to activate the minute repeater.

The Admiral's Cup Minute Repeater Tourbillon 45 underscores the technical prowess of the company's craftsmen with the introduction of a complex new caliber that integrates a tourbillon and a minute repeater, two of horology's most challenging complications.

Corum is already well known in the watchmaking industry for mastering high complications, but this is the first time the brand has merged two major high complications in one model. A chiming timepiece designed for mariners is quite unusual, but it meshes perfectly with the life of a sailor, says Antonio Calce, company CEO. "Ringing bells provide the soundtrack of a sailor's life, from action stations in the morning to the evening ring. This special timepiece brings together the worlds of boating and horology in a creative way, paying tribute to the passions that drive both."

Corum extends the sophisticated ingenuity used to create the movement to the watch's 12-sided bezel, a signature feature of the Admiral's Cup since 1982. Typically, a sliding switch or button on the case activates a repeater. Because the anniversary watch is intended to be worn during sporty activities, the repeater's traditional outcropping was at risk of being struck, potentially damaging the mechanism. To avert this possibility, and maintain the watch's clean lines, Corum designed the bezel to rotate 27 degrees clockwise, which engages the repeater. The attention lavished on small details elevates the Admiral's Cup Minute Repeater Tourbillon 45's design to a rarified level.

The sound of the minute repeater illustrates the point. Made of an undisclosed alloy, the gongs are designed specifically to ensure the beauty and power of their individual tones. The gongs are also specially tuned—A on the hours and C-sharp on the minutes—to produce a major third, two tones that combine to create a bright, harmonious sound.

The repeater's action can be seen through the smoke-tinted sapphire crystal used for the dial. Its transparency also allows for close inspection of the cutting-edge tourbillon oscillating at 5:00. To guarantee the movement's precision and durability, the mechanism integrates an escapement and pallets made of Silicium.

Corum takes special care to make sure that the technical achievements evinced by Caliber CO 010 don't outshine the movement's visual beauty, adorning its surfaces with circular graining and a Côtes de Genève finish on the bottom bridges.

Much has changed since 1960, when the Admiral's Cup debuted in a square case. Its look has matured into a round case decorated with nautical pennants, while its complications have grown to include chronographs, tourbillons and a model that indicates precious information about the tides. Yet the watch's original spirit of adventure has not changed since the Admiral's Cup first set sail on the winds of time.

Corum designed the new Admiral's Cup bezel to rotate 27 degrees clockwise to safely engage the repeater.

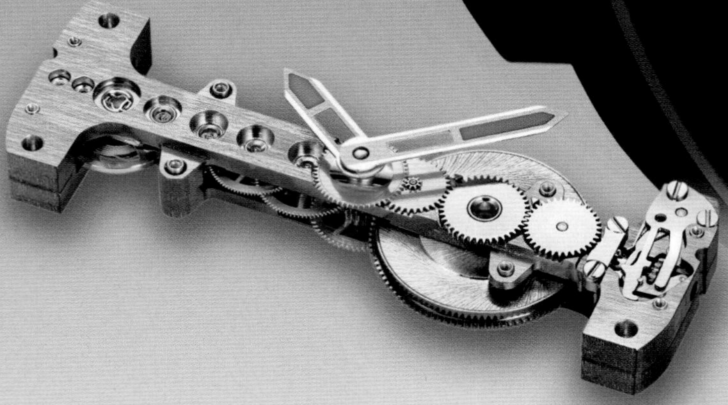

ABOVE LEFT Caliber CO 007 features a large barrel with a snailed finish and is anchored to the Black Ti-Bridge's case by four triangular casing clamps.

ABOVE RIGHT Curved to maximize comfort, the Black Ti-Bridge's 42.5x41.5 case is coated entirely in black PVD and polished to add a gleaming counterpoint to the satin-finished flange, bridge and clamps.

The Black Ti-Bridge's generously proportioned titanium case casts an imposing shadow, while its openworked design uses space confidently and to dramatic effect. A PVD-coated upper bridge bisects the tonneau-shaped case horizontally, providing a satin-finished perch for the skeletonized minute and hour hands.

Caliber CO 007 is suspended beneath, anchored to the case by four triangular casing clamps. Much of the "baguette" movement plays peek-a-boo behind the upper bridge, while its large barrel stands out prominently thanks to both its size and snailed finish. A clear view of the gears in motion is available through a slender opening on the caseback, which is engraved with the Corum logo. To complete the timepiece's contemporary look, it comes on a black rubber strap with a folding clasp made of titanium.

The Corum Bridge represents one of what the brand calls the "four pillars" of its collection (Admiral's Cup, Corum Bridges, Romvlvs and Artisans). Production of this special all-black, titanium version is limited to 250 pieces.

The 5N red-gold Ro
Tourbillon has no dial
casing a black PVD-
movement decorate
Côtes de Genève and
lar graining patterns

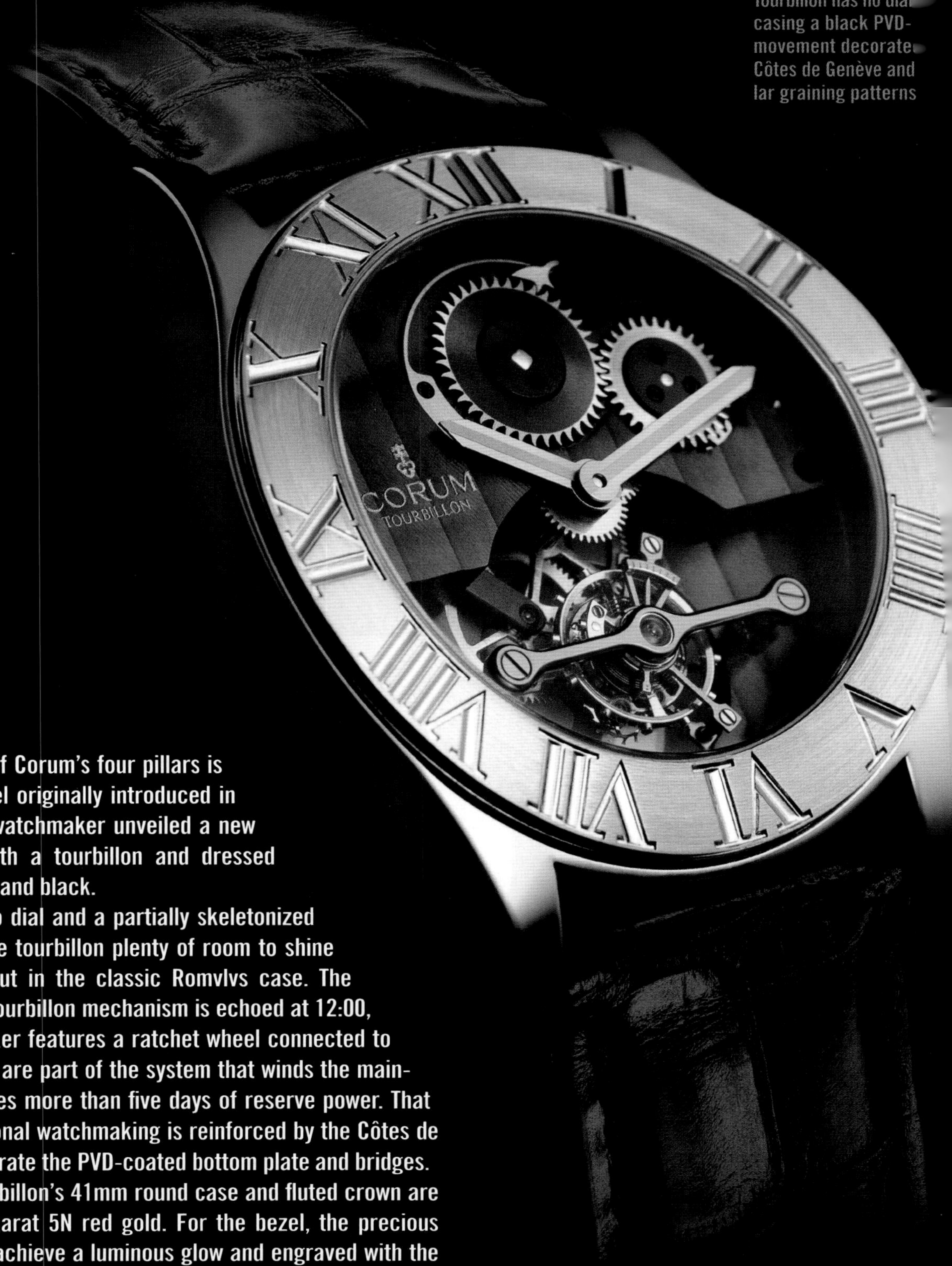

A third member of Corum's four pillars is he Romvlvs, a model originally introduced in 966. Last fall, the watchmaker unveiled a new ersion endowed with a tourbillon and dressed elegantly in red gold and black.

The watch has no dial and a partially skeletonized novement, giving the tourbillon plenty of room to shine as it makes its debut in the classic Romvlvs case. The ound shape of the tourbillon mechanism is echoed at 12:00, where the watchmaker features a ratchet wheel connected to a crown wheel. Both are part of the system that winds the main-spring, which provides more than five days of reserve power. That dedication to traditional watchmaking is reinforced by the Côtes de Genève used to decorate the PVD-coated bottom plate and bridges.

The Romvlvs Tourbillon's 41mm round case and fluted crown are both crafted in 18-karat 5N red gold. For the bezel, the precious metal is brushed to achieve a luminous glow and engraved with the Romvlvs' trademark Roman numerals.

Only ten Romvlvs Tourbillons will be released, making this time-piece a true rarity.

With the latest additions to its exceptional Bridges and Romvlvs collections, as well as the Admiral's Cup Minute Repeater Tourbillon 45 anniversary model, it's clear Corum has plenty to celebrate

ADMIRAL'S CUP CHRONOGRAPH 50 LHS   REF. 753.231.06/0371 AN12

Movement: automatic chronograph CO 753; 48-hour power reserve; 28,800 vph; 27 jewels; COSC certified; special CORUM finish.
Functions: hours, minutes; small seconds at 3, 30-minute counter at 9; date at 6.
Case: Ø 50mm; titanium; vulcanized rubber bezel; crown in titanium with black PVD; crown engraved with CORUM key; exclusive black PVD-coated titanium pushers at 8 and 10; cambered dodecagonal antireflective sapphire crystal; titanium screwed case-

back with molded rubber and raised engraving of Admiral's Cup trophy; water resistant to 30atm.
Dial: black; 12 nautical pennant hour-markers; Superluminova chevron markers and minute numerals; center chronograph seconds hand with counterweight shaped like CORUM key; faceted hands with Super-luminova.
Strap: black vulcanized rubber; molded CORUM inscription; width: 25/24mm; titanium tongue buckle engraved with CORUM logo.
Notes: limited edition 888 pieces; member of left-handed series (LHS).
Suggested price: $8,500
Also available: 18K red gold with crocodile strap ($29,000; limited edition 88 pieces) or platinum ($59,000; limited edition 18 pieces).

ADMIRAL'S CUP CHRONOGRAPH SPORT 48   REF. 753.935.06/V791 AN52

Movement: automatic chronograph CO 753; 48-hour power reserve; 28,800 vph; 27 jewels; rhodium plated; special CORUM finish engraved rotor; COSC certified. **Functions:** hours, minutes; 30-minute counter at 3, 12-hour counter at 6, small seconds at 9; date at 4:30. **Case:** Ø 48mm; satin-finished grade-5 titanium; polished horns; vulcanized rubber bezel and crown protector; grade-5 titanium crown engraved with CORUM key; faceted dodecagonal antireflective sapphire crystal; screwed grade-5 titanium caseback with black vulcanized rubber and engraving of Admiral's Cup trophy medallion in stainless steel; water resistant to

30atm. **Dial:** black; brass with Côtes de Genève; rhodium-coated minutes and chevrons with black Superluminova; "cool gray" nautical pennant hour-markers and minute-circle transferred on fitted flange; rhodium-coated faceted hour and minute; rhodium-coated dauphine-style counter hands; rhodium-coated, center chronograph seconds hand with counterweight shaped like CORUM key; all hands (except chronograph seconds) with black Superluminova. **Bracelet:** grade-5 titanium and black vulcanized rubber; grade-5 titanium tongue buckle and cover with engraved CORUM logo; three laser-soldered links; triple-folding clasp with opening and fastening system using two pushers.
Note: limited production 750 pieces.
Suggested price: $8,100
Also available: titanium on vulcanized rubber strap ($7,000); 18K red gold on vulcanized rubber black strap ($20,900); 18K red gold on bracelet with black vulcanized rubber center links ($30,900).

ADMIRAL'S CUP CHRONOGRAPH 48   REF. 753.936.55/0081 AN32

Movement: automatic chronograph CO 753; 48-hour power reserve; 28,800 vph; 27 jewels; rhodium plated; special CORUM finish engraved rotor; COSC certified. **Functions:** hours, minutes; 30-minute counter at 3, 12-hour counter at 6, small seconds at 9; date at 4:30. **Case:** Ø 48mm; satin-finished 5N 18K red-gold case and bezel; polished horns; vulcanized rubber crown protector; 5N 18K red-gold crown engraved with CORUM key; 18K red-gold corrector at 10 and pushers at 2 and 4 with security locks; faceted dodecagonal antireflective sapphire crystal; screwed

antireflective open caseback; water resistant to 5atm.
Dial: black-lacquered brass; 5N red gold-coated minutes and minute chevrons; nautical pennant hour-markers and transferred minute-circle transferred on fitted flange; 5N red gold-coated dauphine-style counter and small seconds hands; 5N red-gold, center chronograph seconds hand with counterweight shaped like CORUM key; all hands (except chronograph seconds) with Superluminova. **Strap:** black crocodile leather; curved loop; 18K red-gold tongue buckle; triple-folding clasp with opening and fastening system using two pushers; 5N 18K red-gold cover engraved with CORUM logo. **Note:** limited production 125 pieces.
Suggested price: $23,900
Also available: 5N 18K red-gold on matching bracelet ($41,900).

ADMIRAL'S CUP BLACK HULL 48   REF. 753.934.95/0371 AN92

Movement: automatic chronograph CO 753; 48-hour power reserve; 28,800 vph; 27 jewels; rhodium plated; special CORUM finish; COSC certified.
Functions: 60-minute counter at 3, 12-hour counter at 6, small seconds at 9; date at 4:30.
Case: Ø 48mm; black PVD-coated titanium; vulcanized rubber bezel; black PVD-coated titanium crown engraved with CORUM key; lever pushers at 2 and 4 with

exclusive security locks; faceted dodecagonal anti-reflective sapphire crystal; black PVD-coated titanium screwed caseback with molded rubber and raised engraving of Admiral's Cup trophy; water resistant to 30atm.
Dial: black lacquered; chevrons and minute numerals with black Superluminova; nautical pennant hour-markers transferred on the fitted flange; faceted hour and minute hands with black Superluminova; black center chronograph seconds hand with counterweight shaped like CORUM key.
Strap: black vulcanized rubber; black PVD-coated titanium pin buckle engraved with CORUM logo.
Note: limited edition 999 pieces.
Suggested price: $8,000

ADMIRAL'S CUP TIDES 48   REF. 277.931.91/V791 AN32

Movement: automatic CO 277; exclusive CORUM Tides Module.
Functions: hours, minutes, seconds; date at 3; time of the tide at 6; height of the tide and strength of the current at 9; moonphase and strength of the tide at 12.
Case: Ø 48mm; 5N 18K red gold; bezel, caseback and crown protectors in vulcanized rubber; 5N 18K red-gold screwed-crown; faceted dodecagonal antireflective sapphire crystal; screwed caseback engraved with Admiral's Cup trophy; water resistant to 5atm.
Dial: matte-black lacquered; nautical pennant hour-markers transferred on the fitted flange; Superluminova hour and minute hands; seconds hand with counter-weight shaped like CORUM key.
Bracelet: 5N 18K red gold; black vulcanized rubber center links; 5N 18K red-gold tongue buckle.
Note: limited production 150 pieces.
Suggested price: $32,000
Also available: 18K red gold on strap ($22,000).

ADMIRAL'S CUP TOURBILLON 44   REF. 009.697.55/0081 AN12

Movement: manual-winding CO 107; 130-hour power reserve; 21,600 vph; 21 jewels; bridges and bottom plate decorated with Côtes de Genève; circular graining.
Functions: hours, minutes; tourbillon.
Case: Ø 44mm; satin-finished 5N 18K red-gold bezel and crown protector; crown engraved with CORUM key; polished horns; faceted dodecagonal antireflective sapphire crystal; screwed antireflective open caseback; water resistant to 3atm.
Dial: black brass; 5N red gold-coated minute and minute chevrons; nautical pennant hour-markers on PVD-coated 18K gold fitted flange; 5N red gold-coated faceted hour and minute hands with white Superluminova.
Strap: black crocodile leather; curved loop; 5N 18K red-gold tongue buckle.
Note: limited edition 25 pieces.
Suggested price: $112,000

ADMIRAL'S CUP BLACK CHALLENGE 44   REF. 753.691.98/F371 AN12

Movement: automatic chronograph CO 753; 48-hour power reserve; 28,800 vph; 27 jewels; special CORUM finish; COSC certified.
Functions: hours, minutes, seconds; chronograph; 30-minute counter at 3, 12-hour counter at 6, small seconds at 9; date at 4:30.
Case: Ø 44mm; black PVD-coated stainless steel case and crown; crown engraved with CORUM key; faceted dodecagonal antireflective sapphire crystal; PVD-coated steel screwed caseback with raised engraving of Admiral's Cup trophy; water resistant to 10atm.
Dial: black; chevrons and minute numerals with Superluminova; monochromatic nautical pennant hour-markers painted on flange; faceted hour and minute hands and counter hands with Superluminova; center seconds hand with counter-weight shaped like CORUM key.
Strap: black vulcanized rubber; black PVD-coated steel triple-folding clasp engraved with CORUM logo.
Note: limited edition 300 pieces.
Suggested price: $7,000
Also available: white dial (limited edition 200 pieces).

ADMIRAL'S CUP CHALLENGE 44 BLACK & GOLD   REF. 753.691.83/F371 AK12

Movement: automatic chronograph CO 753; 48-hour power reserve; 28,800 vph; 27 jewels; special CORUM finish; COSC certified.
Functions: hours, minutes; chronograph 30-minute counter at 3, 12-hour counter at 6, small seconds at 9; date at 4:30.
Case: Ø 44mm; gray PVD-coated stainless steel; 5N 18K red-gold bezel and crown; crown engraved with CORUM key; faceted dodecagonal antireflective sapphire crystal; gray PVD-coated steel open caseback (1300 Vickers); water resistant to 10atm.
Dial: gray; 5N red gold-coated chevrons and minute numerals with Superluminova; monochromatic nautical pennant hour-markers on flange; 5N red-gold faceted hour and minute hands and counter hands with Superluminova; 5N red-gold center seconds hand with counterweight shaped like CORUM key.
Strap: black vulcanized rubber; gray PVD-coated steel triple-folding clasp with engraved with CORUM logo.
Note: limited edition 128 pieces.
Suggested price: $10,000
Also available: with black PVD treatment and black dial (limited edition 200 pieces).

ADMIRAL'S CUP GMT 44   REF. 383.330.20/0F81 AA12

Movement: automatic CO 383; 42-hour power reserve; 28,800 vph; 21 jewels; special CORUM finishing.
Functions: hours, minutes, seconds; date at 3; second time zone.
Case: Ø 44mm; stainless steel; stainless steel crown engraved with CORUM key; faceted dodecagonal antireflective sapphire crystal; screwed steel caseback with raised engraving of Admiral's Cup trophy; water resistant to 10atm.

Dial: black; transferred nautical pennant hour-markers on flange; transferred 24-hour second time zone indication; chevrons, minute numerals and hands with Superluminova; red second time-zone hand with Superluminova; center seconds hand with counterweight shaped like CORUM key.
Strap: black genuine crocodile leather; stainless steel triple-folding clasp engraved with CORUM logo.
Note: limited production 2,000 pieces.
Suggested price: $4,800
Also available: stainless steel on bracelet ($5,500); 18K red gold on strap ($15,500) or bracelet ($25,500); 18K red gold and steel on strap ($7,200).

ADMIRAL'S CUP CHRONOGRAPH 40 DIAMONDS   REF. 984.970.47/F371 AN12

Movement: automatic chronograph CO 984; 42-hour power reserve; 28,800 vph; 37 jewels; special CORUM finishing; COSC certified.
Functions: hours, minutes; small seconds at 3, 12-hour counter at 6, 30-minute counter at 9; date at 4:30.
Case: Ø 40mm; stainless steel; bezel set with 66 diamonds (0.924 carat); crown engraved with CORUM key; faceted dodecagonal antireflective sapphire crystal;

screwed antireflective open caseback; water resistant to 10atm.
Dial: black; nautical pennant hour-markers transferred on the fitted flange; chevrons, minute numeral and hands with Superluminova; center seconds hand with counterweight shaped like CORUM key.
Strap: black rubber.
Suggested price: $9,500
Note: limited production 700 pieces.
Also available: 18K red gold ($23,000).

TI-BRIDGE   REF. 007.400.04/0F81 0000

Movement: manual-winding mechanical baguette movement CO 007; titanium; 72-hour power reserve; 28,800 vph; 21 jewels; satin-finished bridges with engraved CORUM logo; flange with black PVD coating; barrel with snailed finish; four triangular casing clamps.
Functions: hours, minutes.
Case: 42.5x41.5mm; tonneau-shaped titanium case; polished top; two sand-casted

grooves; fluted titanium crown with satin and polished finishes, adorned with CORUM key; antireflective sapphire crystal; 6-screw satin-finished caseback with engraved CORUM logo, open to reveal movement; water resistant to 5atm.
Dial: no dial; baton-shaped hour and minute hands with Superluminova.
Strap: black leather strap.
Note: limited production 750 pieces.
Suggested price: $12,900
Also available: Black Ti-Bridge with PVD treatments ($14,000, limited production 250 pieces).

GOLDEN BRIDGE LADY   REF. 113.353.69/0081 0019G

Movement: manual-winding mechanical baguette movement CO 113; 40-hour power reserve; 28,800 vph; 19 jewels; white-gold hand-engraved plates and bridges; slipping spring mechanism; variable inertia balance adjustable by screws.
Functions: hours, minutes.
Case: 41x34mm; 18K white gold; set with 72 diamonds (1.6 carats); fluted crown at 3 adorned with white mother-of-pearl; antireflective sapphire crystal; water resistant to 3atm.

Dial: no dial; flange set with 108 diamonds; openworked, leaf-shaped hour and minute hands.
Strap: black crocodile leather; 18K white-gold tongue buckle.
Note: limited production 175 pieces.
Suggested price: $35,000
Also available: 18K red gold with round diamonds and on white strap ($34,200).

ROMVLVS TOURBILLON   REF. 009.510.55/0001 0000

Movement: manual-winding tourbillon CO 107; 130-hour power reserve; 21,600 vph; 21 jewels; Côtes de Genève and circular graining.
Functions: hours, minutes; tourbillon.
Case: Ø 41mm; 5N 18K red gold; wave-profile bezel with 12 Roman numerals; fluted 5N 18K red-gold crown with engraved CORUM key; antireflective sapphire crystal; 6-screw open caseback; water resistant to 3atm.
Dial: no dial; 18K red gold-coated baton-shaped hour and minutes hands.
Strap: black crocodile leather strap (a second brown crocodile strap is delivered with the watch) with 5N 18K red-gold tongue buckle with CORUM logo.
Note: limited edition 10 pieces.
Suggested price: $107,000

GOLDEN BRIDGE BLACK TITANIUM   REF. 113.700.94/0001 0000

Movement: manual-winding mechanical baguette movement CO 113; 40-hour power reserve; 28,800 vph; 19 jewels; slipping spring mechanism; 18K red gold hand-engraved mainplate and bridges; variable inertia balance adjustable by screws.
Functions: hours, minutes.
Case: 34x51mm; black PVD-coated titanium; tonneau shaped; fluted titanium crown at 6 decorated with CORUM key; antireflective sapphire crystal; water resistant to 3atm.
Dial: no dial; black skeleton, baton-shaped hour and minute hands.
Strap: hand-stitched black crocodile leather strap (a second brown crocodile strap is delivered with the watch); titanium tongue buckle.
Note: limited edition 138 pieces.
Suggested price: $22,800

GOLDEN TOURBILLON PANORAMIQUE GREY SAPPHIRE   REF. 382.870.59/0F01 0000

Movement: manual-winding tourbillon CO 382; 90-hour power reserve; 21,600 vph; 17 jewels; gray sapphire plates and bridges.
Functions: hours, minutes, tourbillon.
Case: 38x53mm; 18K white gold; tonneau-shaped case; fluted 18K gold crown at 6 engraved with CORUM key; antireflective sapphire crystal top and sides; 4-screw open caseback with antireflective treatment; water resistant to 3atm.
Dial: transparent; skeleton hour and minute hands.
Strap: black crocodile leather; 18K white-gold folding clasp.
Note: limited edition 18 pieces.
Suggested price: $169,000
Also available: 18K red gold; 18K red gold set with round diamonds; 18K white gold set with round diamonds; 18K white gold set with baguette and round diamonds.

$20 DOUBLE EAGLE GOLD COIN   REF. 082.355.56/0001 MU51

Movement: automatic CO 082.
Case: Ø 36mm; water resistant to 3atm.
Dial: authentic vintage 22K $20 "Double Eagle" US gold coin.
Strap: black crocodile leather; 18K yellow-gold tongue buckle.
Note: introduced in 1964.
Suggested price: $13,000

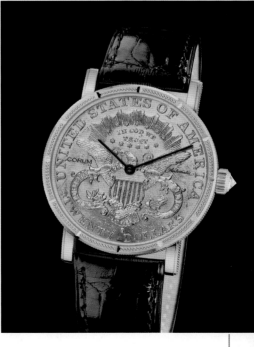

Cuervo y Sobrinos

LA HABANA 1882

Last fall, Cuervo y Sobrinos returned to Cuba, the island nation where the Cuervo family founded the famed international watch brand more than a century ago. Now based in Switzerland, the company comes full circle, launching a boutique and museum across the street from its original headquarters in Havana's historic district.

LEFT   The Ø 41mm rose-gold Historiador Chronograph was bestowed the honor of housing the rare, fully restored vintage Venus 188 movement. Just 50 examples of the movement were acquired by Cuervo y Sobrinos, thereby limiting the watch's production to 50 pieces.

RIGHT   Cuervo y Sobrinos reproduced a movement from the 1940s for its Torpedo Historiador Semanal. It displays the day, date, month, hour, and the week number via five ring indicators.

Visitors to the 19th-century building on Muralla Street are transported back to Havana's golden age of the 1880s, when bon vivants and personalities from around the world were drawn to the "Pearl of the Caribbean" in search of the good life. Inside, the Art Deco space evokes the spirit of bygone eras with displays of antique watches, writing instruments and other memorabilia, including the original vault from the family's store.

But the boutique offers more than a comfortable place for a nostalgic look back while sipping cafecito or seven-year-old Havana Club rum. The luxurious space also showcases a full complement of Cuervo y Sobrinos timepieces from the company's current collection.

Reconnecting with its past is a significant moment for the brand, says Marzio Villa, president of Cuervo y Sobrinos. "Yes we are a Swiss corporation and we can say unequivocally that we have no ties to the Cuban government. But forever we will have ties to the island of Cuba and the city of Havana. This is our heritage and it is important for people to know about our proud origins. And for this, we have made a strong statement and affirmation of our heritage by restoring this site. Now absolutely everyone who visits the museum will understand our continuity and enduring historic roots."

LEFT Along with timepieces from the current Cuervo y Sobrinos collection, the museum also features the vault from the Cuervo family's original jewelry store.

BELOW Cuervo y Sobrinos returned to Havana, the city in which it was founded more than a century ago, opening a boutique and museum across the street from where its original head-quarters stood.

BOTTOM Ambassadors from Switzerland, Spain and Italy were on hand when El Reloj Cuervo y Sobrinos was christened last fall.

'This is our heritage and it is important for people to know about our proud origins.' —*Villa*

The Cuervo family opened its boutique in 1882 on Quinta Avenida (Fifth Avenue), in one of Havana's most prestigious neighborhoods. Nearby embassies and mansions provided an appropriate backdrop for the refined and timeless designs found in the company's showcases.

The business took root and thrived there for years before expanding its operations to Germany, France and La Chaux-de-Fonds in the heart of Switzerland's historic watchmaking region. As Cuervo y Sobrinos grew, so did its status among an international clientele passionate about fine watches.

After 70 years, however, Cuervo y Sobrinos was shuttered during the political upheaval that engulfed Cuba in the late 1950s. Much to the delight of watch collectors, the brand was revived in 2002, returning to rebuild its reputation and lay claim to future glories.

Even though Cuervo y Sobrinos is now based in Switzerland, Havana's hypnotic spell still holds sway. The influence is obvious with models named after famous cuts of cigars, like Robusto, Espléndidos, Torpedo, and Prominente. Deeper still, it seeps down to the core of the current collection, which includes watches based on finished movements and unrealized designs retrieved from the old store.

As it proudly reestablishes a presence in the country of its origin, Cuervo y Sobrinos continues to prove its authenticity with timepieces tailored to transcend trends.

TORPEDO PIRATA GMT

REF. 3052.1NLE

Movement: self-winding ETA 2893-2 movement.
Functions: hours, minutes, seconds; 24-hour second time-zone; anchor markers on inner GMT dial.
Case: bronze, polished/burnished steel and titanium; grooved cannoball-shaped crown; sapphire crystal caseback with antireflective coating and engraved with two swords surrounding the classic CYS crest; water resistant to 5atm.

Dial: black; inner second time-zone circle with alternating Arabic numerals and anchor motifs.
Strap: black rubber with bronze stitching on front; bronze on the back.
Suggested price: $6,500
Note: limited edition of 125 pieces; sold in "treasure chest" humidor/watch box and accompanied by a deck of Cuervo y Sobrinos playing cards.
Also available: in 18K gold, polished/burnished steel and titanium case (25 pieces, $15,900).

PROMINENTE CRONOGRAFO

REF. 1014.9TLE

Movement: self-winding ETA 2094 movement; 33 jewels; 42-hour power reserve.
Functions: hours, minutes, small seconds; date; chronograph: 12-hour, 30-minute, and seconds with central hand.
Case: 18K rose gold; Ø 23.3mm, height: 5.5mm; sapphire crystal caseback with anti-reflective coating; water resistant to 3atm.
Dial: 18K gold.

Strap: hand-stitched Louisiana alligator leather; 18K rose-gold pin buckle.
Suggested price: $19,500
Note: limited edition of 28 pieces.

TORPEDO HISTORIADOR SEMANAL

REF. 2853.1B

Movement: self-winding ETA 2853 movement; 27 jewels; 44-hour power reserve.
Functions: hours, minutes, small seconds; date; day of the week, week of the year; month, year.
Case: stainless steel; Ø 45mm, height: 13.55mm; sapphire crystal caseback with antireflective coating; water resistant to 3atm.
Dial: white.

Strap: hand-stitched Louisiana alligator leather; stainless steel pin buckle.
Suggested price: $6,900

TORPEDO POWER RESERVE

REF. 3051.5RLE

Movement: self-winding CYS 3051 caliber; 25 jewels; 42-hour power reserve.
Functions: hours, minutes, seconds; date; power reserve at 3; chronograph: 12-hour, 30-minute, and central hands.
Case: bronze, titanium and brushed steel; Ø 45mm, height: 15.5mm; cannon-shaped pushers; grooved cannonball-shaped crown; sapphire crystal caseback with antireflective coating; caseback engraved with two swords surrounding the classic CYS crest; water resistant to 5atm.
Dial: black.
Strap: black rubber on front; light gray with bronze stitching and CYS crest printing on back; titanium pin buckle.
Suggested price: $8,900
Note: limited edition of 200 pieces.

ROBUSTO PERPETUALE MOONPHASE   REF. 2825.9CEL

Movement: self-winding CYS 2824 caliber; 21 jewels; 40- to 44-hour power reserve.
Functions: hours, minutes; seconds; perpetual calendar: date, day of the week and month, leap year and moonphase.
Case: 18K rose gold; Ø 43mm, height: 11.95mm; sapphire crystal caseback with anti-reflective coating; water resistant to 3atm.
Dial: mother-of-pearl counters.
Strap: hand-stitched Louisiana alligator leather; 18K rose-gold pin buckle.
Suggested price: $31,000
Note: limited edition of 10 pieces.

TORPEDO CRONÓGRAFO BIG DATE   REF. 3045.1CN

Movement: self-winding Dubois-Dépraz 4500 caliber; 49 jewels; 40- to 44-hour power reserve.
Functions: hours, minutes, small seconds; big date; chronograph: 12-hour counter, 30-minute, and seconds with double central hand for tachymeter functions (speed measurement) and pulsometer (heartbeat measurement).
Case: stainless steel; Ø 44mm, height: 11.35mm; sapphire crystal caseback with anti-reflective coating; water resistant to 5atm.
Strap: hand-stitched Louisiana alligator leather; stainless steel pin buckle.
Suggested price: $5,900

HISTORIADOR CRONÓGRAFO   REF. 3188.9B

Movement: manual-winding chronograph Venus 188 movement; 17 jewels; 44-hour power reserve.
Functions: hours, minutes, small seconds; chronograph: 30-minute and central seconds; tachymeter functions (speed measurement).
Case: 18K rose gold; Ø 41mm, height: 12.5mm; domed sapphire crystal caseback with antireflective coating.
Strap: hand-stitched Louisiana alligator leather; 18K rose-gold pin buckle.
Suggested price: $19,900
Note: engraved CYS crest; limited edition of 50 pieces.

ESPLÉNDIDOS DON RAMÓN DUALTIME   REF. 2451.8SLE

Movement: self-winding TT 651 ETA 2892-A2 movement; 25 jewels; 42-hour power reserve.
Functions: hours, minutes, small seconds; big date; second time zone.
Case: 18K rose gold; 37x47mm, height: 12.75mm; sapphire crystal caseback with antireflective coating;
Dial: skeleton; Don Ramón Cuervo engraving.
Strap: hand-stitched Louisiana alligator leather; 18K rose-gold pin buckle.
Suggested price: $15,000
Note: tribute to Don Ramón Cuervo (founder of Cuervo Y Sobrinos); limited to 28 pieces.

de GRISOGONO
GENEVE

After seven years of creating exquisite jewelry, the Genevan brand **de GRISOGONO** leapt with both feet into the world of watchmaking in 2000.

Since then, the company has released 22 watch collections for women and men, all marked by the exuberant creativity of Fawaz Gruosi, the founder of the brand who still manages the brand's technical and aesthetic directions with a masterly hand. Watch lovers of the world have proved their affection and esteem, awarding the Public Prize to the Meccanico dG watch during the latest Grand Prix d'Horlogerie de Genève.

In the watch world microcosm, winning a prize at the Grand Prix d'Horlogerie de Genève is one of the greatest recognitions a watchmaker can receive. That recognition takes on an even more exceptional dimension when the prize is awarded by the public. Nine years after entering the field of horology, Gruosi walked up to the stage at the Grand Théâtre de Genève on November 17, 2009, for the very first time to accept the Public Prize. The moment was a true recognition for a man who has always, in watches as in jewelry, chosen to claim new horizons rather than content himself with reinterpreting already existing concepts.

THIS PAGE
Recognized by those who love timepieces that combine technique and design, the Meccanico dG won the Public Prize at the Grand Prix d'Horlogerie de Genève 2009.

FACING PAGE
Accepting the Public Prize for Meccanico dG at the Grand Prix d'Horlogerie de Genève in 2009, Fawaz Gruosi graciously thanked his "providers, who had the strength and the courage to continue on this adventure."

meccanico dG

Grand Prix d'Horlogerie de Genève

Prix du Public · 2009

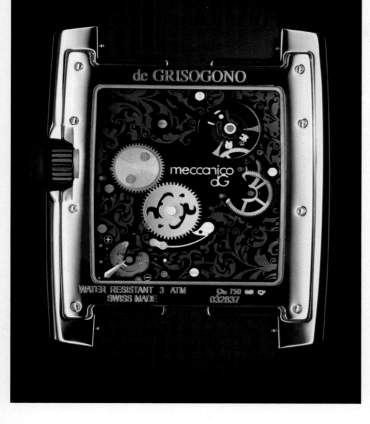

The Meccanico dG is the remarkable illustration of the art of living as cultivated by Gruosi and evident in each of his creations. The timepiece draws on the deepest horological tradition in order to propel that tradition into the future. Its mechanical movement, displaying two time zones—in a totally exclusive, mechanical dual analog and digital display—is one of the most complex ever. The mechanism foresees the horology of tomorrow clothed in a very contemporary design.

Though Gruosi has never been the timid sort, nor doubted the success of even his craziest undertakings, to take on something like this required an exceptional dose of courage chased with a dash of recklessness. Building a digital display powered by an entirely mechanical system? No watchmaker had ever attempted such a thing. As a brilliant wink at the history of horology and the one-time threat of quartz movements, the Meccanico dG builds a bridge between these two systems of thought, at the same time bringing about the accession of a completely original horological innovation.

The manual-winding movement is full of micro-systems—extremely sophisticated mechanisms with gears and rotating discs—and contains 651 components. The top half of the dial features an analog hour and minute display, and the bottom half shows a digital display of the time in the second time zone. The digital display shows the hours and minutes with mobile micro-segments animated by an ensemble of 23 cams and gears, aided by a device for disengagement and synchronization.

The exceptional mechanics unveiled by the Meccanico dG are equaled by a very distinguished contemporary aesthetic. With its extra-large masculine dimensions (56x48mm!), the curved case is available in rose gold, titanium, titanium and rubber, titanium and rose gold, or titanium and platinum. This fusion of materials is in perfect harmony with the innovative character of the timepiece, futuristic down to the smallest details: setting the hour of the analog display is performed with the rubber-covered crown, while the second time zone is adjusted by two correctors that are also crafted in vulcanized rubber. The heart of the watch, including the systems of discs and gears, is visible through the transparent dial. The colored indexes for telling time on the analog system seem to hang suspended, partially revealing the mechanism. As is the case with all movements employed by de GRISOGONO, the Meccanico dG's is blackened and carefully finished. Despite the power necessary to drive the dual display and the instantaneous rotations of the micro-segments, the caliber boasts a power reserve of approximately 35 hours, which is displayed via a hand across a 90° arc on the back of the movement and visible through a curved sapphire crystal revealing the brand's iconic scrolls. To complete such a mechanical masterpiece, one can easily imagine the vast amounts of patience and ingenuity de GRISOGONO must have had to apply. The long, intensive effort is touched with a grain of madness that makes every creation from the brand an immediately recognizable—and exclusive—object. The limited edition of just 177 numbered pieces is now available in de GRISOGONO's 16 boutiques and those of the brand's retail partners.

FACING PAGE
The Meccanico dG in rose gold and rubber is a sport-chic timepiece with an imposing size that opens up a new dimension in haute horology.

THIS PAGE
The emblematic scrolls of de GRISOGONO adorn the movement of the Meccanico dG, one of the most complex movements available.

de GRISOGONO
through the years...

1993   Fawaz Gruosi opens his first store at 104 rue du Rhône in Geneva. He calls it de GRISOGONO and specializes in the creation of jewels and the sale of objets d'art.

2000   de GRISOGONO presents its first watch collection, Instrumento Nº Uno, at the Basel Fair. It is the first watch company to use galuchat for its straps, and the only to offer a movement in blackened steel.

2001   Gruosi launches his second line: Instrumentino, a feminine version of the Instrumento.

2002   The brand creates Instrumento Doppio, a complicated watch that boasts the unusual combination of two dials and just one movement.

2003   de GRISOGONO releases two new watches, Instrumento Doppio Tre with a third time zone and Instrumento Tondo.

2004 The brand raises the veil on three new models: Instrumentino Steel & Diamonds, Instrumento Chrono, and Lipstick.

2005 de GRISOGONO launches the Instrumento Grande, the Power Breaker, and the complicated Occhio Ripetizione Minuti. Equipped with a 12-shutter diaphragm that opens to show the movement as the time sounds and then closes afterwards, this extremely limited edition (only 50 examples were made) met with immediate success.

2006 The brand presents four new watches: the Instrumento Grande Open Date, the Uno Grande Seconde, the complicated FG One, and the Be Eight.

2007 The Instrumento Novantatre and the Piccolina are added to de GRISOGONO's collections. The company moves into a new, larger watchmaking workshop with room for high-performance machinery.

2008 The Meccanico dG arrives on the scene and the brand also presents the Boule Watch, a combination of Gruosi's jewelry and horological savoir-faire.

2009 The Genevan house releases its 22nd watch collection: Fuso Quadrato, which boasts a diaphragm with 12 titanium shutters and a dual time zone. Meccanico dG wins the Public Prize at the Grand Prix d'Horlogerie de Genève.

FACING PAGE

LEFT   Instrumento N° Uno is an iconic watch that marked de GRISOGONO's entry into the watch world in 2000. Shown here is the Instrumento Doppio Tre version, released in 2003.

RIGHT   Shown in steel and diamonds, the Instrumentino (the feminine version of the very first timepiece from de GRISOGONO) was re-released in 2009 with glamorous updated style.

THIS PAGE

TOP   Presented in 2004, the Lipstick unites in one piece the brand's jewelry and horological expertise.

BOTTOM   Unveiled in 2005, the unusual mechanism of the Ripetizione Minuti delighted the universe of haute horology. Produced in a limited edition, the watch was reissued in 2009 with a sparkling case set with baguette diamonds.

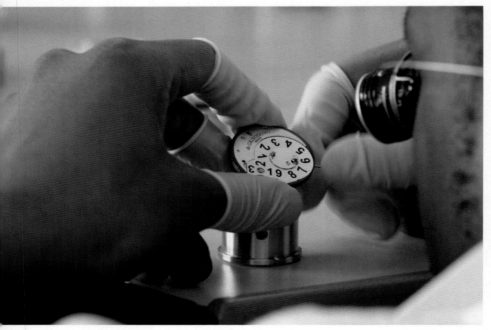

THIS PAGE
Every de GRISOGONO timepiece is the collaborative fruit of the research and development team and in-house assembly workshop.

FACING PAGE
The Fuso Quadrato is more evidence of Gruosi's creative energy. The diaphragm system was reinterpreted to reveal a completely innovative display of the second time-zone function.

BEHIND THE SCENES AT de GRISOGONO

The house reached an important turning point in its history when it acquired an horological workshop just a few hundred meters from its headquarters at Plan-les-Ouates, not far from Geneva. Since 2007, the workshop has been housed in a space of 850 square meters. Here, throughout three luminous, refined floors, a six-person department of research and development advances the company's many innovations. Thanks to the research conducted by these engineers and watchmakers, de GRISOGONO has many patents, notably one relating to two analog displays on opposite sides, and one for a large date-display device. Though the company does not yet create its own movements, it excels in creating additional modules. Its work is also distinguished by the PVD-blackening of each movement. Thanks to the acquisition of new digital machines three years ago, the atelier created a new unit devoted to the finishing of small series and prototypes, with the objective of improving its reactivity and taking one more step towards the complete in-house production of watches—a dazzling evolution for this brand, which in just ten years has made an enviable place for itself in the universe of haute horology.

DIOR HORLOGERIE

OR THE HERITAGE OF THE ART OF HAUTE COUTURE

Designed in the Avenue Montaigne studios, the Dior Christal, La D de Dior And Chiffre Rouge timepieces are continually reinventing and reviving the same **spirit of creativity, excellence and exceptionalness** that has animated the fashion house since 1947.

Time is precious in an Haute Couture house. The closer it gets to the day of the show, the more every second counts, the more every idea fuses together. And the more the seamstresses are seen making miracles—cutting, draping, sewing, embroidering and embellishing the most exceptional dresses imaginable. For Christian Dior in Paris, all the floors at 30 Avenue Montaigne live in step with the exciting and bustling rhythm of the design studio. Time is precious. In the real and in the figurative sense, since this house now creates haute horlogerie in the same spirit of creativity, excellence and exceptionalness that animates the elaboration of an haute couture dress. Dior Haute Horlogerie is in a permanent state of creation. The house's artistic directors are given free rein of their imaginations, making sketches and expressing their desires. Then, they pass the baton to expert Swiss watchmakers who translate their ideas into terms of feasibility.

In 2001, Dior set up its own production unit at Chaux-de-Fonds, the legendary cradle of all that is finest in

Swiss timekeeping. Two years later, these workshops, including a team of watchmaking craftsman and development experts, proved their capacity to combine creation, tradition and innovation with the development of the La D de Dior. Victoire de Castellane had dreamed of a watch with a dual personality. On the one hand, she imagined a classic, almost masculine design in sparse, 1970s-inspired lines; on the other hand, a more vivacious style created by precious stones in seductive colors in the same mode as the high jewelry she designs for the House of Dior. The following year, the watchmaking workshops at Chaux-de-Fonds set their time to the radical chic of Dior Homme. This was another universe with a whole other story, yet here again designers and technicians knew how to team their talents and know-how, producing the Chiffre Rouge timepiece that attracted the admiration of connoisseurs as soon as it was launched. Finally in 2005, another challenge, another innovation: John Galliano sought to transpose the ultra-femininity of his designs into the world of watchmaking.

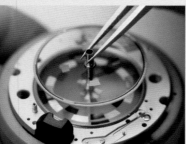

The floors at 30 Avenue Montaigne live in step with the exciting and bustling rhythm of the design studio.

Famous for his fondness for fashion twists, the designer now launched a new take on sapphire crystal, the traditional material for a watch's glass, by using it to inlay the bezel and bracelet with inserts and pyramids. From the very outset, the couture allure of the Dior Christal wristwatch compelled recognition.

In 2008, its preciousness was accentuated even further with the launch of the Dior Christal Tourbillon fitted with one of the greatest watchmaking movements and enhanced by the unusual transparent design of the mechanism.

DIOR IN TIME:
WITH THE GREAT WATCHMAKERS

Watchmaking innovation and savoir-faire in the service of creation and new ideas: in fact, it took Dior very little time to propose timepieces that renew traditional watchmaking. It's a question of style…and of haute couture as well as an haute horlogerie mindset, since both of these domains devoted to exceptional craftsmanship have more than one thing in common. As the show draws closer, the seamstresses of a fashion house can neither do nor know how to do absolutely everything, so Dior turns to outside specialized artisans for the feather work or the making of lace and embroidery. In the same way, when a designer imagines a watch requiring a specific technology, mechanism or effect not within the competence of the workshops at Chaux-de-Fonds, Dior Horlogerie never hesitates to call upon specialists' talents. This was notably the case last year for the launch of the Dior Christal "mystérieuse." John Galliano

had wanted a completely transparent movement. This technology existed for clocks but not for wristwatches. At least, not until the Quinting manufacture proposed an electro-mechanical solution that met the challenge made by the House of Dior's designer.

Time is stimulating and precious in all its forms of creation, yet paradoxically these are crafts that never count the hours it takes to achieve the sublime. Beautiful workmanship, exquisite embellishment and meticulous festooning or paving are all extremely important details. Therefore, Dior Horlogerie turned to the Maison Bunter in Geneva, recognized by the entire profession for the precious stone settings of its haute horlogerie. For the mechanisms, it called upon another choice partner, the Zenith manufacture, for the making of the "irreducible" movement in the Chiffre rouge limited series, for its hand-wound elite movement in the 42mm La D de Dior timepiece, as well as for the automatic version of the Dior Christal Diamonds. For the development of its tourbillon caliber, Dior also teamed up with the conceiver of the Concepto movement.

All these mechanical feats perfectly illustrate the spirit of haute horlogerie inhabiting these treasures of precision that push back the boundaries of the impossible again and again. This is also the spirit of haute couture, a spirit constantly questioning itself, never hesitating to break with habit while tirelessly aiming for perfection.

FACING PAGE
TOP   Dior Christal Tourbillon Rubis

THIS PAGE
TOP CENTER   Dior Christal "Serti neige"

BOTTOM   Chiffre Rouge I02

DIOR CHRISTAL TOURBILLON   REF. CD115962M001

Movement: manual-winding DIOR tourbillon calibre; 80-hour power reserve.
Functions: hours, minutes.
Case: 18K white gold; Ø 42mm; bezel set with 54 baguette diamonds (3.62 carats) and 18 baguette rubies (1.35 carats); crown set with a rose-cut diamond (0.34 carat); water resistant to 5atm.
Dial: red-mineral glass set with 43 baguette diamonds (0.96 carat).

Bracelet: 18K white gold set with 116 baguette diamonds (28.5 carats) and 48 baguette rubies (6.7 carats).
Note: one-of-a-kind piece.

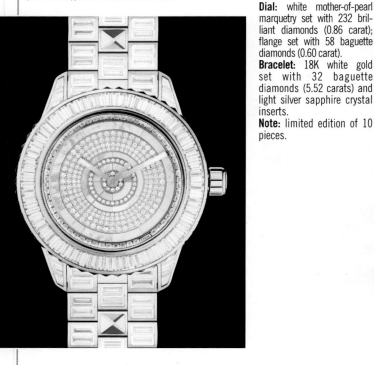

DIOR CHRISTAL TOURBILLON   REF. CD115961A001

Movement: manual-winding DIOR tourbillon calibre; 80-hour power reserve.
Functions: hours, minutes.
Case: 18K white gold; Ø 42mm; bezel set with 25 baguette diamonds (1.68 carats) and 7 black sapphire crystal inserts; crown set with a rose-cut diamond (0.34 carat); water resistant to 5atm.
Dial: transparent shaded-gray sapphire crystal set with 43 baguette diamonds (0.96 carat).
Strap: hand-made double-sided alligator; ardillon buckle set with 13 baguette diamonds (1 carat).
Note: limited edition of 15 pieces.

DIOR CHRISTAL BAGUETTE DIAMONDS   REF. CD114561M001

Movement: automatic movement Elite calibre by Zenith for DIOR; oscillating weight inlaid with mother-of-pearl insert; 50-hour power reserve.
Functions: hours, minutes, seconds.
Case: 18K white gold; Ø 38mm; bezel set with 79 baguette diamonds (3.09 carats); horns set with 12 baguette diamonds (1.10 carats); crown set with a rose-cut diamond (0.34 carat); water resistant to 5atm.

Dial: white mother-of-pearl marquetry set with 232 brilliant diamonds (0.86 carat); flange set with 58 baguette diamonds (0.60 carat).
Bracelet: 18K white gold set with 32 baguette diamonds (5.52 carats) and light silver sapphire crystal inserts.
Note: limited edition of 10 pieces.

DIOR CHRISTAL MYSTERIEUSE   REF. CD116411M001

Movement: electromechanical movement by Quinting Manufacture for DIOR.
Functions: hours, minutes.
Case: stainless steel; Ø 44mm; set with 52 diamonds (0.91 carat) and 11 black sapphire crystal inserts.
Dial: six plates decorated with white & Tahiti mother-of-pearl inserts and black & golden metallization; one plate set with 28 diamonds (0.42 carat).

Bracelet: stainless steel set with pyramid-cut black sapphire crystal inserts.
Note: limited edition of 100 pieces.

DIOR CHRISTAL RED   REF. CD11311HM001

Movement: ETA Swiss quartz.
Functions: hours, minutes, seconds; date.
Case: stainless steel; Ø 33mm; set with 97 diamonds (0.58 carat) and red sapphire crystal inserts; water resistant to 5atm.
Dial: red lacquered set with 16 diamond indexes (0.08 carat).
Bracelet: stainless steel set with pyramid-cut red sapphire crystal inserts.

DIOR CHRISTAL AUTOMATIC BLACK   REF. CD113513M001

Movement: ETA Swiss automatic; 40-hour power reserve.
Functions: hours, minutes, seconds; date.
Case: stainless steel; Ø 33mm; case set with 172 diamonds (1.35 carats); bezel set with 80 diamonds (1 carat) and 16 black sapphire crystal inserts; water resistant to 5atm.
Dial: black lacquered and silver set with 97 diamonds (0.39 carat).
Bracelet: stainless steel set with pyramid-cut black sapphire crystal inserts.

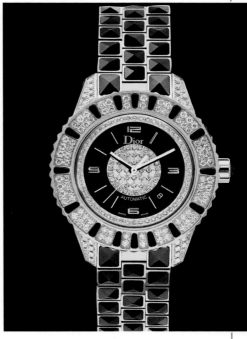

DIOR CHRISTAL PINK GOLD   REF. CD114370R001

Movement: ETA Swiss quartz.
Functions: hours, minutes, seconds; date; chronograph.
Case: 18K pink gold; Ø 38mm; set with 76 diamonds (1.14 carats) and white sapphire crystal inserts; water resistant to 5atm.
Dial: white lacquered.
Strap: white genuine rubber set with one row of white sapphire crystal inserts.

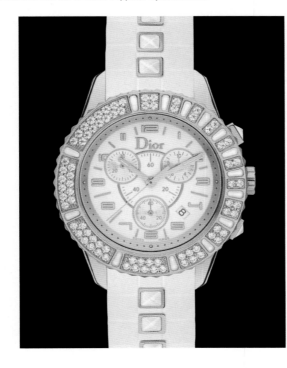

DIOR CHRISTAL AUTOMATIC BLACK   REF. CD115510M01

Movement: ETA Swiss automatic; 42-hour power reserve.
Functions: hours, minutes, seconds; date.
Case: stainless steel; Ø 42mm; set with black sapphire crystal inserts.
Dial: black lacquered.
Bracelet: stainless steel set with pyramid-cut black sapphire crystal inserts.

LA D DE DIOR "SNOW SET" DIAMONDS REF. CD045960A001

Movement: manual-winding movement Elite calibre by Zenith; 50-hour power reserve.
Functions: hours, minutes.
Case: 18K white gold; Ø 42mm; bezel set with 72 diamonds (1.08 carats); crown set with 19 diamonds (0.19 carat); water resistant to 3atm.
Dial: 18K white gold set with 330 diamonds (3.54 carats).
Strap: black genuine satin; 18K white gold ardillon buckle set with 60 diamonds (0.53 carat).

LA D DE DIOR MITZA REF. CD043154A001

Movement: ETA Swiss quartz.
Functions: hours, minutes.
Case: 18K yellow gold; Ø 38mm; bezel set with 72 yellow sapphires (0.65 carat); water resistant to 3atm.
Dial: golden and black lacquered set with 184 yellow sapphires (0.81 carat).
Strap: shiny black alligator.

LA D DE DIOR REF. CD043111M001

Movement: ETA Swiss quartz.
Functions: hours, minutes.
Case: stainless steel; Ø 38mm; bezel set with 72 diamonds (0.65 carat); water resistant to 3atm.
Dial: silver sun-brushed.
Bracelet: stainless steel.

LA MINI D DE DIOR REF. CD040150A001

Movement: ETA Swiss quartz.
Functions: hours, minutes.
Case: 18K yellow gold; Ø 19mm; bezel set with 40 diamonds (0.32 carat); crown set with 13 diamonds (0.03 carat); water resistant to 3atm.
Dial: white mother-of-pearl.
Strap: black satin.

CHIFFRE ROUGE I03   REF. CD084850M001

Movement: automatic chronograph chronometer calibre Irreductible by Zenith for DIOR; COSC certified; oscillating weight in sapphire crystal and gold; 50-hour power reserve.
Functions: hours, minutes, seconds; date; chronograph.
Case: 18K yellow gold; Ø 38mm; set with 25 diamonds (0.31 carat); transparent sapphire crystal caseback; water resistant to 5atm.
Dial: golden set with 4 princess diamonds (0.06 carat).
Bracelet: 18K yellow gold.
Note: limited edition of 15 pieces.

CHIFFRE ROUGE I02   REF. CD084860M001

Movement: automatic chronograph chronometer calibre Irreductible by Zenith for DIOR; COSC certified; 50-hour power reserve.
Functions: hours, minutes, seconds; date; chronograph.
Case: 18K white gold; Ø 38mm; set with 27 diamonds (0.24 carat); milk-white tinted sapphire crystal caseback; water resistant to 5atm.
Dial: white lacquered set with 4 baguette diamonds (0.12 carat).
Bracelet: 18K white gold.
Note: limited edition of 30 pieces.

CHIFFRE ROUGE D02   REF. CD085540R001

Movement: ETA Swiss automatic; 42-hour power reserve.
Functions: hours, minutes, seconds; date.
Case: stainless steel; Ø 42mm; molded with black rubber; crown protecting arm and unlocked by caseback; screw-in crown; translucent red sapphire crystal caseback; water resistant to 30atm.
Dial: black sun-brushed.
Bracelet: stainless steel molded with black rubber.

CHIFFRE ROUGE A03   REF. CD084510M001

Movement: ETA Swiss automatic; 42-hour power reserve.
Functions: hours, minutes, seconds; date.
Case: stainless steel; Ø 36mm; black tinted sapphire crystal caseback; water resistant to 5atm.
Dial: black sun-brushed.
Bracelet: stainless steel.

EBEL
THE ARCHITECTS OF TIME

Ebel watches epitomize architectural ideals, employing sculptural curves, balanced proportions and fine craftsmanship to create timeless designs prized by an international following. As Ebel approaches its centenary, it's clear that a distinctive vision of refined elegance and sensual luxury has served the company well.

In fact, one of the most popular creations to emerge recently from Ebel's La Chaux-de-Fonds workshop harkens back to 1912, when the company issued its very first timepiece. The spirit of that barrel-shaped debut lives on today in the Beluga Tonneau.

Introduced in 2002, its voluptuous case tapers gradually as it stretches out toward the matching triple-row bracelet. The center links are smooth, like pebbles polished by the currents of a racing stream. That organic shape stands out against the geometric pieces on either side, producing an appealing visual contradiction.

A graduated procession of diamonds travels vertically from lug to lug, accentuating the case's generous arc. That glittering outline resonates on the dial, where diamonds are also used for the watch's hour-markers.

The Beluga Tonneau is offered in two sizes, both available exclusively with diamond-set cases. The 26.8mm version is dressed in either stainless steel or yellow gold with a mother-of-pearl dial. For women who prefer a watch with a larger profile, the 31.4mm version comes exclusively in stainless steel with a dial that is either silver or white mother-of-pearl with a guilloché center.

The Tonneau follows the breakthrough success of the original Beluga. Launched in 1985 with a round case, it quickly became one of the company's signature pieces. Today, Ebel offers the Beluga in two sizes, 26mm and 30.5mm, both available exclusively with diamond-set cases crafted in either yellow gold or stainless steel.

Ebel watches transcend utility to the level of **time-less artistry.**

Ebel added a vibrant twist to its stylish two-tone models last year by introducing 5N red gold to the Brasilia Mini collection.

The precious metal's warm glow plays a prominent role on the mother-of-pearl dial, where it's used for: the hour and minute hands; the Roman 12 and 6; the EBEL logo; and the ten diamond hour-markers' settings. The radiant red gold punctuates the Brasilia Mini's stainless steel bracelet, interspersed between the H-shaped links.

Used for the recessed crown, red gold also enhances the elegance of the sleek, stainless steel case, which features a row of 17 brilliant-cut diamonds on both the left and right sides.

Along with the aforementioned quartz models, Ebel also makes a mechanical timepiece for women, satisfying their desires for distinctive design and technical excellence.

The Ebel Classic's brushed stainless steel case is outfitted with an ETA 2000-1 automatic movement with a date function displayed at 3:00 on the white mother-of-pearl dial. There, 11 diamonds set in 5N red gold are used for the hour-markers. The rich combination is repeated on the red-gold bezel, which is set with 42 white brilliants.

The bracelet's wave-pattern, introduced in 1977 with the Sport Classic, is one of the brand's most iconic designs. For the latest version of the Ebel Classic, the two-tone bracelet mixes stainless steel with red gold, adding a contemporary flourish to an ageless look.

With all its horological inventions, Ebel reveals an unyielding resolve to create watches that transcend mere utility and ascend to the level of timeless artistry.

FACING PAGE

FROM LEFT The Beluga's 30.5mm stainless steel case edges showcase progressive gem settings totaling 48 white brilliants. The stainless steel Beluga Tonneau (31.4mm) is featured with a white mother-of-pearl dial. Both models include diamond hour-markers and are water resistant to 5atm.

THIS PAGE

LEFT Ebel adds 5N red-gold touches to the Brasilia Mini collection, accenting the dial and bracelet. The diamond-set case houses a Swiss-made quartz movement.

RIGHT Highlighted with 5N red gold, the Ebel Classic is equipped with an ETA 2000-1 automatic movement that includes a date function.

EBEL CLASSIC AUTOMATIC LADY STEEL & 5N RED GOLD   REF. 1215928

Movement: Swiss automatic.
Functions: hours, minutes; date at 3; sweep seconds hand.
Case: stainless steel and 18K 750 5N red gold; 42 brilliant-cut VVS-IF Top Wesselton diamonds (0.34 carat); sapphire crystal with antireflective treatment on both sides; water resistant to 5atm.
Dial: white mother-of-pearl; 11 diamond markers.

Bracelet: stainless steel and 18K 750 5N red gold; brushed finish.
Suggested price: $6,950

EBEL BRASILIA MINI STEEL & 5N RED GOLD   REF. 1215922

Movement: Swiss quartz.
Functions: hours, minutes.
Case: stainless steel and 18K 750 5N red gold; full-polished finish; 34 brilliant-cut VVS-IF Top Wesselton diamonds (0.54 carat); sapphire crystal with antireflective treatment on both sides; water resistant to 5atm.
Dial: white mother-of-pearl; 10 diamond markers; hand-applied Roman numerals.

Bracelet: stainless steel and 18K 750 5N red gold; polished gold cap for the five central links and the head piece; alternating brushed/polished finish.
Suggested price: $5,990

EBEL BELUGA ROUND LADY   REF. 1215874

Movement: Swiss quartz.
Functions: hours, minutes.
Case: 18K 750 yellow gold; 48 VVS-IF Top Wesselton diamonds (6 different diameters for a total of 0.62 carat); sapphire crystal with antireflective treatment on both sides; water resistant to 5atm.
Dial: mother-of-pearl; 12 diamond markers.

Bracelet: 18K 750 yellow gold; polished finish.
Suggested price: $22,900

EBEL BELUGA TONNEAU LADY   REF. 1215924

Movement: Swiss quartz.
Functions: hours, minutes.
Case: stainless steel; full-polished finish; 44 brilliant-cut VVS-IF Top Wesselton diamonds (6 different diameters for a total of 0.59 carat); sapphire crystal with antireflective treatment on both sides; water resistant to 5atm.
Dial: white mother-of-pearl; 13 diamond markers; gadroon-decorated hands.

Bracelet: stainless steel; polished finish.
Suggested price: $6,450

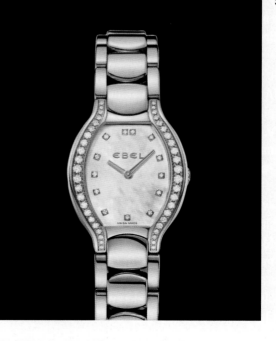

EBEL CLASSIC HEXAGON CHRONOGRAPH   REF. 1215931

Movement: Swiss automatic chronograph movement (Dubois-Dépraz 4500).
Functions: hours, minutes, seconds; big date at 12; chronograph function with two subdials at 3 and 9; total 12-hour counter with window opening at 6.
Case: monohull case; stainless steel; alternating brushed/polished finish; push-buttons; sapphire crystal with antireflective treatment on both sides; water resistant to 5atm.
Dial: silver-colored; double-layered; "Clous de Paris" decorated counters; facetted diamond-polished hands; 12 hand-applied hour-markers; painted EBEL logo.
Strap: hand-stitched brown alligator leather; EBEL folding clasp.
Suggested price: $5,450

EBEL CLASSIC HEXAGON DAY, RETROGRADE DATE, POWER RESERVE   REF. 1215835

Movement: Swiss automatic (SOPROD 9094).
Functions: hours, minutes, seconds; day-date calendar; power reserve.
Case: 18K 750 4N rose gold; alternating brushed/polished finishing; sapphire crystal with antireflective treatment on both sides; water resistant to 5atm.
Dial: silver-colored; galvanic; retrograde date indicator at 3; power-reserve indicator with "Clous de Paris" pattern at 6; hand-applied day counter with "Clous de Paris" pattern at 9; facetted diamond-polished hands; 12 hand-applied hour-markers; hand-applied EBEL logo.
Strap: hand-stitched brown alligator leather; EBEL pin buckle.
Suggested price: $16,900

EBEL 1911 DISCOVERY   REF. 1215794

Movement: Valjoux 7750 — Day-Date, Swiss automatic chronograph movement; COSC-certified chronometer.
Functions: hours, minutes, seconds; day-date at 3; chronograph functions with subdial indicators at 12, 6 and 9; tachymeter scale on the outside bezel in black.
Case: stainless steel; alternating brushed/polished finish; tachymeter on aluminum bezel ring; dedicated screwed in crown and pushers; sapphire crystal with antireflective treatment on both sides; water resistant to 10atm.
Dial: black; galvanic finishing; hand-applied hour-markers and applied counters; Super-LumiNova on flange (dots) and hands; dedicated hands with color contrast.
Bracelet: stainless steel; alternating brushed/polished finish; EBEL folding clasp.
Suggested price: $4,500

EBEL 1911 BTR 137   REF. 1215863

Movement: Swiss EBEL automatic chronograph caliber 137; COSC-certified chronometer.
Functions: hours, minutes, seconds; date at 4; chronograph functions with subdial indicators at 3, 6 and 9; tachymeter scale on the flange.
Case: stainless steel; alternating brushed/polished finish; dedicated screwed in crown and pushers; sapphire crystal with antireflective treatment on both sides; sapphire crystal caseback; water resistant to 10atm.
Dial: black; hand-applied hour-markers; SuperLumiNova on the hour-markers and hands.
Strap: black alligator leather; white hand stitching; EBEL folding clasp.
Suggested price: $6,950

ETERNA

Nothing but Watchmaking.
Since 1856.

For over a century and a half, Eterna has been known for its exceptional technical expertise, as well as its innovative designs that enhance the appeal of the movements within. The brand's history, which started in 1856, has been littered with breakthroughs—including a rotor system mounted on ball bearings, which revolutionized watchmaking in the 20th century. The brand continues to experiment and triumph, leaving no doubt as to its prominent place in the industry.

Eterna has come as close as any manufacture could to resolving a major sticking point (no pun intended) for the design of mechanical watches. Instead of requiring lubricating oil, Eterna's Spherodrive movement uses zirconium oxide ball bearings for the spring barrel, a major innovation.

This original solution is well served by its placement in the Madison Three-Hands, an elegant piece of business housed in a stainless steel case and featuring a black sunray-brushed dial. The compelling simplicity of the watch's aesthetic makes an ideal stage for showing off technical achievements—an opening at 6:00 proudly displays the ball bearings.

The Madison Three-Hands' dial makes a special point of revealing the miniature ball bearings with which Eterna's manufacture has revolutionized watch construction.

THE ETERNA SPHERODRIVE is by no means the first time Eterna has broken ground with its use of ball bearings. In 1948, the company developed a ball bearing-mounted low-friction rotor system for automatic movements and dubbed it the "Eterna · Matic." The brand is enjoying a 60-year history of pioneering the latest and greatest in ball-bearing technology…who knows what mutations of the Eterna DNA could follow?

Twenty years of simulated aging in Eterna's laboratories resulted in very little wear on the Eterna Spherodrive mechanism.

With the vast majority of watches, the issue of friction between the arbor and the spring barrel is resolved with a drop of lubricating oil, but even with this palliative, the two pieces wear on each other over time, resulting in a less efficient, less accurate, shorter-lived spring barrel. Eterna, however, has revolutionized this aspect of watchmaking, pioneering the use of ultra-precise miniature ball bearings for mounting the spring barrel. This system extends the life of the spring barrel, as the rolling movement mitigates the pressures of the watch's internal workings. Twenty years of simulated aging in Eterna's laboratories resulted in very little wear on the mechanism.

Mature elegance dominates the Vaughan Big Date: the convex dial is shaped to fit snugly above the lens-shaped movement, allowing for extremely smooth contours when it comes to the case; the movement within is the flattest movement to ever power a big date function. The minimalist hour indexes, barely-there minute markings, and classical dauphine hands combine to create an impression of hyper-refined sensuality. The date function switches over at midnight in under a second, and unlike more conventional date displays, the Vaughan Big Date allows the wearer to adjust both time and date over 24 hours.

Eterna's watchmakers have gone to the bleeding edge of horological technology, completely reworking the Eterna 1504 caliber and using a photolithographic process for creating the main components of the movement. This technology allowed the expert watchmakers to create with pinpoint accuracy the complex components responsible for key functions, in extremely hard nickel or phosphor alloys. Using these materials makes for a very long-lived watch. The watchmakers combine this daring technology with the historical horological arts; the rotor shimmers with the Côtes de Genève pattern.

TOP   Eterna's 3505 movement obviates the need for lubrication by using virtually maintenance-free zirconium oxide ball bearings.

BOTTOM   The Vaughan Big Date epitomizes the savoir-faire of Eterna's manufacture, with the clean, harmonious lines of its case housing an extremely flat, large date movement, the Eterna 3030.

RIGHT The streamlined stainless steel Contessa case recalls elegant Art Deco design.

BELOW Every Contessa watch is set with a 0.06-carat diamond in the crown for a touch of discreet glamour.

BOTTOM RIGHT The diamond-set Contessa model in stainless steel comes with an elegant white lizard strap.

The Contessa picks up Eterna's proud 80-year-old feminine tradition and runs with it. The rectangular stainless steel case is nuanced with subtle slopes and the crosspieces on the top and back of the case are chamfered. The luxurious finishing on the diagonal band bars recalls the refined yet opulent aesthetic of the Art Deco movement. This new model is available with a choice of white dial—one with rhodanized indexes or one with a sunray pattern with rhodanized Roman numerals—on a polished stainless steel bracelet, a white or light brown lizard leather strap, or a dark brown alligator leather strap. Art Deco influences the bracelet design as well.

Believing that every woman is worthy of a precious gem, Eterna graces each Contessa with a 0.06-carat Top Wesselton VVS diamond, bringing a new note of subtle luxury to the piece. Still luxurious but less subtle are the versions with diamond-adorned bezels—46 diamonds in all—and mother-of-pearl dials, which can be paired with 12 diamond indexes. The 18-karat rose-gold version of the Contessa comes with two quickly interchangeable straps: a dark brown alligator leather strap, and a white stingray strap for special occasions.

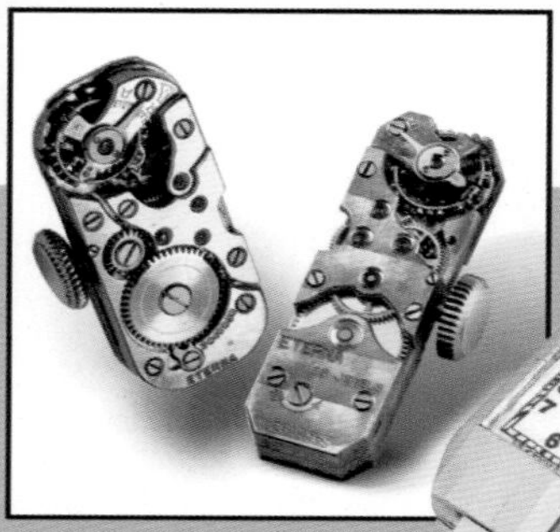

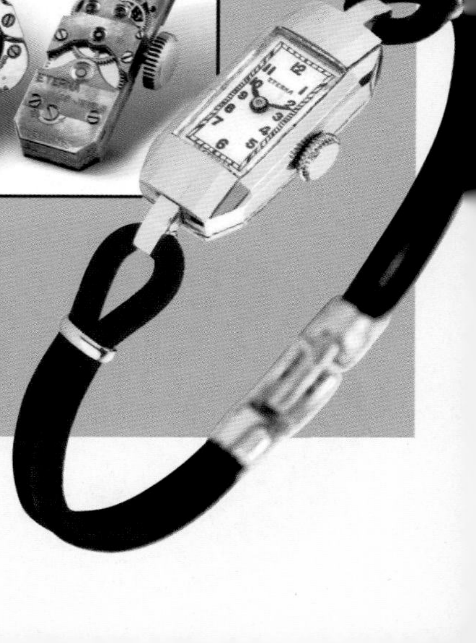

BACK IN THE 1930s, when women's watches were universally teeny tiny, Eterna jumped to the head of the pack with the world's smallest baguette-shaped movement, allowing its designers that much more space to express their creativity.

In 1950, Eterna produced a world's first with its smallest self-winding movement ever, seducing seductresses such as Gina Lollobrigida and Brigitte Bardot.

In 1947, Norwegian explorer Thor Heyerdahl sailed from South America to the Polynesian Islands on a simple raft named the Kon-Tiki, built only with the materials and technology that would have been available to the inhabitants of pre-Columbian America. The stalwart Scandinavians wore Eterna watches over the entire two-month journey, and the hardy timepieces kept perfect time throughout.

The KonTiki line was named in honor of this epic voyage, and its rugged sports aesthetic continues the homage. The face of the KonTiki has been totally revamped for the new KonTiki Date—the dial, available in either black or white, limns an outline of Raroia, the atoll in French Polynesia where Heyerdahl's craft eventually alit. The KonTiki Date's dial also features a very subtle aperture for the date at 4:30. The bold design of the dial, with its reliance on straightforward triangles and rectangular bars, also shows up in the KonTiki Four-Hands (the fourth hand is for the date), its XXL version and the KonTiki Chronograph.

The distinctive contours of Eterna's personality shine through every collection it creates. From the rugged style and history of the KonTiki line, to the understated glamour of the Contessa and clean, classic elegance of the Madison and Vaughan collection, Eterna operates with a sublime confidence that comes from over 150 years of being a leader in the industry. Behind the daring aesthetic lies (sometimes literally) the dazzling horological mastery and innovation that has ensured Eterna's continued success in three centuries.

TOP   In 1947, Thor Heyerdahl set sail on his Kon-Tiki raft, which inspired Eterna's KonTiki line, to research the possibility that French Polynesia had been settled by migrants from pre-Columbian South America.

CENTER   The Eterna KonTiki Date's flat dial and lack of a dial ring lend a modern tone to the timepiece and make its face appear larger.

LEFT   The dial of the KonTiki Date features a depiction of Raroia, where the original Kon-Tiki landed.

229

The Cobra Chronograph Large Date Automatic is presented on a rubber strap that mimics the look of the scales found on a snake's underside.

The flowing lines that characterize Franc Vila's timepieces interlace to form a round bezel atop an ellipse-shaped case, a figure that is elegantly incongruent and remarkably fresh. That daring silhouette—executed in a range of materials—plays host to a growing number of highly evolved movements.

Now entering its fifth year, the company skillfully combines contemporary style with traditional watchmaking acumen in a pair of limited edition chronographs that capture Franc Vila's unique spirit.

The Cobra Chronograph Large Date Automatic is first, a brawny timepiece that is water resistant to 300 meters (984 feet). A balance of strength and sophistication, the case and bezel mix carbon fiber with red gold or DieHard Extreme Steel.

The carbon fiber's crosshatch pattern extends to the dial, where the chronograph's subsidiary minute and hour dials are positioned at 6:00 and 9:00 respectively. The button located at 2:00 on the side of the case stops and starts the chronograph, while a second pusher at 4:00 resets the timer. These red-gold buttons are located on opposite sides of the watch's sizeable crown, an arrangement that makes the case subtly larger than other Franc Vila models.

A transparent curved sapphire crystal is used for the caseback, revealing the traditional hand-wrought decoration that adorns the automatic movement (FV8Ch). Fixed to a central arbor, the watchmaker's exclusive "gold concept rotor" spins when the watch is worn, replenishing the caliber's 42-hour power reserve.

Franc Vila will produce only 88 pieces of the Cobra Chronograph Large Date Automatic.

The second standout chronograph model presented by the watchmaker is the Cuarto Tourbillon Chronograph SuperLigero Concept. It expands on the innovations introduced in 2008's SuperLigero model, which featured a movement made with Lightnium. First used in aerospace applications, this aluminum-lithium alloy provides an inimitable mix of strength and lightness perfectly suited for manufacturing watch movements.

In addition to using that innovative material, the Cuarto Tourbillon Chronograph SuperLigero Concept also adapts the latest advances in nanotechnology. The watch's bridges are inspired by the molecular structure of graphene, a newly discovered material that is substantially less dense than steel, yet stronger by a factor of 10. In fact, it is the only known material able to support its own weight infinitely.

"I wanted to take what we achieved with Lightnium and go a step further," says Franc Vila, the company's founder. "I was able to translate graphene's hexagonal atomic structure to create a tourbillon that is extremely shock resistant."

More than an experiment in chemical engineering, the Cuarto Tourbillon Chronograph SuperLigero Concept is a showcase for haute horlogerie expertise. Adding an unusual technical twist, the mechanism that controls the column-wheel monopusher chronograph is visible from the skeletonized dial. The chronograph's atypical construction allows the wearer to watch the machinations unfold when the button on the caseband is pressed.

In keeping with the watchmaker's dedication to exclusivity, Franc Vila will produce only eight of these prized timekeepers.

The rarity of his watches, Vila says, is a natural result of his passion for technical perfection. "I focus on watches that reflect my uncompromising standards for quality and convey a strong visual personality that respects the past, but lives in the present," he says. "The exclusivity comes because I'm adamant about excellence."

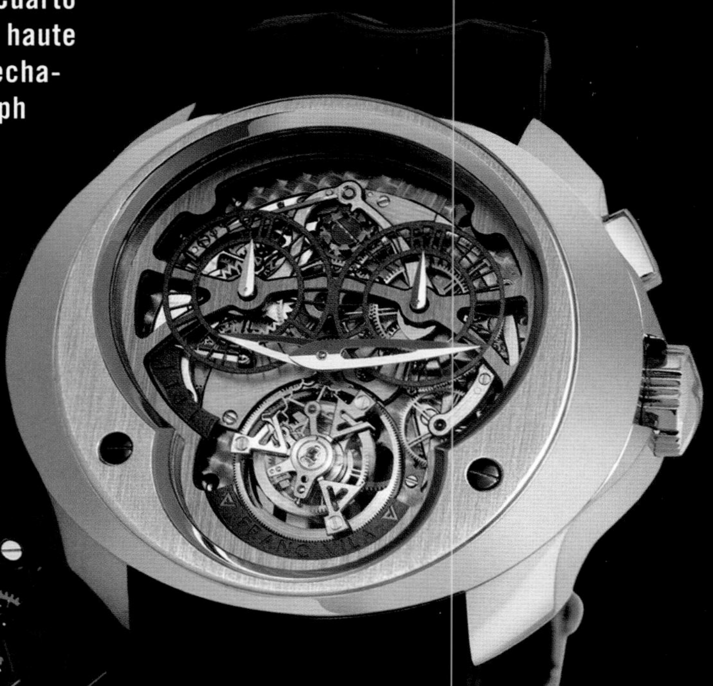

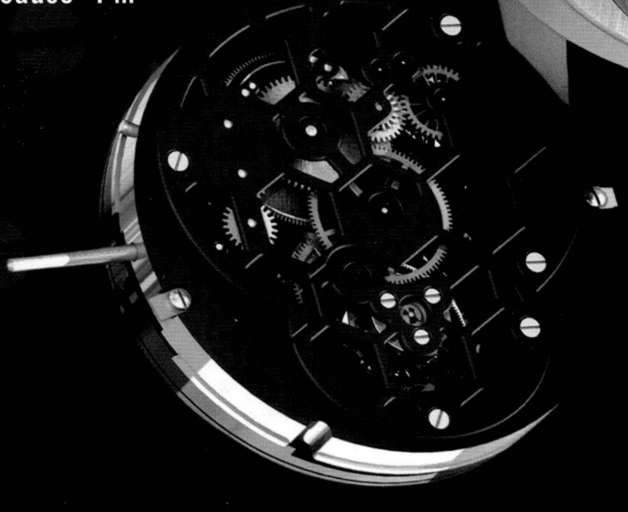

FV EVOS 8 "COBRA" CHRONOGRAPH LARGE DATE AUTOMATIC

Movement: high-grade, mechanical automatic, hand-finished complicated caliber FRANC VILA 8Ch; exclusive "gold concept rotor"; 42-hour power reserve.
Functions: hours, minutes, seconds; large date via central windows; chronograph start/stop pusher at 2, reset pusher at 4, minutes at 6, hours at 9.
Case: red gold and carbon fiber; "Esprit Unique" shape with elliptic and circular bezel; sapphire crystal and caseback with double-sided antireflective treatment; water resistant to 30atm.
Dial: carbon fiber and guilloché.
Strap: comes with both crocodile and black rubber strap with red-gold deployant clasp.
Suggested price: $58,000
Note: limited edition of 88 pieces.
Also available: bezel in DHES or red gold and carbon fiber; case in DHES; red gold; titanium.

FVA8.1QA QUANTIÈME ANNUAL GRAND DATE AUTOMATIC

Movement: high-grade, mechanical automatic, hand-finished complicated caliber FRANC VILA 8Qa; exclusive "gold concept rotor"; 42-hour power reserve.
Functions: hours, minutes, seconds; large date via central windows; month window and seconds indication in subsidiary dial at 6.
Case: titanium and red gold; "Esprit Unique" shape with elliptic and circular bezel; sapphire crystal and caseback with double-sided antireflective treatment; water resistant to 10atm.
Dial: blackened meteorite and sapphire decorated with brand's logos.
Strap: comes with both crocodile and black rubber strap with DieHard Extreme Steel deployant clasp.
Suggested price: $40,000
Note: limited edition of 88 pieces.
Also available: DHES; black DHES; red gold; white gold; titanium.

FVA15 COLUMN REGULATOR AUTOMATIC

Movement: high-grade, mechanical automatic, hand-finished complicated caliber FRANC VILA 15; exclusive "gold concept rotor"; 42-hour power reserve.
Functions: hours, minutes, seconds; date at 3.
Case: titanium; "Esprit Unique" shape with elliptic and circular bezel in DieHard Extreme Steel; sapphire crystal and caseback with double-sided antireflective treatment; water resistant to 10atm.
Dial: meteorite; mother-of-pearl and sapphire glass.
Strap: comes with both crocodile and black rubber sports strap with steel deployant clasp.
Suggested price: $19,000
Note: limited edition of 88 pieces.
Also available: case in DHES; black DHES; red gold; white gold; titanium.

FVA N° 6 TOURBILLON PLANÉTAIRE SKELETON SUPERLIGERO CONCEPT

Movement: mechanical manual-winding; flying tourbillon with inertial moment control system and wheel differential system; "Esprit Unique" shape, hand-made and decorated; bridge and plate made in blue Lightnium; 120-hour power reserve.
Functions: hours, minutes; power-reserve indicator at 9.
Case: black titanium; 24 rubies; "Esprit Unique" shape with elliptic and circular bezel; sapphire crystal and caseback with double-sided antireflective treatment; water resistant to 10atm.
Dial: sapphire with hours and minutes indications.
Strap: comes with both crocodile and black rubber strap.
Suggested price: $245,000
Note: ultra-limited edition of 8 pieces.
Also available: red or orange Lightnium details.

FVA N° CUATRO TOURBILLON CHRONOGRAPH SUPERLIGERO CONCEPT

Movement: caliber FRANC VILA N° Cuatro SuperLigero; flying tourbillon with inertial moment control system and wheel differential system; 262 components; chronograph monopushing function with dial-side column wheel directly coupled with tourbillon; "Esprit Unique" shape, hand-made and decorated; 120-hour power reserve.
Functions: hours, 30 minutes at 10, 60 seconds at 2; chronograph monopusher at 2; power-reserve indicator at 9.
Case: white gold; 33 rubies; "Esprit Unique" shape with elliptic and circular bezel; sapphire crystal and caseback with double-sided antireflective treatment.
Strap: comes with both crocodile and black rubber strap.
Suggested price: $355,000
Note: limited edition of 8 pieces.
Also available: DHES; black DHES; white gold; titanium.

FVA N° CUATRO TOURBILLON DIAL-SIDE COLUMN WHEEL MONOPUSHER CHRONOGRAPH

Movement: mechanical manual-winding caliber FRANC VILA N° Cuatro; 21,600 vph; flying tourbillon with inertial moment control system and wheel differential system; 262 components; chronograph monopushing function with dial-side column wheel directly coupled with tourbillon; "Esprit Unique" shape, hand-made and decorated 120-hour power reserve.
Functions: hours; monopusher chronograph seconds at 2, minutes at 10; power-reserve at 9.
Case: red gold; 32 rubies; "Esprit Unique" shape red-gold with elliptic and circular bezel; sapphire crystal and caseback with double-sided antireflective treatment; water resistant to 10atm.
Dial: sapphire with filet.
Strap: comes with both crocodile and rubber strap with red gold deployant clasp.
Suggested price: $325,000
Note: ultra-limited edition of 8 pieces.
Also available: DHES; black DHES; red gold; white gold; titanium.

FVA9 CHRONOGRAPH MASTER QUANTIÈME AUTOMATIC

Movement: high-grade, mechanical automatic, hand-finished complicated caliber FRANC VILA a9; exclusive "gold concept rotor"; 42-hour power reserve.
Functions: moonphase at 3; minutes and day of the week at 6; hours and month at 9; seconds and date at 12.
Case: titanium and red gold; "Esprit Unique" shape with elliptic and circular bezel; sapphire crystal and caseback with double-sided antireflective treatment; water resistant to 30atm.
Dial: carbon fiber and guilloché.
Strap: comes with both crocodile and rubber strap with DieHard Extreme Steel deployant clasp.
Suggested price: $38,000
Note: limited edition of 88 pieces.
Also available: DHES; black DHES; black DHES and red gold; titanium and DHES, red gold or white gold.

FVA11 CHRONOGRAPH FLY-BACK PERPETUAL AUTOMATIC

Movement: high-grade, mechanical automatic, hand-finished complicated caliber FRANC VILA 11; exclusive "gold concept rotor"; 42-hour power reserve.
Functions: moonphase at 3; hours and day of the week at 6; minutes, month and leap year at 9; seconds and date at 12; flyback chronograph.
Case: titanium and red gold; "Esprit Unique" shape with elliptic and circular bezel; sapphire crystal and caseback with double-sided antireflective treatment; water resistant to 10atm.
Dial: carbon fiber and guilloché.
Strap: comes with both crocodile and rubber strap with DieHard Extreme Steel deployant clasp.
Suggested price: $75,000
Note: limited edition of 48 pieces.
Also available: DHES; black DHES; black DHES and red gold; 18K red or white gold; titanium and DHES, red gold or white gold.

![Frederique Constant crest logo]

FREDERIQUE CONSTANT
GENEVE

When Peter and Aletta Stas founded Frédérique Constant in 1988, they considered the Geneva-based company a labor of love. In the more than two decades since, the husband-and-wife team has developed the brand, nurturing it from an original creative spark to a collection that boasts a manufacture tourbillon with a silicon escapement wheel.

Drawing on their ancestors' horological prowess (Peter is a direct descendant of Constant Stas, one of the company's namesakes), Peter and Aletta began with six prototypes they designed and dubbed "The 18th Century Collection." The line's early success fueled momentum as the family worked to create a collection of attractively priced mechanical timepieces crafted in Switzerland.

"At Frédérique Constant's workshop in Geneva, we've streamlined production and maximized efficiency to keep costs under control," Peter Stas explains. "This business model allows us to create complicated timepieces finished by experienced craftsmen and offer them at sensible price points."

The brand made its entrance on a larger stage in 1995 when Frédérique Constant first presented at the Basel Watch Fair. Demand soared as a result of this exposure and the company expanded to its current factory, which can produce up to 90,000 watches a year.

Frédérique Constant keeps close tabs on every step of watch production. The brand's watches are designed either in-house or by a carefully hand-chosen selection of designers working on series-specific projects. These timepieces call for the consummate expertise used in creating the tiny yet crucial components that power and adorn the highest-quality Swiss mechanical watches. Frédérique Constant appeals to an underserviced portion of the population: watch lovers who want expertly produced timepieces at sensible prices.

ABOVE   Frédérique Constant founders, Peter and Aletta Stas.

RIGHT   The Manufacture Tourbillon Moonphase Date 24 Silicium's 44mm rose-gold case is nattily attired with a black dial, the center of which is decorated with guilloché.

The Heart Beat Trilogy sold for almost $35,000, contributing to the ONLY WATCH '09 auction's total of nearly $3,350,000 raised for medical research.

Frédérique Constant caused a stir at BaselWorld 2008 when it debuted the company's first proprietary tourbillon movement. The admirable technical feat was made all the more impressive by the fact that the tourbillon boasted a cutting-edge silicon escapement.

Last summer, Frédérique Constant went a step further and unveiled a new tourbillon movement enhanced with moon-phase, date, and a 24-hour indicator. Based on the brand's acclaimed Heart Beat movement and conceived in Frédérique Constant's Geneva workshop, the newly developed FC-985 movement powers the Manufacture Tourbillon Moonphase Date 24 Silicium.

Reflecting an appreciation for traditional craftsmanship and a keen attention to detail, the highly refined finishing techniques lavished on the automatic movement include Côtes de Genève and perlage decoration, chamfer and rhodium plating on all the bridges, plus blued steel screws.

To ensure the timepiece's exclusivity, the company will produce only 188 pieces in rose gold and 88 in white gold.

Introduced in 1994, Frédérique Constant's Heart Beat collection has become one of the brand's most popular and recognizable thanks to a key visual feature. Each Heart Beat features an openworked design that exposes the balance—the "heart" of the movement—as it oscillates steadily.

The Heart Beat Manufacture Automatic Pavée is the latest member to join that esteemed collection. This feminine model is presented in a 41mm stainless steel case with a mother-of-pearl dial set with more than 280 white diamonds weighing more than 2.5 carats.

In September of 2009, Frédérique Constant participated in one of the watch industry's most prestigious charity events—the ONLY WATCH '09 Charity Auction—held to raise money for research into Duchenne Muscular Dystrophy, a genetic disorder that affects one in every 3,500 boys born. Frédérique Constant's contribution was the stellar Heart Beat Trilogy, consisting of three one-of-a-kind timepieces designed by women for women: the Heart Beat Manufacture Automatic Pavée, the Double Heart Beat Chocolate Pavée and the Love Heart Beat. The three elements of this unique triptych share an exquisite jewel box. The Heart Beat Trilogy sold for almost $35,000, contributing to the event's total of nearly $3,350,000 for medical research.

LEFT The Lady Heart Beat Manufacture Automatic Pavée's mother-of-pearl dial is awash in sparkle provided by more than 280 diamonds.

CENTER The new 34mm 18-karat rose-gold Lady Chocolate Double Heart Beat Automatic Pavée reveals the workings of the movement through two heart-shaped openings on the dial.

RIGHT Bearing 64 diamonds (0.2 carat), this stunning new Ladies Love Heart Beat Automatic is housed in an 18-karat rose-gold-plated case fitted on a vanilla satin strap. This piece also comes in a special ONLY WATCH '09 edition in solid 18-karat rose gold.

DELIGHT

REF. FC-220WAD2ECD2B

Movement: high-precision quartz FC-220 caliber.
Functions: hours, minutes; date.
Case: stainless steel; Ø 35x28mm; rose-gold-plated crown; antireflective convex sapphire crystal; antireflective sapphire crystal caseback; each case individually numbered; water resistant to 3atm.
Dial: mother-of-pearl; fine hearts guilloché decor in silver dial center; applied, rose-gold-plated Arabic numerals; eight H-color diamond indexes.
Strap: satin strap; rose-gold-plated bracelet.
Also available: bi-colored stainless steel and rose-gold-plated bracelet in special box.

CARREE SAPPHIRE

REF. FC-303V4C29

Movement: automatic-winding FC-303 caliber.
Functions: hours, minutes, seconds; date.
Case: 18K rose gold; Ø 47x30.7mm; antireflective convex sapphire crystal; antireflective sapphire crystal caseback secured with six screws; sapphire block visible through the case sides; each case individually numbered; water resistant to 3atm.
Dial: silver; Côtes de Genève decor in dial center; rose-gold numerals; rose-gold-plated hands.
Strap: brown crocodile calf leather; water-resistant lining.

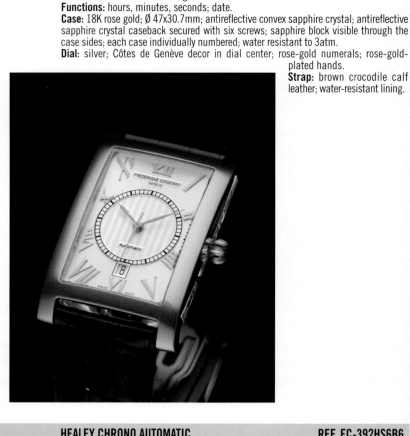

LADIES "LOVE HEART BEAT" AUTOMATIC

REF. FC-310LHB2PD4

Movement: automatic-winding FC-310 caliber; 42-hour power reserve; perlage finishing on the balance's bridge opening.
Case: rose-gold-plated case; bezel set with 48 full-cut H-color diamonds convex; sapphire crystal; screw-down transparent caseback; water resistant to 6atm.
Dial: hearts guilloché decoration; Heart Beat Love aperture at 12; set with 64 diamonds (0.2 carat).
Strap: sweet vanilla satin; water-resistant lining.

HEALEY CHRONO AUTOMATIC

REF. FC-392HS6B6

Movement: automatic-winding FC-392 caliber; 42-hour power reserve.
Functions: chronograph counters: hours, minutes, seconds.
Case: polished stainless steel; Ø 43mm; convex sapphire crystal; transparent caseback secured by six screws; Austin Healey Conclave—Kingston 2009 logo engraving on the caseback; each case individually numbered; water resistant to 10atm.
Dial: silver and blue; applied luminous Arabic numbers; date window at 6; Healey logo at 3; hand-polished stainless steel hands with white luminescent center.
Strap: dark blue calf racing; optional folding clasp; water-resistant lining.
Note: limited edition of 1,888 pieces.

RUNABOUT   REF. FC-392RM6B4

Movement: automatic-winding FC-392; 42-hour power reserve.
Functions: chronograph counters: hours, minutes, seconds; date at 6.
Case: rose-gold-plated case; polished; Ø 43mm; convex sapphire crystal; transparent caseback secured by six screws; water resistant to 10atm.
Dial: silvered; central Pavé de Paris guilloché decoration; shiny, hand-polished, applied rose-gold-plated Arabic applied numerals; shiny, hand-polished rose-gold-plated hands; white luminescent center.
Strap: dark brown calf; rose-gold-plated buckle; water-resistant lining.
Note: limited edition of 1,888 pieces.

LADY HEART BEAT MANUFACTURE PAVÉE   REF. FC-930ASD4HPV6

Movement: automatic-winding proprietary FC-930 caliber.
Functions: hours, minutes.
Case: stainless steel; Ø 41mm; set with 235 full-cut H-color diamonds (2.54 carats); antireflective convex sapphire crystal; antireflective sapphire crystal caseback secured with six screws; each case individually numbered; water resistant to 3atm.
Dial: silvered; FC crest decor in dial center; heart beat aperture at 6; Roman numerals set with 52 full-cut H-color diamonds (0.16 carat); black steel hands.
Strap: gray satin; water-resistant lining.
Note: limited edition of 888 pieces.

MANUFACTURE TOURBILLON MOONPHASE DATE   REF. FC-985ABS4H9

Movement: automatic-winding proprietary FC-985 caliber (conceived, developed and produced entirely in-house); 48-hour power reserve; one-minute tourbillon; balance-cock on dial side; 28,800 vph; 33 jewels; Incabloc anti-shock system; Glucydur balance; Nivarox No. 1 balance spring; bridges decorated with Côtes de Genève and perlage, anglage and rhodiage finishing; 208 components; each movement individually numbered.
Functions: hours, minutes, seconds; date; moonphase; 24-hour indication.
Case: 18K rose gold; two-piece case; Ø 44mm, thickness: 12.2mm; antireflective convex sapphire crystal; sapphire crystal caseback secured with six screws; water resistant to 3atm.
Dial: black; FC Crest guilloché dial center; fine, applied rose-gold-plated steel indexes; rose-gold-plated hands.
Strap: genuine hand-stitched alligator; water-resistant lining; additional folding buckle included.

MAXIME   REF. FC-700MS5M6

Movement: automatic-winding proprietary Maxime FC-700 caliber; 42-hour power reserve.
Functions: date counter at 6.
Case: steel; Ø 42mm; convex sapphire crystal; transparent caseback secured by four screws; water resistant to 5atm.
Dial: silvered; central guilloché decoration; shiny, hand-polished, applied steel Roman numerals; shiny, hand-polished steel hands with white luminescent center.
Strap: black alligator; stainless steel deployment buckle; water-resistant lining.

GF
GREUBEL FORSEY

INVENTEURS HORLOGERS

Robert Greubel and Stephen Forsey blend art and science to create imaginative watches that blur the lines between horology and architecture. Designed to captivate, each Greubel Forsey timepiece is envisioned through an architectural prism, exhibiting a highly developed sense of proportion, style and history.

One of its latest, the Quadruple Tourbillon, represents the company's crowning achievement thus far. Taking five years to perfect, this superlative timekeeper contains four separate tourbillons—a world's first—working in virtuosic concert to produce exceptional accuracy.

Conceived by Greubel Forsey, this visionary, three-dimensional construction places two independently regulated oscillators inside separate tourbillons, each inclined 30 degrees and rotating once a minute. Each tourbillon is then mounted inside a second tourbillon that rotates once every four minutes. All four members of this "whirlwind" quartet are positioned so that it's virtually impossible for them to be in a position that would negatively affect accuracy.

"The spherical differential doubles the chronometric performance of the two regulating organs by transmitting the averaged results of two oscillators to the time display," Forsey explains.

The watchmakers grandly showcase this immense technical invention in an asymmetrical case. It gently curves outward at 8:00 to accommodate a pair of tourbillons and across the dial, where the small seconds and power-reserve indicator are located.

The Quadruple Tourbillon is presented in two versions, one in platinum with a silvered gold dial and the other in rose gold with a black dial.

Greubel Forsey wants to redefine the frontiers of technical accomplishments in watchmaking. The message could not be clearer: it's engraved, in so many words, on Invention Piece 3's dial.

More importantly, it's obvious from this limited edition's sophisticated design. Gone are the minute and hour hands cracking a smile when they reach 10:10. Instead, the movement's plates are subversively transformed into a multi-level dial, where the hour and minute scales nestle together in concentric circles and are read with rotating arrows. Offering another sly wink to convention, the watchmakers subvert the traditional small seconds by subtly nudging it from its customary post at 6:00.

That artistic design is all visual preamble for Invention Piece 3's truly groundbreaking tourbillon. Pitched at 25 degrees, the cage rotates to the deliberate rhythm of once every 24 seconds. This assault on custom, however, is not made simply for the sake of marching to a different drummer. The remarkable deviations ensure high levels of accuracy and performance. Even so, it's easy to forget all of that and just gaze at its purposeful spinning through the convex crystal on the side of the case.

To maintain its exclusivity, Greubel Forsey will permit only 33 pieces to be produced, 11 each in 5N red gold, white gold, and platinum.

THIS PAGE
Invention Piece 3 offers a three-dimensional design that uses the movement's plates for the dial. The 24-hour scale is articulated with a red arrow, while the minutes are indicated with one in blue. The entire dial is decorated with a unique engraved message from the watchmakers.

FACING PAGE
CENTER To guarantee an exceptional level of accuracy, the Quadruple Tourbillon harnesses the precision achieved by its four tourbillons in two double cages.

BOTTOM LEFT A convex sapphire crystal window on the side of the asymmetrical case provides a view of a team of tourbillons at work.

Greubel Forsey opened its
new headquarters and
workshops last summer
in La Chaux-de-Fonds.

Horological Architecture

With its groundbreaking Double Tourbillon Technique, Greubel Forsey borrows the Double Tourbillon 30°, but that's where the similarities end—construction and mode differ, and the Double Tourbillon Technique pushes the boundaries of horology even further with the addition of four co-axial barrels that ensure five days of reserve power.

Not only does the power-reserve indicator at 3:00 indicate the barrels' status, its open design also reflects the watchmaker's passion for showcasing the balanced arrangement of the movement's dynamic architecture. The kinetic splendor of the Double Tourbillon Technique's mechanical intricacies captivates the eye, compelling it along a three-dimensional journey to discover the heart of the mechanism.

To enhance that unfettered visibility, the watch uses openworked hands to indicate the time with metallic indexes on a transparent sapphire ring that encircles the movement. The combination provides a spectacular view of the barrels rotating as they wind and unwind, which drives the spherical differential connected to the power-reserve indicator.

Mirroring the movement's elegant machinations, the watch's finishing is equally exquisite. Presented in white gold, the 47.5mm round case features a gold plate attached around the crown engraved with a message from the watchmakers, as well as another gold plate on the other side of the case at 9:00.

The company recently moved from its workshops at the Ancien Manège—its primary home for six years—to a new location in La Chaux-de-Fonds, Switzerland. Situated near the city's airport, the site houses Greubel Forsey's headquarters and workshops, where around 65 watchmakers, artisans and staff members work.

The grounds include two buildings. The first is a 17th-century farmhouse that receives guests and accommodates the company's Unique Timepieces Workshop. Gilles Tissot, an expert in Neuchâtel-style architecture, renovated the building, preserving many historic features and decorative flourishes. Among the highlights are a vaulted cellar, a carved doorway that dates to 1668 and a charming sundial, the perfect symbol of the building's new purpose.

In stark contrast, the main building, designed by Pierre Studer, is a marvel of modern architecture. Home to Greubel Forsey's development and production workshops; the glazed building seems to ascend from the Earth, creating the image of Greubel Forsey's meteoric rise. The striking form is also designed to mimic the geological phenomenon of buckling strata commonly found in the surrounding Jura Mountains.

The structure was conceived to maximize visual impact and function, including a glazed atrium that allows natural light to flood into the workspace. It also incorporates green technologies and construction techniques that minimize its environmental effect. One of the most noticeable is the sloped roof, which is covered with grass to increase thermal and noise insulation. Less obvious, but just as important, are the numerous environmentally friendly ventilation systems at work, such as the double windows aimed at creating a cool breeze in the summer, and retaining heat in the winter.

With the christening of both these buildings, Greubel Forsey finds a new home that aptly reflects its watchmaking philosophy by expressing its reverence for the past and its vision for the future.

FACING PAGE
The openworked architecture of the Double Tourbillon Technique allows a clear view of much of the watch's complex mechanics, including its double tourbillon. Also on display are the watch's four barrels, which generate five days of reserve power.

THIS PAGE
Greubel Forsey opened its new headquarters and workshops last summer in La Chaux-de-Fonds. It features a 17th-century farmhouse that encompasses the reception area and Unique Timepieces workshop. Subtly linked nearby, a dazzling glass-walled building is home to the company's main workshop, research and development facilities.

GΞ | GUY ELLIA

Few contemporary elite watchmakers design both jewelry and timepieces. One notable exception is Guy Ellia. The avant-garde designer whose innovations create some of the most complicated watches in the industry considers horology his main passion, yet his bejeweled background is evident in every watch he designs—right down to the beautiful mechanical movements that are as stunning as they are precise.

As a diamond dealer and jewelry designer, Guy Ellia launched his first innovative line of timepieces in 1999, which immediately rocketed him into the realm of watchmaking royalty. Collaborating with such prestigious movement designers as Parmigiani, Piguet and, most recently, Christophe Claret, Guy Ellia's extraordinary creative vision continuously emerges in surprising ways through his watch designs. Ellia's Répétition Minutes Zephyr, introduced in Basel two years ago, is a marvel of form and function. The watch's transparency and extraordinarily high complications—yet ethereal with dreamlike visage—made it an instant classic for men.

"Creation is a delicate thing," says Ellia. "Watch designs must be trendy, yet timeless. Each year, we must show something different; but luxury watches must be perfect. There is a constant need to create new and better technology." Because of the level of complication in Ellia's designs, his watches can take five or six years to develop.

Ethereal with dreamlike visage, the **Répétition Minutes Zephyr** became an instant classic for men.

In his offices on the glamorous rue de la Paix in Paris, Ellia's relaxed demeanor belies his opulent luxury businesses. Dressed in jeans, his striking white hair casually wind-tousled, Ellia exudes a blend of understated elegance, bohemian charm and quintessential French intellectualism. It is this combination of characteristics that identifies Ellia and informs his designs.

"Guy Ellia is one of the best in the business for getting ideas and finding the techniques to make his complicated designs happen," says Carla Chalhoui, owner of the celebrated haute joaillerie and haute horlogerie boutiques, Arije, in Paris.

While Ellia declares that, "watches are one of the most difficult businesses in the luxury world," he also concedes that haute timepieces seem to be one of the few niches relatively impervious to financial hardship: a watch is often the only accessory a man will allow himself; without a watch encircling her wrist, a woman still feels naked. In an era when watches are no longer necessities, the timepiece a person chooses to wear tells much more about that person than ever before. Men and women who favor Guy Ellia are hip, yet refined, savvy and individualistic—more likely to start their own trends than to join in on someone else's.

Incredibly selective when it comes to choosing retailers, Guy Ellia is enjoying ever-increasing attention around the globe. In the popular film *L'Emmerdeur*, which was released in December 2008, the lead character sports a Guy Ellia watch. Some of the biggest names in French cinema are said to own Ellia designs, including Jean Reno, Gérard Darmon and Gérard Lanvin. With his latest designs, Guy Ellia offers watches that transcend time.

FACING PAGE AND TOP The Répétition Minutes Zephyr features an exclusive manual-winding Christophe Claret caliber GEC 88, visible through both sides of the case.

RIGHT The Tourbillon Zephyr is fitted with a GES 97 manual-winding movement.

REPETITION MINUTE ZEPHYR

Movement: mechanical manual-winding Christophe Claret caliber GEC 88; cage: 41.2x38.2mm, thickness: 9.41mm; 48-hour power reserve; flat balance-spring: 18,000 vph; 720 pieces; 72 jewels; gear wheels with different platings; five-position adjustment.
Functions: hour, minute; power-reserve indicator; minute repetition function; five time zones with day/night indicators.

Case: 18K white-gold sides (70.76g); convex case; 53.6x43.7mm, thickness: 14.8mm; sapphire glass; sapphire and 18K gold crown set with a Ø 2.2mm diamond; water resistant to 3atm.
Strap: rubber or alligator; width case / buckle: 33x24mm; 18K solid white-gold folding buckle (17.27g).
Note: limited edition of 20 numbered pieces.
Also available: pink gold and titanium.

TOURBILLON ZEPHYR

Movement: mechanical manual-winding Christophe Claret caliber GES 97; cage: 37x37mm, thickness: 6.21mm; 110-hour power reserve; flat balance-spring: 21,600 vph; 233 pieces; 17 jewels; winding ring set with 36 baguette-cut diamonds (1.04 carats) or engine turning; one-minute tourbillon; entirely hand-chamfered cage; bottom plate and bridges in blue sapphire; five-position adjustment.

Functions: hour, minute; tourbillon.
Case: 950 platinum sides (54.9g); convex case; 54x45.3mm, thickness: 15.4mm; white sapphire glass with thermal counter-shock marking; transparent caseback, hearth engraving; crown set with a Ø 1mm diamond; water resistant to 3atm.
Strap: alligator; width case / buckle: 37x22mm; 18K solid white-gold folding buckle (15.64g).
Note: limited edition of 12 numbered pieces.
Also available: white gold.

JUMBO CHRONO

Movement: mechanical automatic-winding Frédéric Piguet caliber PGE 1185; cage: Ø 26.2mm, thickness: 5.5mm; chronograph with column wheel; 45-hour power reserve; five-position adjustment; Côtes de Genève-finished bridges with rhodium plating; GUY ELLIA logo engraved on rotor with rhodium plating.
Functions: hour, minute at 12; day by coloration at 2; 30-minute counter at 3; small seconds at 6; 12-hour counter at 9; central chronograph sweep seconds.

Case: 18K black-gold case (87g); Ø 50mm, thickness: 11.5mm; sapphire glass with thermal counter-shock marking; water resistant to 3atm.
Strap: alligator; width case / buckle: 26x20mm; 18K black-gold folding buckle (16g).
Also available: set black-gold bezel; full-set black gold; white gold; set white-gold bezel; full-set white gold; pink gold; set pink-gold bezel; full-set pink gold.

TIME SPACE

Movement: mechanical manual-winding Frédéric Piguet caliber PGE 15; cage: Ø 35.64mm, thickness: 1.9mm; 43-hour power reserve; 21,600 vph; 20 jewels; five-position adjustment; Côtes de Genève-finished bridges with black PVD treatment; "GE" logo engraved on stippled plate with black PVD treatment.
Functions: hour, minute.
Case: 18K pink gold 33.5g; Ø 46.8mm, thickness: 4.9mm; sapphire glass with thermal counter-shock marking; water resistant to 3atm.

Strap: alligator; width case / buckle: 26x18mm; 18K white-gold pin buckle (4.73g).
Also available: set pink-gold bezel; full-set pink gold; white gold; set white-gold bezel; full-set white gold; black gold; set black-gold bezel; full-set black gold.

TOURBILLON MAGISTERE TITANIUM

Movement: mechanical manual-winding Christophe Claret caliber TGE 97; cage: 37.4x29.9mm, thickness: 5.4mm; 110-hour power reserve; flat balance spring: 21,600 vph; 20 jewels; mysterious winding; one-minute tourbillon; skeletonized barrel and ratchet-wheel; entirely hand-chamfered cage; titanium bottom plate and bridges.
Functions: hour, minute.
Case: titanium (18.2g); biconvex case; 43.5x36mm, thickness: 10.9mm; sapphire glass with thermal counter-shock marking; crown set with a Ø 1mm diamond; water resistant to 3atm.
Strap: alligator; width case / buckle: 24x20mm; 18K solid white-gold folding buckle (9.65g) and titanium hood.

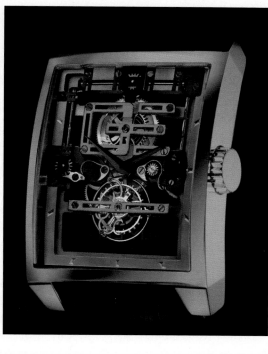

TOURBILLON MAGISTERE II

Movement: mechanical manual-winding Christophe Claret caliber MGE-97; cage: 38.40x30.9mm, thickness: 5.71mm; 90-hour power reserve; flat balance spring: 21,600 vph; 266 pieces, 33 jewels; mysterious winding; one-minute tourbillon; skeleton ratchet and wheels with curved arms and wolf-teeth; entirely hand-chamfered cage; barrel bridges and tourbillon in 18K gold.
Functions: hour, minute.
Case: 18K 5N red gold (97.54g); biconvex case 44.2x36.7mm, thickness: 15mm; sapphire glass with antireflective treatment; transparent caseback; water resistant to 3atm.
Strap: alligator; 18K 5N red-gold folding buckle (14.61g).
Note: limited edition of 12 numbered pieces.
Also available: white gold.

TIME SPACE QUANTIEME PERPETUEL

Movement: mechanical manual-winding Frédéric Piguet caliber PGE 5615 D; cage: Ø 35.64mm, thickness: 4.7mm; 43-hour power reserve; 21,600 vph; 20 jewels; five-position adjustment; Côtes de Genève-finished bridges with black PVD treatment; GE logo engraved on stippled plate with black PVD treatment; watch box with an integrated specific automatic winder.
Functions: hour, minute; day, date, month; moonphases; leap years.
Case: 18K black gold (32.87g); Ø 46.8mm, thickness: 7.75mm; white sapphire middle case ring; sapphire glass with thermal counter-shock marking; water resistant to 3atm.
Strap: alligator; width case / buckle: 26x18mm; 18K black-gold pin buckle (4.73g).
Also available: set black-gold bezel; full-set black gold; white gold; set white-gold bezel; full-set white gold; pink gold; set pink-gold bezel; full-set pink gold.

CIRCLE

Movement: Frédéric Piguet caliber PGE 820; cage: Ø 18.8mm, thickness: 1.95mm
Functions: hour, minute.
Case: 18K polished white gold (83.86g); bezel set with 124 diamonds (diamonds: Ø1.5mm); Ø 52mm, thickness: 7mm; sapphire glass with thermal counter-shock marking; crown set with one Ø 2.8mm diamond; mirror-polished bottom cover set with a Ø 0.95mm diamond on the "i" of ELLIA; water resistant to 3atm.
Dial: 18K white-gold mirror; markers set with 168 brilliants (1 carat); dauphine-shaped 18K white-gold hands.
Strap: alligator; 18K solid white-gold pin buckle set with 86 diamonds (0.384 carat); pin set with one Ø 0.9mm diamond; width case / buckle: 31.6x20mm.
Also available: Case: set, matte white-gold bezel; full-set white gold. Dial: matte black; shiny black; opalin; matte gold. Markers: shiny black; mirror-polished gold; outline gold; polished copper outline.

H. Moser & Cie.

Watchmaker Heinrich Moser left Switzerland in 1827, building an horological empire in Russia before returning to his native Schaffhausen 20 years later as a driving force behind the city's industrialization. When Dr. Jürgen Lange and Moser's great-grandson Roger Nicholas Balsiger relaunched H. Moser & Cie. in 2002, they adopted the two principles that guided Moser's success.

The pair began with Moser's philosophy that those who have the best suppliers make the best watches. This runs contrary to the current trend of watchmakers eager to tout their ability to produce an entire watch in-house. Before it was in vogue, Moser eschewed this line of thinking, claiming that an experienced specialist was more efficient and delivered more interesting results.

Today, H. Moser & Cie. collaborates with horology's best on a number of projects, but it also has expanded its own manufacturing capabilities, opening a new facility in Neuhausen am Rheinfall. The move not only allows the company to satisfy growing demand for its remarkable creations, but also ensures a steady supply of the complex components it uses in its timepieces.

Moser's second principle was to specialize in movements whose sophisticated engineering precludes large-scale production and ensures exclusivity. To achieve this goal in its current collection, H. Moser & Cie. uses true bevel wheels in the winding train along with pallets and escape wheels made of gold.

The company's breakthrough success is a testament to Heinrich Moser's foresight. In under a decade, H. Moser & Cie. has already inspired a dedicated following. It has also earned a number of accolades, including winning the Complicated Watch category at the Grand Prix d'Horlogerie in 2006, a major achievement for such a young brand.

ABOVE A reproduction of Heinrich Moser's 1875 biography was reissued in 2009.

RIGHT To meet increasing demand, H. Moser & Cie. recently opened a new production facility in Neuhausen am Rheinfall, Switzerland.

The company's breakthrough success is a testament to **Heinrich Moser's foresight.**

H. Moser & Cie. introduced one of its most important inventions in 2007, a complex component helping revolutionize escapement design it calls the Straumann Double Hairspring.

In mechanical watchmaking, the escapement's role is to ensure the watch's accuracy by maintaining a steady rate. The challenge is gravity, whose constant pull distorts the escapement's balance spring and reduces its accuracy.

H. Moser and Cie. watchmakers remedied this age-old conundrum with the Straumann Double Hairspring, an exclusive design that uses two balance springs oscillating against one another in order to equalize gravitational error at its point of origin.

The invention not only improves day-to-day performance, but its construction also proves invaluable when the time comes to clean and adjust the escapement. A watchmaker simply loosens two screws, removes the entire module and replaces it with one that's pre-adjusted. When the watchmaker is finished servicing the original, the owner can have it reinstalled or continue using the new module. This innovation represents a major improvement in customer service that translates into the watch spending more quality time with its owner—and not the repair shop.

The Straumann Double Hairspring can be found oscillating within a number of H. Moser & Cie. finest timepieces, including the Henry Rosso and Monard Fumé.

Since its 2002 revival, H. Moser & Cie. has climbed quickly to the apex of horology, empowered by its founder's wisdom from the past and inspired by the promise of future generations.

TOP LEFT   This Henry Rosso's rose-gold case is paired with a black dial featuring small seconds. A transparent caseback reveals the movement's decoration and a display for the watch's four-day power reserve.

TOP RIGHT   The groundbreaking Straumann Double Hairspring from H. Moser & Cie. uses two hairsprings oscillating against one another to achieve a high level of accuracy.

ABOVE   The Monard Fumé dial boasts clean lines and a smoky hue. Its 40.8mm case is made of palladium, a metal whose rich luster is equaled only by its rarity.

MAYU BLACK — REF. 321.503-007

Movement: manual-winding HMC 321.503 caliber; 80-hour power reserve; bevel wheels; interchangeable escapement module.
Function: hours, minutes, seconds; seconds with stop function.
Case: 18K rose gold; Ø 38.8mm, thickness: 9.3mm; power-reserve display on movement side; antireflective sapphire crystal caseback.
Dial: black lacquered; applied faceted diamond-polished indexes; pocket-watch seconds hand.

Strap: crocodile leather; solid rose-gold clasp.
Suggested price: $12,000

MAYU FUMÉ — REF. 325.503-010

Movement: manual-winding HMC 321.503 caliber; 80-hour power reserve; bevel wheels; Straumann double hairspring; interchangeable escapement module.
Function: hours, minutes, seconds; seconds with stop function.
Case: palladium; Ø 38.8mm, thickness: 9.3mm; power-reserve display on movement side; convex sapphire glass; antireflective sapphire crystal caseback.
Dial: fume; applied faceted diamond-polished indexes; pocket-watch seconds hand.

Strap: crocodile leather; solid rose-gold clasp.
Suggested price: $16,800

MONARD BLACK — REF. 343.505-017

Movement: manual-winding HMC 343.505 caliber; 7-day power reserve; bevel wheels; dual barrel; interchangeable escapement module.
Function: hours, minutes, seconds; seconds with stop function.
Case: 18K rose gold; Ø 40.8mm, thickness: 10.85mm; power-reserve display on movement side; convex sapphire glass; antireflective sapphire crystal caseback.
Dial: black lacquered.

Strap: crocodile leather; solid rose-gold clasp.
Suggested price: $15,800

MONARD FUMÉ — REF. 343.505-016

Movement: manual-winding HMC 343.505 caliber; 7-day power reserve; bevel wheels; dual barrel; Straumann double hairspring; interchangeable escapement module.
Function: hours, minutes, seconds with stop function.
Case: palladium; Ø 40.8mm, height: 10.85mm; power-reserve display on movement side; antireflective sapphire crystal caseback.
Dial: fume; fine sun pattern ground finish.

Strap: crocodile leather; solid palladium clasp.
Suggested price: $21,100

MONARD DATE
REF. 342.502-002

Movement: manual-winding HMC 342.502 caliber; 7-day power reserve; bevel wheels; dual barrel; Straumann hairspring; interchangeable escapement module.
Function: hours, minutes, seconds stop functions; date; large date; calendar adjustable forwards and backwards via crown; double pull crown mechanism.
Case: 18K white gold; Ø 40.8mm, thickness: 10.85mm; power-reserve display on movement side; convex sapphire glass; antireflective sapphire crystal caseback.
Dial: rhodium-plated; sun pattern ground finish.
Strap: crocodile leather; solid white-gold clasp.
Suggested price: $20,700

MONARD DATE
REF. 342.502-003

Movement: manual-winding HMC 342.502 caliber; 7-day power reserve; bevel wheels; dual barrel; Straumann hairspring; interchangeable escapement module.
Function: hours, minutes, seconds stop function; date; large date; calendar adjustable forwards and backwards via crown.
Case: 18K rose gold; Ø 40.8mm, thickness: 10.85mm; double pull crown mechanism; power-reserve display on movement side; convex sapphire glass; antireflective sapphire crystal caseback.
Dial: silver-plated; sun pattern ground finish.
Strap: crocodile leather; solid rose-gold clasp.
Suggested price: $20,700

HENRY DOUBLE HAIRSPRING, PLATIN
REF. 324.607-006

Movement: manual-winding rectangular shaped HMC 324.006 caliber; 4-day power reserve; bevel wheels; large volume barrel; Straumann double hairspring; interchangeable escapement module.
Function: hours, minutes, seconds; seconds stop function.
Case: palladium tonneau; Ø 44x38.6mm, thickness: 10.4mm; power-reserve display on movement side; sapphire glass convex in two directions; antireflective sapphire crystal caseback.
Dial: fume; fine sun pattern ground finish; Moser pocket-watch seconds hand.
Strap: crocodile leather; solid palladium clasp.
Suggested price: $27,500

PERPETUAL
REF. 341.501-004

Movement: manual-winding HMC 341.501 caliber; 7-day power reserve; bevel wheels; dual barrel; Straumann hairspring with stabilized Breguet over coil; interchangeable escapement module.
Function: hours, minutes, seconds; seconds stop function; month, date, power reserve; perpetual flash calendar display; calendar adjustable forwards and backwards via crown independently of movement.
Case: 18K rose gold; Ø 40.8mm, thickness: 11.05mm; double pull crown mechanism.
Dial: silver-plated; sun pattern ground finish.
Suggested price: $34,700

HERMÈS
PARIS

The Hermès legacy is leather. Yet the Parisian house's tradition as a watchmaker can be traced back nearly a century to the late 1920s, when it began offering the first Hermès watches at its store.

Before opening its Swiss-based watch factory in 1978, the company spent 50 years collaborating on timepieces with many of the world's finest watchmakers. Today, the company is busy at work on the next generation of Hermès watches, which it says will feature a growing number of mechanical models. To help it reach that milestone, the company purchased a stake in the celebrated Swiss movement maker Vaucher, which is now making calibers for Hermès.

In another move, La Montre Hermès recently expanded its workshops to include an atelier specializing in leather straps. There, 13 craftsmen are dedicated to creating the company's luxurious straps using Hermès's exclusive tanning techniques. The expansion combines two of the company's areas of expertise—leather and horology—in one location.

Hermès evokes the joy of sailing the open waters with its Clipper Chrono Titanium, an automatic mechanical chronograph whose ridged bezel recalls a style of porthole common among 19th-century sailboats. Beyond its aesthetic value, the texture makes it easier to rotate the bezel so it can be used to track elapsed times.

The bezel surrounds a dark gray dial where red-accented chronograph indicators line up along a vertical axis to enhance legibility. The arrangement is easily read from top to bottom, starting with the 30-minute counter and ending with the 12-hour counter. The color repeats on the right side of the dial, where a red triangle points to the date.

Made from titanium, the rugged case (44mm diameter) is light on the wrist and water resistant to 200 meters; a sporty combination at home at sea or on land.

THIS PAGE

TOP   After collaborating with Switzerland's finest watchmaker for 50 years, Hermès opened its own watch atelier in Biel, Switzerland, in 1978.

BOTTOM   In 2006, Hermès added a workshop at its atelier where craftsmen use exclusive tanning techniques to create the sensuous straps used for the brand's watches.

FACING PAGE

An orange rubber strap imbues the Clipper Chrono Titanium with a supremely self-confident look that is enhanced by its robust titanium case.

The Clipper Chrono Titanium's ridged bezel recalls a style of porthole **common among 19th-century sailboats.**

Hermès spotlights its mechanical watchmaking prowess with the Dressage Perpetual Calendar, a model equipped with one of the brand's in-house movements, the Hermès H1936.

The caliber's nearly 400 elements come together in a rose-gold case with a dark gray dial that encompasses a retrograde arc for the date, plus rotating discs for the day, month, leap year and moonphase.

The case, which measures 40mm in diameter, includes a transparent caseback to view the automatic movement, whose bridges and oscillating weight are decorated with an interlocking H-pattern.

With its Arceau Skeleton, Hermès again highlights the watch's movement, this time through an openworked dial. As the caliber performs its mechanical ballet below, three blued hands rotate above, indicating the time on a brown chapter ring. A matching brown alligator strap attached to the stainless steel case completes this striking design. Hermès also offers this model in white gold with a slate-gray chapter ring.

TOP LEFT   The rose-gold Dressage Perpetual Calendar includes a retrograde arc for the date, along with rotating discs for the leap year, month, moonphase and day.

ABOVE   The Dressage Perpetual Calendar's transparent caseback reveals the decoration used on the bridges and rotor of the Hermès H1936 movement.

RIGHT   The Arceau Skeleton's 41mm stainless steel case features an openworked dial framed by a brown chapter ring with a perforated inner edge.

Hermès expresses its mastery of both horology and leather goods with two distinctive ladies' models that celebrate exquisite craftsmanship.

The company unveiled a stainless steel version of the Cape Cod Tonneau last year, its barrel-shaped case adorned with 64 diamonds. The case's flowing lines culminate at the lugs, which secure a number of strap options ranging from classic black alligator to a daring calfskin version that wraps around the wrist twice.

The second model, the Kelly watch, is a perennial favorite. Its unique look plays off the coveted Hermès Kelly, an iconic handbag named after Princess of Monaco Grace Kelly. According to legend, the bag—originally launched by Hermès in the '30s—received its royal sobriquet in the '50s after Kelly was repeatedly photographed camouflaging her pregnancy with the bag's tailored shape.

For the watch, Hermès transforms the bag's signature padlock into a diamond-set stainless steel case. A metal loop secures the "lock clock" to a black Barenia leather strap.

With all its timepieces, Hermès demonstrates its ability to harness its expertise in two luxurious realms to create a singular style.

ABOVE A quartz movement enlivens the Cape Cod Tonneau's white mother-of-pearl dial. The 33.5x30mm stainless steel case is set with 64 white diamonds.

LEFT The Kelly watch features a quartz movement inside a stainless steel, diamond-set padlock, a design that recalls the brand's legendary Kelly bag.

KELLY DIAMONDS

Movement: quartz.
Functions: hours, minutes.
Case: 20x20mm; steel with full-cut diamonds; mineral glass.
Dial: natural white mother-of-pearl; four brilliant hour-markers.
Strap: black Box calf.
Suggested price: $9,425

Also available: other straps.

HEURE H TGM

Movement: quartz.
Functions: hours, minutes, seconds; date at 3.
Case: 30.5x30.5mm; steel; antireflective sapphire crystal.
Dial: guilloched silver.
Strap: natural Barenia.
Suggested price: $1,825

Also available: other sizes and straps.

DRESSAGE PERPETUAL CALENDAR

Movement: mechanical self-winding Hermès H1936 caliber; 55-hour power reserve; 393 components; 28,800 vph.
Functions: hours, minutes, seconds via central hands; retrograde date on an angular sector of 225°; days at 9; month at 3; year at 12; retrograde perpetual calendar (day, date, month, year); moonphase.
Case: Ø 40mm; rose gold; transparent sapphire crystal and caseback; water resistant to 5atm.
Dial: dark gray.
Strap: Havana alligator.
Suggested price: $59,950
Also available: white gold with white dial.

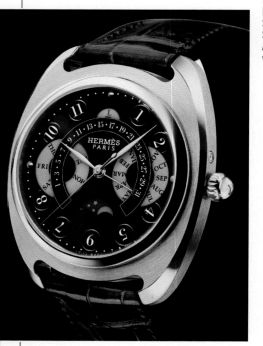

CLIPPER CHRONO TITANIUM

Movement: mechanical self-winding chronograph Valjoux 7750; 46-hour power reserve; 28,800 vph.
Functions: hours, minutes, small seconds at 9; simple calendar at 3; chronograph: hour counter at 6, minute counter at 12, second counter in the center.
Case: Ø 44mm; titanium and steel; transparent antireflective sapphire crystal and caseback; water resistant to 20atm.
Dial: dark gray.
Strap: orange rubber; pin safety folding clasp in steel of 20mm.
Suggested price: $5,950
Also available: other dials and straps.

CAPE COD TONNEAU STEEL & DIAMONDS

Movement: quartz.
Functions: hours, minutes.
Case: 33.5x30mm; steel with diamonds; antireflective sapphire crystal; water resistant to 5atm.
Dial: natural white mother-of-pearl.
Strap: black alligator.
Suggested price: $11,850
Also available: other sizes and straps.

ARCEAU SKELETON

Movement: mechanical self-winding skeleton ETA 2892 movement; 42-hour power reserve; 28,800 vph.
Functions: hours, minutes, seconds.
Case: Ø 41mm; steel; antireflective sapphire crystal and caseback; water resistant to 3atm.
Dial: brown skeleton; beige Arabic numerals; blued hands.
Strap: Havana alligator; steel safety folding clasp.
Suggested price: $7,250
Also available: white gold with slate-gray skeleton dial.

ARCEAU CHRONOGRAPH EBONY

Movement: mechanical self-winding; 42-hour power reserve; 269 components; 37 jewels; 28,800 vph.
Functions: hours, minutes, seconds; date; chronograph: seconds counter in the center, hour counter at 6, minute counter at 9.
Case: Ø 43mm; steel; antireflective sapphire crystal on bezel; water resistant to 5atm.
Dial: ebony colored; etoupe indexes; steel hour and minute hands; orange-lacquered steel seconds and counter hands.
Strap: Hermès ebony-colored Barenia calfskin; folding safety clasp.
Suggested price: $4,600

MEDOR

Movement: quartz.
Functions: hours, minutes.
Case: 24x23mm; steel; antireflective sapphire crystal.
Dial: silvered.
Strap: gold Epsom calf.
Suggested price: $3,075
Also available: other sizes and straps.

Founded on **Carlo Crocco's foresight and expanded by Jean-Claude Biver's vision,** Hublot has made a practice of redefining the boundaries of its industry.

Hublot raised eyebrows among traditionalists and expectations among collectors in 1980 when the company began producing timepieces defined by the artful juxtaposition of unusual materials. Since its debut, the company has emerged on horology's leading edge, where it continues to synthesize the lessons of the past and the technologies of the future to create distinctly original timepieces.

In fact, its willingness to embrace contrasts is the common thread running through Hublot's universe. This is particularly evident in the King Power, which combines the brawny proportions of a 48mm Big Bang case with the performance finesse of a split-seconds foudroyante chronograph.

The watch's all-black design projects confidence. Its case and bezel are made of ceramic that has been microblasted to achieve a distinctive matte finish. The same technique is used on the multilayered dial for both chronograph counters, including the foudroyante display, which allows the wearer to time events to an eighth of a second.

Hublot continues its focus on dark designs with a second chronograph, the limited-edition Big Bang All Black Blue. Instantly recognizable for its futuristic aesthetic, the watch's 44.5mm case combines black ceramic elements with several dark blue accents, including an alligator strap injected with black rubber for a comfort and style.

Among the Big Bang All Black Blue's technical achievements is the smooth operation of the more than 250 components that make up the watch's automatic chronograph movement. Despite its mechanical complexity, the chronograph's pushers—both fitted with blue rubber inserts—make it easy to operate.

Hublot edges away from dark tones with the Big Bang Earl Gray, a chronograph whose bezel can be enhanced with either 48 white diamond baguettes or paved with 114 round brilliants.

Those sparkling facets reflect the dynamic interplay between light and shadow found on the dial, where the bright rhodium-plated figures appear to jump off the tantalum-colored dial through the sapphire crystal.

Whether black, blue or gray, this trio of Big Bang chronographs intensifies the company's reputation for bold aesthetics

CLOCKWISE FROM TOP

Befitting its name, King Power's 48mm case commands respect. Its multilevel dial serves as a dynamic background for the split-seconds foudroyante chronograph's subdials.

The contrasting finishes found on the Big Bang Earl Gray's stainless steel case extend to its bracelet, which integrates inserts made of composite resin.

The limited-edition Big Bang All Black Blue combines black ceramic elements and dark blue accents to conjure a chic, ultramodern design.

Tantalizing women, Hublot presents the delicious design of its Black Tutti Frutti collection, which includes the Big Bang Apple Black, Big Bang Black Lemon and Black Pink Bang.

Each vibrant member is offered in a black ceramic Big Bang case, whose trademark porthole bezel is embellished with colorful gems that match the watch's rubber-alligator strap. For its Big Bang Apple Black, Hublot sets the bezel with 48 gleaming green tsavorites. The same number of sapphire baguettes adds color-coordinated sparkle to both the Big Bang Black Lemon and Black Pink Bang.

All three of these automatic chronographs are equipped with identical movements and feature dials with the same black-on-black color scheme. To ensure legibility, designers have selected a matte finish for the dial to contrast with the brightly polished hands, hour markers and subdial indexes.

With its Black Tutti Frutti models, Hublot presents a high level of visual and mechanical sophistication in fun, lively wrappers.

CLOCKWISE FROM TOP

Part of the Black Tutti Frutti collection, the Big Bang Apple presents a daring mixture of green tsavorites, black ceramic and rubber. Its 41mm Big Bang case houses an automatic chronograph movement.

Bright yellow sapphires frame the Big Bang Black Lemon's dial, which combines matte and polished elements for easy legibility. Behind the dial, an automatic chronograph provides 42 hours of power reserve.

The pink alligator strap and case accents complement the 48 pink sapphire baguettes that encircle the Black Pink Bang's bezel.

From high horology to high athletic performance, Hublot expands its universe beyond watchmaking with the All Black collection, which includes limited-edition lines of racing skis and bikes. Designed for speed and style, both embrace the company's signature look while tapping into its expertise at blending unusual materials in effective ways.

Hublot produced 111 numbered pairs of the All Black Ski with Swiss ski-maker Zai. Echoing the Big Bang, these hand-made skis feature an all-black design that fuses carbon fiber, fiberglass, steel, rubber, and locally mined gneiss stone. Rubber cloaks the ski tops, its matte finish a visual reference to Hublot's trademark straps. Optimized by Zai's skilled team to deliver dynamic handling, the All Black Ski is much more than just eye candy for the slope. The second addition to the All Black line is the All Black Bike. Hublot partnered with bicycle-manufacturer BMC to create a racing bike that shares the watch-maker's focus on lightness, quality, and rarity in particular—production is limited to just 30 bikes.

Like a watch's movement, this bike's components are engineered precisely to maximize the transfer of energy. The All Black Bike also incorporates materials used in watchmaking, including ceramic pedal bearings to reduce friction and a carbon-fiber frame for strength and rigidity.

The bold leap into other realms seems a natural step for Hublot. Founded on Carlo Crocco's foresight and expanded by Jean-Claude Biver's vision, the company has made a practice of redefining the boundaries of its industry.

TOP LEFT

The All Black Bike is the latest addition to Hublot's new All Black collection. Designed with BMC, the first bike was race-tested in Monaco at the 2009 World Stars Cycling Criterium on the eve of the Tour de France.

ABOVE

Mirroring the signature style of Hublot's rubber watchstraps, the All Black Skis were produced in collaboration with Swiss ski-maker Zai. Only 111 numbered pairs have been made.

KING POWER ALL BLACK
REF. 715.CI.1110.RX

Movement: HUB 4144 self-winding split-second foudroyante chronograph.
Case: black ceramic; black ceramic and rubber bezel.
Dial: black.
Strap: black rubber.
Note: 500 numbered pieces.
Suggested price: $22,900

BIG BANG ALL BLACK II
REF. 301.CI.1110.C.I

Movement: HUB 4100 mechanical automatic-winding chronograph.
Case: Big Bang; sandblasted black ceramic; 44.5mm; sandblasted black ceramic bezel with 6 H-shaped black PVD-coated steel screws, sunken, polished and blocked; water resistant to 10atm.
Dial: matte black; applied black nickel numerals and indexes.
Bracelet: sandblasted black ceramic.

Note: 500 numbered pieces.
Suggested price: $17,500

KING POWER CHRONO TOURBILLON ALL BLACK
REF. 708.CI.0110.RX

Movement: HUB 4144 self-winding split-second foudroyante chronograph.
Case: zirconium; zirconium and black rubber bezel.
Dial: black.
Strap: black rubber.
Note: 28 numbered pieces.
Suggested price: $210,000

KING POWER BLACK MAGIC
REF. 715.CI.1123.RX

Movement: HUB 4144 mechanical self-winding split-seconds foudroyante chronograph; developed with La Joux-Perret.
Case: King Power; Ø 48mm; microblasted black ceramic; microblasted black ceramic bezel with black rubber molding and 6 H-shaped black PVD-coated raised titanium screws.
Dial: multipiece with matte-black microblasted additional counters and flange; rhodium-plated and red SuperLumiNova hands and indexes; red SuperLumiNova™ transfers.
Strap: jointed black rubber.
Note: 500 numbered pieces.
Suggested price: $22,900

BIG BANG BLACK APPLE   REF. 341.CG.1110.LR.1922

Movement: HUB 4300 mechanical self-winding chronograph.
Case: black ceramic; PVD-coated white-gold bezel set with 48 baguette tsavorites; water resistant to 10atm.
Dial: black.
Strap: green alligator leather with rubber lining.
Suggested price: $21,900

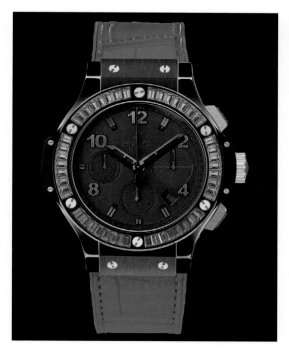

BIG BANG APPLE   REF. 341.PG.2010.LR.1922

Movement: HUB 4300 mechanical self-winding chronograph.
Case: Big Bang; Ø 41mm; 5N gold; 5N gold bezel with 6 H-shaped titanium screws, sunken, polished and blocked, and set with 48 baguette tsavorites; water resistant to 10atm.
Dial: white; satin-finished 5N gold-plated numerals and applied indexes; diamond-polished faceted 5N gold hands with white luminescent coating.
Strap: green alligator leather with rubber lining.
Suggested price: $21,900
Also available: black ceramic; matte-black dial with black numerals and applied indexes; black nickel hands without luminescent coating.

BIG BANG HAZELNUT   REF. 341.PC.2010.LR.1903

Movement: HUB 4300 self-winding chronograph.
Case: 18K red gold; 18K red-gold bezel set with baguette chocolate garnets.
Dial: white.
Strap: chocolate alligator leather with rubber lining.
Suggested price: $29,900

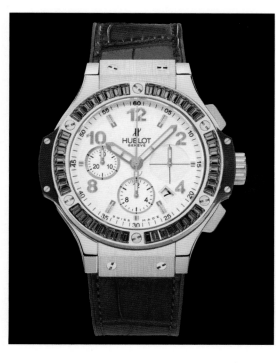

BIG BANG BLACK PURPLE   REF. 341.CX.1110.RV.1905

Movement: HUB 4300 self-winding chronograph.
Case: black ceramic; PVD-coated white-gold bezel set with 48 baguette amethysts.
Dial: black.
Strap: purple alligator leather with rubber lining.
Suggested price: $21,900

BIG BANG COMMANDO JUNGLE   REF. 301.CI.8610.NR

Movement: HUB 4100 mechanical automatic-winding chronograph.
Case: Big Bang; sandblasted black ceramic; 44.5mm; sandblasted black ceramic bezel with 6 H-shaped black PVD-coated steel screws, sunken, polished and blocked; water resistant to 10atm.
Dial: jungle camouflage transfer with matte green numerals and applied indexes; diamond-faceted high-gloss black nickel hands with luminous green markings.
Strap: stitched Nomex® fiber; jungle camouflage on black rubber.
Note: 250 numbered pieces.
Suggested price: $14,500

BIG BANG COMMANDO DESERT   REF. 301.CI.8710.NR

Movement: HUB 4100 mechanical automatic-winding chronograph.
Case: Big Bang; sandblasted black ceramic; 44.5mm; sandblasted black ceramic bezel with 6 H-shaped black PVD-coated steel screws, sunken, polished and blocked; water resistant to 10atm.
Dial: desert camouflage transfer with matte black numerals and applied indexes; diamond-faceted high-gloss black nickel hands with luminous orange markings.
Strap: stitched Nomex® fiber; desert camouflage on black rubber.
Note: 250 numbered pieces.
Suggested price: $14,500

GUMMY BANG BLACK TOURBILLON   REF. 305.RX.1910.RX

Movement: HUB 6000 manual-winding tourbillon.
Case: black rubber; black rubber bezel.
Dial: black rubber.
Strap: black rubber.
Note: 28 pieces.
Suggested price: $120,000

KING POWER ZIRCONIUM   REF. 715.ZX.1127.RX

Movement: HUB 1400 CT manual-winding tourbillon-chronograph with direct coupling on cage; 120-hour power reserve with chronograph stopped.
Functions: flying tourbillon; chronograph.
Case: King Power; Ø 48mm; microblasted black ceramic; microblasted black ceramic bezel with black rubber molding and 6 H-shaped black PVD-coated raised titanium screws; water resistant to 10atm.
Dial: multipiece sapphire; index markers with black nickel treatment; black SuperLumiNova transfers; brilliant black nickel chronograph hand; brilliant black nickle hour, minute and counter hands with black SuperLumiNova.
Strap: jointed black rubber.
Note: 50 numbered pieces.
Suggested price: $20,800

AYRTON SENNA FOUDROYANTE

REF. 315.CI.1129.RX.AES09

Movement: HUB 4144 self-winding split-second chronograph.
Case: black ceramic; black ceramic bezel.
Dial: black.
Strap: black rubber.
Note: 500 numbered pieces.
Suggested price: $27,500

BIG BANG ALL BLACK BLUE

REF. 301.CI.1190.GR.ABB09

Movement: HUB 4100 mechanical automatic-winding chronograph.
Case: Big Bang; Ø 44.5mm; sandblasted black ceramic; sandblasted black ceramic bezel with 6 H-shaped black PVD-coated steel screws, sunken, polished and blocked; water resistant to 10atm.
Dial: matte black; applied blue nickel indexes and numerals; matte-blue faceted hands.
Strap: blue gummy alligator leather.
Note: 500 numbered pieces.
Suggested price: $14,500

RED DEVIL BANG II

REF. 318.PM.1190.RX.MUN09

Movement: HUB 45 mechanical automatic-winding 45-minute chronograph; 42-hour power reserve.
Case: Big Bang; Ø 44.5mm; 5N gold; satin-polished black ceramic bezel with 6 H-shaped titanium screws, sunken, polished and blocked; 5N gold and antireflective sapphire cyrstal caseback with opaque Manchester United logo; water resistant to 10atm.
Dial: matte black; microblasted; applied red indexes; yellow motion work; date at 6; 45-minute counter with yellow figures at 9; Red Devil logo in counter at 3; brilliant black hands with yellow luminescence; red chronograph hand.
Strap: adjustable black Gummy alligator leather.
Note: 99 numbered pieces.
Suggested price: $14,900

AERO BANG MORGAN

REF. 310.CK.1140.RX.MOR08

Movement: HUB 44 SQ skeleton-like automatic-winding chronograph.
Case: Big Bang; Ø 44.5mm; black ceramic; satin-finished tungsten bezel; water resistant to 10atm.
Dial: black; sandblasted skeleton cut-out; satin-finished ruthenium-colored indexes and Morgan logo at 9; sandblasted, ruthenium chronograph hand with H-shaped counterpoise.
Strap: black rubber.
Note: 500 numbered pieces.
Suggested price: $18,500

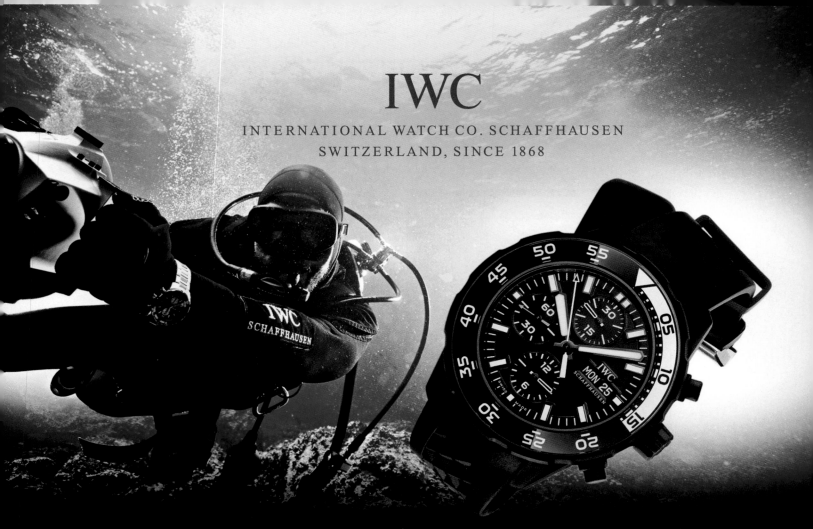

IWC

INTERNATIONAL WATCH CO. SCHAFFHAUSEN
SWITZERLAND, SINCE 1868

Divers have trusted IWC's Aquatimer watches to guide them safely through watery depths for more than 40 years. With its latest generation of Aquatimers, IWC embraces change, raising the bar with technical and aesthetic innovations.

The Aquatimer Chronograph Edition Galapagos Islands' 44mm case is clad in black rubber. Like all of the new Aquatimers, it sports a newly developed external unidirectional bezel that is adjusted easily while the user is wearing diving gloves.

Amid the transformations to the Aquatimer family, it's appropriate that evolution is the focus of one of those timepieces, the Chronograph Edition Galapagos Islands. Issued in 2009 to mark the 200th anniversary of Charles Darwin's birth, it highlights IWC's ongoing support of the Charles Darwin Foundation, a non-profit group dedicated to studying and preserving the cloistered Galapagos habitat that provided the basis for Darwin's theory of evolution. A portion of the proceeds from the sale of this watch will help fund the foundation's mission.

The new wave of Aquatimers features four other models: Deep Two, Automatic 2000, Chronograph, and Chronograph in red gold. All of the watches share several common characteristics, including a newly developed rotating bezel. Now placed outside the case, the unidirectional ring not only allows a diver to set the bezel while wearing diving gloves, but also prevents unintentional rotation while diving. The 4mm-wide bezel provides legibility even in murky environments thanks to a luminescent coating that brightly illuminates the numbers.

Another functional attribute shared by the Aquatimers is a quick-change bracelet system, developed by IWC under a patent license from Cartier. Requiring no tools, the bracelet or strap is released from the case by pushing the lug's underside. The replacement simply snaps into the lug, finishing the operation in only a few seconds. The straightforward process makes it easy to transform an Aquatimer from a reliable underwater instrument into a bold

IWC demonstrates its expertise on land and at sea.

Beyond their mutual technical changes, the Aquatimers now also feature larger cases, expanding to 44mm in diameter except for the Deep Two, which measures 46mm.

With its impressive Portuguese Minute Repeater, IWC demonstrates its mastery of haute horlogerie's most intricate complication. Few brands possess the skills to create a minute repeater, fewer still the expertise to produce a classic like the Portuguese.

The latest limited edition—500 in platinum, 500 in red gold—offers two variations on past models, moving the small seconds from 9:00 to 6:00, while expanding the case diameter by 2mm to a total of 44mm. The repeater includes an "all-or-nothing" mechanism that prevents the chiming sequence unless the slide on the case middle is pressed properly. The aural delight of the Portuguese's finely tuned gongs is matched visually by a view of the finely decorated movement through the crystal caseback.

While the Portuguese's heritage can be traced to the first repeaters IWC introduced in the 1980s, the digital display used for the Da Vinci Perpetual Calendar Digital Date-Month has roots that go back more than century. Back to the Schaffhausen manufacture's early days, when—for a short time—it produced pocket watches that displayed the time digitally. Unlike those prized collectibles of yore, however, this Da Vinci wristwatch reveals both the date and month in digital format.

To provide the large amount of power required to advance the date and month discs without negatively affecting the watch's performance, IWC developed an instantaneous jumping date. When the date changes at midnight, the system diverts and stores a portion of the energy intended to move the date to a separate power reserve. At the end of each month, that reserve energy is used to advance the month.

With the innovations exhibited by the Da Vinci Perpetual Calendar Digital Date-Month, Portuguese Minute Repeater, and the Aquatimer family, IWC demonstrates its expertise on land and at sea.

TOP LEFT
CLOCKWISE FROM TOP These three updated members of the Aquatimer family—Chronograph, Deep Two, and Automatic 2000—feature the new quick-change bracelet system. All of the Aquatimer cases have grown to 44mm in diameter, except the Deep Two, which is presented in a 46mm stainless steel case.

ABOVE The limited edition Portuguese Minute Repeater's 44mm case houses IWC's 98959 movement, a striking caliber visible through the sapphire crystal caseback. In previous Portuguese models, the small seconds was located at 9:00; here it is found in the classic 6:00 position.

BELOW Along with digital displays for the date and month, the Da Vinci Perpetual Calendar Digital Date-Month also features a flyback chronograph. Its tonneau case is available in rose gold or a limited edition (500 pieces) platinum version.

IWC AQUATIMER CHRONOGRAPH   REF. IW376701

Movement: mechanical 79320 caliber with chronograph; 28,800 vph; 44-hour power reserve; 25 jewels.
Functions: day and date display at 3; small seconds at 6; hacking seconds at 9; chronograph at 12; small seconds hand with stop function.
Case: stainless steel; Ø 44mm, thickness: 15mm; external mechanical rotating bezel; sapphire crystal, antireflective on both sides; water resistant to 12 bar.

Dial: rhodium-plated black dial; white luminescent indexes.
Bracelet: stainless steel.
Also available: on black rubber strap; with blue/orange dial on blue rubber strap.
Suggested price: $5,300–$6,300

IWC DA VINCI PERPETUAL CALENDAR EDITION KURT KLAUS   REF. IW376205

Movement: mechanical automatic-winding IWC 89360 caliber with double-pin winding device and seconds-stopping system; column wheel; 28,800 vph; 68-hour power reserve; 40 jewels.
Functions: hours, minutes, small seconds at 6; date at 6; chronograph with 3 counters.
Case: rose-gold three-piece case in tonneau shape; 44x43mm, thickness: 14.4mm; polished and brushed finish; domed sapphire crystal, antireflective on both sides; screw-down crown; rocking pushers; caseback fastened by 6 screws, displaying the movement through a sapphire crystal; water resistant to 3atm.

Dial: black dial; extra-long markers; simple baton hands.
Strap: black crocodile leather; rose-gold clasp.
Note: limited to 1,000 pieces.
Also available: stainless steel (limited to 1,000 pieces).
Suggested price: $36,400

IWC AQUATIMER CHRONOGRAPH   REF. IW376903

Movement: mechanical IWC 89360 caliber with chronograph; 28,800 vph; 68-hour power reserve; 40 jewels.
Functions: hours, minutes and seconds; day and date display at 3; mechanical chronograph with stop function; small seconds at 6; combined hour and minute counters at 12.
Case: rose gold; Ø 44.5mm, thickness: 15.5mm; external mechanical rotating bezel; sapphire crystal, antireflective on both sides; exhibition caseback; water resistant to 12 bar.

Dial: black; white luminescent indexes.
Strap: black rubber.
Suggested price: $19,900

IWC DEEP TWO   REF. IW354701

Movement: mechanical 30110 caliber; 28,800 vph; 21-hour power reserve; 40 jewels.
Functions: central seconds hand with stop function; mechanical depth gauge from 6 to 12; date at 3.
Case: stainless steel; external mechanical rotating bezel; sapphire crystal, antireflective on both sides; screw-in caseback.
Dial: rhodium-plated black dial; white luminescent indexes; depth gauge.

Bracelet: stainless steel.
Also available: on black rubber strap.
Suggested price: $14,900–$15,900

IWC AQUATIMER AUTOMATIC 2000   REF. IW356802

Movement: mechanical 30110 caliber; 28,800h vph; 21-hour power reserve; 40 jewels.
Functions: central seconds with stop function; date at 3.
Case: stainless steel; external mechanical rotating bezel; sapphire crystal, antireflective on both sides; screw-in caseback.
Dial: rhodium-plated black dial; white luminescent indexes.
Strap: black rubber.
Also available: on stainless steel bracelet; white dial on black rubber strap or stainless steel bracelet.
Suggested price: $4,400–$5,400

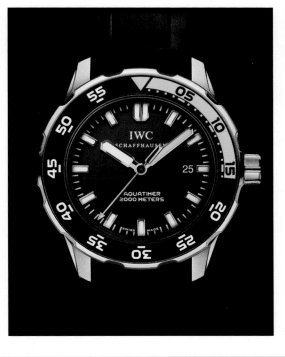

IWC DA VINCI PERPETUAL CALENDAR DIGITAL DATE-MONTH   REF. IW376101

Movement: mechanical 89800 caliber with chronograph and perpetual calendar; 28,800 vph; 68-hour power reserve; 52 jewels.
Functions: chronograph; perpetual calendar; small seconds hand with stop function; large month display at 3; small seconds at 6; large date at 9; combined hour and minute counters at 12.
Case: platinum; sapphire crystal, antireflective on both sides; exhibition caseback.
Dial: rhodium-plated silver dial.
Strap: black crocodile leather.
Note: limited to 500 pieces.
Also available: in rose gold on brown crocodile leather strap.
Suggested price: $44,300–$70,000

IWC INGENIEUR CHRONOGRAPH   REF. IW378401

Movement: mechanical IWC 89360 caliber with chronograph; 28,800 vph; 68-hour power reserve; 40 jewels.
Functions: hours, minutes and seconds; date display at 3; mechanical chronograph with stop function and flyback hand; small seconds at 6; combined hour and minute counters at 12.
Case: stainless steel; Ø 45.5mm; sapphire crystal, antireflective on both sides.
Dial: rhodium-plated black dial; recessed silver subdials.
Strap: black crocodile leather.
Also available: rose gold; platinum (limited to 250 pieces).
Suggested price: $13,300–$45,200

IWC INGENIEUR AUTOMATIC MISSION EARTH   REF. IW332601

Movement: mechanical IWC 80110 caliber; 28,800 vph; 44-hour power reserve; 28 jewels.
Functions: central seconds hand with stop function; date at 3.
Case: stainless steel; sapphire crystal, antireflective on both sides.
Dial: rhodium-plated black dial; Arabic numerals and indexes.
Strap: black rubber.
Suggested price: $6,900
Also available: on stainless steel bracelet.

IWC INGENIEUR AUTOMATIC MISSION EARTH EDITION ADVENTURES ECOLOGY REF. IW323603

Movement: mechanical IWC 80110 caliber; 28,800 vph; 44-hour power reserve; 28 jewels.
Functions: central seconds hand with stop function; date at 3.
Case: stainless steel; sapphire crystal, antireflective on both sides.
Dial: rhodium-plated blue dial; orange Arabic numerals and indexes.
Strap: blue rubber.

Note: limited to 1,000 pieces.
Suggested price: $7,900

BIG PILOT'S WATCH EDITION ANTOINE DE SAINT EXUPERY REF. IW500420

Movement: mechanical 51111 caliber with Pellaton automatic-winding system; 21,600 vph; 168-hour power reserve; 42 jewels; beryllium alloy balance with high-precision adjustment cam on the balance bars.
Functions: central seconds hand with stop function; 7-day power-reserve display at 3; date at 6.
Case: white gold; Ø 46mm; convex sapphire crystal, antireflective on both sides.
Dial: rhodium-plated sepia dial; white Arabic numerals.
Strap: brown buffalo strap.
Note: limited to 250 pieces.
Also available: platinum (limited to 1 piece); rose gold (limited to 500 pieces); stainless steel (limited to 1,149 pieces).
Suggested price: $15,700–$31,000

IWC INGENIEUR AUTOMATIC: VINTAGE COLLECTION REF. IW323301

Movement: mechanical 80111 caliber with Pellaton automatic-winding system; 28,800 vph; 44-hour power reserve; 28 jewels.
Functions: hours, minutes, seconds; date at 3.
Case: stainless steel; Ø 42.5mm, thickness: 14.5mm; crossed out, antireflective sapphire crystal; sapphire crystal caseback; screw-down crown; water resistant to 12atm.

Dial: rhodium-plated black dial; dot-and-line markers (the dots are luminescent); dauphine hands.
Strap: black crocodile leather; stainless steel clasp.
Also available: platinum (limited to 500 pieces); rose gold; white gold.
Suggested price: $7,300-$38,000

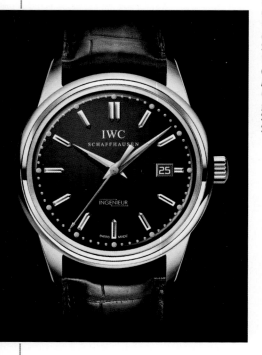

IWC PORTOFINO HAND-WOUND: VINTAGE COLLECTION REF. IW544801

Movement: mechanical manual-winding 98800 caliber; 18,800 vph; 46-hour power reserve; 18 jewels; Breguet spring.
Functions: hours, minutes, small seconds at 6; moonphase at 12.
Case: stainless steel; Ø 46mm, thickness: 11mm; crossed out, antireflective sapphire crystal; sapphire crystal caseback; water resistant to 3atm.
Dial: black dial with elongated Roman-style numerals.

Strap: black crocodile leather; stainless steel clasp.
Also available: platinum (limited to 500 pieces); rose gold; white gold.
Suggested price: $10,900–$44,000

IWC PILOT'S WATCH HAND-WOUND: VINTAGE COLLECTION   REF. IW325401

Movement: mechanical manual-winding 98300 caliber; 18,000 vph; 46-hour power reserve; 18 jewels.
Functions: hours, minutes, small seconds at 6.
Case: stainless steel; Ø 44mm, thickness: 12mm; antireflective sapphire crystal; sapphire crystal caseback; rotating bezel with pointer; water resistant to 6atm.
Dial: black dial with the classical IWC cockpit-style design; luminescent hands and numerals.
Strap: brown buffalo strap; stainless steel clasp.
Also available: platinum (limited to 500 pieces); rose gold; white gold.
Suggested price: $8,900-41,600

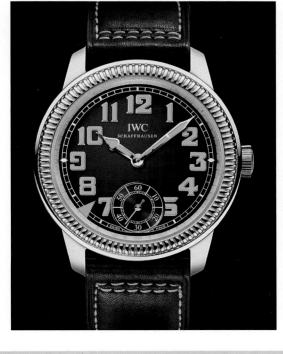

IWC PORTUGUESE PERPETUAL CALENDAR   REF. IW502213

Movement: mechanical IWC 51612 caliber with Pellaton automatic-winding system; 21,600 vph; 7-day power reserve, 64 jewels; balance with Breguet spring; rotor with 18K yellow-gold weight.
Functions: perpetual calendar; perpetual moonphase display with four-digit year display at 12; double phase of the moon for the northern and southern hemispheres, countdown indicator until the next full moon; power-reserve display at 3; monthly calendar display at 6; weekly calendar display at 9; small seconds hand with stop function.
Case: 18K rose-gold three-piece case; Ø 44.2mm; thickness 15.5mm; polished and brushed finish; exhibition sapphire crystal caseback.
Dial: silver; subdial decorated with circular beads; applied gilded Arabic numerals.
Strap: hand-stitched crocodile leather; rose-gold fold-over clasp.
Suggested price: $30,500-$35,000
Also available: in white gold on brown crocodile strap.

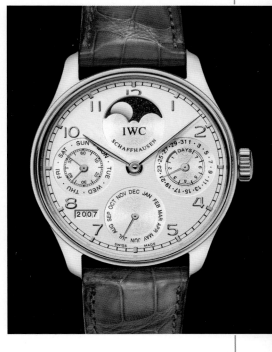

IWC PORTUGUESE CHRONO-AUTOMATIC   REF. IW371402

Movement: mechanical automatic-winding IWC 79350 caliber; 28,800 vph; 44-hour power reserve; 31 jewels.
Functions: hours, minutes; chronograph with two counters: minutes at 12, small seconds at 6.
Case: 18K white-gold three-piece case; Ø 40.9mm, thickness: 12.3mm; polished and brushed finish; convex, antireflective sapphire crystal; water resistant to 3atm.
Dial: ardoise; railway-style minute chapter ring; applied gilded Arabic numerals; recessed subdials for the minutes and seconds counters; rhodium plated.
Strap: dark brown hand-stitched crocodile leather; white-gold fold-over clasp.
Suggested price: $6,800-$15,800
Also available: with all-silvered or black dial; in yellow gold with silvered dial; in stainless steel with white dial; in rose gold with black or silvered dial.

IWC PILOT'S WATCH CHRONO-AUTOMATIC   REF. IW371701

Movement: mechanical automatic-winding IWC 79320 caliber; 28,800 vph; 44-hour power reserve; 25 jewels.
Functions: hours, minutes; small seconds hand with stop function; day and date indicator, stopwatch at 6, 9 and 12.
Case: stainless steel three-piece case; Ø 42mm, thickness: 14.7mm; soft iron for protection against magnetic fields; convex, antireflective sapphire crystal resistant against pressure drop.
Dial: black; applied Arabic numerals; chapter ring; propeller-like hands.
Strap: black hand-stitched crocodile leather; stainless steel fold-over clasp.
Suggested price: $4,400-$14,500
Also available: on a stainless steel bracelet equipped with folding clasp and special IWC bracelet system that allows for quick adjustment; in rose gold on a brown hand-stitched crocodile leather strap with rose-gold fold-over clasp.

IWC BIG PILOT'S WATCH   REF. IW500401

Movement: mechanical automatic-winding IWC 51110 caliber; 21,600 vph; 7-day power reserve; 44 jewels; balance with Breguet spring.
Functions: hours, minutes; date at 6; power-reserve display at 3; central seconds hand with stop function.
Case: stainless steel three-piece case; Ø 46.2mm, thickness: 15.8mm; soft iron for protection against magnetic fields; convex, antireflective sapphire crystal resistant against pressure drop.
Dial: black; applied Arabic numerals; propeller-like hands.
Strap: black hand-stitched crocodile leather; stainless steel fold-over clasp.
Suggested price: $13,500-$26,500
Also available: 18K gold on a dark brown hand-stitched crocodile leather strap.

IWC PORTUGUESE AUTOMATIC   REF. IW500106

Movement: mechanical IWC 51010 caliber with Pellaton automatic-winding system; 21,600 vph; 7-day power reserve; 44 jewels; balance with Breguet spring; rotor with 18K yellow-gold weight.
Functions: power-reserve display at 3; date display at 6; small seconds hand with stop function at 9.
Case: 18K white-gold three-piece case; Ø 42.3mm, thickness: 13.9mm; convex, anti-reflective sapphire crystal.
Dial: rhodium-plated; ardoise; railway-style minute chapter ring; applied gilded Arabic numerals; recessed subdials for the minutes and seconds counters.
Strap: dark brown hand-stitched crocodile leather; white-gold fold-over clasp.
Suggested price: $10,900-$20,500
Also available: in rose gold on a brown hand-stitched crocodile leather strap; in stainless steel on a blue or black hand-stitched crocodile strap.

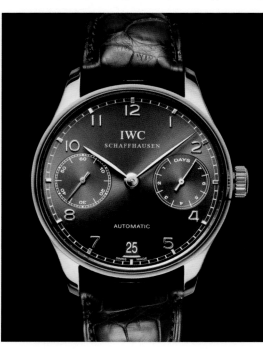

IWC AQUATIMER CHRONOGRAPH EDITION GALAPAGOS   REF. IW376705

Movement: mechanical 79320 caliber with chronograph; 28,800 vph; 44-hour power reserve; 25 jewels.
Functions: chronograph function and small seconds hand with stop function; day and date display at 3; small seconds at 6; hacking seconds at 9; chronograph at 12.
Case: stainless steel coated in vulcanized rubber; Ø 44mm, thickness: 15mm; external rotating mechanical bezel; sapphire crystal, antireflective on both sides; water resistant to 12 bar.
Dial: rhodium-plated black dial; white luminescent indexes.
Strap: black rubber.
Note: limited to 1,000 pieces.
Suggested price: $6,500

PILOT'S WATCH DOUBLE CHRONOGRAPH EDITION TOP GUN   REF. IW379901

Movement: mechanical automatic-winding IWC 79230 caliber (integral chronograph modified for the split-second feature) with a seconds-stopping system; 28,800 vph; 44-hour power reserve; 29 jewels.
Functions: hours, minutes, center seconds; day and oversized date at 3; split-second chronograph with 3 counters: hour at 6, small second at 9, minute at 12.
Case: black ceramic and natural titanium; two-piece case; Ø 46mm, thickness: 17.8mm; matte finish; additional ductile iron inside for the deviation of magnetic fields; very thick, curved sapphire crystal, antireflective on both sides, highly depressurization-resistant; screw-down crown and pushers with case protection (the one for the split-second chronograph at 10 in titanium); titanium screw-on caseback in titanium with Top Gun logo; water resistant to 6atm.
Dial: matte black; chronograph subdials decorated with circular beads; white Arabic numerals; triangular and bâton markers, luminescent at quarters; luminescent matte-black lozenge hands; split-second counter with white hands and red counterweights; minute track.
Strap: black fabric; brushed titanium clasp.
Suggested price: $10,900

IWC DA VINCI AUTOMATIC: VINTAGE COLLECTION REF. IW546101

Movement: mechanical 80111 caliber with Pellaton automatic-winding system; 28,800 vph; 44-hour power reserve; 28 jewels.
Functions: hours, minutes, seconds; date at 3.
Case: stainless steel; Ø 41mm, thickness: 13.5mm; antireflective sapphire crystal; sapphire crystal caseback; screw-down crown; water resistant to 3atm.
Dial: black dial with extra-long markers and simple bâton hands.
Strap: black crocodile leather; stainless steel clasp.
Also available: platinum (limited to 500 pieces); rose gold; white gold.
Suggested price: $7,300–$38,000

PILOT'S WATCH MARK XVI REF. IW325501

Movement: mechanical automatic-winding IWC 30110 caliber; 28,800 vph; 42-hour power reserve; 21 jewels.
Functions: hours, minutes, seconds; date at 3.
Case: stainless steel three-piece case; Ø 39mm, thickness: 11.5mm; soft iron for protection against magnetic fields; convex, antireflective sapphire crystal resistant against pressure drop.
Dial: black; Arabic numerals; propeller-like hands.
Strap: hand-stitched black crocodile leather; stainless steel fold-over clasp.
Also available: on stainless steel bracelet with special IWC system enabling quick adjustment.
Suggested price: $3,500–$4,900

BIG INGENIEUR REF. IW500503

Movement: mechanical 51113 caliber with Pellaton automatic-winding system; 21,600 vph; 7-day power reserve when fully wound; 42 jewels.
Functions: hours, minutes, seconds; power-reserve display at 3; date at 6.
Case: rose gold; Ø 45.5mm, thickness: 15mm; convex, antireflective sapphire crystal; sapphire crystal caseback; screw-down crown; water resistant to 12atm.
Dial: rhodium-plated silvered dial; gold indexes.
Strap: brown crocodile leather.
Also available: stainless steel; platinum (limited to 500 pieces).
Suggested price: $11,800–$42,000

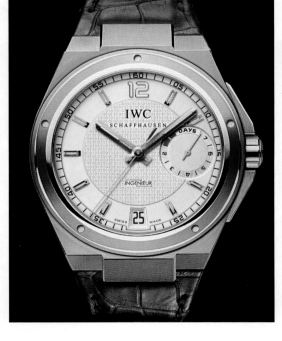

IWC PORTUGUESE HAND-WOUND: VINTAGE COLLECTION REF. IW544501

Movement: mechanical manual-winding 98295 caliber; 18,000 vph; 46-hour power reserve; 18 jewels; Breguet spring.
Functions: hours, minutes, small seconds at 6.
Case: stainless steel; Ø 44mm, thickness: 10mm; antireflective, crossed out sapphire crystal and sapphire crystal caseback; water resistant to 3atm.
Dial: rhodium-plated black dial; silvered indexes; railway-style minute chapter ring; applied gilded Arabic numerals.
Strap: black leather.
Also available: platinum (limited to 500 pieces); rose gold; white gold.
Suggested price: $9,900–41,500

After years spent crafting jewelry for an elite circle of trendsetters and celebrities, Jacob Arabo introduced his unique vision of luxury to the world of mechanical timepieces in 2002. Jacob & Co. has since earned a lofty place among Swiss watchmakers with its technical innovation and incomparable style.

The company recently expanded one of its most popular designs—the Epic—with several interpretations of the original. The first is a tourbillon model enhanced with multiple time zones, which have been an important part of the brand's identity from the start. The company says the function is a reflection of the jet-set lifestyle enjoyed by Jacob & Co.'s celebrity clientele, which counts among its members Tom Cruise, Sir Elton John, Sean Combs, David Beckham, and Derek Jeter.

The Epic Tourbillon's 47mm round case houses the same sophisticated movement unveiled in the acclaimed Rainbow Tourbillon. The outstanding caliber displays 24 time zones in addition to the reference time while providing five days of reserve power. Jacob & Co. offers the Epic Tourbillon in a number of case materials, including black ceramic, stainless steel, white or rose gold.

With the Epic v2 series, Jacob & Co. presents sleek sequels to its Epic I and Epic II chronographs. Slimmer and more compact than its predecessor, the Epic I v2's square case remains substantial on the wrist, measuring 17mm thick. The generously sized case houses the company's automatic chronograph movement, which allows the wearer to measure elapsed time with a central seconds and 30-minute and 12-hour counters. The same caliber is also found in the Epic II v2, a chronograph whose round case is more than 8mm smaller in diameter than the original model.

ABOVE Soccer star David Beckham (left) and actor Tom Cruise (right) sport the Epic II from Jacob & Co.

TOP RIGHT The 47mm round Epic II v2 is equipped with Jacob & Co. 2121 automatic chronograph, which provides 48 hours of reserve power.

RIGHT The Epic I v2's geometrically shaped chronograph counters express a fusion of art and skill that imbue the watch with its unique personality.

FAR RIGHT Available in black ceramic, stainless steel, and white or rose gold, the 47mm Epic Tourbillon is stylish in any one of its featured 24 time zones.

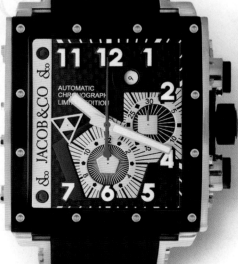

Ruby and sapphire versions of the Crystal Tourbillon now join the original white-diamond edition.

Jacob and Co. is renowned for haute jewelry timepieces that glitter with high-carat glamour. The company carries on the tradition, expanding the precious palette of its Crystal Tourbillon with colorful new cousins.

First introduced in 2007, the Crystal Tourbillon features a skeletonized tourbillon movement that leaves nothing to the imagination with a clear dial, caseback and sapphire bridges. The design's clarity highlights the complexities of the tourbillon, positioned at 6:00 and topped with the company logo.

Jacob & Co. turns a sparkling spotlight on that technical prowess with a 47mm case lavished with precious gemstones. Recently, the Ruby Crystal Tourbillon and the Sapphire Crystal Tourbillon joined the original white-diamond limited edition.

In an elegant demonstration of Arabo's extensive experience in the diamond industry, all three use an invisible setting that focuses attention on the natural beauty of the gems.

The watchmaker went full-spectrum in 2005 with its Rainbow Tourbillon, the first limited edition collection in the world to combine a tourbillon with a multiple-time-zone display. One version displays 12 time zones, the other twice that, running the gamut from New York City to Kamchatka, Russia. All of these watches share a multicolor tourbillon movement, which can be examined through the transparent caseback. Jacob & Co. offers a limited number of Rainbow Tourbillon watches in platinum or white, yellow or rose gold.

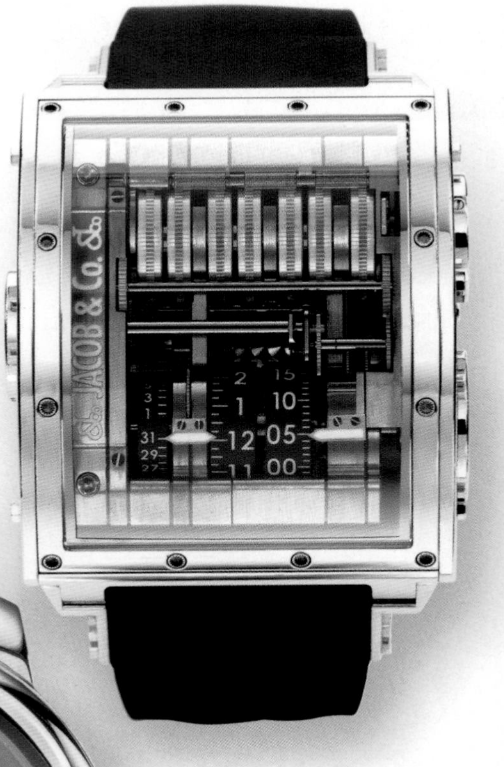

TOP LEFT   The Ruby Crystal Tourbillon includes more than 18 carats of ruby baguettes on the bezel, movement and crown.

TOP RIGHT   The Sapphire Crystal Tourbillon's clear bridges and dial reveal the intricacies of the skeletonized movement.

CENTER   The Quenttin emphasizes technical sophistication with a rare vertical movement by Jacob & Co. that generates a 31-hour power reserve via seven barrels, each equipped with multiple mainsprings. Vertical discs assembled coaxially are used for the hours and minutes as well as the power reserve. Arabo calls the Quenttin the most advanced timepiece yet by Jacob & Co.

RIGHT   The Rainbow Tourbillon's 47.5mm rose-gold case surrounds a neutral-colored dial where 24 time zones and the corresponding cities from around the world are displayed on rotating discs.

EPIC I — REF. Q2B

Movement: Jacob & Co. 2121 automatic chronograph movement; 48-hour power reserve; Incabloc shock-absorption system.
Functions: chronograph: 30 minutes, 12 hours, center seconds; date; early seconds.
Case: black PVD; 51x47x18mm.
Dial: six-layer multi-tiered dial; signature Jacob & Co. geometric subdials and hands.
Strap: rubber.

Approximate price: $16,800
Also available: 18K rose gold or stainless steel.

EPIC II — REF. E2RGCP

Movement: Jacob & Co. 2121 automatic chronograph movement; 48-hour power reserve; Incabloc shock-absorption system.
Functions: chronograph: 30 minutes, 12 hours, center seconds; date; early seconds.
Case: 18K rose gold; ceramic bezel; 47mm.
Dial: six-layer multi-tiered dial; signature Jacob & Co. geometric subdials and hands.
Strap: rubber.

Approximate price: $27,000
Also available: stainless steel or black PVD.

EPIC TOURBILLON — REF. ET3

Movement: mechanical manual-winding tourbillon device featuring multiple time zones.
Functions: hours, minutes; 12- and 24-hour time zones.
Case: black PVD; 47mm.
Dial: six-layer multi-tiered dial; signature Jacob & Co. geometric subdials and hands.
Strap: rubber.

Approximate price: $200,000
Also available: 18K rose gold or stainless steel.

QUENTTIN — REF. QUENTTIN

Movement: Jacob & Co. vertical mechanical movement; 31-day power reserve; winding escapement with Swiss anchor mounted in tourbillon cage; cage suspended without roller bearings and positioned vertically; winding via integrated key, external hand key or motorized in the box.
Functions: hours, minutes; power reserve made by vertical discs assembled coaxially.

Case: 18K white gold; carbon-fiber applications on casesides; 56x47x21.5mm.
Strap: rubber.
Approximate price: $360,000
Also available: 18K rose gold or magnesium with carbon-fiber applications on casesides.

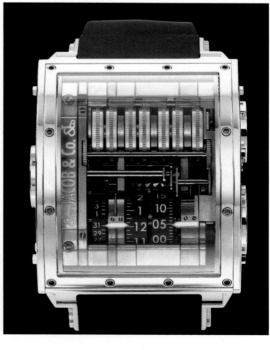

NAPOLEON REF. NT5WG

Movement: mechanical manual-winding Jacob & Co Caliber 8005; 652 components; sapphire bridges.
Functions: hours, minutes
Case: 18K white gold; 46mm; exhibition caseback.
Dial: transparent sapphire disc revealing skeletonized tourbillon cage with Jacob & Co. logo.
Strap: alligator.
Approximate price: $195,000
Also available: 18K rose gold.
Note: limited edition of 18 pieces for each version.

CRYSTAL TOURBILLON REF. CRYSTAL TOUR

Movement: Jacob & Co. 7 Caliber movement; skeleton; 32.6x5.2mm; set with baguette diamonds (1.6 carats); sapphire bridges; crafted, assembled, and decorated by hand to the highest Jacob & Co. quality standards.
Functions: hours, minutes.
Case: 18K white gold; 47mm (with crown guard), thickness: 14mm; baguette diamonds (17.48 carats); transparent caseback.
Dial: transparent; skeleton tourbillon movement.
Strap: alligator; baguette diamonds on the buckle (2.22 carats).
Approximate price: $900,000
Note: limited edition of 18 pieces.

NAPOLEON QUADRA REF. QUADB

Movement: mechanical manual-winding Jacob & Co. Caliber 8082; four 60-second tourbillon escapements; 78 jewels; 652 components; sapphire bridges.
Functions: hours, minutes; four time zones.
Case: black PVD; 55.5mm, thickness: 10.05mm; exhibition caseback.
Dial: transparent sapphire disc revealing four skeletonized tourbillon escapements and four time-zone apertures.
Strap: alligator.
Approximate price: $540,000
Also available: 18K white gold or 18K rose gold.
Note: limited edition of 18 pieces of each version.

RAINBOW TOURBILLON REF. R5RG

Movement: mechanical manual-winding tourbillon device featuring multiple time zones; five-day power reserve.
Functions: hours, minutes; 12- and 24-hour time zones.
Case: 18K rose gold; 47.5mm; exhibition caseback with multi-row Rainbow Tourbillon movement.
Dial: painted and embossed with a special guilloché; leaf-shaped hands in steel with gun-color treatment.
Strap: alligator.
Approximate price: $240,000
Also available: 18K white or yellow gold, or platinum; various dial designs: multi-colored, natural and black with white timers.

LEVIEV®

EXTRAORDINARY DIAMONDS

The Leviev empire continued its global expansion this spring when the company opened locations in Dubai and Singapore. The first boutique resides in the Burj Dubai Mall beneath the Khalifa Tower, the world's largest man-made structure. The second occupies nearly half of the new Yafriro showroom in the lobby of the Marina Bay Sands Casino and Resort in Singapore. Decorated lavishly with Leviev fixtures, chandeliers, and antique Venetian mirrors, this high-profile space also offers a private Leviev salon.

These openings are but the latest chapters in the Leviev saga, which began in 1956 when its founder Lev Leviev was born in Uzbekistan. As a young boy, he immigrated to Israel where he first discovered the art of cutting diamonds in a neighbor's workshop. The fateful experience inspired Leviev to dream of one day becoming a captain of industry.

He soon brought his fantasy to life. Through tenacity, industriousness and an exceptional business sense, he successfully broke De Beers's negotiating monopoly on the world diamond trade by acquiring 30 percent of the world's diamond production.

Old Bond Street in London is home to many jewelers, yet one stands out conspicuously from the others. Peer into Leviev's window and one soon discovers that this store shelters more carats than all the other stores combined—4,000 carats valued at more than 200 million pounds sterling when the boutique opened in 2006. The same is true for Leviev's other boutiques in New York City, Moscow and Dubai.

LUXURY WITHOUT EQUAL

Leviev emerged as the world's largest cutter and polisher of diamonds by controlling the entire chain of diamond production. In fact, the company supplies many luxury jewelry brands that do not own their diamonds, but rather purchase their regular assortments, whether to set in engagement rings or to set on watches.

When it comes to diamonds larger than five carats, the industry-wide practice is to rely on consignments. Indeed, it makes no economic sense for a luxury brand to tie up millions of dollars in a single display of large, rare diamonds. When they do occasionally display one or two such exceptional diamonds, chances are that they are on loan from a diamond producer such as Leviev.

After supplying the industry for years, Leviev decided to launch his eponymous brand in 2005, allowing his company to sell directly to diamond collectors and connoisseurs alike. Today, the company is well positioned in the "über-luxury" market—not the mass luxury market. But Leviev did not stop there.

THIS PAGE
An artist's rendering of Leviev's new boutique inside the Yafriro showroom in the lobby of the Marina Bay Sands Casino and Resort in Singapore.

FACING PAGE
TOP   Leviev's Moscow boutique.

BOTTOM   Interior of the Madison Avenue in New York City.

Leviev emerged as the world's largest cutter and polisher of diamonds **by controlling the entire chain of diamond production.**

A great admirer of the watch industry, he decided to create his own brand watches for his pleasure and that of his customers. To help make it happen, iev enlisted the help of Thierry Chaunu, a widely respected executive who ked previously at Cartier and Chopard. Now president and COO of Leviev, aunu set about creating a line of exceptional Swiss timepieces that would er to a discerning clientele.

Chaunu began in 2006 and quickly contracted the renowned Swiss watchmaker istophe Claret, who devised the Double Eagle Platinum and Diamond Tourbillon Leviev. The COSC-certified chronometer is one of the only watches in the world ipped with a power reserve that exceeds 100 hours.

INDULGENT DIAMONDS AND TIMEPIECES THAT REDEFINE RARITY

Each precious piece is produced in extremely limited quantities and stamped with interlocking Ls—the brand's symbol and its founder's initials. "To mark the fact that they are from a master of gems," Chaunu says, "all have at least one diamond on the crown or in the case. Luxury market analysts have placed the Leviev brand in the über-luxury category, which is the top of the pyramid. Our brand caters to the elite of the elites." When it comes to timepieces, the prices of the first women's day-time models range from $16,000 to $200,000, and the tourbillon model is currently the most complex in the catalog.

"So far, the men's collection has included the GMT Alarm with a specially decorated movement, the GMT Chrono, and the GMT Chrono Mega Yacht, whose success has been resounding," Chaunu explains. "This is why we created a second version called the GMT Chrono Mega Yacht 2. As in the others, the latter is equipped with a movement, A. Schild 5008, to which we added an additional module from the Lajoux-Perret workshops to obtain the hours, minutes, seconds, chronograph, second time-zone and date functions." The most recent introduction, the Double Barillet, houses an automatic Muller-Laville mechanical movement. As its name indicates, it draws energy from a pair of barrels offering a total reserve of 120 hours. Equipped with hours, minutes, seconds and a retrograde date function, the Double Barillet boasts a partially diamond-set dial and a diamond on the crown. Carefully skeletonized, it reveals the escapement and features a delicate guilloché sun whose center is at 9:00. The interlocking L symbol serves as a counterweight on the seconds hand. For women, Leviev invented a uniquely shaped case framed by two symmetrically placed Ls. Named the Double Elle, the collection offers models whose bezels are set with one or two rows of diamonds, and whose dials are often decorated with mother-of-pearl.

Judging from the meteoric rise of the Leviev empire, one may expect the brand to extend its reach to the remaining continents before too long.

ABOVE Created by the Swiss watchmaker Christophe Claret, the Leviev Double Eagle Platinum and Diamond Tourbillon boasts an exceptional power reserve exceeding 100 hours.

BELOW The GMT Alarm in 18-karat pink gold.

TOP The Double Barillet model has a maximum power reserve of 120 hours and its automatic mechanical movement is a COSC-certified chronometer.

FAR LEFT The Double Elle models are equipped with quartz movements from Swiss manufacturer ETA.

LEFT Each series of the Double Elle collection has 8 to 12 numbered pieces.

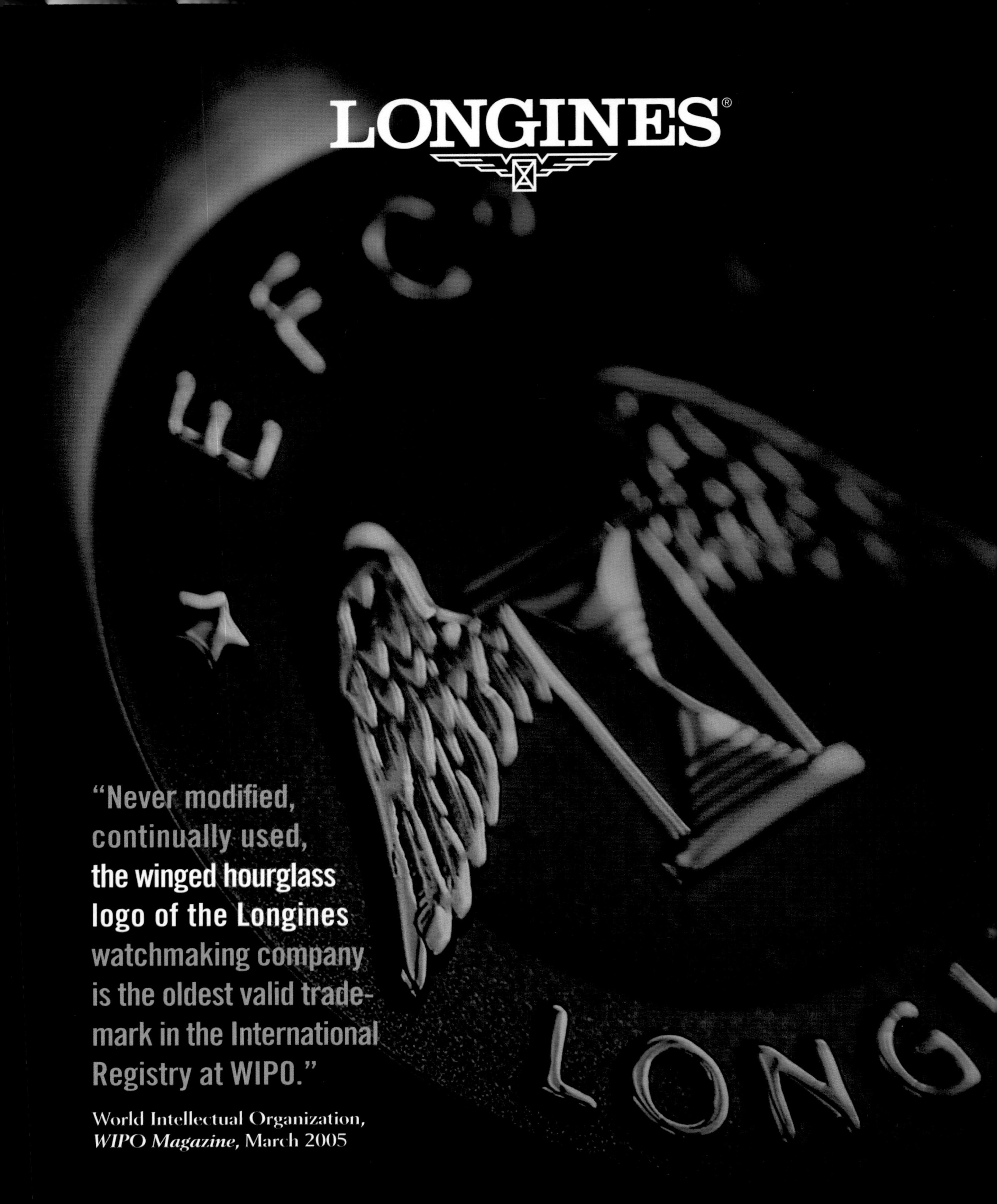

LONGINES®

"Never modified,
continually used,
**the winged hourglass
logo of the Longines**
watchmaking company
is the oldest valid trademark in the International
Registry at WIPO."

World Intellectual Organization,
WIPO Magazine, March 2005

On October 1st, 2009, Longines celebrated the 120th anniversary of the registration of a logo that the famous Saint-Imier watchmaker still uses today.

Protected since 1889 in Switzerland (FOIP), this factory trademark comprising a winged hourglass and the name Longines is the oldest of its kind still active, in its original form, in the international registers kept by the World Intellectual Property Organization (WIPO). To mark the 120th anniversary of its logo, the brand has organized a themed exhibition in the Cité du Temps in Geneva, published a study about the symbol, and created two exceptional limited series of timepieces numbered from 1 to 120.

On May 27th, 1889, Ernest Francillon registered a factory mark consisting of a winged hourglass within a double circle which contained the signature EFCo (Ernest Francillon & Compagnie) and the name Longines. This mark was registered with the Swiss authority that dealt with the protection of trademarks at the time, namely the Federal Office for Intellectual Property (FOIP). For Longines, the 1889 registration was the start of an important tradition of graphic and symbolic signatures since, for the first time, a trademark whose use and protection in its original form continued beyond the 21st century was legally recognized. The protection of the trademark was ensured at an international level in 1893 and makes Longines' the oldest trademark still valid in its original form in the international registers of the World Intellectual Property Organization (WIPO).

The registration of this logo was part of the industrialization of watchmaking in Switzerland in the last third of the 19th century, in which Longines played a leading role. Initially, the trademark chosen by Longines—the winged hourglass—served to authenticate the company's products. But it quickly became a means of fighting against counterfeiters who hoped to take advantage of the excellent reputation built up by the Saint-Imier watch manufacture. Subsequently, the factory mark was used in other contexts apart from on the product itself and began to determine the visual identity of the brand. This logo, registered in 1889, has therefore been part and parcel of the development and construction of the Longines brand which, in line with its watchmaking heritage, continues to use it to this day.

Longines PrimaLuna

The Longines PrimaLuna collection with its rounded, delicate lines is a tribute to the moon. Inspired by femininity, the famous Saint-Imier watchmaker is launching an exquisitely fine interpretation of elegance, grace and carefree femininity: the Longines PrimaLuna.

The soft silhouette of the Longines PrimaLuna is enhanced by the exquisite purity of the dial and its whole is illuminated by a play of sparkling diamonds. The collection offers models in stainless steel, rose or yellow gold, and rose gold and steel on sleek bracelets of steel, gold, or rose gold and steel or leather straps. A selection of delicate dials is also available: white, silvered, or mother-of-pearl decorated with hour symbols, Arabic or Roman numerals, or diamonds. And finally, three hands, blued, gilded or rose, mark the passing of time. As multifaceted as the modern woman, the Longines PrimaLuna range offers a selection of models in four sizes. Resolutely elegant and subtle, the new Longines PrimaLuna offers to every woman, to every modern Sheherazade, to each luminous and unique female, a magical world represented by this new collection of exquisite models.

A whole day was devoted to a photo shoot and a film documenting this new collection of women's watches. Who other than the stunning Aishwarya Rai could play the starring role? The well known Swiss watchmaker has surrounded the beauty, who has been its Ambassador of Elegance for the past ten years, with a host of Indian stars. The lineup included Farrokh Chothia, by far the country's leading fashion photographer, and Kiiran Deohans, the unquestioned master of advertising films in India, to shoot a film about the Longines PrimaLuna advertising campaign. The result is exactly what one might expect: Aishwarya, the queen of a mysterious and exotic world, radiates beauty and charm. The superb Indian star is without question the perfect embodiment of Longines' slogan "Elegance is an attitude."

Longines Lindbergh's Atlantic Voyage Watch

In 1933 the American aviator Charles Lindbergh set off with his wife on a trip of 47,000 km around the North Atlantic. Having achieved a remarkable technical and human feat in being the first man to fly nonstop across the North Atlantic in his Spirit of St. Louis, Lindbergh wanted to explore possible future air routes across the far north before returning to the USA via Cape Verde and Brazil. The equipment Lindbergh took with him on his long expedition included a wrist chronograph created specially by Longines for this very purpose. Today, Longines is reissuing this exceptional timepiece called the Longines Lindbergh's Atlantic Voyage Watch in tribute to the historical feat achieved by this pioneer of the skies.

This timepiece had a wristwatch chronograph movement with a 30-minute counter. It measured time to the fifth of a second and the chronograph mechanism also had a tachometer that could measure speeds of up to 500 kph. With the flying conditions that were experienced by the Lindberghs, a reliable timepiece was one of the final safeguards as far as navigational instruments were concerned.

Now Longines reissues the timepiece under its original name, the Longines Lindbergh's Atlantic Voyage Watch, a tribute to the long trip undertaken by the couple across the far north. This mechanical wrist chronograph has a diameter of 47.5mm and a self-winding movement. Just like the original model, it has small seconds at 9:00 and a 30-minute counter at 3:00. The time and time measurements are displayed via hands of blued steel on a silvered dial with a white ring, and the watch has a tachometer for measuring speeds of up to 500 kph. The model has a sapphire glass and a solid case-back that protects a transparent back cover through which the workings of the movement can be admired. The watch is mounted on a brown genuine alligator strap. The new versions are in either steel or rose gold. The Longines Lindbergh's Atlantic Voyage Watch stands as an exquisite contemporary of a timepiece that was part of a great aeronautical adventure.

LONGINES DOLCEVITA — REF. L5.155.0.16.6

Movement: quartz caliber L178.2.
Functions: hours, minutes, small seconds at 6.
Case: rectangular; polished stainless steel; bezel set with 32 Top Wesselton VVS diamonds (0.32 carat); cambered scratch-resistant sapphire crystal; water resistant to 30 meters (100 feet).
Dial: matte white; applied rhodium-plated Arabic numeral 12; ten applied, rhodium-plated drop-shaped hour-markers; rhodium-plated hands; small seconds at 6.
Bracelet: polished stainless steel with triple-folding clasp.

LONGINES PRIMALUNA — REF. L8.112.0.87.6

Movement: quartz caliber L129.2.
Functions: hours, minutes, seconds; date at 3.
Case: stainless steel; Ø 30mm; 48 Top Wesselton VVS diamonds (0.403 carat); sapphire crystal with antireflective coating; water resistant to 30 meters (100 feet).
Dial: white mother-of-pearl set with 11 diamonds; rhodium-plated, blued steel hands; date at 3.
Bracelet: stainless steel with folding safety clasp and pushpieces.

THE LONGINES MASTER COLLECTION — REF. L2.673.4.78.5

Movement: mechanical self-winding caliber L678; 13¼ lines; 25 jewels; 28,800 vph; 42-hour power reserve.
Functions: hours, minutes, seconds; 24 hours at 9; date, day of the week and month; moonphase at 6; chronograph: center 60-second hand, 12-hour totalizer at 6, 30-minute totalizer at 12.
Case: stainless steel; Ø 40mm; scratch-resistant sapphire crystal; transparent caseback; water resistant to 30 meters (100 feet).
Dial: silver-finished stamped "barleycorn"; nine Arabic numerals; blued steel hands; central hand featuring blue moon; black painted minute track, 31-day calendar; moonphase at 6; day and month aperture at 12; 24-hour indicator and small seconds at 9.
Strap: dark brown genuine leather with triple-folding or standard clasp.

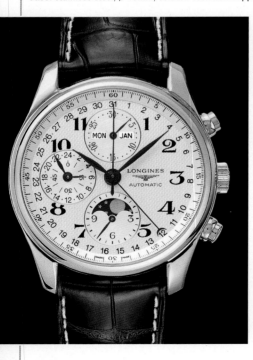

THE LONGINES MASTER COLLECTION — REF. L2.717.4.78.5

Movement: mechanical self-winding caliber L698; 16½ lines; 25 jewels; 28,800 vph; 46-hour power reserve.
Functions: hours and minutes; four retrograde functions: day, date, seconds, and second time zone on a 24-hour scale.
Case: stainless steel; Ø 44mm; scratch-resistant sapphire crystal; transparent sapphire crystal caseback; water resistant to 30 meters (100 feet).
Dial: silver-finished stamped "barleycorn"; 11 Arabic numerals and black painted minute track; six blued steel hands.
Strap: dark brown genuine alligator strap with triple-folding safety clasp.

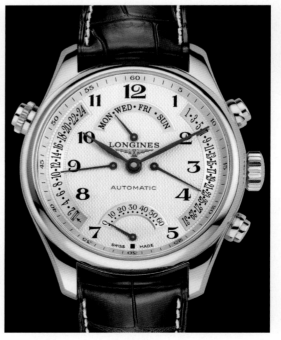

LONGINES EVIDENZA   REF. L2.643.4.73.4

Movement: mechanical self-winding caliber L650; 12½ lines; 37 jewels; 28,800 vph; 46-hour power reserve.
Functions: hours, minutes, seconds; date at 6; chronograph: central 60-second hand, 30-minutes totalizer at 9, 12-hour totalizer at 6.
Case: stainless steel; tonneau-shaped; domed, scratch-resistant and antireflective crystal; water resistant to 30 meters (100 feet).
Dial: silvered "flinqué"; 12 blue painted Arabic numerals; small seconds at 3; date at 6; blued steel hands.
Strap: dark brown genuine leather strap with optional deployment buckle.

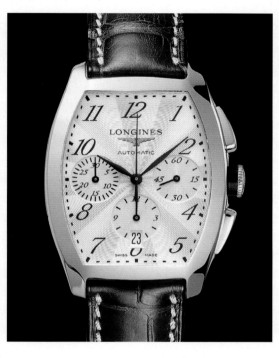

LONGINES LINDBERGH'S ATLANTIC VOYAGE WATCH   REF. L2.730.4.11.0

Movement: mechanical self-winding caliber L705; 16½ lines; 27 jewels; 28,000 vph; 46-hour power reserve.
Functions: hours, minutes, small seconds; chronograph; 30-minute counter; tachymeter.
Case: stainless steel; Ø 47.50mm; scratch-resistant sapphire crystal; solid caseback over transparent sapphire glass back cover; crown with pushpiece function for opening the caseback; water resistant to 30 meters (100 feet).
Dial: polished white lacquer/silvered; ten black Arabic numerals; black tachymeter, 500-60 kph; blued steel Breguet hands (hours and minutes); blued steel counter-weight line pear (fly-back hand); blued steel arrow (30-minute counter); blued steel counter-weight stick pear (small seconds).
Strap: genuine brown alligator strap with buckle.

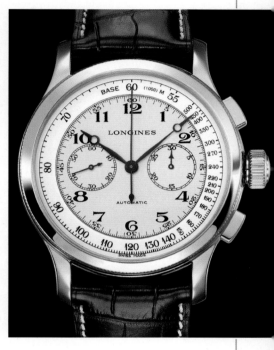

LONGINES CONQUEST   REF. L3.661.4.56.7

Movement: mechanical self-winding caliber L667; 13¼ lines; 27 jewels; 28,800 vph; 46-hour power reserve.
Functions: hours, minutes, small seconds at 9; date at 3; chronograph: center second hand, 30-minute counter at 12, 12-hour counter at 6.
Case: stainless steel; Ø 41mm; black ceramic bezel; black ceramic cabochon; screw-in crown with crown protection sapphire crystal with antireflective coating; screw-down caseback; water resistant to 300 meters (1,000 feet).
Dial: black lacquered; silver "large 12" Arabic numeral; 11 indexes; date opening at 3; small seconds at 9; polished rhodium-plated hands.
Bracelet: stainless steel bracelet with black ceramic links with triple-folding safety clasp.

LONGINES ADMIRAL   REF. L3.670.4.56.6

Movement: mechanica self-winding caliber L686; 13¼ lines; 25 jewels; 28,800 vph; 46-hour power reserve.
Functions: hours, minutes, seconds; date; second time zone; chronograph: center seconds, 30-minute counter at 12, 12-hour counter at 6.
Case: stainless steel; Ø 42mm; stainless steel bezel with tachymeter; screw-in crown and pushpieces with protective shoulder; sapphire crystal with antireflective coating; screw-in caseback; water resistant to 100 meters (300 feet).
Dial: black dial with a "large 12" in Arabic numeral; eight applied, polished rhodium-plated hour-markers coated with SuperLumiNova, plus 24-hour graduations in Arabic numerals on the flange; date aperture at 3; small seconds at 9; polished, rhodium-plated hands with SuperLumiNova coating; red 24-hour hand with SuperLumiNova coating.
Bracelet: stainless steel bracelet with triple-folding safety clasp.

LOUIS MOINET
1806

Louis Moinet captivated the world's wealthiest and most influential people in the 1800s with the genius of his watchmaking. Having withstood the test of time, his visionary designs are reborn and his legacy perpetuated in the modern Louis Moinet collection.

Michael Brader-Araje, President of Louis Moinet North America, notes that those who wear a Louis Moinet watch join an exclusive group whose membership has included royalty, presidents and emperors. "Today's owners will go on to have their own great achievements," he says, "and just like in the past, Louis Moinet will be right there with them to mark the time of those achievements."

To preserve the watch's exclusive allure, the family-owned company will produce no more than 1,000 pieces every year.

Among those rarified offerings are two limited editions inspired by Jules Verne, the French author considered by many to be the father of science fiction. The Jules Verne Instrument 1 and Instrument 2 both pay tribute to the writer's influential works about space travel: *From the Earth to the Moon* (1865) and its sequel *Round the Moon* (1870).

They feature technically advanced chronographs that employ a patent-pending lever system to secure their stop and start mechanisms. The Instrument 2, however, is a rattrapante chronograph and able to time multiple events simultaneously.

As a subtle reminder of how far mankind has traveled and how far it has yet to go, Louis Moinet watchmakers embed a piece of the moon into each watch. The lunar memento is visible through a porthole on the side of the titanium case. The company will produce 120 of each Jules Verne model, 60 with black dials and 60 with silver dials.

With these watches, Louis Moinet pays fitting homage to two contemporaries whose imaginative foresight about the future continues to resonate in the here and now.

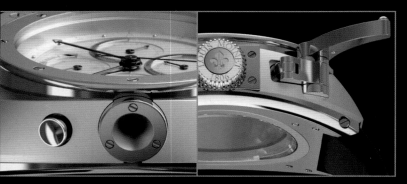

ABOVE LEFT   A porthole on the side of the 46.3x54mm titanium case shows off a piece of the moon integrated into every Jules Verne watch.

ABOVE RIGHT   The Jules Verne Instrument 1 and 2 both feature an innovative lever system to secure the chronographs' stop and start mechanisms.

RIGHT   The Jules Verne Instrument 2 is equipped with a rattrapante chronograph, allowing it to time multiple events concurrently.

The Jules Verne Instrument 1 and Instrument 2 pay tribute to the writer's influential works about space travel.

Another fitting example of Moinet's influence on the present can be found in the company's Twintech Chronograph, whose 41x54mm stainless steel case is one of the founder's original designs.

Inside, the watch features the Louis Moinet LM07, an automatic movement that comprises more than 150 parts. Its intricate arrangement controls the hours and minutes as well as the chronograph counters.

Designers balance those outstanding technical aspects with stylish appointments, including black or silver dials decorated superbly with the Côtes du Jura's elegant undulations.

The company also offers a third model dubbed the Twintech Chronograph Racing. Its black and red color scheme and its carbon-fiber dial both evoke the style and materials from the world of auto racing. Only 60 of each Twintech Chronograph will be produced.

Moinet's spirit can also be seen in a winding box the company recently introduced. Shaped like two leather-bound books, the box recalls the watchmaker's famous Treatise on Watchmaking that was published in 1848.

A lithium ion battery, expected to provide five years of uninterrupted service, powers the system, offering an environmentally friendly touch that results in fewer batteries in landfills. "Our watchwinder box," Brader-Araje says, "is yet another example of the way Louis Moinet strives to create a luxury experience for our watches' owners while continuing to innovate the industry, just like our namesake did during the 19th century."

TOP LEFT   Louis Moinet will limit production of its Twintech Chronograph models to 60 pieces each.

TOP RIGHT   Côtes du Jura decorate the Twintech Chronograph's black dial, providing a distinctive background for the chronograph counters.

BOTTOM LEFT   This unique watchwinder box is designed to look like the groundbreaking Treatise on Watchmaking Louis Moinet published in 1848.

BOTTOM RIGHT   The winder offers a variety of settings to accommodate the winding needs of just about any automatic timepiece.

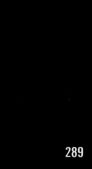

DATOSCOPE

Movement: exclusive mechanical automatic LM03 caliber with date; 42-hour power reserve; 25 jewels; 28,000 vph; blued steel screws; oscillating weight and shield shaped in Côtes du Jura motif; engraved with individual numbers and Louis Moinet markings.
Function: hours, minutes; central seconds; calendar.
Case: 316L polished stainless steel; 45mm; caseback secured with four screws; two sapphire crystals; water resistant to 3atm.

Dial: burgundy; decorated with Côtes du Jura; applied date indicator; rhodium-plated hands coated with SuperLumiNova; linden-tree color hands.
Strap: hand-sewn Louisiana alligator leather; 316L folding clasp with Louis Moinet symbol.
Suggested price: $6,900
Note: limited edition of 60 pieces worldwide.

TEMPOGRAPH

Movement: exclusive mechanical automatic LM05 caliber; 42-hour power reserve; 27 jewels; 28,800 vph; 125 parts; blued steel screws; oscillating weight shaped in Côtes du Jura motif.
Function: hours; 10-second retrograde mechanism.
Case: rose and yellow gold; 47mm; two sapphire crystals; water resistant to 3atm.
Dial: black; decorated with Côtes du Jura engraving; composed of 48 different parts;

galvanic blue or rose gold-plated hands; fitted with a cap.
Strap: hand-sewn Louisiana alligator leather; steel 316L or 18K rose-gold folding clasp with Louis Moinet symbol.
Suggested price: $59,000
Also available: black dial, titanium and steel; silver dial, titanium and steel ($28,000); black dial, rose gold and titanium; silver dial, rose gold and titanium ($36,000).
Note: limited edition of 60 pieces.

TWINTECH CHRONOGRAPH SILVER DIAL

Movement: exclusive mechanical automatic LM07 chronograph caliber; 44-hour power reserve; 25 jewels; 28,800 vph; blued steel screws; oscillating weight; casing ring engraved with Côtes du Jura.
Functions: hours, minutes; small seconds at 9; 60-second chronograph in the center; 30-minute chronograph counter at 3; 12-hour chronograph counter at 6.
Case: 316L polished stainless steel; 41x54mm; two sapphire crystals; caseback secured with four screws; engraved with individual numbers and Louis Moinet markings; water resistant to 3atm.

Dial: silver; decorated with Côtes du Jura; seven applied zones; rhodium-plated hands, coated with SuperLumiNova.
Strap: hand-sewn crocodile leather; carbon finish; 316L folding clasp with Louis Moinet symbol.
Suggested price: $9,900
Note: limited edition of 60 pieces worldwide for each dial.

TWINTECH CHRONOGRAPH CARBON FIBER RACING DIAL

Movement: exclusive mechanical automatic chronograph LM07 caliber; 44-hour power reserve; 25 jewels; 28,800 vph; blued steel screws; oscillating weight; casing ring engraved with Côtes du Jura.
Functions: hours, minutes; small seconds at 9; 60-second chronograph in the center; 30-minute chronograph counter at 3; 12-hour chronograph counter at 6.
Case: 316L polished stainless steel; 41x54mm; two antiglare sapphire crystals; caseback secured with four screws; engraved with individual numbers and Louis Moinet markings; water resistant to 3atm.

Dial: carbon fiber; decorated with Côtes du Jura and seven applied zones; rhodium-plated hands, coated with SuperLumiNova.
Strap: hand-sewn crocodile leather; carbon finish; 316L folding clasp with Louis Moinet symbol.
Suggested price: $9,900
Note: limited edition of 60 pieces worldwide for each dial.

TWINTECH

Movement: exclusive mechanical automatic Louis Moinet Twin Barrel LM01 caliber manufacture movement; 120-hour power reserve; 37 jewels; 28,800 vph; blued steel screws; engraved with individual numbers and Louis Moinet markings.
Functions: hours, minutes, seconds; retrograde date; power-reserve indicator.
Case: 316L polished stainless steel; 40x54mm; two sapphire crystals; caseback secured with four screws; water resistant to 3atm.
Dial: silver; rhodium-plated; coated with SuperLumiNova; linden-tree color hands.
Strap: hand-sewn Louisiana alligator leather; 316L folding clasp with Louis Moinet symbol.
Also available: old rose, black, ivory and chocolate dials.
Suggested price: $12,900
Note: limited edition of 60 pieces worldwide.

VERTALIS TOURBILLON

Movement: exclusive LM06 caliber; tourbillon movement; 80-hour power reserve; consists of 50 parts; 19 jewels; 21,600 vph; Côtes du Jura engraving; blued steel screws.
Functions: hours, minutes.
Case: 47mm; two sapphire crystals; water resistant to 3atm.
Dial: black; decorated with Côtes du Jura engraving; rose-gold-plated hands.
Strap: hand-sewn Louisiana alligator leather; 18K rose-gold folding clasp with Louis Moinet symbol.
Suggested price: $199,500
Note: limited to only 12 pieces worldwide.

JULES VERNE INSTRUMENT I BLACK

Movement: exclusive mechanical automatic LM 08 caliber; 44-hour power reserve; 25 jewels; 28,800 vph; blued steel screws; oscillating weight decorated with Côtes du Jura motif.
Functions: hours, minutes, seconds; 60-second chronograph in the center; 30-minute chronograph counter at 12; 12-hour chronograph counter at 6; date by hand at 3; second time zone by hand at 9.
Case: grade-5 titanium and 316L; 18K rose-gold 5N; 46.3x54mm; two sapphire crystals; water resistant to 5atm.
Dial: black; decorated with Côtes du Jura and applied half-circles; rhodium-plated and galvanic blue hands; dial featuring a real piece of the moon (Lunar Meteorite Dhofar 459).
Strap: hand-sewn crocodile leather; carbon finish 316L stainless steel folding clasp with Louis Moinet symbol.
Suggested price: $18,900
Also available: silver dial.
Note: limited edition of 60 pieces worldwide for each dial version.

JULES VERNE INSTRUMENT II SILVER DIAL

Movement: exclusive mechanical automatic LM09 caliber; 44-hour power reserve; 25 jewels; 28,800 vph; blued steel screws; oscillating weight decorated with Côtes du Jura motif.
Functions: hours, minutes, seconds; 60-second chronograph in the center; 30-minute chronograph counter at 12; 12-hour chronograph counter at 6; rattrapante split-second hand in the center.
Case: grade-5 titanium and 316L stainless steel and 18K rose gold 5N; 46.3x54mm; two sapphire crystals; water resistant to 5atm.
Dial: silver; decorated with Côtes du Jura motif and applied half-circles; rhodium-plated and galvanic blue hands; featuring a real piece of the moon (Lunar Meteorite Dhofar 459).
Strap: hand-sewn crocodile leather; carbon finish; 316L stainless steel folding clasp with Louis Moinet symbol.
Suggested price: $19,600
Also available: black dial.
Note: limited edition of 60 pieces worldwide for each dial version.

Exclusivity is key for Manufacture Contemporaine du Temps.

Denis Giguet, the founder and creative force behind MCT, announced last year that the company expects to produce only 50 watches a year until 2017, when it will conclude all four limited-edition versions of the Sequential One. "I am not interested in high-volume production and do not expect to ever produce more than 300 pieces a year," Giguet said in a statement.

Indeed, the Sequential One is a rare horological fruit grown in the rich vineyards of Geneva and Neuchâtel, where Giguet and an elite cadre of experienced artisans tend to it fastidiously.

It is the first design from MCT, a young company founded in 2007 that boldly claimed changing the way we read time as one of its primary missions. According to Giguet's statement, "We consider ourselves to be in the vanguard of a new wave of exciting Swiss watchmakers."

The Sequential One is a work of true originality. It successfully articulates a new perspective on time with an instantly recognizable design that displays the hours on rotating prisms and the minutes on a "jumping dial."

For the hours, MCT divides 20 triangular prisms into four sections, arranging them around the dial like the points on a compass. The hour travels counterclockwise around the dial, starting with 12 in the north position. Every 60 minutes it moves from one section of prisms to the next, completing a rotation once every four hours.

It's easy to get caught up in watching the hour change. Halfway through the hour, the prisms in the adjacent section slowly begin rotating to show the upcoming hour.

MCT's method of indicating the minutes is equally impressive. Fixed at the center of the dial, a hand travels counterclockwise, pointing to the correct minute on an arc-shaped index made of brushed sapphire crystal. Once the minute hand reaches the 60, the entire crystal rotates 90 degrees. The jump not only returns the minute counter to zero, but also shifts the crystal so that it frames the new hour.

In contrast to its system's complexity, the Sequential One delivers at-a-glance readability.

THIS PAGE

ABOVE Made of brushed sapphire crystal, the minute index rotates counterclockwise, jumping 90 degrees every 60 minutes. The index's open section highlights the hours, displayed below on five rotating prisms.

RIGHT Manufacture Contemporaine du Temps founder Denis Giguet.

FACING PAGE
Sandwiched between the 45mm Sequential One's complex, rounded square case is a generous section of sapphire crystal, which conducts light and improves legibility of the watch's prisms.

The Sequential One is a **rare horological fruit** grown in the rich vineyards of Geneva and Neuchâtel.

Made exclusively of Swiss-crafted parts, the Sequential One comes to life in the hands of master watchmaker Jerome Marcu and his skilled team. Together, they orchestrate the nearly 500 components and countless hours of finishing it takes to transform this original vision into an elegant reality.

Developed by MCT, the movement is a powerhouse equipped with a system designed to store and deliver the vast amounts of energy it takes to animate the minute disc and hour prisms. In fact, the company recently submitted the innovative mechanism for a patent.

Another leading-edge invention making its home in the Sequential One is the Straumann Double Hairspring. The escapement delivers a steady rate, eliminating gravitational error with a pair of carefully matched balance springs that oscillate against one another.

MCT asserts that combining all of these technical milestones into one integrated design poses an horological challenge far knottier than the creation of a tourbillon.

More nontraditional twists unfold on the Sequential One's 45mm-wide case. A complexity in its own right, its design entails 41 pieces. A number of those are dedicated to the lug collars, an original design devised by MCT to enhance comfort and beauty. The lugs are one of the three features currently being considered for a patent.

A look at the watch's profile reveals another functional element that also contributes to the timepiece's aesthetics. A generous section of sapphire crystal is pressed between the case's upper and lower halves, bisecting it with what appears to be a slice of light. According to the company, the crystal functions as a window that focuses more light on the movement, illuminating its curious architecture and improving readability of the prisms.

The Sequential One's formed case is generously proportioned. Its supple lines arch modestly to form a rounded square whose thickness peaks in the middle at 15mm, tapering to less than half that at its edges. MCT will offer two white-gold versions of the Sequential One, one with light prisms and the other with dark prisms. Likewise, the company will produce two pink-gold versions with light and dark prisms. Production of each is limited to 99 pieces.

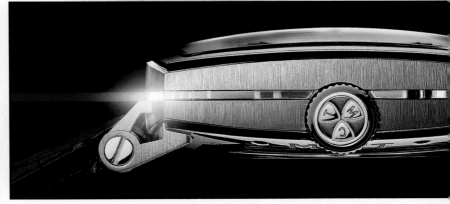

TOP   MCT will make 99 of each member of the Sequential One family by 2017.

LEFT   Responsible for the watch's steady rate, the Straumann Double Hairspring escapement can be seen from the back of the watch. The Côtes de Genève pattern adorns the movement's bridges.

ABOVE   A slice of sapphire crystal divides this rose-gold case, allowing light to pour in and illuminate the movement from the inside.

BLANC

The Nicolas Rieussec Chronograph made its debut in 2008—this was Montblanc's first timepiece to feature a movement developed completely in-house by the company after more than a decade of producing timepieces at its factory in Le Locle, Switzerland.

Montblanc named the watch for Nicolas Rieussec, the French inventor who created the first chronograph in the early 19th century. Primitive yet effective, his design marked the elapsed time on two rotating discs using ink-filled styli. With its modern incarnations, Montblanc evokes Rieussec's legacy—albeit without the inky nibs—using a pair of spinning discs to display the elapsed seconds and minutes. The result is an unconventional watch whose retro inspiration stands out among today's chronographs.

The latest addition to the fold is the Montblanc Nicolas Rieussec Open Date. Arriving last winter, this monopusher chronograph uses skeletonized elements to offer glimpses of Montblanc's latest in-house movement (MB R110).

Inside the standard time display, the company places a rotating date disc with large open sections that reveal the Geneva stripes decorating the caliber's mainplate. The same cutout technique is also used on the chronograph's discs, offering another view of the movement.

Between those discs, the skeletonized design showcases the chronograph's classic column wheel and its innovative vertical clutch. A single button at 8:00 on the side of the case controls the system. The watch's designers cleverly chose the pusher's position to avoid unintentional activation of the chronograph when winding or adjusting the time.

Montblanc offers the Nicolas Rieussec Open Date in 5N red gold or stainless steel, as well as a special platinum version limited to 25 pieces.

ABOVE Montblanc began producing watches in 1997 at its state-of-the-art facility in Le Locle, Switzerland.

RIGHT The Nicolas Rieussec Open Date's openworked date and chronograph counters show off the company's latest manufacture movement, the MB R110. In addition to this stainless steel version, Montblanc also offers the watch in 5N red gold as well as a limited edition platinum version.

It's apropos that this company's first manufacture calibers would be chronographs—**the function whose name literally means "time-writer."**

When Montblanc unveiled the Nicolas Rieussec Monopusher two years ago in Geneva, it introduced two manufacture chronograph movements: a manual (MB R100) and an automatic (MB R200).

The brand released the first caliber in a limited edition model that features the date indicator nestled inside the round, off-center time display. The watch's power-reserve indicator, visible through a transparent caseback, clearly displays how much of the watch's 72-hour reserve remains.

Montblanc houses the automatic movement in a stainless steel case, creating a dazzling variation with a gray dial that features a date aperture next to the crown and a day-night indicator at 9:00. Offered on a hand-stitched alligator strap, the watch is also available with a stainless steel bracelet.

Together, these movements mark a turning point for the brand. Not only do they signal Montblanc's arrival as a manufacture, Lutz Bethge, CEO Montblanc International says they also demonstrate the company's continued dedication to cultivating European craftsmanship while maintaining the tradition of manufacturing watches by hand.

For a company renowned for its elegant writing instruments, it's apropos that Montblanc's first manufacture calibers would be chronographs—the function's name literally means "time-writer."

With all three Nicolas Rieussec models, Montblanc intertwines the company's heritage with its unquenchable passion for discovery.

TOP LEFT The MB R100 movement, produced exclusively at Montblanc's Swiss-based factory, powers the Nicolas Rieussec Monopusher Chronograph.

TOP CENTER Released in 2008, the Nicolas Rieussec Monopusher Chronograph is the first watch that Montblanc created entirely in-house.

TOP RIGHT The Nicolas Rieussec Monopusher Automatic features a pair of horn-shaped apertures on its gray dial, one a day-night indicator and the other a date display.

VILLERET 1858 GRAND TOURBILLON HEURES MYSTÉRIEUSES   REF. 104874

Movement: manual-winding MBM 65.60 caliber; 45-hour power reserve; 28 jewels; 18,000 vph.
Functions: hours, minutes indicated on mysterious sapphire crystal discs; tourbillon cylindrical spiral; tourbillon at 12.
Case: 18K white gold; Ø 47mm, thickness: 13.3mm; crown with mother-of-pearl Montblanc logo; elliptic swell at 6; cambered sapphire crystal; screwed caseback; water resistant to 3atm.
Dial: 18K white gold; hand-guilloché decoration; hour and minute hands indicated on mysterious sapphire crystal discs.
Strap: black hand-stitched alligator; 18K white-gold prong buckle.
Suggested price: $266,000
Note: limited to 8 pieces.
Also available: 18K red gold, limited to 8 pieces, $252,700 (Ref. 104873).

VILLERET 1858 GRAND CHRONOGRAPHE RÉGULATEUR   REF. 104863

Movement: manual-winding MBM 16.30 caliber; 55-hour power reserve; 33 jewels; 18,000 vph; two chatons on the chronograph bridge; two chatons set on the horizontal clutch.
Functions: monopusher chronograph regulator; subsidiary indications: home/time, indication day/night and special power reserve with indication of the emergency reserve.
Case: 18K white gold; Ø 47mm, thickness: 15mm; crown with mother-of-pearl Montblanc logo; cambered sapphire crystal; screwed, domed, sapphire crystal caseback; hinged cuvette with a patented release mechanism; water resistant to 3atm.
Dial: black and white guilloché.
Strap: black hand-stitched alligator; 18K white-gold prong buckle.
Suggested price: $93,100
Note: limited to 8 pieces.
Also available: 18K red gold with black guilloché dial, limited to 58 pieces, $86,500 (Ref. 104865); 18K red gold with silver guilloché dial on brown hand-stitched alligator strap, limited to 58 pieces, $86,500 (Ref. 104866).

NICOLAS RIEUSSEC CHRONOGRAPH AUTOMATIC   REF. 102336

Movement: MB R200 caliber; chronograph with column-wheel control and vertical disc clutch; 72-hour power reserve; 300 parts; 40 jewels; 28,800 vph; large balance wheel with screws; flat hairspring; rhodium-plated and circular-grained plates; rhodium-plated bridges with Geneva striping; wheel train with special toothing.
Functions: hours, minutes; date; second time zone with day/night display; chronograph functions: 30-minute and 60-second counters with rotating discs.
Case: stainless steel; Ø 43mm, thickness: 14.8mm; 22/20mm distance between horns and clasp; non-screw crown with one O-ring; fixed bezel; domed sapphire crystal with double antireflective coating; sapphire crystal caseback; water resistant to 3atm.
Dial: anthracite; black numerals on appliqué hour circle; feuille and baton-shaped hands.
Bracelet: stainless steel; triple-folding clasp.
Suggested price: $10,000
Also available: stainless steel on black alligator strap with double-folding clasp, $9,700 (Ref. 102337).

NICOLAS RIEUSSEC MONOPUSHER CHRONOGRAPH   REF. 102332

Movement: MB R100 caliber; chronograph caliber with column-wheel control and vertical disc clutch; 286 parts; 72-hour power reserve; 33 jewels; 28,800 vph; large balance wheel with screws; flat hairspring; rhodium-plated and circular-grained plates; rhodium-plated bridges with Geneva striping; wheel train with special toothing. **Functions:** hours, minutes; date display by hand; chronograph functions: 30-minute and 60-second counters with rotating discs. **Case:** platinum; Ø 43mm, thickness: 14.8mm; 22/20mm distance between horns and clasp; non-screw crown with one O-ring; mother-of-pearl Montblanc signet; fixed bezel; domed sapphire crystal with double antireflective coating; sapphire crystal caseback; water resistant to 3atm.
Dial: silver; black numerals on appliqué hour circle; feuille- and baton-shaped hands.
Strap: black alligator; 18K white-gold double-folding clasp.
Suggested price: $52,700
Note: limited to 25 pieces.
Also available: 18K white gold with anthracite dial on black alligator strap with 18K white-gold double-folding clasp, limited to 75 pieces, $32,100 (Ref. 102333); 18K red gold with beige dial on brown alligator strap with 18K red-gold double-folding clasp, limited to 125 pieces, $30,600 (Ref. 102334); 18K yellow gold with beige dial on brown alligator strap with 18K yellow-gold double-folding clasp, limited to 75 pieces, $30,600 (Ref.102335).

NICOLAS RIEUSSEC MONOPUSHER CHRONOGRAPH MANUAL (OPEN DATE)   REF. 104981

Movement: manual-winding MB R110 caliber; 72-hour power reserve; 33 jewels; 28,800 vph; monopusher chronograph.
Functions: hours, minutes; date; 30-minute and 60-second counters with rotating discs; date by disc; power-reserve display on caseback.
Case: stainless steel; Ø 43mm, thickness: 14.8mm; 22/20mm distance between horns and clasp; non-screw crown with one O-ring; fixed bezel; domed sapphire crystal with double antireflective coating; sapphire crystal caseback; water resistant to 3atm.
Dial: anthracite; black numerals on appliqué hour circle; feuille- and baton-shaped hands.
Strap: black alligator; double-folding clasp.
Suggested price: $13,450
Also available: platinum with silver-colored dial on black alligator strap with 18K white-gold double-folding clasp, limited to 50 pieces, $57,340 (Ref.104980); 18K red gold with beige dial on brown alligator strap with 18K red-gold double-folding clasp, $34,400 (Ref. 104705).

TIMEWALKER RED GOLD CERAMIC CHRONOGRAPH AUTOMATIC   REF. 104668

Movement: automatic 4810/502 caliber; 46-hour power reserve; 27 jewels; 28,800 vph; COSC certified.
Functions: hours, minutes, small seconds; chronograph functions: 12-hour and 30-minute totalizers, stop seconds; date by disc.
Case: 18K red gold; Ø 43mm, thickness: 14.4mm; 22/20mm distance between horns and clasp; non-screw crown with one O-ring, black ceramic with Montblanc emblem; fixed black ceramic bezel; domed sapphire crystal with double antireflective coating; sapphire crystal caseback; water resistant to 3atm.
Dial: black with red-gold plated hands and numerals; red-gold-plated baton shaped hands filled with white SuperLumiNova.
Strap: black alligator; 18K red-gold pin buckle.
Suggested price: $15,250
Also available: fixed white ceramic bezel and white dial on white alligator strap, $15,250 (Ref. 104669).

TIMEWALKER RED GOLD DIAMONDS CHRONOGRAPH AUTOMATIC   REF. 104283

Movement: automatic 4810/502 caliber; 46-hour power reserve; 27 jewels; 28,800 vph; COSC certified.
Functions: hours, minutes, small seconds; chronograph functions: 12-hour and 30-minute totalizers, stop seconds; date by disc.
Case: 18K red gold; Ø 43mm, thickness: 14.4mm; 22/20mm distance between horns and clasp; non-screw crown with one O-ring; mother-of-pearl Montblanc emblem; fixed 18K red-gold bezel with 72 white Top Wesselton VVS diamonds (1.16 carats); domed sapphire crystal with double antireflective coating; sapphire crystal caseback; water resistant to 3atm.
Dial: white; red-gold plated hands and numerals; red-gold plated baton-shaped hands filled with white SuperLumiNova.
Strap: white alligator; 18K red-gold pin buckle.
Suggested price: $23,600
Also available: fixed 18K red-gold bezel and black dial on black alligator strap, $23,600 (Ref. 104282).

TIMEWALKER CERAMIC CHRONOGRAPH AUTOMATIC   REF. 103094

Movement: automatic 4810/502 caliber; 46-hour power reserve; 27 jewels; 28,800 vph.
Functions: hours, minutes, small seconds; chronograph functions: 12-hour and 30-minute totalizers, stop seconds; date by disc.
Case: stainless steel; Ø 43mm, thickness: 14.5mm; 22/22mm distance between horns and clasp; non-screw crown with one O-ring; black ceramic; fixed black ceramic bezel; domed sapphire crystal with double antireflective coating; sapphire crystal caseback; water resistant to 3atm.
Dial: black; luminescent hands and indexes.
Bracelet: stainless steel and black ceramic; triple-folding clasp.
Suggested price: $6,300
Also available: black alligator strap with stitching, $5,900 (Ref. 102365).

SPORTS DLC CHRONOGRAPH AUTOMATIC   REF. 104279

Movement: automatic 4810/501 caliber; 46-hour power reserve; 25 jewels; 28,800 vph.
Functions: hours, minutes, small seconds; chronograph functions: 12-hour and 30-minute totalizers, stop seconds; date display with magnifying glass.
Case: black DLC-coated stainless steel; Ø 44mm, thickness: 14.9mm; 22/20mm distance between horns and clasp; unidirectional turning bezel, details in relief; screw-down crown with two O-rings; flat sapphire crystal with double antireflective coating; screwed black DLC-coated stainless steel caseback; water resistant to 2atm.
Dial: black; luminescent indexes; black luminescent hands.
Strap: black alligator strap; triple-folding clasp.
Suggested price: $5,350

SPORT CHRONOGRAPH AUTOMATIC   REF. 104659

Movement: automatic 4810/501 caliber; 46-hour power reserve; 25 jewels; 28,800 vph.
Functions: hours, minutes, small seconds; chronograph functions: 12-hour and 30-minute totalizers, stop seconds; date display with magnifying glass.
Case: stainless steel; Ø 44mm, thickness: 14.9mm; 22/22mm distance between horns and clasp; unidirectional turning bezel, details in relief; screw-down crown with two O-rings; flat sapphire crystal with double antireflective coating; screwed stainless steel caseback; water resistant to 2atm.
Dial: black; luminescent indexes; rhodium-plated luminescent hands.
Bracelet: stainless steel; triple-folding clasp.
Suggested price: $4,630
Also available: silver-colored dial on black alligator strap, $4,400 (Ref. 104280).

STAR 4810 CHRONOGRAPH AUTOMATIC   REF. 102378

Movement: automatic 4810/501 caliber; 46-hour power reserve; 25 jewels; 28,800 vph.
Functions: hours, minutes, small seconds; chronograph functions: 60-second counter, 30-minute and 12-hour counter; date display.
Case: stainless steel; Ø 44mm, thickness: 14.5mm; fixed bezel; 22/20mm distance between horns and clasp; non-screw crown with one O-ring; domed sapphire crystal with double antireflective coating; sapphire crystal caseback; water resistant to 3atm.
Dial: silver guilloché; sword- and baton-shaped luminescent hands.
Strap: brown alligator; triple-folding clasp.
Suggested price: $3,830
Also available: black guilloché dial on stainless steel bracelet, $4,050 (Ref.102376); black guilloché dial on black alligator strap, $3,830 (Ref.102377).

STAR XL AUTOMATIC   REF. 104182

Movement: automatic 4810/401caliber; 42-hour power reserve; 21 jewels; 28,800 vph.
Functions: hours, minutes, seconds; calendar date display.
Case: stainless steel; Ø 40mm, thickness: 12mm; 21/18mm distance between horns and clasp; fixed bezel; non-screw crown with one O-ring; domed sapphire crystal with double antireflective coating; stainless steel caseback; water resistant to 30atm.
Dial: black guilloché; feuille- and baton-shaped rhodium-plated hands.
Strap: black alligator; triple-folding clasp.
Suggested price: $1,870

PROFILE LADY ELEGANCE ETOILE SECRETE   REF. 104264

Movement: quartz 4810/110 caliber; 5 jewels; battery: 317/1.5V.
Functions: hours, minutes.
Case: 18K red gold (38.4g) set with 113 Top Wesselton VVS Diamonds (0.616 carat); 23x35mm, thickness: 8.3mm; 18/16mm distance between horns and clasp; non-screw crown with one O-ring; mother-of-pearl Montblanc emblem; domed sapphire crystal with double antireflective coating; 18K red-gold caseback; water resistant to 3atm.
Dial: white mother-of-pearl; 124 Top Wesselton VVS diamonds (0.466 carat); Montblanc diamond at 12 (0.1 carat); red-gold-plated baton-shaped hands.
Strap: white satin; 18K red-gold pin buckle.
Suggested price: $26,500
Note: limited to 10 pieces.
Also available: brown mother-of-pearl dial on brown satin strap, limited to 10 pieces, $26,500 (Ref.104263).

STAR PLUIE D'ETOILES WHITE GOLD DIAMONDS AUTOMATIC   REF. 104304

Movement: automatic 4810/401 caliber; 42-hour power reserve; 21 jewels; 28,800 vph.
Functions: hours, minutes, seconds.
Case: 18K white gold (62g); Ø 36mm, thickness: 11.7mm; 19/17mm distance between horns and clasp; non-screw crown with one O-ring; 18K white gold with Montblanc diamond (0.055 carat); fixed bezel set with 80 baguette diamonds (1.41 carats); domed sapphire crystal with double antireflective coating; 18K white-gold caseback; water resistant to 3atm.
Dial: black mother-of-pearl; 218 Top Wesselton VVS diamonds (0.584 carat); flange set with 80 diamonds (0.17 carat); rhodium-plated feuille- and baton-shaped hands.
Strap: black alligator; 18K white-gold pin buckle.
Suggested price: $47,220
Note: limited to 10 pieces.
Also available: white mother-of-pearl dial on white alligator strap, limited to 10 pieces, $47,220 (Ref.104305).

STAR ETERNAL WHITE GOLD DIAMONDS   REF. 104310

Movement: quartz 4810/103 caliber; 7 jewels; battery: 397/1.5V.
Functions: hours, minutes, seconds; end-of-life indicator for battery.
Case: 18K white gold (67g) set with 20 Top Wesselton VVS diamonds (0.15 carat); Ø 36mm, thickness: 11.6 mm; 19/17mm distance between horns and clasp; non-screw crown with one O-ring; mother-of-pearl Montblanc emblem; fixed bezel set with 42 Top Wesselton diamonds (1.766 carats); domed sapphire crystal with double antireflective coating; 18K white-gold caseback; water resistant to 3atm.
Dial: white mother-of-pearl; 112 Top Wesselton VVS diamonds (0.30 carat); Montblanc diamond at 12 (0.055 carat), flange set with 80 diamonds (0.17 carat); rhodium-plated feuille- and baton-shaped hands.
Strap: white alligator; 18K white-gold pin buckle.
Suggested price: $27,000
Note: limited to 20 pieces.
Also available: black mother-of-pearl on black alligator strap, limited to 20 pieces, $27,000 (Ref. 104311).

MINISTAR RED GOLD   REF. 102352

Movement: quartz 4810/103 caliber; 7 jewels; battery: 397/1.5V.
Functions: hours, minute, seconds; end-of-life indicator for battery.
Case: 18K red gold (36.55g); Ø 32mm, thickness: 10.3mm; 17/16mm distance between horns and clasp; fixed bezel; non-screw crown with one O-ring; mother-of-pearl Montblanc signet; domed sapphire crystal with double antireflective coating; 18K red-gold caseback; water resistant to 3atm.
Dial: white mother-of-pearl; 10 Top Wesselton VVS diamonds (0.09 carat); red-gold-colored feuille- and baton-shaped hands.
Strap: brown satin; 18K red-gold pin buckle.
Suggested price: $9,300
Also available: 18K yellow gold on white satin strap, $9,300 (Ref. 102351).

MOVADO

While Movado watches have embodied modernism's uncluttered aesthetic for more than a century, the company's creative scope goes far beyond design.

For decades, Movado has supported the arts through its work with the Lincoln Center for the Performing Arts, New York City Ballet, John F. Kennedy Center for the Performing Arts, and the Miami International Film Festival. In 1987, the brand became entrenched with the arts on a very personal level when it formed the Movado Artists' Series, inviting Andy Warhol to create a special dial for the Movado Museum Watch to serve as the series' inaugural piece. Since then, this collection of limited editions has showcased an eclectic group of artists such as James Rosenquist, Max Bill, and Arman, each transforming dials from blank canvases into miniature works of art.

Last year, Kenny Scharf joined the select list, introducing six dials designed by the American painter and sculptor. Renowned for his thought-provoking mix of pop culture and fine art, Scharf began as one of the first graffiti artists in New York City. After rising to prominence in the 1980s alongside Keith Haring and Jean-Michel Basquiat, Scharf has exhibited his work in museums and galleries around the world.

Instead of a single design, Scharf created six for Movado, each reflecting his blend of surrealism and abstract expressionism. The company frames the silk-screened dials with stainless steel cases that feature engraved casebacks. Each watch comes with a pair of interchangeable leather straps that are coordinated to complement the dial's color scheme. Movado produced 100 of each model to be sold separately, plus 25 box sets that contain all six of Scharf's designs. Watches numbered 1 to 25 are reserved for the complete collections.

Like the Movado Artists' Series, many of the brand's collections remain popular decades after their releases. In fact, Movado recently revisited its archives to design the first watch in its new Collectors' Edition Series. An update of the original Datron introduced in 1970, the Series 800 Datron Chronograph offers a clean, modern dial without losing the retro charm of its predecessor's tonneau-shaped case. At the top of the dial, the square date window from years past is replaced by a round opening that echoes the dot found on the Museum dials.

Housed within a 40mm steel case is an automatic ETA 2894.2 movement that provides nearly two days of reserve power. The contrasting finishes of the brushed case and polished bezel continue to the bracelet, which is secured with a butterfly clasp. The dial comes in two handsome color schemes: silver for the main dial with black small seconds and chronograph subdials, or the opposite configuration.

Scharf's designs reflect his **blend** of surrealism and abstract expression.

FAR LEFT   The Movado Master's textured black dial continues the rubber strap's grid pattern. Hinged lugs and a black sapphire bezel enhance the 44mm stainless steel case's muscular design.

LEFT   The all-white design of this Movado Master for women features a round bezel set with 130 white diamonds. Its 34mm stainless steel case is water resistant to 5atm.

BELOW LEFT   Offered with a black or silver dial, the 40mm version of the Sub-Sea combines baton hour-markers with a day-date display. All members of the Sub-Sea collection are water resistant to 20atm.

BELOW RIGHT   The Sub-Sea Chronograph is equipped with a unidirectional rotating bezel capable of tracking elapsed times. The watch's 42mm case and bracelet are made of Movado's trademarked Performance Steel.

The Movado Master exemplifies fresh design from the brand's artists. Crafted in polished stainless steel, the tonneau-shaped case is available in versions for men (44mm) and women (34mm). Both case sizes are equipped with convenient hinged lugs that adjust to the wearer's wrist to provide a custom fit.

Offering a new slant on the minimalist design of the Museum Watch, the Movado Master's dial combines a textured, off-center circle with graduated hour-markers to emphasize its tastefully skewed perspective. Even Movado's iconic dot gets a new look thanks to the addition of a convex contour.

Shifting from refined style to rugged elegance, Movado welcomes the Sub-Sea collection. The hardy construction of these sporty timepieces includes cases and bracelets made from Movado's trademarked Performance Steel.

Among the line's highlights is a men's chronograph with a rotating bezel to measure elapsed time, along with a trio of women's models with stylish diamond-set dials. All of the watches included in the Sub-Sea collection are well suited for water sports thanks to a screw-down crown and a solid design that is water resistant to depths of 200 meters.

Proving that good things come in small packages, the ultra-petite watches of Movado's Festa collection deliver outsized glamour with colorful designs and decadent details.

Measuring just 22mm in diameter, the Festa's chic design projects feminine allure. Its white-gold bezel is studded with white brilliants, while the Museum dial is crafted from a colorful array of natural stones like lavender jade and aventurine. Festa slinks around ladies' wrists on python-skin straps color-coordinated to match the dials. For true opulence, Movado also offers a Festa paved entirely with white diamonds.

The Festa's shining beauty gives way to a star on the rise as Movado introduces its latest brand ambassador, Amanda Seyfried. The actress is known for her performances in *Dear John* (2010), *Mamma Mia!* (2008) and *Mean Girls* (2004). She also appears regularly in the critically acclaimed HBO series, *Big Love*.

Just as the selection of cultural programs sponsored by Movado represents art in its various forms, the brand's diverse collection expresses its own unique artistry.

ABOVE   Movado offers an haute joaillerie version of the Festa that is paved completely with diamonds.

LEFT   Measuring just Ø 22mm, Festa's Museum dials are made from a colorful range of natural stones and accessorized with python-skin straps.

The pasts of vintage yacht Eilean and Officine Panerai intersected long before their paths. Renowned Scottish boat maker Fife built the Bermudian ketch in 1936, the same year that the Florentine watchmaker began producing wristwatches for the Italian Navy. Each proceeded to chart a separate course until 2006, when Panerai discovered the boat in disrepair on the island of Antigua.

Intent on restoring Eilean, the brand transported the yacht—inside a cargo ship—to Italy in 2007. There, craftsmen spent nearly three years returning her to pristine condition, preserving the original Burmese teak hull, upgrading the engine room and finely appointing living quarters to accommodate ten people.

Much as Italian artisans enriched Eilean's value with their earnest dedication to details, watchmakers elevate Panerai timepieces to a rarified category with their focus on horology's finer points. The company's passion is manifest in several one-of-a-kind sailing instruments it created exclusively in honor of Eilean. The set includes a barometer, hygrometer, thermometer and wall clock, each sporting the brand's signature cushion-shaped case and black dial.

Panerai draws on its rich nautical heritage, equipping the boat with a marine chronometer, a precision instrument used for generations by sailors navigating the Seven Seas. COSC certified, the OP XX chronometer is encased in brushed stainless steel and housed in a square teak case that matches the ship's timber.

Eilean was formally dedicated in La Spezia during a ceremony provided by the Italian Navy in October 2009.

Panerai unveiled three new proprietary movements in 2009.

In 2005, Panerai introduced its first proprietary movement. In the five years since, the company has presented eight calibers made entirely in-house, including three unveiled just last year: the P.9000, P.9001, and P.9002.

All three movements in the P.9000 family share the same automatic-winding function equipped with three-day power reserve and each mechanism boasts a modern, hard-edged aesthetic.

Panerai uses the P.9000 in five Luminor 1950 Marina 3 Days Automatic models, all with cases measuring 44mm. The steel models possess black dials and an alligator or calf strap or steel bracelet, while those with titanium cases feature brown dials and are offered on an alligator strap or titanium bracelet. P.9000 is also at home in the Luminor 1950 Submersible 3 Days Automatic, a titanium diving watch whose 47mm case is water resistant to 300 meters and has a bezel scale for calculating immersion times.

Panerai equips two versions of the Luminor 1950 3 Days GMT Automatic with the second movement, P.9001. The first comes on an alligator strap and the other on a stainless steel bracelet. Both use a centrally fixed arrow to display the second time zone on the black dial, where a small seconds and date window appear. An indicator on the back of the watch reveals the movement's remaining power.

The family's third member, P.9002, is used in the Luminor 1950 3 Days GMT Power Reserve Automatic. Available on a bracelet or alligator strap, the 44mm stainless steel model contains the same functions as the previous model. The one exception is that the power-reserve indicator is viewed on the dial side, rather than the back.

Panerai eagerly embraces its independence and its future with its expanding collection of manufacture movements. With Eilean, the watchmaker honors the marine pedigree that ensures its enduring legacy. For both journeys, Panerai's hand is steady at the helm.

FACING PAGE

LEFT   Panerai created a marine chronometer in brushed stainless steel especially for Eilean. This piece is housed in a teak box that matches the boat's decking.

TOP RIGHT   Panerai CEO Angelo Bonati, center, was involved in the several stages of Eilean's restoration.

BOTTOM RIGHT   Made from seasoned Alaskan spruce, the main mast affords a panoramic view of the newly refurbished Eilean. In the early 1980s, the ship was the perfect stage for Duran Duran's music video "Rio."

THIS PAGE

TOP LEFT   Panerai's proprietary P.9002 caliber pictured here equips the PAM00321 Luminor 1950 3 Days GMT Power Reserve Automatic, which reveals the movement's remaining power reserve through an indicator on the dial.

TOP CENTER   The PAM00305 Luminor 1950 Submersible 3 Days Automatic's 47mm, brushed titanium case is water resistant to 300 meters. A small seconds counter at 9:00 is positioned opposite the date window.

TOP RIGHT   The PAM00320 Luminor 1950 3 Days GMT Automatic includes a reset function for the seconds, enabling it to be synchronized to another timekeeper.

LUMINOR 1950 MARINA 3 DAYS AUTOMATIC   REF. PAM00312

Movement: automatic Panerai P.9000; 3-day power reserve.
Functions: hours, minutes, small seconds at 9; date at 3.
Case: brushed 316L steel; 44mm; trademark crown-protecting device; antireflective sapphire crystal; sapphire crystal caseback; water resistant to 300 meters.
Dial: black; sandwich style; luminescent markers and Arabic numerals.
Strap: black PANERAI-personalized alligator leather; second strap supplied with strap-changing tool.
Suggested price: $7,400
Also available: on PANERAI-personalized steel bracelet (PAM00328, $8,600); polished steel with new style black dial and PANERAI-personalized leather strap (PAM00359, $7,400); brushed and polished titanium with brown dial and PANERAI-personalized leather strap (PAM00351, $8,000); brushed and polished titanium with brown dial on PANERAI-personalized titanium bracelet (PAM00352, $9,300).

LUMINOR 1950 SUBMERSIBLE 3 DAYS AUTOMATIC   REF. PAM00305

Movement: automatic Panerai P.9000; 3-day power reserve.
Functions: hours, minutes, small seconds at 9; date at 3; calculation of immersion time.
Case: brushed titanium; 47mm; trademark crown-protecting device; unidirectional bezel with graduated scale to calculate immersion time and ratchet click at minute intervals; antireflective sapphire crystal; sapphire crystal caseback; water resistant to 300 meters.
Dial: black; applied dots and hour-markers.
Strap: PANERAI-personalized rubber; second strap supplied with strap-changing tool.
Suggested price: $9,600

LUMINOR 1950 3 DAYS GMT AUTOMATIC   REF. PAM00329

Movement: automatic Panerai P.9001; 3-day power reserve.
Functions: hours, minutes, small seconds at 9; date at 3; seconds reset; second time zone.
Case: brushed 316L steel; 44mm; trademark crown-protecting device; power-reserve indicator on back; antireflective sapphire crystal; sapphire crystal caseback; water resistant to 300 meters.

Dial: black; sandwich style; luminescent markers and Arabic numerals; second time zone GMT hand.
Bracelet: PANERAI-personalized steel with bracelet removal tool.
Suggested price: $9,950
Also available: on brown PANERAI-personalized alligator leather strap (PAM00320, $8,900).

LUMINOR 1950 3 DAYS GMT POWER RESERVE AUTOMATIC   REF. PAM00321

Movement: automatic Panerai P.9002; 3-day power reserve.
Functions: hours, minutes, small seconds at 9; date at 3, power-reserve indicator at 5; seconds reset; second time zone.
Case: brushed and polished 316L steel; 44mm; trademark crown-protecting device; antireflective sapphire crystal; sapphire crystal caseback; water resistant to 300 meters.

Dial: black; sandwich style; luminescent markers and Arabic numerals; second time zone GMT hand.
Strap: black PANERAI-personalized alligator leather; second strap supplied with strap-changing tool.
Suggested price: $8,900
Also available: brushed and polished steel with black dial on PANERAI-personalized metal bracelet (PAM00347, $9,950).

LUMINOR 1950 8 DAYS GMT   REF. PAM00233

Movement: mechanical manual-winding Panerai P.2002; 8-day power reserve; 247 components; three barrels.
Functions: hours, minutes; small seconds and 24-hour indicator at 9; date at 3; linear power-reserve indicator at 6; seconds reset; second time zone.
Case: brushed 316L steel; 44mm; trademark crown-protecting device; antireflective sapphire crystal; sapphire crystal caseback; water resistant to 100 meters.
Dial: black; sandwich style; luminescent markers and Arabic numerals; second time zone hand.
Strap: black PANERAI-personalized vintage calf leather; second strap supplied with strap-changing tool.
Suggested price: $14,700

LUMINOR 1950 8 DAYS GMT PINK GOLD   REF. PAM00289

Movement: mechanical manual-winding Panerai P.2002; 8-day power reserve; 247 components; three barrels.
Functions: hours, minutes; small seconds and 24-hour counter at 9; date at 3; linear power-reserve indicator at 6; seconds reset; second time zone.
Case: brushed and polished 18K pink gold; 44mm; trademark crown-protecting device; antireflective sapphire crystal; sapphire crystal caseback; water resistant to 100 meters.
Dial: brown; sandwich style; luminescent markers and Arabic numerals; second time-zone GMT hand.
Strap: brown PANERAI-personalized alligator leather; second strap supplied with strap-changing tool.
Suggested price: $30,200

RADIOMIR 8 DAYS   REF. PAM00268

Movement: mechanical manual-winding Panerai P.2002/3; 8-day power reserve; 247 components; three barrels.
Functions: hours, minutes, small seconds at 9; date at 3; linear power-reserve indicator at 6.
Case: polished 316L steel; 45mm; OP-personalized screw-down crown and patented wire-loop strap attachments; antireflective sapphire crystal; sapphire crystal caseback; water resistant to 100 meters.
Dial: black; sandwich style; luminescent markers and Arabic numerals.
Strap: black PANERAI-personalized alligator leather.
Suggested price: $11,900

LUMINOR 1950 10 DAYS GMT   REF. PAM00270

Movement: mechanical automatic Panerai P.2003; 10-day power reserve; 296 components; three barrels.
Functions: hours, minutes; small seconds and 24-hour indicator at 9; date at 3; linear power-reserve indicator at 6; seconds reset; second time zone.
Case: brushed 316L steel; 44mm; trademark crown-protection device; antireflective sapphire crystal; sapphire crystal caseback; water resistant to 100 meters.
Dial: black; sandwich style; luminescent markers and Arabic numerals; second time zone GMT hand.
Strap: brown PANERAI-personalized alligator leather; second strap supplied with strap-changing tool.
Suggested price: $17,300

LUMINOR 1950 TITANIUM CHRONO MONOPULSANTE 8 DAYS GMT   REF. PAM00311

Movement: mechanical manual-winding Panerai P.2004; 8-day power reserve; 321 components; three barrels.
Functions: hours, minutes; single-button chronograph with two counters; small seconds and 24-hour indicator at 9; date at 3; linear power-reserve indicator at 6; second time zone.
Case: brushed titanium; 44mm; trademark crown-protecting device; antireflective sapphire crystal; sapphire crystal caseback; water resistant to 100 meters.
Dial: brown; sandwich style; luminescent markers and Arabic numerals; second time zone GMT hand.
Strap: brown PANERAI-personalized alligator leather; second strap supplied with strap-changing tool.
Suggested price: $21,100
Also available: brushed 316L steel with black sandwich-style dial and black PANERAI-personalized alligator leather strap (PAM00275, $20,200).

LUMINOR 1950 CERAMIC CHRONO MONOPULSANTE GMT 8 DAYS   REF. PAM00317

Movement: mechanical manual-winding Panerai P.2004/B; 8-day power reserve; 321 components; three barrels.
Functions: hours, minutes; single-button chronograph with two counters; small seconds and 24-hour indicator at 9; date at 3; linear power-reserve indicator at 6; second time zone.
Case: black ceramic; 44mm; trademark crown-protecting device; antireflective sapphire crystal; sapphire crystal caseback; water resistant to 100 meters.
Dial: black; sandwich style; luminescent markers and Arabic numerals; second time zone GMT hand.
Strap: PANERAI-personalized leather; bridges and buckles treated with special hard black coating; second strap supplied with strap-changing tool.
Suggested price: $25,600

RADIOMIR TOURBILLON GMT   REF. PAM00330

Movement: mechanical manual-winding Panerai P.2005; power reserve; 239 components; three barrels.
Functions: hours, minutes; small seconds and tourbillon at 9; 24-hour indicator at 3; second time zone.
Case: polished 18K pink gold; 48mm; OP-personalized screw-down winding crown and patented wire-loop strap attachments; antireflective sapphire crystal; sapphire crystal caseback, revealing tourbillon and power-reserve indicator; water resistant to 100 meters.
Dial: brown; sandwich style; knurled pink-gold ring around outer edge; luminescent markers and Arabic numerals; second time zone GMT hand.
Strap: brown PANERAI-personalized alligator leather.
Suggested price: $133,000
Also available: brushed and polished titanium with brown sandwich-style dial and brown PANERAI-personalized alligator leather strap (PAM00315, $122,700); platinum with black sandwich-style dial and black PANERAI-personalized alligator leather strap (PAM00316, $137,000).

LUMINOR 1950 TOURBILLON GMT   REF. PAM00276

Movement: mechanical manual-winding Panerai P.2005; power reserve; 239 components; three barrels.
Functions: hours, minutes; small seconds and tourbillon at 9; 24-hour indicator at 3; second time zone.
Case: brushed and polished 316L steel; 47mm; trademark crown-protecting device; antireflective sapphire crystal; sapphire crystal caseback, revealing tourbillon and power-reserve indicator; water resistant to 100 meters.
Dial: black; sandwich style; knurled pink-gold ring around outer edge; luminescent markers and Arabic numerals; second time zone GMT hand.
Strap: black PANERAI-personalized alligator leather; second strap supplied with strap-changing tool.
Suggested price: $119,100
Also available: brushed and polished titanium with brown sandwich-style dial and brown PANERAI-personalized alligator strap.

LUMINOR 1950 8 DAYS RATTRAPANTE PINK GOLD   REF. PAM00319

Movement: mechanical manual-winding Panerai P.2006/3; 8-day power reserve; 356 components; three barrels.
Functions: hours, minutes; two counters: minutes at 3, small seconds at 9; central chronograph and split-seconds hand; linear power-reserve indicator at 6.
Case: brushed and polished 18K pink gold; 47mm; trademark crown-protecting device; antireflective sapphire crystal; sapphire crystal caseback; water resistant to 100 meters.
Dial: brown; sandwich style; luminescent markers and Arabic numerals.
Strap: brown PANERAI-personalized alligator leather; second strap supplied with strap-changing tool.
Note: limited edition of 300 pieces.
Suggested price: $43,000

RADIOMIR ORO ROSA   REF. PAM00336

Movement: mechanical manual-winding Panerai P. 999; swan's neck regulator; 60-hour power reserve; 154 components.
Functions: hours, minutes, small seconds at 9.
Case: brushed and polished 18K pink gold; 42mm; OP-personalized screw-down winding crown and patented removable wire-loop strap attachments; antireflective sapphire crystal; sapphire crystal caseback; water resistant to 100 meters.
Dial: brown; sandwich style; luminescent markers and Arabic numerals.
Strap: PANERAI-personalized alligator strap; polished 18K pink-gold buckle.
Note: limited edition of 500 pieces.
Suggested price: $17,400
Also available: polished steel with black sandwich-style dial and PANERAI-personalized brown alligator strap (PAM00337, $7,400); brushed titanium with black sandwich-style dial and PANERAI-personalized black alligator strap (PAM00338, $8,100).

LUMINOR 1950 CHRONO MONOPULSANTE 8 DAYS ORO ROSA   REF. PAM00344

Movement: mechanical manual-winding Panerai P.2004/6; 8-day power reserve; 313 components; three barrels.
Functions: hours, minutes; single-button chronograph with two counters: minutes at 3, small seconds at 9; seconds reset; central chronograph hand.
Case: brushed and polished 18K pink gold; 44mm; 18K brushed pink-gold trade-marked crown-protecting device; antireflective sapphire crystal; sapphire crystal caseback: water resistant to 100 meters.
Dial: brown; sandwich style; luminescent markers and Arabic numerals; circular power-reserve indicator at 6.
Strap: PANERAI-personalized alligator strap; brushed 18K pink-gold buckle; second strap supplied with strap-changing tool. second strap supplied with strap-changing tool.
Note: unique edition of 150 pieces.
Suggested price: $35,800

RADIOMIR COMPOSITE MARINA MILITARE 8 GIORNI   REF. PAM00339

Movement: mechanical manual-winding Panerai P.2002/7 caliber; 8-day power reserve; 191 components; three barrels.
Functions: hours, minutes, small seconds at 9.
Case: brown Panerai composite material; 47mm; personalized screw-down winding crown and patented wire-loop strap attachments; antireflective sapphire crystal; brown Panerai composite caseback; water resistant to 100 meters.
Dial: brown; sandwich style; luminous Arabic numerals and hour markers.
Strap: PANERAI-personalized brown alligator leather; large-size brown Panerai composite buckle.
Note: special edition.
Suggested price: $14,900

PATEK PHILIPPE
GENEVE

As Patek Philippe marches steadily toward its second century, the watchmaker's Calatrava cross is recognized around the world as iconic shorthand for timeless elegance. Seasoned by the comings and goings of generations of watchmakers, the company's state-of-the-art workshops are well prepared for the future.

Patek Philippe recently introduced new rose-gold editions of several popular designs, including the return of the Calatrava officer's watch, its hinged hunter-case newly christened in the precious metal.

Rose gold is a fitting choice for the company. Favored for its warm tone, the gold and copper alloy gained prominence during the early days of the Art Deco movement, an era whose distinctive style informs several of Patek Philippe's most successful models, the Chronometro Gondolo in particular.

Introduced in 2007, this watch follows the design cues of a 1920s model. The flowing lines of its tonneau case extend to a pair of precisely shaped sapphire crystals. One reveals the movement's curvaceous flourishes, including an S-shaped bridge that spans the caliber.

The other crystal opens onto the watch's cambered dial. The work of dedicated craftsmen, the complex guilloché pattern used to embellish the dial is wrought by hand through labor-intensive techniques seldom seen today. An oval ring of light brown gilt punctuates the elaborate design and serves as a background for a railroad-style minute scale and Breguet numerals, both hand-painted in dark brown.

In fact, the Chronometro Gondolo's history dates back to the '20s, when an early version was available exclusively in Brazil. But like a secret that's too good to keep, the design's popularity has caught on around the world.

For a glamorous twist, the bezels of **Twenty~4** can be set with diamonds.

Now available in rose gold, the Chronometro Gondolo's flowing curves draw inspiration from the Art Deco era.

Patek Philippe's most popular ladies' watch, the Twenty~4 celebrated ten years with a new yellow-gold model with a clean bezel. The gray Night Glow and brown Autumn Gold dials were created specifically for this yellow-gold model.

The luxury brand stays in the Jazz Age for the Twenty~4®. The original was envisioned as a modern reinvention of the Gondolo, Patek Philippe's Art Deco classic, and the new design quickly became the company's best-selling ladies' watch. To honor the tenth anniversary of that achievement, the company presented the first-ever Twenty~4 in yellow gold with a sleek bezel or the option of opulent diamonds in 2009.

The dial—Timeless White, Night Glow (gray gradation), or Autumn Gold (brown gradation)—is decorated with ten diamond hour-markers and two yellow-gold Roman numerals. A pair of baton-style hands made of yellow gold completes the look of feminine elegance.

When it debuted in 1999, the Twenty~4 was embraced by a generation of women who wanted a versatile watch that could accommodate their 24-hour lifestyles and the brand capitalized on the line's slogan "Who will you be in the next 24 hours?" Women found a stylish companion in the Twenty~4, whose modern-classic look is the perfect complement in the office or out on the town.

This new version of the Twenty~4 joins a fashionable family that includes siblings in stainless steel, rose gold and white gold. For a glamorous twist, the bezels of these earlier models can be set with diamonds.

This glittering possibility is one of many in Patek Philippe's diverse collection. Despite the wide range of styles and complications, the one thing that links all of the company's watches is its dedication to the traditions of Genevan watchmaking.

AQUANAUT EXTRA-LARGE REF. 5167R

Movement: mechanical automatic-winding 324 S C caliber; 45-hour power reserve; 213 parts; 29 jewels; 28,800 vph; unidirectional-winding 21K gold central rotor; Gyromax balance; flat balance spring.
Functions: hours, minutes, sweep seconds; date at 3; three-position crown to wind, correct date, and set time.
Case: 5N 18K rose gold; Ø 40mm, thickness: 8.95mm; bezel and flanks with vertical

satin finish; screw-down crown; screwed-on sapphire-crystal caseback; water resistant to 12atm.
Dial: black perimeter/brown center; structured dial with exclusive Aquanaut pattern; 12 baton-style markers and 11 applied 18K rose-gold Arabic numerals with luminescent coating; baton-style hour and minute hands with luminescent coating; white transfer-printed counterbalanced seconds hand.
Strap: chocolate "Tropical" composite integrated with case; exclusive Aquanaut pattern; 18K rose-gold Aquanaut double-security fold-over clasp with Calatrava cross.

AQUANAUT LUCE REF. 5087/1A

Movement: quartz; caliber E23 S C; 100 parts; 7 jewels.
Functions: hours, minutes, sweep seconds; date at 3; three-position crown to operate, correct date, and stop movement / set time.
Case: steel; Ø 36mm, thickness: 8.2mm; set with 46 Ø 1.8mm flawless rare white Top Wesselton round diamonds totaling approx. 1 carat; screw-down crown; water resistant to 12atm.

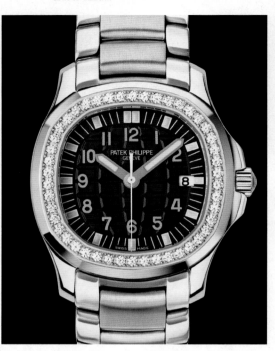

Dial: Mysterious Black; 11 applied 18K white-gold Arabic numerals; 13 baton-style hour-markers and hour and minute hands with luminescent coating; white transfer-printed counterbalanced seconds hand.
Bracelet: steel; fold-over clasp with Calatrava cross.
Also available: Pure White dial; complementing 18K white gold rings set with 21 flawless rare white Top Wesselton round diamonds (Ø 1.5mm) totaling approx. 0.32 carat and featuring two interchangeable composite inserts in Mysterious Black and Pure White.

CALATRAVA SQUELETTE REF. 5180/1G

Movement: mechanical automatic-winding extra-flat Patek Philippe 240 SQU manufacture caliber; 27 jewels; skeletonized; chased; rhodium-plated; decorated by hand and beveled; balance bridge in the shape of the Calatrava cross; engraved; 22K gold off-center micro-rotor; hallmarked with the Geneva Seal.
Functions: hour, minute.
Case: 18K white-gold two-piece case; Ø 39mm, thickness: 6.85mm; polished finish;

with an aperture on the movement; curved sapphire crystal; crown in white gold; screwed-on caseback displaying the movement through a sapphire crystal with blue fumé border; water resistant to 3atm.
Dial: baton hands on the aperture; blued gold leaf-style hands.
Bracelet: white gold; invisible white-gold double-security fold-over clasp.

CALATRAVA OFFICER'S WATCH REF. 5153

Movement: mechanical automatic-winding 324 S C caliber; 45-hour power reserve; 213 parts; 29 jewels; 28,800 vph; unidirectional-winding 21K gold central rotor; Gyroma balance; flat balance spring.
Functions: hours, minutes, sweep seconds; date at 3; three-position crown to wind, set date, and set time.
Case: officer style; 18K yellow gold; Ø 38mm, thickness: 10.97mm; 20mm between

lugs; screwed-on sapphire-crystal caseback; hinged dust cover; crown protector; sealed turban-style crown; water resistant to 3atm.
Dial: silvery opaline; two zones; center with manual guilloche; new arrangement of golden cartouche with PATEK PHILIPPE GENEVE signature at 12; gilt minute pearls; 12 applied 18K yellow-gold arrow markers; 18K yellow-gold dauphine hour and minute hands with two lapped facets; 18K yellow-gold counterbalanced seconds hand.
Strap: brown large-scale alligator leather; hand-stitched; 18K yellow-gold buckle.

NAUTILUS   REF. 7010/1

Movement: quartz; caliber E23 S C; 100 parts; 7 jewels.
Functions: hours, minutes, sweep seconds; date at 3; three-position crown to operate, correct date, and stop movement/set time.
Case: 18K rose-gold three-piece case; 35.4x35x32mm, thickness: 6.9mm; bezel with 46 Top Wesselton round diamonds totaling approx. 0.73 carat; water resistant to 6atm.

Dial: center embossed with horizontal Nautilus pattern; inner minute scale; 10 applied 18K gold baton-style hour-markers, applied 18K gold Arabic numeral 12, and 18K gold baton-style hour and minute hands (designed specifically for the ladies' Nautilus) all with luminescent coating; gold seconds hand.
Bracelet: 18K rose gold; polished center links; satin-finished outer links; 18K rose-gold fold-over clasp.
Also available: 18K white-gold version; white dial; complementary 18K gold Nautilus rings with 48 or 60 flawless Top Wesselton round diamonds totaling approx. 0.4 or 0.5 carat, respectively, and Patek Philippe Nautilus engraving.

NAUTILUS   REF. 7011/1

Movement: quartz; caliber E23 S C; 100 parts; 7 jewels.
Functions: hours, minutes, sweep seconds; date at 3; three-position crown to operate, correct date, and stop movement / set time.
Case: 18K white-gold three-piece case; 35.4x35x32mm, thickness: 6.9mm; satin-finished bezel; water resistant to 6atm.

Dial: center embossed with horizontal Nautilus pattern; inner minute scale; 10 applied 18K gold baton-style hour-markers, applied 18K gold Arabic numeral 12, and 18K gold baton-style hour and minute hands (designed specifically for the ladies' Nautilus) all with luminescent coating; gold seconds hand.
Bracelet: 18K white gold; polished center links; satin-finished outer links; 18K white-gold fold-over clasp.
Also available: 18K rose-gold version; charcoal gray dial; complementary 18K gold Nautilus rings with 48 or 60 flawless Top Wesselton round diamonds totaling approx. 0.4 or 0.5 carat, respectively, and Patek Philippe Nautilus engraving.

NAUTILUS POWER RESERVE MOONPHASE   REF. 5722G

Movement: mechanical automatic-winding Patek Philippe 240 PS IRM C LU manufacture caliber; decorated with a Côtes de Genève pattern and beveled; 22K gold off-center micro-rotor; hallmarked with the Geneva Seal.
Functions: hour, minute, small second; small second at 4; date and moonphase at 7; power reserve between 10 and 11.
Case: 18K white-gold three-piece case; 38x43mm, thickness 9.2mm; polished and brushed finish; octagonal bezel set with 36 baguette-cut diamonds (5.7 carats); flat sapphire crystal; 2 correctors on the middle; screw-down crown with shoulder case protection; screwed-on sapphire crystal caseback displaying movement; water resistant to 6atm.

Dial: black perimeter/ blue center; embossed horizontal linear decoration; luminescent applied white-gold baton markers; luminescent white-gold baton hands; secondary hands in white enameled gold.
Strap: navy blue alligator leather; hand-stitched; integral with the case; double-security fold-over clasp.

LADIES' ANNUAL CALENDAR   REF. 4937R

Movement: mechanical automatic-winding Patek Philippe 315 S QA LU manufacture caliber; decorated with a Côtes de Genève pattern and beveled; 21K gold rotor; hallmarked with the Geneva Seal.
Functions: hour, minute, second; annual calendar; month at 3; moonphase and date at 6; day of the week at 9; takes the days of a month into account over an entire year.
Case: 18K pink-gold three-piece case; Ø 37mm, thickness: 11.5mm; pavé with 431 brilliant-cut diamonds (2.79 carats); four correctors on the middle; crown in pink gold and brilliants (1 row, 0.07 carat); curved sapphire crystal; screwed-on sapphire crystal caseback displaying movement; water resistant to 3atm.

Dial: white mother-of-pearl; engraved Calatrava cross at 6; applied pink-gold Breguet markers; black painted minute track with 11 applied pink-gold cabochons; luminescent pink-gold leaf-style hands.
Strap: white alligator leather; hand-stitched; pink-gold clasp with 27 brilliants (0.2 carat).
Also available: in white gold.

PIAGET

For the Piaget Polo, life began in the spotlight. Often seen on the wrists of the powerful and famous, the watch's instantly recognizable profile caused a sensation upon its release that has since graduated into an honored icon.

The Piaget Polo's evolution, from its 1979 launch to last year's anniversary, illustrates Piaget's capacity for refined elegance and reliable precision, two keys fueling the brand's longevity.

The timeless form of Piaget Polo's signature bracelet reveals Piaget's glamorous flair, one fostered by a desire to equal its horological achievements with innovations that redefine the art of gem setting.

Piaget marks the Piaget Polo's 30th anniversary with diamonds, transforming the classic Piaget Polo into a bold statement of luxury. Limited to 150 pieces each for men and women, these white-gold Piaget Polo watches are set generously with rows of brilliant-cut stones. Piaget enlivens its historical design with more than 200 diamonds on the women's model and more than 250 on the men's.

For another limited edition anniversary model, Piaget updates the original by replacing the trademark bracelet with a leather strap. Despite the fundamental change, the result is positively Piaget Polo.

With the men's model, the Piaget Polo family resemblance appears in the alternating satin and brushed finishes applied to the white-gold bezel, which is bookended by a pink-gold case. Piaget tailors a smaller version for women, marking the bezel's familiar valleys with white diamonds.

The Piaget Polo also continues to provide sporty stages for Piaget's proprietary complications, including tourbillon and chronograph models that exalt the company's heritage as an illustrious movement maker. The brand welcomed a new generation of Piaget Polos last year with the Piaget Polo FortyFive, a line of sporty timepieces made from unusual materials and powered by complicated movements born in the company's La Côte-aux-Fées manufacture.

ABOVE   Marcos Heguy captains Piaget's polo team, Pilara. A special 45-piece limited edition Polo FortyFive has been created in his honor.

RIGHT   The Piaget Polo FortyFive Chronograph is powered by Piaget's 880P movement, which features a flyback chronograph, small seconds, date and dual time zone.

The Piaget Polo continues to set sporty stages for the brand's proprietary complications.

The Piaget Polo FortyFive Chronograph and Piaget Polo FortyFive Automatic both feature titanium cases, a first for Piaget. They also share the same strap, a rubber design armored with steel inserts that approximate the original's mix of brushed and polished finishes. It is fitted with a buckle that offers two positions, one for summer when the wrist is naturally thinner, and another for winter.

For the Piaget Polo FortyFive Chronograph, Piaget drew on more than a of century of mechanical prowess to create the 880P movement, a combination of flyback chronograph, date and second time zone. The movement is thoroughly detailed, enriched by the hands of craftsmen schooled in elegant finishing techniques passed down for generations.

IN THE LIMELIGHT

Piaget Limelight Paradise brings the company's expertise in the realm of gem setting into sharp focus with a collection of women's watches that evoke sailing, warm seas and tropical flowers.

Aquamarine and beryl reflect the vivid shades of oceans and lagoons with the Piaget Limelight Tropical Seas. This extravagantly jeweled cuff-watch shines with 274 white brilliants that pave its case and dial, and strings together 1,402 diamonds and 80 white Akoya pearls for a triple-row bracelet. Piaget also lavishes luxurious details on complementing Piaget Limelight Tropical Seas earrings.

With its inimitable collection, Piaget masters both the eccentricities of mechanical watchmaking and the savoir-faire of haute jewelry, establishing itself as a force in both worlds.

TOP ROW   Aaron Eckhart wearing a Piaget Polo FortyFive; Alec Baldwin; Matt Dillon; J. Renner.
ABOVE   Mickey Rourke; John Hamm wearing a Piaget Polo FortyFive with Piaget CEO Philippe Léopold-Metzger.
BOTTOM LEFT   Teri Hatcher; Jessica Alba; Andie McDowell, wearing her Magic Hour watch.

BELOW   Limelight Paradise Tropical Seas theme cuff watch and earrings.

PIAGET EMPERADOR COUSSIN PERPETUAL CALENDAR   REF. GOA33018

Movement: mechanical automatic-winding Piaget 855P perpetual calendar; Ø 28.4mm, thickness: 5.6mm; 38 jewels; 21,600 vph; approx. 72-hour power reserve; circular Côtes de Genève; circular-grained plate; bridges beveled and drawn with a file; blued screws; oscillating weight engraved with the Piaget coat of arms.
Functions: hours, minutes, small seconds at 4; retrograde date indicator at 3; dual time at 8; retrograde day indicator at 9; month/leap year at 12.

Case: 18K white gold; sapphire crystal caseback revealing the movement.
Dial: silvered; satin-finished counters; applied 18K white-gold hour-markers.
Strap: black alligator leather; 18K white-gold pin buckle.

PIAGET EMPERADOR   REF. GOA33070

Movement: mechanical automatic-winding Piaget 551P; Ø 20.5mm, thickness: 4.95mm; 27 jewels; 21,600 vph; approx. 40-hour power reserve; circular Côtes de Genève; beveled hand-drawn bridges; blued screws.
Functions: hours, minutes, small seconds at 10; power-reserve indicator at 6.
Case: 18K pink gold.
Dial: silvered sunburst dial; applied 18K pink-gold hour-markers and the Piaget coat of arms.
Strap: brown alligator leather; 18K pink-gold pin buckle.

PIAGET POLO TOURBILLON RELATIF   REF. GOA31123

Movement: manual-winding Piaget 608P tourbillon; thickness: 3.28mm; thickness including hand fitting: 9.14mm; caging: 11 1/2''' (Ø 25.6mm); 27 jewels; 21,600 vph; approx. 70-hour power reserve; oscillating organ—balance: Ø 7.75mm; mainplate, bridges and carriage beveled and drawn out by hand with a file; circular Côtes de Genève finishing; blued screws.
Note: flying tourbillon: the minute hand, which has its center of rotation at the center of the watch, performs one complete rotation per hour; the 0.2g tourbillon carriage with three titanium bridges, suspended on the minute hand, spins once per minute on its own axis.
Functions: hour, minute, second.
Case: 18K white gold.
Dial: silvered dial; white-gold applied Arabic numerals and hour-markers.
Strap: black alligator leather; 18K white-gold folding clasp.
Also available: diamond-set version.

PIAGET POLO FORTYFIVE CHRONOGRAPH   REF. GOA34002

Movement: mechanical automatic-winding Piaget 880P chronograph; 12'''; Ø 26.8mm, thickness: 5.6mm; 35 jewels; 28,800 vph (balance with screws); approx. 50-hour power reserve (double barrel); circular Côtes de Genève finishing; circular-grained mainplate; beveled bridges; blued screws.
Functions: hour, minute, small seconds at 6; dual 24-hour time zone at 9; flyback chronograph function (30-minute counter) at 3.

Case: large model; titanium; titanium bezel with alternating satin-brushed surfaces and polished steel godrons; titanium and rubber screw-lock crown; sapphire crystal caseback; water resistant to 10atm.
Dial: black; luminescent hour-markers.
Strap: rubber with steel inserts; steel triple-folding safety clasp with summer/winter position.

PIAGET ALTIPLANO   REF. GOA33112

Movement: mechanical manual-winding, ultra-thin Piaget 838P; Ø 26.8mm, thickness: 2.5mm; 19 jewels; 21,600 vph; approx. 65-hour power reserve; circular Côtes de Genève; circular-grained plate; bridges beveled and drawn with a file; blued screws.
Functions: hour, minute, small seconds at 10.
Case: large model; 18K white gold.
Dial: silver colored; black bâton hour-markers; bâton hands.
Strap: black alligator leather; 18K white-gold pin buckle.

PIAGET ALTIPLANO DOUBLE JEU   REF. GOA32152

XL model: two superimposed cases on black alligator leather strap with 18K white-gold folding clasp.

UPPER CASE: 18K white gold; caseback fitted with sapphire crystal revealing the movement.
Movement: mechanical manual-winding, ultra-thin Piaget 838P; Ø 26.8mm, thickness: 2.5mm; 19 jewels; 21,600 vph; approx. 65-hour power reserve; circular Côtes de Genève finishing; circular-grained main-plate; bridges beveled and drawn out; blued screws.
Functions: hour, minute, small seconds at 10.
Dial: silver-color; black bâton hour-markers; bâton hands.

LOWER CASE: 18K white gold; caseback engraved with the Piaget coat of arms.
Movement: mechanical manual-winding, ultra-thin Piaget 830P; Ø 26.8mm, thickness: 2.5mm; 19 jewels; 21,600 vph; approx. 65-hour power reserve; circular Côtes de Genève finishing; circular-grained mainplate; bridges beveled and drawn out; blued screws.
Functions: hour, minute.
Dial: slate-gray; black and silver hour-markers; bâton hands.

PIAGET LIMELIGHT TWICE   REF. GOA34137

One watch, two dials: two quartz 56P movements; total of 332 brilliant-cut diamonds (approx. 6 carats), on black satin strap with reversible integrated clasp.

FIRST DIAL:
Case: 18K white gold; sunburst motif composed of 226 brilliant-cut diamonds (approx. 4.6 carats).
Dial: black.
Clasp: 18K white gold set with 54 brilliant-cut diamonds (approx. 0.2 carat).

SECOND DIAL:
Case: 18K white gold; 52 brilliant-cut diamonds (approx. 1.2 carats).
Dial: silver colored; black Roman numerals.
Clasp: 18K white gold.

PIAGET LIMELIGHT MAGIC HOUR   REF. GOA32096

Movement: Piaget 56P quartz.
Case: 18K pink gold; set with 36 brilliant-cut diamonds (approx 1.1 carats).
Note: an invisible mechanism developed in-house endows this timepiece with the unique power to be three watches in one: when positioned horizontally, the ellipse provides a generous dial opening with timeless style; with a gentle touch, the oval swivels to take an impish slant; with another 45° turn, diamond-set golden numerals are revealed.
Strap: white satin; 18K pink-gold pin buckle.
Also available: in white gold on black strap.

PORSCHE DESIGN
TIMEPIECES
P'6000

Good design simplifies. This notion guides the work of Ferdinand Alexander Porsche, who designed several successful models for his family's renowned auto company before opening the Porsche Design Studio. The company debuted in 1972 with a chronograph that gave rise to a growing collection of intuitive designs that marry form and function in cutting-edge watches.

Among the most important is the Indicator P'6910 from Porsche Design, a timepiece whose unfussy operation belies the intricacy of its advanced movement, a chronograph that ensures superior readability with a jumping digital display combined with large luminous numerals and openworked hands.

Designers left no assumption unchallenged when looking for ways to increase the watch's utility, improving legibility by raising the seconds-hand toward the sapphire crystal where the minute-scale was printed. For the watch's design, the company turned to its automotive roots, taking inspiration from the Carrera GT's pedals for the pushers and its tires for the inside of the rubber strap. Visually, the dial's honeycomb motif echoes a pattern commonly used in racecar construction.

On the surface, the chronograph's balanced display personifies Porsche's approach to design. The 6036 movement below, however, tells a far more complicated story. Designed and produced by Swiss watchmaker Eterna, its construction involves approximately 800 pieces. Among those are four spring barrels. One powers the watch while the other three provide the large amount of energy needed to change the chronograph's digital display in the blink of an eye.

The Porsche Design Indicator P'6910 is encased in a titanium, PVD-coated titanium or rose-gold case, the latter fitted with a PVD-coated titanium bezel and caseback.

As the brand nears its 40-year anniversary, the Porsche Design Studio's success continues to grow.

One key to the Porsche Design Studio's success is its ability to draw inspiration from both emotion and reason to create timepieces that balance tradition with innovation. An apt example of this delicate alchemy is the P´6920 Rattrapante, a watch that contrasts modern case production with a classic complication.

The Ø 45mm case is made from titanium, a metal prized for its lightness, strength and resistance to corrosion. The Porsche Design Studio applies an attractive black coating to the metal using PVD technology, a vacuum-based process that leaves behind a uniform layer of metal nitride "condensation."

Inside this rugged construction, Porsche Design presents a split-second chronograph whose ability to measure multiple times is controlled by a trio of pushers on the sides of the case. The French term Rattrapante (catch up) refers to the seconds. When the chronograph is activated, a red-tipped seconds hand begins to rotate. Pushing the button on the left side of the case stops a green-tipped seconds hand hidden below as the red hand continues. After reading the measurement, pushing the button again causes the green hand to "catch up" with the red hand.

Porsche Design has created two versions of the limited edition P´6920 Rattrapante, 200 examples with cases entirely in PVD and 50 with PVD-coated cases and 18-karat rose-gold 4N bezels and casebacks.

FACING PAGE

LEFT   Produced by Eterna, the 6036 is the first mechanical chronograph that displays the stop-time in a digital manner.

RIGHT   Generously proportioned, the 49mm case used for this Indicator P´6910 is made from rose gold and fitted with a PVD-coated titanium bezel and caseback.

THIS PAGE

ABOVE   This P´6920 Rattrapante's case and bezel are both made of PVD-coated titanium. Four screws are used to secure the bezel and caseback to the 45mm case.

RIGHT   When the P´6920 Rattrapante is engaged, pressing the button on the left will stop a green-tipped seconds hand and allow for a reading. Pressing the button again sends the green hand back under the red-tipped hand.

The Porsche Design Studio puts the world at one's fingertips with the Worldtimer P´6750.

A patented module developed by Eterna empowers the movement's practical and unique ability to transfer the second time zone from the digital display to the central hands by pushing a button integrated into the crown at 2:00.

Arranged horizontally across the center of the dial, the second time zone is read quickly from two apertures. On the left, a rotating 24-hour indicator shows the time in one of the 24 cities displayed opposite using the local airport abbreviation. As a reminder for weary travelers, the caseback is engraved with the 24 reference cities available for display.

The brand's emphasis on effortless function translates aesthetically into a minimalist design whose uncluttered composition complements the clarity of the display. The Worldtimer's 45mm round case—shaped similarly to a pressure gauge—is offered in either rose gold, titanium with a matte finish, or PVD-coated titanium.

ABOVE A push of the button at 2:00 on the Worldtimer P´6750 instantly swaps the reference time with the second time zone.

LEFT Developed by Swiss watchmaker Eterna, the patented 6037 movement's second time-zone function displays the time in one of 24 different cities, each indicated by the appropriate airport abbreviation.

Beyond cutting-edge production techniques, the Porsche Design Studio is also known for exploring non-traditional watchmaking materials, particularly with its designs for the Dashboard and Flat Six collections.

With a dial that channels the graphic clarity of a Porsche Dashboard, the first collection presents an automatic chronograph cased in a range of materials. Each conjures a distinct style, such as sophisticated elegance with black PVD; classic glamour with rose gold and diamonds; and sporty with titanium and rubber.

For its Flat Six collection, the Porsche Design Studio returns to the automobile for inspiration, evoking the automaker's celebrated flat six-cylinder engine in name while visually referencing the shape of a piston with the watch's grooved case.

The company produces the Flat Six as either a chronograph or a basic automatic with date. Each is available in a number of configurations designed to please a range of discerning tastes.

As the brand nears its 40-year anniversary, the Porsche Design Studio's success continues to grow, driven by an outstanding and diverse collection of timepieces. Each luxurious creation is dedicated to making life easier through better design.

RALPH LAUREN

WATCH AND JEWELRY CO.

The year 2009 marked Ralph Lauren's entry into horology, one of the luxury industry's most prestigious segments. Of course, his are not just any watches—eschewing trendy designs and licensing agreements, the New York enterpreneur has chosen to partner with the Richemont Group to stake a claim to the only place worthy of watches bearing his name: the high end.

Since creating his brand in 1967, Lauren has proved that he is a man who does nothing halfway when he plays, he plays to win. His extraordinary success is proof of that: from his wide "Polo" ties in the late 1960s to the empire he runs today, Lauren's path has been strewn with recognition, success and countless awards. The Council of Fashion Designers of America granted him the American Fashion Legend Award in 2007, crowning his fabulous career with his most prestigious award to date. In 40 years of creative endeavors, Lauren has tried his hand at everything: ready-to-wear, haute couture, perfumes, accessories... actually, a more apt phrase may be "almost everything," as one choice element was missing from his empire until now: watches. At a time when almost every luxury brand has released at least one timepiece, one might wonder why Ralph Lauren has waited so long to take this step when he easily could have done it so long ago.

THE RIGHT PARTNER AT THE RIGHT TIME

"Creating something legendary, something timeless—that is what I aspire to. That means taking risks and following my intuitions, without ever losing sight of my project or of my convictions." "Intuition" and "conviction" are words that have a particular sound when voiced by Lauren, and they certainly explain why he wanted to wait for the right time to dive into the adventure of true horology.

That time finally came when he met Johann Rupert, another watch lover and head of Richemont. The two men bonded over their shared conceptions of excellence, timelessness and savoir-faire, creating a business in which they would be equal partners financially and otherwise. Lauren, an avid watch collector, would be involved personally in the design of each model, whereas Rupert would call on three of his most prestigious manufactures—IWC, Piaget and Jaeger-LeCoultre—to provide the watches' heartbeats. Far from a stroke of opportunism, this was the dawn of a common project built for the long term by two major players in the luxury world and with a strong strategy for development.

This rose-gold Ralph Lauren Sporting World Time possesses a rare complication: world time advises the wearer of the time in any of 24 time zones and specifies, of course, am or pm. This watch also displays the power reserve on the dial.

Ralph Lauren's initial three lines, Sporting, Slim Classique and Stirrup, speak to different genres of watch enthusiasts.

The Ralph Lauren Sporting steel chronograph is equipped with the RL750 caliber, an automatic movement developed for Ralph Lauren by Jaeger-LeCoultre.

The RL750 caliber is a chronograph with column-wheel engagement, a sign of great precision and a characteristic of very high-end chronographs. It has a power reserve of 48 hours.

INIMITABLE DESIGN AND MANUFACTURE MOVEMENTS

The result is a sumptuous collection that marks Ralph Lauren's arrival in the closed circle of haute horology. The brand's initial three lines—Sporting, Slim Classique and Stirrup—speak to different genres of watch enthusiasts.

The feeling of remarkable power dominates any first impression of the Ralph Lauren Sporting collection, from its masculine 44.8mm case middle to the six screws that hold the bezel in place. High-tech as well as elegant and sporty, the first of three versions displays hours, minutes and small seconds, and is powered by the RL98295 movement specially made by IWC. Mostly visible through a transparent caseback, this manual-winding mechanical movement is decorated in tribute to watchmaking traditions, blending Côtes de Genève, hand-chamfered bridges and a stippled bottom plate. Ralph Lauren's two complicated Sporting models are powered by Jaeger-LeCoultre movements: the chronograph is equipped with the RL750 caliber, an automatic mechanical movement with a 48-hour power reserve and column-wheel engagement (the ultimate in precision that regulates only the most high-end chronographs); and the third Sporting model depends on its automatic RL939 movement for a function that is as practical as it is rare: world time, a function that allows the user to view the time in any one of 24 time zones on demand.

The 18-karat rose-gold Ralph Lauren Slim Classique is an extra-flat piece of absolute classic elegance on an alligator leather strap. It beats to the rhythm of the RL430 movement, one of the flattest in the world with a thickness of only 2.1mm. The RL430 was developed by Piaget.

The Ralph Lauren Slim Classique model is exceptionally elegant. The harmony of its curves lends it the smooth shape of a polished pebble. The guilloché decoration that adorns its bezel and dial, its Breguet-style hands, its restrained dial showing only the hour and the minute—everything adds to the impression of extreme refinement and supreme simplicity. The piece is equipped with the RL430, an extra-flat manual mechanical movement specially developed by Piaget, a manufacture known for its ultra-slim calibers.

The third model is already well on its way to becoming an icon of haute horology.

Unmistakably recognizable, the Ralph Lauren Stirrup is homage to that upon which the Ralph Lauren universe is based: the equestrian world. Also powered by Piaget or Jaeger-LeCoultre movements according to the model, the Ralph Lauren Stirrup showcases ultimate luxury in diamond-studded versions.

Ralph Lauren Sporting, Slim Classique and Stirrup are three pieces of exceptional horology that rival timepieces from the most prestigious manufactures.

ABOVE LEFT This 18-karat rose-gold Ralph Lauren Stirrup chronograph exhibits just how well this model bears its complication. The Stirrup perfectly blends the classicism of its lines and the sportier side of its functions.

ABOVE RIGHT The Ralph Lauren Stirrup is created in masculine and feminine versions and is Ralph Lauren's first collection to bear diamonds. This small 18-karat white-gold model is equipped with an ultra-flat RL430 movement developed by Piaget.

RAYMOND WEIL

GENEVE

The Swiss family firm RAYMOND WEIL, founded in Geneva in 1976, enjoys a special position in the exclusive world of luxury watchmaking. RAYMOND WEIL stands out for its dynamism and pioneering character, striving constantly to create timepieces which reflect the brand's values of independence, creativity and watchmaking savoir-faire—at attractive prices.

RAYMOND WEIL is a modern, diversified brand which has positioned its watches in an **attractively priced market sector.**

RAYMOND WEIL is present across the globe and has enjoyed spectacular and constant growth in every market. Under the leadership of Olivier Bernheim, President & CEO—latterly joined by his two sons Elie (Marketing Director) and Pierre (Sales Director), both grandsons of company founder Monsieur Raymond Weil—the firm has continued to expand and innovate in the fields of Product Research & Development, Marketing and Communication. The Geneva watchmaker has also expanded into markets like China and India, mindful of their economic potential and the brand's strong local reputation.

The strategy adopted in recent years has assuredly contributed to RAYMOND WEIL's impact on the watchmaking world. Key factors in the firm's success include the constant renewal of its product range, with the introduction of new, increasingly sophisticated mechanical timepieces; strengthening collections at the lower end of the price range; a wider-reaching communications strategy; and the launch of the RW Club (the first club to be set up by a luxury watchmaking brand).

FACING PAGE AND LEFT

The freelancer pink gold date chronograph is shown with a sober dial in matte black, a case in brushed, polished 18-karat pink gold, and a subtle blend of harmonious lines with practical day and date indications, giving this new version of the freelancer a daring, original look.

RAYMOND WEIL timepieces stand out for their high quality, precious materials (diamonds, gold, alligator skin, precious stones) and their emphasis on aesthetic appeal. They reflect a modern, diversified brand which has also chosen to position its watches in an attractively priced sector of the market.

Men's watches—notably the nabucco, freelancer and don giovanni così grande collections—powerfully confirm RAYMOND WEIL reputation as a brand that dares to combine originality and technical proficiency. The appeal of the recently launched don giovanni così grande heure sautante lies in its refined character and mechanical sophistication. It is a timepiece which reflects RAYMOND WEIL's resolutely contemporary approach to the world of luxury.

ABOVE

don giovanni così grande jumping hour has an avant-garde spirit and displays immense appeal. The dial of this elegant and refined timepiece entices the eye with its jumping hour display.

RIGHT

nabucco rivoluzione's perfect proportion of steel, titanium and hi-tech carbon fiber conveys an architectural power to the timepiece, symbolizing the quintessence of masculine elegance. The blue chronograph hand and the subdials provide a striking contrast to the deep black beauty of the nabucco rivoluzione with a 46mm case.

Ladies' collections like the shine and noemia jewelry watches, and the free-lancer dame mechanical timepieces, occupy major roles in the brand's international range. With its dial fitting snugly between the delicate curves of its diamond-spangled case, the brand's latest female collection—the aesthetically harmonious noemia—is Sensuality Incarnate…while subtly alluding to RAYMOND WEIL's family values.

LEFT

noemia is the epitome of feminine grace with the delicate curves of its polished steel case set with sparkling diamonds, and the flawless elegance of its sophisticated dial studded with four Roman numerals and eight full-cut diamonds. noemia's crown, with its intriguing midnight-blue dome, adds a final note of harmony to the design.

The RW Club is an exchange-platform (www.raymond-weil.com/club) between RAYMOND WEIL and its various target publics, aiming to enhance the special relationship between the independent brand with a human face and its clientele. In line with the brand's motto, INDEPENDENCE is a state of mind, the RW Club also aims to discover new talent(s) and to support the arts. Competitions staged each year as the International Photography Prize help RAYMOND WEIL assist young talents in expressing their creativity and raising their profiles. In this way RAYMOND WEIL continues to strengthen its historical ties with the world of Art and Culture.

RICHARD MILLE

Devotees of the brand always love to expound on the concepts that make Richard Mille's creations so special. Fueled by Mille's bold fusion of the latest technology with watch design that has made the horological world sit up and take notice, the discussions about his watches will never leave you cold—they embody far too much passion and vision for merely a neutral response.

THE WORLD OF RICHARD MILLE

Richard Mille reveals that he was "always astonished at how the industry was using 21st-century materials and techniques such as Cadcam to make 19th-century watches. Many of these products are fantastic, and I respect them, but," he notes, "in my opinion, if we are going to use today's materials and technology, then we have to make contemporary watches." And he consequently set out to do just that by elevating the industrial-derived techniques of stamping and CNC machining to brand new forms of modern art. The signature tonneau shape of his watchcases requires, for instance, a staggering 28 stamping operations even before the actual cutting and shaping can begin. Nevertheless, this does not mean that Mille rejects the past; in actuality, quite the contrary is true. "My watches have more hand finishing than you will find in the majority of high-end watches," he contends. "You can see it in the hand beveling of screws and the black polish on my tourbillons; even my watch hands are hand finished! At the same time, you will also see a wide use of advanced techniques. This is exactly how F1 cars are created," he explains. "A modern engine is created using Cadcam, but many parts of it will always be hand finished, polished and adjusted." In Mille's view, only by uniting the best of both worlds can the highest performance possible be achieved.

The fact that he had to focus on creating legitimacy for his products makes it doubly important that Mille's watches reflect an extreme dedication to quality. "When you don't have a name that is 200 years old, you have to provide other factors in order to prove yourself to the collectors and lovers of fine watchmaking," he points out. Mille has a firm belief that the timing was just right for him when the high-end luxury market shifted its focus. "Twenty years ago, a brand name in itself was the only thing that defined status. Today, such status is accorded almost solely to the actual product. People will buy something if it is the very best, even if the brand is not known. This has opened up avenues for me." Above all, it is his deepest desire to advance technology and luxury beyond existing confines that has brought Mille to the lofty ranks of high-end watchmaking.

FACING PAGE
With one of the flattest tourbillon movements ever created, the new RM 017 Ultra Flat Tourbillon carries the lines set by the first rectangular watch of the Richard Mille collection, the RM 016 Automatic. Via a special pusher in the crown, the functions for Winding, Neutral and Handsetting can be activated. In addition, the setting "S" allows one to change the hour hand quickly and independently of the minute hand with a single click.

'If we are going to use today's materials and technology, **we have to make contemporary watches.'**

– Mille

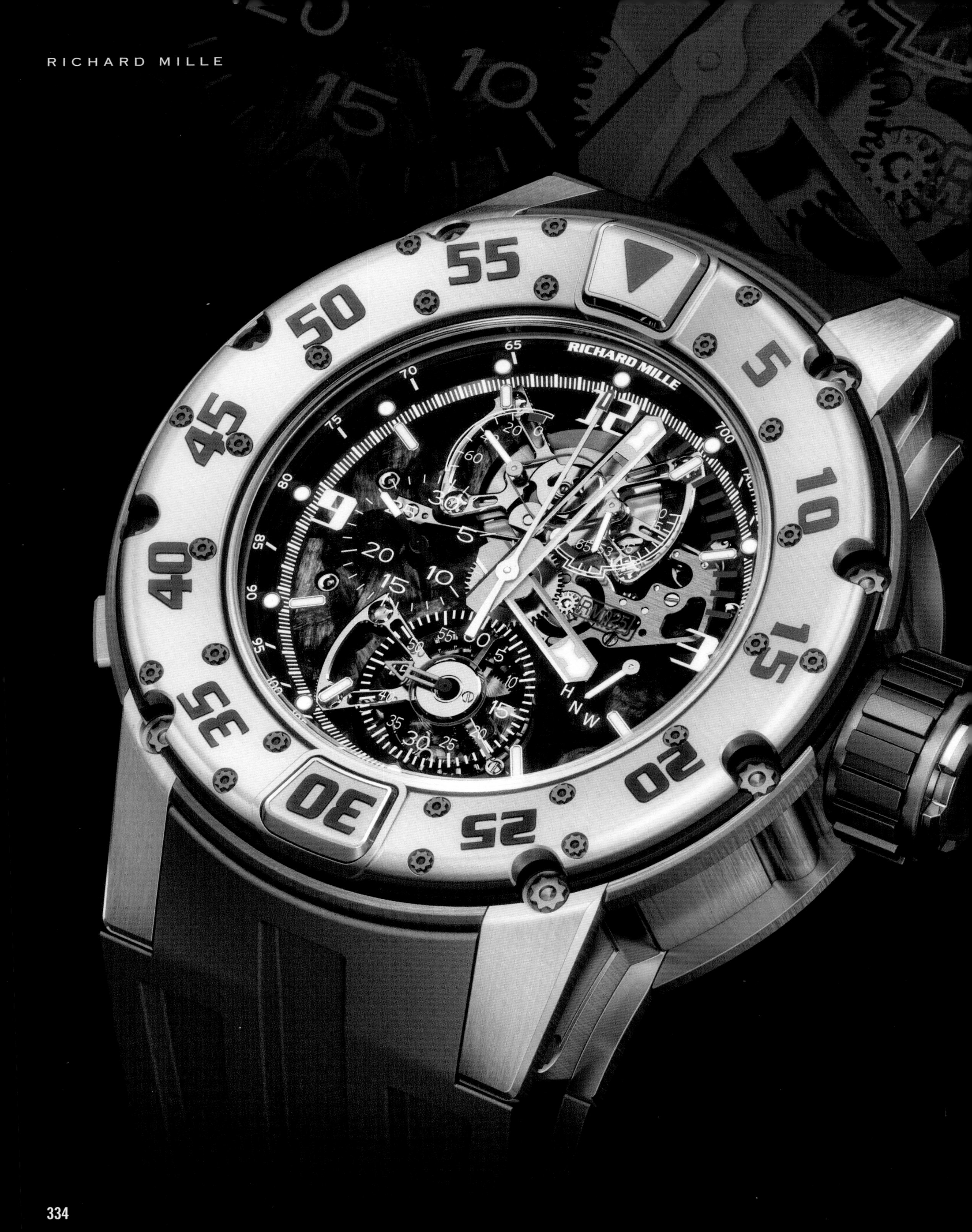
RICHARD MILLE

With specially designed watertight pushers and a screwed down crown, the RM 025 is a tourbillon-chronograph that is ready for action under extreme conditions. Waterproof to 300 meters, all versions have 18-karat red-gold lugs with a titanium central case-band and turning bezel. The bezel is constructed of three layers, connected with 24 screws, and has a unidirectional rotation following ISO 6425 norms in order to avoid timing miscalculations. In addition, the entire bezel system is screwed to the case. The RM 025 was recipient of the Grand Prix d'Horlogerie de Genève 2009 in the Sports Watches category.

THE LIGHTNESS OF PURE LUXURY

Ergonomics stand at the center of Mille's vision. The brand is the only one in which every model has a specially curved case profile, which means they will fit comfortably on any wrist, large or small. It might at first appear a rather simple issue, yet the creation of this wrist-fitting ergonomic design is a costly endeavor, as the cases are not forced into shape but milled from solid pieces of metal. Their streamlined, aerodynamic look and contrasting brushed/polished surfaces and detailing make them among the most complex watchcases produced in Switzerland today.

"An ergonomic fit has always been at the center of my attention," reveals Mille. "People who buy my watches wear them because they are very comfortable. My new diver's watch, the RM 025, is a big beast, but a beast that fits very, very well on the wrist. I push my people to the limit on these kinds of issues. It's very difficult to make a watch ergonomic, but I fight like mad to do so, including the crowns. We've all had watches that made you want to kill the designer because winding them was a nightmare. I've also fought against this marketing concept of 'perceived value'—the idea that the watch must weigh a lot to have a value. To me, that's nonsense. In fact, it costs much more to manufacture a watch in titanium than the same one in gold. It's very difficult to work with titanium. When I came out with watches in titanium that were as expensive as a gold timepiece, people said I was crazy. But a lot of customers appreciated that it was very comfortable. Now it is accepted that a light watch can cost as much as a heavy watch. After all, who is going to say, 'My car weighs five tons, so it should cost more than a car that weighs one ton?' Everybody is fighting against weight today. And to fight against weight costs a fortune. Just look at satellites and F1 cars, where every gram has to be accounted for; they have been busy with this subject for years already."

With specially designed watertight pushers and a screwed down crown, the RM 025 is a tourbillon-chronograph that is ready for action under extreme conditions. Waterproof to 300 meters, all versions have 18-karat red-gold lugs with a titanium central caseband and turning bezel. The bezel is constructed of three layers, connected with 24 screws, and has a uni-directional rotation following ISO 6425 norms in order to avoid timing miscalculations. In addition, the entire bezel system is screwed to the case. The RM 025 was recipient of the Grand Prix d'Horlogerie de Genève 2009 in the Sports Watches category.

RM 017

"You know it is funny," muses the watchmaker, "originally, when I started my brand, I wanted to make a rectangular model. But to fit all of the movement's mechanism inside, I had to enlarge it into a tonneau. In my first drawing of the RM 001, the watch was rectangular! So when the RM 016, the visual predecessor of the RM 017 tourbillon, was released it was like 'returning home' in a way."

New for 2010, the RM 017 Ultra Flat Tourbillon continues the development of the highly successful rectangular RM 016 case that joined the ranks of the Richard Mille Watches collection two years ago. The rectangular models proudly take their place alongside the uniquely curvaceous Richard Mille tonneau shape, providing a variation on a theme that combines elegant curves with the freshness of straight lines, a symbiosis of laid-back 1970s' stylishness and 21st-century cutting edge. With a total thickness comprising a mere 8.7mm, its new ultra-flat manual-winding movement is amongst the thinnest tourbillon constructions ever created. The RM 017's dimensions of 49.8x38mm retain a proportional harmony with the other cases in the collection and, of course, the same wrist-fitting curvature and tapering thickness towards 12:00 and 6:00 that every Richard Mille fan has come to admire.

Increasingly higher levels of development in the automotive and aerospace industries have been achieved under the strong influences and inspiration gleaned from regular contact with new materials. ALUSIC, ceramics, carbon nanofiber, LITAL, silicium and many more materials are no longer seen as exclusively the domain of such industries, thanks to Mille's vision of watchmaking's future. Materials such as these offer the watchmaking industry tremendous possibilities for growth and development.

The new RM 017, for instance, uses a movement baseplate in carbon nanofiber, a major innovation first tested with great success in the RM 006, an experimental model. Carbon nanofiber, not to be confused with common carbon fiber, is an isotropic composite material created from carbon nanofibers molded under a high pressure of 7,500 N/cm2 and a temperature of 2000° C, resulting in a material with high mechanical, physical and chemical stability in all environments. A ribbed perimeter around the movement plate assures the highest rigidity between the plate and bridges. Carbon nanofiber composite structures such as this are amorphous, chemically neutral and dimensionally constant within a very wide range of operating temperatures, including those outside of normal ranges. This stability assures the highest integrity of the movement's going train under all conditions.

The technical results of its first horological application, presented in the RM 006, were so remarkable that Richard Mille decided to extend the use of carbon nanofiber further to the entire tourbillon range. This is just one small example of how developments in the application of new materials for horology have marked Richard Mille Watches as an innovative leader of 21st-century watchmaking.

The use of carbon nanofiber, however, is not all that is new for the RM 017. A new capability has been added to the function selector that first premiered in the RM 002: in addition to this gearbox concept embodied in the separate states of the crown via a special pusher for Winding, Neutral and Hand-setting, the RM 017 adds a quick-setting second-time-zone-adjustment function "S," which allows one to change the hour hand independently of the minute hand with a single click.

Cutting-edge technology combined with elegance and exceptional lines, useful functionality and unmistakable recognition: the RM 017 Ultra Flat Tourbillon is Richard Mille Watches personified.

RM 028

After conquering the racetrack and the open seas, Richard Mille entered the ocean depths with his premiere diver's watch, the RM 025 tourbillon chronograph. This exceptional piece also marked the first appearance of a round case within the collection. Today the brand presents a new automatic diver's watch, the RM 028 Automatic, with a slightly smaller diameter of 47mm. Mirroring the lines of the RM 025, the new RM 028 with its exceptional case and skeletonized movement possesses all the incontestable qualities that typify the watches of Richard Mille.

Following diver's watch ISO norms 6425 with its water resistance of 300 meters (30atm) and a unidirectional bezel, the seemingly simple lines of the round case of the RM 028 conceal a considerable amount of technical expertise. The exceptional water resistance is achieved with a three-part case construction and torque screws, with complete integration of the lugs into the case system. With unidirectional rotation to prevent miscalculations whilst diving, the bezel is composed of three sections assembled with 22 torque screws, making it impossible to accidentally dislodge from the case. The skeletonized automatic movement of the RM 028 utilizes a rotor with variable geometry, a major innovation of Richard Mille that allows the level of automatic winding to be adjusted to the user's lifestyle via the setting of two 18-karat white-gold wings.

The skeletonized RM 023 uses an asymmetrical layout with Roman numerals in appliqué on sapphire with an unusual, sculpted, Alcryn collared crown. Designed for both men and women, this new model unites everything essential in Richard Mille's philosophy with a sophisticated appearance, convincing as well as comfortable under all imaginable conditions from the racetrack to the concert hall. For 2010 some new variants of the RM 023 are presented with polished or brushed bezels and different color combinations of interior flanges.

RM 022 'AERODYNE' DUAL TIME

Keeping track of home base—family, friends and colleagues—when flying around the globe is not always easy for today's business traveler. And a traveler's life is already stressful enough without having to deal with a lot of buttons and dials in order to figure out what time it is somewhere else in the world.

Now, Richard Mille has been able to continue the expansion and application of truly unique materials to watchmaking, successfully combining them with a user-friendly second time zone function in the new RM 022. This tourbillon wristwatch is the first to combine a time-zone function with a composite baseplate utilizing a titanium exterior framework in combination with honeycombed orthorhombic titanium aluminides and carbon nanofiber.

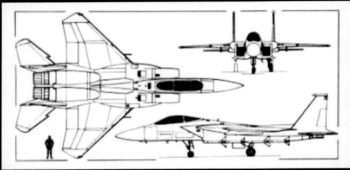

Orthorhombic titanium aluminides form a new group of alloys, developed from the main class of titanium aluminides, which possesses a specific crystalline molecular structure ordered on the orthorhombic phase of Ti2AlNb. Its use within a honeycombed geometrical pattern was originally the subject of research by NASA for application as a core material of supersonic aircraft wings, where resistance to extremely high temperatures and torsion is paramount. The alloy in this honeycombed form has unparalleled stiffness, a low thermal expansion coefficient and exceptional torsion resistance. The actual shape of the baseplate itself as seen from the dial side resembles the trench-like V-shaped profile

of a flying wing aircraft where the wing tips are positioned higher than the central body of the aircraft itself. The winding barrel and the tourbillon are both placed in the central depth of this aerodynamic structure, balancing on light and airy bridges with four arms on two sides. The RM 022 "Aerodyne" Dual Time represents the extraordinary union of all the aspects that comprise the Richard Mille philosophy of watchmaking—now and in the future.

The second time-zone indicator uses a highly sophisticated mechanism that is very simple to use. At the center of the dial, a transparent sapphire crystal hour-disc turns continuously, driven by the movement. The numbers on this disc come into view only when they are suspended above the light colored field located at 3:00. For setting the second time zone, a finely finished pusher is located at 9:00. Each push advances the second time zone by one hour. Changing the time zone several times during a trip with such ease is an ultimate luxury of well-planned horological design.

Combined with a tourbillon movement possessing exceptional chronometric characteristics, the RM 022 represents an exceptional synthesis of useful functionality and the best of high-end 21st-century watchmaking.

The alloy used in the RM 022 "Aerodyne" Dual Time baseplate construction uses a honeycombed structure with unparalleled stiffness, a low thermal expansion coefficient and exceptional torsion resistance. The actual shape of the baseplate itself as seen from the dial side resembles the V-shaped profile of a flying wing aircraft where the wing tips are positioned slanting up from the central body of the aircraft. The winding barrel and the tourbillon are both placed in the central depth of this aerodynamic structure, balancing on light and airy bridges with four arms on two sides. The pusher at 9:00 activates the second time-zone indication on a white field at 3:00.

TOURBILLON — RM 002-V2

Movement: mechanical manual-winding tourbillon caliber RM 002-V2; carbon nanofiber baseplate; approx. 70-hour power reserve; variable inertia balance with overcoil hairspring; fast rotating barrel; function selector gearbox with indicator; ceramic tourbillon endstone; central bridge in rigidified ARCAP; spline screws in grade-5 titanium for the bridges and case; winding barrel and third pinion's teeth with central involute profile; jewels set in white-gold chatons.

Functions: hours, minutes; power-reserve and torque indicators; function indicator.
Case: 18K red-gold, anatomically curved tripartite case; 45x38.3x11.95mm; assembled with 12 spline screws in grade-5 titanium; sapphire crystal front and back with double-sided antiglare coating; water resistant to 50 meters.
Dial: sapphire with double-sided antiglare treatment; protected with eight silicon braces in grooved edges.
Strap: leather or crocodile attached via titanium screws to the case; with matching buckle individually engraved with model number.
Also available: in titanium, 18K white gold or platinum.

TOURBILLON — RM 002-V2 ALL GRAY

Movement: mechanical manual-winding "gray" tourbillon caliber RM 002-V2; gray PVD-coated carbon nanofiber baseplate; approx. 70-hour power reserve; variable inertia balance with overcoil; fast rotating barrel; function selector gearbox with indicator; ceramic tourbillon endstone; central bridge in rigidified ARCAP; spline screws in grade-5 titanium for the bridges and case; winding barrel and third pinion's teeth with central involute profile; jewels set in white-gold chatons.

Functions: hours, minutes; power-reserve and torque indicators; function indicator.
Case: microblasted titanium, anatomically curved tripartite case; 45x38.3x11.95mm; assembled with 12 spline screws in grade-5 titanium; sapphire crystal front and back with double-sided antiglare coating; water resistant to 50 meters.
Dial: sapphire with double-sided antiglare treatment; protected with eight silicon braces in grooved edges.
Strap: special composite strap; attached via titanium screws to the case; matching buckle individually engraved with model number.

TOURBILLON — RM 003-V2

Movement: mechanical manual-winding tourbillon caliber RM 003-V2; carbon nanofiber baseplate; approx. 70-hour power reserve; variable inertia balance with overcoil hairspring; fast rotating barrel; function selector gearbox with indicator; ceramic tourbillon endstone; central bridge in rigidified ARCAP; spline screws in grade-5 titanium for the bridges and case; winding barrel and third pinion's teeth with central involute profile; jewels set in white-gold chatons.

Functions: hours, minutes, second time zone; power-reserve and torque indicators; function indicator.
Case: 18K white-gold, anatomically curved tripartite case; 48x39.3x13.84mm; tripartite case assembled with 12 spline screws in grade-5 titanium; sapphire crystal front and back with double-sided antiglare coating; water resistant to 50 meters.
Dial: sapphire with double-sided antiglare treatment; protected with eight silicon braces in grooved edges.
Strap: leather or crocodile attached via titanium screws to the case; with matching buckle individually engraved with model number.
Also available: in titanium, 18K red gold or platinum.

TOURBILLON — RM 003-V2 ALL GRAY

Movement: mechanical manual-winding "gray" tourbillon caliber RM 003-V2; gray PVD-coated carbon nanofiber baseplate; approx. 70-hour power reserve; variable inertia balance with overcoil; fast rotating barrel; function selector gearbox with indicator; ceramic tourbillon endstone; sapphire glass disc for second time zone; central bridge in rigidified ARCAP; spline screws in grade-5 titanium for the bridges and case; winding barrel and third pinion's teeth with central involute profile; jewels set in white-gold chatons.

Functions: hours, minutes; second time zone; power-reserve and torque indicators; function indicator.
Case: microblasted titanium, anatomically curved tripartite case; 48x39.3x13.84mm; assembled with 12 spline screws in grade-5 titanium; sapphire crystal front and back with double-sided antiglare coating; water resistant to 50 meters.
Dial: sapphire with double-sided antiglare treatment; protected with eight silicon braces in grooved edges.
Strap: special composite strap; attached via titanium screws to the case; matching buckle individually engraved with model number.

SPLIT SECONDS CHRONOGRAPH   RM 004-V2

Movement: mechanical manual-winding caliber RM 004-V2; carbon nanofiber baseplate; approx. 60-hour power reserve; titanium column wheel, gear wheels and lever; split seconds mechanism with improved and patented functions; fast rotating barrel; function indicator; variable inertia balance with overcoil hairspring; newly designed three-tiered titanium bridge with lever escapement; spline screws in grade-5 titanium for the bridges and case; winding barrel and third pinion's teeth with central involute profile.

Functions: hours, minutes, seconds; split seconds; chronograph minute counter; power-reserve and torque indicators; function indicator.

Case: 18K red-gold, anatomically curved tripartite case; 48x39.7x14.95mm; assembled with 20 spline screws in grade-5 titanium; sapphire crystal front and back with double-sided antiglare coating; water resistant to 50 meters.

Dial: sapphire with double-sided antiglare treatment; protected with eight silicon braces in grooved edges.

Strap: leather or crocodile; attached via titanium screws to the case; with matching buckle individually engraved with model number.

Also available: in titanium, 18K white gold or platinum.

SPLIT SECONDS CHRONOGRAPH   RM 004-V2 ALL GRAY

Movement: mechanical manual-winding movement; RM 004-V2 "gray" caliber with gray PVD-coated carbon nanofiber baseplate; approx. 60-hour power reserve; titanium column wheel, gear wheels and lever; split seconds mechanism with improved and patented functions; fast rotating barrel; variable inertia balance with overcoil; newly designed three-tiered titanium bridge with in-line lever escapement; spline screws in grade-5 titanium for the bridges and case; winding barrel and third pinion's teeth with central involute profile.

Functions: hours, minutes, seconds; split seconds; chronograph minute counter; power-reserve and torque indicators; function indicator.

Case: microblasted titanium, anatomically curved tripartite case; 48x39.7x14.95mm; assembled with 20 spline screws in grade-5 titanium; sapphire crystal front and back with double-sided antiglare coating; water resistant to 50 meters.

Dial: sapphire with double-sided antiglare treatment; protected with eight silicon braces in grooved edges.

Strap: special composite strap; attached via titanium screws to the case; matching buckle individually engraved with model number.

FELIPE MASSA SPLIT SECONDS CHRONOGRAPH   RM 004-V2 FM

Movement: mechanical manual-winding RM 004-V2 caliber with carbon nanofiber baseplate; approx. 60-hour power reserve; titanium column wheel, gear wheels and lever; split seconds mechanism with improved and patented functions; fast rotating barrel; function indicator; variable inertia balance with overcoil; newly designed three-tiered titanium bridge with inline lever escapement; spline screws in grade-5 titanium for the bridges and case; winding barrel and third pinion's teeth with central involute profile.

Functions: hours, minutes, seconds; split seconds; chronograph minute counter; power-reserve and torque indicators; function indicator.

Case: microblasted titanium, anatomically curved tripartite case; 48x39.7x14.95mm; assembled with 20 spline screws in grade-5 titanium; sapphire crystal front and back with double-sided antiglare coating; water resistant to 50 meters.

Dial: sapphire with double-sided antiglare treatment; protected with eight silicon braces in grooved edges.

Strap: special composite strap; attached via titanium screws to the case; matching buckle individually engraved with model number.

AUTOMATIC (TITANIUM VERSION)   RM 007

Movement: mechanical self-winding caliber RM 007; approx. 38-hour power reserve; rotor fitted with a patented auto-reverse system integrated into the rotor ball bearing; grade-5 titanium screws; date aperture at 6 with sapphire crystal calendar disc treated with double-sided antiglare coating; crown with double-seal O-ring and collar in Alcryn; teeth with central involute profile.

Functions: hours, minutes; date.

Case: titanium, anatomically curved tripartite case; 45x31x10.09mm; assembled with 12 spline screws in grade-5 titanium; sapphire crystal front and back with double-sided antiglare coating; water resistant to 50 meters.

Strap: leather, crocodile and various fabrics; attached via titanium screws to the case; with matching buckle individually engraved with model number.

AUTOMATIC — RM 007 TITALYT

Movement: mechanical self-winding caliber RM 007; approx. 38-hour power reserve; rotor fitted with a patented auto-reverse system integrated into the rotor ball bearing; grade-5 titanium screws; date aperture at 6 with sapphire crystal calendar disc treated with double-sided antiglare coating; crown with double-seal O-ring and collar in Alcryn; teeth with central involute profile.
Functions: hours, minutes; date.

Case: titanium, anatomically curved tripartite case with Titalyt surface treatment; 45x31x10.09mm; assembled with 12 spline screws in grade-5 titanium; sapphire crystal front and back with double-sided antiglare coating; water resistant to 50 meters.
Strap: leather, crocodile and various fabrics; attached via titanium screws to the case; with matching buckle individually engraved with model number.

AUTOMATIC (DIAMOND VERSION) — RM 007

Movement: mechanical self-winding caliber RM 007; approx. 38-hour power reserve; rotor fitted with a patented auto-reverse system integrated into the rotor ball bearing; rotor segment in sandblasted 18K gold with weight comprising more than 100 18K gold micro-balls within a transparent, PVD-coated container; grade-5 titanium screws; date aperture at 6 with sapphire crystal calendar disc treated with double-sided antiglare coating; crown with double-seal O-ring and collar in Alcryn; teeth with central involute profile.
Functions: hours, minutes; date.
Case: 18K white-gold, anatomically curved tripartite case; 45x31x10.09mm; set with white diamonds on bezel and sides with black diamonds on the case columns; assembled with 12 spline screws in grade-5 titanium; sapphire crystal front and back with double-sided antiglare coating; water resistant to 50 meters.
Strap: crocodile or various fabrics; attached via titanium screws to the case; with matching buckle individually engraved with model number or with deployant.

TOURBILLON SPLIT SECONDS CHRONOGRAPH — RM 008

Movement: mechanical manual-winding tourbillon caliber RM 008; titanium baseplate; approx. 60-hour power reserve; titanium column wheel, gear wheels and lever; split seconds mechanism with improved and patented functions; fast rotating barrel; function indicator; variable inertia balance with overcoil hairspring; newly designed in-line lever escapement; spline screws in grade-5 titanium for the bridges and case; winding barrel and third pinion's teeth with central involute profile.

Functions: hours, minutes, seconds, split seconds; chronograph minute counter; power-reserve and torque indicators; function indicator.
Case: 18K red-gold, anatomically curved tripartite case; 48x39.7x14.95mm; tripartite case assembled with 20 spline screws in grade-5 titanium; sapphire crystal front and back with double-sided antiglare coating; water resistant to 50 meters.
Dial: sapphire with double-sided antiglare treatment; protected with eight silicon braces in grooved edges.
Strap: leather or crocodile; attached via titanium screws to case; with matching buckle individually engraved with model number.
Also available: in titanium, 18K white gold or platinum.

FELIPE MASSA LIMITED EDITION — RM 008-V2 FM

Movement: mechanical manual-winding "gray" tourbillon caliber RM 008; gray PVD-coated carbon nanofiber baseplate; approx. 60-hour power reserve; titanium column wheel, gear wheels and lever; split seconds mechanism with improved and patented functions; fast rotating barrel; function indicator; variable inertia balance with overcoil; inline lever escapement; spline screws in grade-5 titanium for the bridges and case; winding barrel and third pinion's teeth with central involute profile.

Functions: hours, minutes, seconds; split seconds; chronograph minute counter; power-reserve and torque indicators; function indicator.
Case: 18K red-gold, anatomically curved tripartite case; 48x39.7x14.95mm; assembled with 20 spline screws in grade-5 titanium; sapphire crystal front and back with double-sided antiglare coating; water resistant to 50 meters.
Dial: sapphire with double-sided antiglare treatment; protected with 8 silicon braces in grooved edges.
Strap: special composite strap; attached via titanium screws to the case; matching buckle individually engraved with model number.

AUTOMATIC   RM 010

Movement: mechanical self-winding skeletonized caliber RM 005-S; approx. 55-hour power reserve; rotor with variable geometry via white-gold wings adjustable to six positions; ceramic rotor ball bearings; PVD-coated titanium baseplate, bridges and balance cock; crown in sandblasted grade-5 titanium with double-seal O-ring and collar in Alcryn; double-winding barrel; grade-5 titanium spline screws for movement and case.

Functions: hours, minutes, seconds; date.

Case: 18K red-gold, anatomically curved tripartite case; 48x39.3x13.84mm; assembled with 12 spline screws in grade-5 titanium; sapphire crystal front and back with double-sided antiglare coating; water resistant to 100 meters.

Dial: sapphire with double-sided antiglare treatment; protected with eight silicon braces in grooved edges.

Strap: leather or crocodile; attached via titanium screws to the case; with matching buckle in titanium, 18K red or white gold or platinum; individually engraved with model number.

Also available: in titanium, 18K white gold or platinum.

AUTOMATIC FLYBACK CHRONOGRAPH   RM 011 FELIPE MASSA

Movement: mechanical with skeletonized self-winding chronograph caliber RM 011; approx. 55-hour power reserve; rotor with variable geometry via white-gold wings adjustable to six positions; ceramic rotor ball bearings; PVD-coated titanium baseplate, bridges and balance cock; large date; double-winding barrel; titanium column wheel, gear wheels and lever; split seconds mechanism with improved and patented functions; crown in sandblasted grade-5 titanium with double-seal O-ring and collar in Alcryn; grade-5 titanium spline screws for movement and case.

Functions: hours, minutes, seconds; flyback chronograph; 60-minute count-down timer; 12-hour totalizer; large date; month.

Case: titanium central case ring, anatomically curved tripartite case; 50x42.5x15.85mm; 18K white-gold bezel; assembled with 12 spline screws in grade-5 titanium; sapphire crystal front and back with double-sided antiglare coating; water resistant to 100 meters.

Dial: sapphire with double-sided antiglare treatment; protected with eight silicon braces in grooved edges.

Strap: leather or crocodile; attached via titanium screws to the case; with matching buckle individually engraved with model number.

Also available: with 18K red-gold front and back bezel or full titanium.

AUTOMATIC FLYBACK CHRONOGRAPH   RM 011 LE MANS CLASSIC

Movement: mechanical with skeletonized self-winding chronograph caliber RM 011; approx. 55-hour power reserve; rotor with variable geometry via white-gold wings adjustable to six positions; ceramic rotor ball bearings; PVD-coated titanium baseplate, bridges and balance cock; large date; double-winding barrel; titanium column wheel, gear wheels and lever; split seconds mechanism with improved and patented functions; crown in sandblasted grade-5 titanium with double-seal O-ring and collar in Alcryn; grade-5 titanium spline screws for movement and case.

Functions: hours, minutes, seconds; flyback chronograph; 60-minute count-down timer; 12-hour totalizer; large date; month.

Case: titanium central case ring, anatomically curved tripartite case; 50x42.5x15.85mm; green interior bezel; assembled with 12 spline screws in grade-5 titanium; sapphire crystal front and back with double-sided antiglare coating; water resistant to 100 meters.

Dial: sapphire with double-sided antiglare treatment; protected with eight silicon braces in grooved edges.

Strap: leather or crocodile; attached via titanium screws to the case; with matching buckle individually engraved with model number.

Note: limited to 150 pieces in titanium.

AUTOMATIC FLYBACK CHRONOGRAPH   RM 011 LE MANS CLASSIC

Movement: mechanical with skeletonized self-winding chronograph caliber RM 011; approx. 55-hour power reserve; rotor with variable geometry via white-gold wings adjustable to six positions; ceramic rotor ball bearings; PVD-coated titanium baseplate, bridges and balance cock; large date; double-winding barrel; titanium column wheel, gear wheels and lever; split seconds mechanism with improved and patented functions; crown in sandblasted grade-5 titanium with double-seal O-ring and collar in Alcryn; grade-5 titanium spline screws for movement and case.

Functions: hours, minutes, seconds; flyback chronograph; 60-minute countdown timer; 12-hour totalizer; large date; month.

Case: 18K red-gold central case ring, anatomically curved tripartite case; 50x42.5x15.85mm; green interior bezel; assembled with 12 spline screws in grade-5 titanium; sapphire crystal front and back with double-sided antiglare coating; water resistant to 100 meters.

Dial: sapphire with double-sided antiglare treatment; protected with eight silicon braces in grooved edges.

Strap: leather or crocodile; attached via titanium screws to the case; with matching buckle individually engraved with model number.

Note: limited to 150 pieces in 18K red gold.

TOURBILLON — RM 014 PERINI NAVI CUP

Movement: mechanical manual-winding marine tourbillon caliber RM 014; carbon nanofiber baseplate; nautical pattern-finished case, screws and crown; approx. 70-hour power reserve; variable inertia balance with Breguet-Phillips spiral; fast rotating barrel; function selector gearbox with indicator; ceramic tourbillon endstone; central bridge in rigidified INOX; spline screws in grade-5 titanium for the bridges and case; winding barrel and third pinion's teeth with central involute profile; jewels set in white-gold chatons.

Functions: hours, minutes; power-reserve and torque indicators; function indicator.

Case: platinum, anatomically curved tripartite case; 45x38.9x11.85mm; assembled with 12 spline screws in grade-5 titanium; sapphire crystal front and back with double-sided antiglare coating; water resistant to 50 meters.

Dial: sapphire with double-sided antiglare treatment; protected with eight silicon braces in grooved edges.

Strap: leather or crocodile; attached via titanium screws to the case; with matching buckle in titanium, 18K red or white gold or platinum; individually engraved with model number.

Also available: 18K red or white gold.

TOURBILLON — RM 015 PERINI NAVI CUP

Movement: mechanical manual-winding marine tourbillon caliber RM 015; carbon nanofiber baseplate; nautical pattern-finished case, screws and crown; approx. 70-hour power reserve; variable inertia balance with overcoil hairspring; fast rotating barrel; function selector gearbox with indicator; ceramic tourbillon endstone; central bridge in rigidified INOX; spline screws in grade-5 titanium for the bridges and case; winding barrel and third pinion's teeth with central involute profile; jewels set in white-gold chatons.

Functions: hours, minutes; second time zone; power-reserve and torque indicators; function indicator.

Case: platinum, anatomically curved tripartite case; 45x38.9x11.85mm; assembled with 12 spline screws in grade-5 titanium; sapphire crystal front and back with double-sided antiglare coating; water resistant to 50 meters.

Dial: sapphire with double-sided antiglare treatment; protected with eight silicon braces in grooved edges.

Strap: leather or crocodile; attached via titanium screws to the case; with matching buckle in titanium, 18K red or white gold or platinum; individually engraved with model number.

Also available: 18K red or white gold.

AUTOMATIC — RM 016

Movement: mechanical self-winding skeletonized RM 005-S caliber; approx. 55-hour power reserve; rotor with variable geometry via white-gold wings adjustable to six positions; ceramic rotor ball bearings; PVD-coated titanium baseplate, bridges and balance cock; crown in sandblasted grade-5 titanium with double-seal O-ring and collar in Alcryn; double-winding barrel; grade-5 titanium spline screws for movement and case.

Functions: hours, minutes, seconds; date.

Case: 18K red-gold, anatomically curved tripartite case; 49.8x38x8.25mm; assembled with 12 spline screws in grade-5 titanium; sapphire crystal front and back with double-sided antiglare coating; water resistant to 50 meters.

Dial: sapphire with double-sided antiglare treatment; protected with eight silicon braces in grooved edges.

Strap: leather or crocodile; attached via titanium screws to the case; with matching buckle in 18K red gold; individually engraved with model number.

Also available: in titanium, 18K white gold or platinum with matching buckle.

AUTOMATIC — RM 016 TITALYT

Movement: mechanical self-winding skeletonized RM 005-S caliber; approx. 55-hour power reserve; rotor with variable geometry via white-gold wings adjustable to six positions; ceramic rotor ball bearings; PVD-coated titanium baseplate, bridges and balance cock; crown in sandblasted grade-5 titanium with double-seal O-ring and collar in Alcryn; double-winding barrel; grade-5 titanium spline screws for movement and case.

Functions: hours, minutes, seconds; date.

Case: titanium, anatomically curved tripartite case with Titalyt surface treatment; 49.8x38x8.25mm; assembled with 12 spline screws in grade-5 titanium; sapphire crystal front and back with double-sided antiglare coating; water resistant to 50 meters.

Dial: sapphire with double-sided antiglare treatment; protected with eight silicon braces in grooved edges.

Strap: leather or crocodile; attached via titanium screws to the case; with matching buckle in 18K red gold; individually engraved with model number.

Also available: in titanium, 18K white gold or platinum with matching buckle.

AUTOMATIC WITH FULL DIAMOND SETTING — RM 016

Movement: mechanical self-winding skeletonized RM 005-S caliber; approx. 55-hour power reserve; rotor with variable geometry via white-gold wings adjustable to six positions; ceramic rotor ball bearings; PVD-coated titanium baseplate, bridges and balance cock; crown in sandblasted grade-5 titanium with double-seal O-ring and collar in Alcryn; double-winding barrel; grade-5 titanium spline screws for movement and case.

Functions: hours, minutes, seconds; date.

Case: 18K white-gold, anatomically curved tripartite case; 49.8x38x8.25mm; assembled with 12 spline screws in grade-5 titanium; sapphire crystal front and back with double-sided antiglare coating; water resistant to 50 meters.

Dial: sapphire with double-sided antiglare treatment; protected with eight silicon braces in grooved edges.

Strap: leather or crocodile; attached via titanium screws to the case; with matching buckle in 18K red gold; individually engraved with model number.

Also available: in titanium, 18K red gold or platinum with matching buckle.

TOURBILLON — RM 017 ULTRA FLAT

Movement: mechanical manual-winding ultra-flat tourbillon 017 caliber with carbon nanofiber baseplate; approx. 72-hour power reserve; variable inertia balance with overcoil; fast rotating barrel; ceramic tourbillon endstone; spline screws in grade-5 titanium for the bridges and case; winding barrel and third pinion's teeth with central involute profile.

Functions: hours, minutes; function selector with indicator.

Case: 18K white-gold, rectangular, anatomically curved; 49.8x38x8.7mm; assembled with 12 spline screws in grade-5 titanium; sapphire crystal front and back with double-sided antiglare coating; water resistant to 50 meters.

Dial: sapphire with double-sided antiglare treatment; protected with eight silicon braces in grooved edges.

Strap: crocodile attached via titanium screws to the case; with matching buckle individually engraved with model number.

TOURBILLON — RM 018 HOMMAGE A BOUCHERON

Movement: mechanical manual-winding tourbillon RM 018 caliber; two-layered synthetic sapphire Al$_2$O$_3$ baseplate construction; wheels created from precious and semi-precious stones; approx. 48-hour power reserve; variable inertia balance with overcoil hairspring; fast rotating barrel; ceramic tourbillon endstone; spline screws in grade-5 titanium for the bridges and case; winding barrel and third pinion's teeth with central involute profile; jewels set in white-gold chatons.

Functions: hours, minutes.

Case: 18K white gold; 48x39.3x13.84mm; assembled with 12 spline screws in grade-5 titanium; sapphire crystal front and back with double-sided antiglare coating; water resistant to 50 meters.

Dial: sapphire with double-sided antiglare treatment; protected with eight silicon braces in grooved edges.

Strap: crocodile; attached via titanium screws to the case; matching buckle individually engraved with model number.

Note: limited to 30 pieces worldwide.

TOURBILLON — RM 019 BLACK ONYX

Movement: mechanical manual-winding tourbillon RM 019 caliber; black onyx baseplate; approx. 48-hour power reserve; variable inertia balance with overcoil hairspring; fast rotating barrel; ceramic tourbillon endstone; spline screws in grade-5 titanium for the bridges and case; winding barrel and third pinion's teeth with central involute profile; jewels set in white-gold chatons.

Functions: hours, minutes; power-reserve indicator.

Case: 18K white gold; 45x38.3x12.15mm; assembled with 12 spline screws in grade-5 titanium; sapphire crystal front and back with double-sided antiglare coating; water resistant to 50 meters.

Dial: sapphire with double-sided antiglare treatment; protected with eight silicon braces in grooved edges.

Strap: leather or crocodile; attached via titanium screws to the case; matching buckle individually engraved with model number.

Also available: in 18K red gold.

Note: limited to 30 pieces.

TOURBILLON POCKET WATCH — RM 020

Movement: mechanical manual-winding tourbillon RM 020 caliber; carbon nanofiber baseplate; approx. 10-day power reserve via two winding barrels; variable inertia balance with overcoil hairspring; fast rotating barrel; function selector gearbox with indicator; ceramic tourbillon endstone; central bridge in rigidified ARCAP; spline screws in grade-5 titanium for the bridges and case; winding barrel and third pinion teeth with central involute profile; jewels set in white-gold chatons.

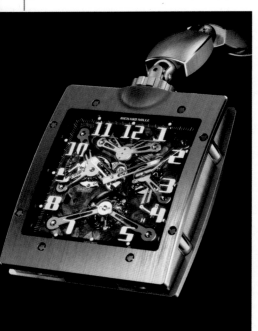

Functions: hours, minutes; power-reserve and torque indicators; function indicator.

Case: titanium central case ring with both front and back bezels in titanium; 62x52x15.6mm; assembled with 12 spline screws in grade-5 titanium; sapphire crystal front and back with double-sided antiglare coating; water resistant to 50 meters.

Dial: sapphire with double-sided antiglare treatment; protected with eight silicon braces in grooved edges.

Note: supplied with specially designed titanium chain with quick release mechanism.

Also available: with front and back bezels in either 18K red or white gold, or platinum.

TOURBILLON — RM 021 AERODYNE

Movement: mechanical manual-winding tourbillon RM 021 caliber; movement baseplate of titanium and honeycombed orthorhombic titanium aluminide with carbon nanofiber; approx. 70-hour power reserve; variable inertia balance with overcoil hairspring; fast rotating barrel; function selector gearbox with indicator; ceramic tourbillon endstone; central bridge in rigidified ARCAP; spline screws in grade-5 titanium for the bridges and case; winding barrel and third pinion's teeth with central involute profile; jewels set in white-gold chatons.

Functions: hours, minutes; power-reserve and torque indicators; function indicator.

Case: 18K white-gold, anatomically curved tripartite case; 48x39.3x13.95mm; assembled with 12 spline screws in grade-5 titanium; sapphire crystal front and back with double-sided antiglare coating; water resistant to 50 meters.

Dial: sapphire with double-sided antiglare treatment; protected with eight silicon braces in grooved edges.

Strap: leather or crocodile attached via titanium screws to the case; with matching buckle individually engraved with model number.

Also available: in titanium and 18K red gold.

RM 022

Movement: mechanical manual-winding tourbillon RM 022 caliber; movement baseplate of titanium and honeycombed orthorhombic titanium aluminide with carbon nanofiber; approx. 70-hour power reserve; variable inertia balance with overcoil hair-spring; fast rotating barrel; function selector gearbox with indicator; ceramic tourbillon endstone; central bridge in rigidified ARCAP; spline screws in grade-5 titanium for the bridges and case; winding barrel and third pinion's teeth with central involute profile; jewels set in white-gold chatons.

Functions: hours, minutes; second time zone; power-reserve and torque indicators; function indicator.

Case: 18K white-gold, anatomically curved tripartite case; 48x39.3x13.84mm; assembled with 12 spline screws in grade-5 titanium; sapphire crystal front and back with double-sided coating; water resistant to 50 meters.

Dial: sapphire with double-sided antiglare treatment; protected with eight silicon braces in grooved edges.

Strap: leather or crocodile attached via titanium screws to the case; with matching buckle individually engraved with model number.

Also available: in titanium and 18K red gold.

AUTOMATIC — RM 023

Movement: mechanical self-winding partially skeletonized caliber; approx. 55-hour power reserve; rotor with variable geometry via white-gold wings adjustable to six positions; ceramic rotor ball bearings; PVD-coated titanium baseplate, bridges and balance cock; crown in sandblasted grade-5 titanium with double-seal O-ring and collar in Alcryn; double-winding barrel; grade-5 titanium spline screws for movement and case.

Functions: hours, minutes, seconds; date.

Case: 18K white-gold anatomically curved tripartite case; 48x39.3x13.84mm; assembled with 12 spline screws in grade-5 titanium; sapphire crystal front and back with double-sided antiglare coating; water resistant to 50 meters.

Dial: sapphire with double-sided antiglare treatment; protected with eight silicon braces in grooved edges.

Strap: leather or crocodile; attached to the case via titanium screws with matching buckle engraved with model number.

Also available: in titanium and 18K red gold.

AUTOMATIC RM 023

Movement: mechanical self-winding partially skeletonized caliber; approx. 55-hour power reserve; rotor with variable geometry via white-gold wings adjustable to six positions; ceramic rotor ball bearings; PVD-coated titanium baseplate, bridges and balance cock; crown in sandblasted grade-5 titanium with double-seal O-ring and collar in Alcryn; double-winding barrel; grade-5 titanium spline screws for movement and case.

Functions: hours, minutes, seconds; date.

Case: 18K red-gold anatomically curved tripartite case; 48x39.3x13.84mm; assembled with 12 spline screws in grade-5 titanium; sapphire crystal front and back with double-sided antiglare coating; water resistant to 50 meters.

Dial: sapphire with double-sided antiglare treatment; protected with eight silicon braces in grooved edges.

Strap: leather or crocodile; attached to the case via titanium screws with matching buckle engraved with model number.

Also available: in titanium and 18K white gold.

AUTOMATIC RM 023

Movement: mechanical self-winding partially skeletonized caliber; approx. 55-hour power reserve; rotor with variable geometry via white-gold wings adjustable to six positions; ceramic rotor ball bearings; PVD-coated titanium baseplate, bridges and balance cock; crown in sandblasted grade-5 titanium with double-seal O-ring and collar in Alcryn; double-winding barrel; grade-5 titanium spline screws for movement and case.

Functions: hours, minutes, seconds; date.

Case: 18K white-gold anatomically curved tripartite case; 48x39.3x13.84mm; assembled with 12 spline screws in grade-5 titanium; sapphire crystal front and back with double-sided antiglare coating; water resistant to 50 meters.

Dial: sapphire with double-sided antiglare treatment; protected with eight silicon braces in grooved edges.

Strap: leather or crocodile; attached to the case via titanium screws with matching buckle engraved with model number.

Also available: in titanium and 18K red gold.

TOURBILLON CHRONOGRAPH RM 025 DIVER'S WATCH

Movement: mechanical manual-winding RM 025 caliber; carbon nanofiber baseplate; approx. 70-hour power reserve; titanium column wheel; gear wheels and lever; chronograph mechanism with improved and patented functions; fast rotating barrel; variable inertia balance with overcoil hairspring; newly designed in-line lever escapement; spline screws in grade-5 titanium for the bridges and case; screwed crown; winding barrel and third pinion's teeth central involute profile.

Functions: hours, minutes, seconds; chronograph minute counter; power-reserve and torque indicators; function indicator.

Case: full titanium, anatomically curved tripartite case; 18K red-gold lugs; Ø 50.7x19.2mm; assembled with 20 torque screws in grade-5 titanium; unidirectional turning timing bezel; screwed crown; sapphire crystal front and back with double-sided antiglare coating; water resistant to 300 meters according to ISO 6425.

Dial: sapphire with double-sided antiglare treatment protected with silicon braces in grooved edges.

Strap: RICHARD MILLE-designed strap of chemically inert KALREZ; fastened to lugs with screws; matching engraved buckle.

AUTOMATIC RM 028 DIVER'S WATCH

Movement: mechanical self-winding partially skeletonized caliber; approx. 55-hour power reserve; rotor with variable geometry via white-gold wings adjustable to six positions; ceramic rotor ball bearings; PVD-coated titanium baseplate, bridges and balance cock; crown in sandblasted grade-5 titanium with double-seal O-ring and collar in Alcryn; double-winding barrel; unidirectional turning and locking tripartite bezel fastened with 22 special spline screws.

Functions: hours, minutes, seconds; date.

Case: titanium, anatomically curved tripartite case; Ø 47x14.6mm (thickest area); assembled with 20 spline screws in grade-5 titanium; sapphire crystal front and back with double-sided antiglare coating; water resistant to 50 meters.

Dial: sapphire with double-sided antiglare treatment; protected with eight silicon braces in grooved edges.

Strap: special rubber strap attached with screws to the case with matching buckle engraved with model number.

In the popular vernacular, the Rolex name is analogous to luxury. Today, its hard-won reputation for enduring style and performance spans the globe. To ensure its independence in the future, the company now controls all aspects of its watchmaking.

Rolex continues its tradition of timeless design with four new versions of the Oyster Perpetual Datejust II. Introduced in 2009 at Basel, they present a subtly redesigned take on one of the world's most iconic timepieces.

For the first time ever, Rolex now offers this 41mm model in yellow or white Rolesor (the brand's term for combinations of stainless steel and gold elements). The first features a stainless steel case, yellow-gold bezel and crown, and a stainless steel bracelet with a yellow-gold middle section. The white Rolesor includes a stainless steel case, bracelet and crown, topped with a white-gold bezel.

These new metal pairings are met with four stylish new dials. The yellow Rolesor version is accompanied by either a slate dial with black Roman numerals outlined in green, or a black dial with white Arabic numerals. The white Rolesor version is offered with a white dial and hour-markers, or with a rhodium dial with blue Arabic numerals.

Rolex matches the Oyster Perpetual Datejust II's luxurious exterior with an innovative movement on the inside. It combines many of Rolex's pioneering achievements in one watch, referencing the Oyster with its water- and dustproof case, the Perpetual with its rotor, and the Datejust with its date window.

The watch also reflects the brand's devotion to precision, equipping the watch with an officially certified Swiss chronometer.

For the first time, Rolex adds fiery facets to its classic Oyster Perpetual Datejust, unveiling eight new models, each with a bezel set with 52 brilliant-cut diamonds. The refined design bears the unmistakable imprint of Rolex's aesthetic personality, delivering a versatile mix of everyday chic and glittering glamour.

The 36mm model is available with a range of dials, including four adorned with a floral motif and Arabic numerals. Mother-of-pearl dials decorated with diamond hour-markers are set within two models—black for the yellow Rolesor and pink for the white Rolesor. Rounding out the list is a wavy green dial set in yellow Rolesor and a wavy rhodium dial set in white Rolesor. Both feature gem-set Arabic numerals.

The beauty of the Oyster Perpetual Datejust extends to its movement, developed and manufactured by Rolex. Chronometer-certified by the Swiss Official Chronometer Testing Institute (COSC), the caliber has passed a battery of demanding tests to guarantee its high level of precision.

All of these new Oyster Perpetual Datejust models come on bracelets, half of which are the Oyster bracelet, fitted with an Oysterclasp and Easylink extension link. The others are equipped with a Jubilee bracelet with a Crownclasp. Both styles are designed to maximize comfort while adding a final, graceful touch.

THIS PAGE
Rolex now offers the ladies' Oyster Perpetual Datejust models with diamond-set bezels. This pink floral version in white Rolesor is one of eight new versions.

FACING PAGE

The handsome detailing of the new yellow Rolesor Oyster Perpetual Datejust II includes a fluted bezel and a slate dial with black Roman numerals edged in green.

The Oyster Perpetual Datejust II **has been revamped in Rolesor** and with four new dials.

Since the 1950s, Rolex has enjoyed a connection to the world of sailing that has grown stronger over the years. Today, the watchmaker is a major sponsor of nearly two dozen international sailing events, including the prestigious Rolex Farr 40 World Championship.

Therefore, it's no surprise that the pleasures of boat racing provide inspiration for the Oyster Perpetual Yacht-Master II. Its certified chronometer movement integrates a regatta chronograph. This complication provides a programmable countdown feature that can be set—from zero to ten minutes—at the starting sequences of each regatta.

To ensure its overall accuracy, the watch contains Rolex's blue Parachrom hairspring. Unlike typical oscillator hairsprings that are susceptible to magnetic fields, this special design is not only impervious to magnetic fields, but its advanced design is also more resistant to knocks and shocks.

Water resistant to 100 meters, the Oyster Perpetual Yacht-Master II is presented in a 44mm case that is available in yellow gold with a blue ceramic bezel or white gold with a platinum bezel.

A marvel of watchmaking ingenuity, the blue bezel is made from Cerachrom. This extremely hard ceramic material is well suited to handle the harsh elements endured by sailors. Resistant to corrosion and virtually scratchproof, the bezel's blue hue remains unchanged by the sun's intense ultraviolet rays.

Equipped with a regatta chronograph, the Oyster Perpetual Yacht-Master II's programmable countdown feature can be set from zero to ten minutes. Its blue bezel is made with Cerachrom, a ceramic material able to endure the harsh elements encountered on the open sea.

Marine sports continue to hold sway at Rolex as it drops anchor and immerses itself into watery depths with two new additions to its Oyster Perpetual Submariner Date collection.

Designed to meet the needs of both professional and recreational divers, the 40mm case is water resistant to a depth of 300 meters. It also sports a new unidirectional bezel used by divers to monitor the amount of air remaining in their tanks. To ensure the user's safety, an anti-reverse click system is used to prevent the bezel from shifting inadvertently during a dive.

The case houses an automatic movement designed and manufactured by Rolex. A certified chronometer, its extensive testing assures reliable and lasting performance.

Both of the new Oyster Perpetual Submariner Date watches are available in yellow Rolesor. The first features a yellow-gold bezel decorated with black Cerachrom and a matching dial. The other pairs a vivid blue Cerachrom bezel and matching dial.

Despite its reputation as a classic, the Submariner continues to evolve and grow. The same is true for Rolex; it is the world's most recognized watchmaker, yet its pursuit of new accomplishments is ceaseless.

Water resistant to a depth of 300 meters, the yellow Rolesor Oyster Perpetual Submariner Date features a new, black, unidirectional bezel to help divers safely monitor their dive times.

Salvatore Ferragamo

TIMEPIECES

Famed Italian designer Salvatore Ferragamo captured women's imaginations for generations with shoes that cradled their soles in peerless quality and visual esprit. After more than eight decades, Salvatore Ferragamo's Florentine empire still thrives and, under his family's direction and the aegis of Timex Group, offers an expanding array of gents' and ladies' timepieces.

The height of precision, the Salvatore Ferragamo F-80's automatic movement has passed the Swiss Chronometer Testing Institute's exhaustive battery of tests to earn its chronometer certification.

The Salvatore Ferragamo F-80 is a bold example of the company's respect for watchmaking's highest standards, from its chronometer certification to its masculine details.

Rigorously tested by the Swiss Chronometer Testing Institute (COSC), the F-80's automatic movement is a precise mechanical instrument. Its meshing gears are visible through the caseback, along with a black rotor decorated with Côtes de Genève and engraved with the Salvatore Ferragamo logo.

The accuracy assured by the F-80's mechanics serves as an apt companion to the dial's confident mix of materials and handsome details. A black ceramic and tungsten bezel tops the 44mm titanium case.

The black carries over to the F-80's flange and textured dial with the chronograph's white and gray subdials adding subtle contrast. The muted palette is punctuated sharply by the dash of red provided by a central seconds hand adorned with Salvatore Ferragamo's signature double-Gancino logo.

Opposite the crown and chronograph pushers, the caseband includes a trio of ridges, a clever reference to one of the shoemaker's most iconic innovations: the wedge heel.

This addition to the F-80 collection stands as a worthy successor to the automatic chronograph GMT model Salvatore Ferragamo introduced last year.

The Ferragamo name first rose to prominence in the 1920s, thanks in part to the shoes Salvatore made by hand for queens of both state and Hollywood. It is rather fitting that Salvatore Ferragamo's heritage of bespoke luxury lives on in its watches, which can be customized according to owners' wishes.

Clients often ask that their watches be decorated with baguette diamonds or diamond pavé, and the brand also produces a few concept watches each year that are prized by collectors.

Salvatore Ferragamo's workshop in Switzerland offers a range of capabilities to help turn a client's dream into reality. For instance, one gentleman wished to give his wife something special for their twelfth anniversary and asked the brand to create a special dial with twelve diamond hour-markers. The result proved that sometimes the simplest ideas have the biggest impact.

Bespoke luxury lives on at the brand's workshop, where clients' dreams become reality.

Keeping her father's beloved icons alive, Salvatore's eldest daughter, Fiamma, followed in his footsteps to become an award-winning shoe designer in her own right. One of Fiamma's most enduring creations—the Vara shoe—and Salvatore's Gancino symbol that she made famous serve as the inspirations behind two great watch models.

The first is the Vara Large. Its case's curvy profile echoes the buckle used on the Vara shoe, a top-seller since its 1978 introduction. For the shoe, the buckle is typically threaded with a grosgrain bow. For the watch, the case is attached to an alligator strap available in various colors.

The Vara Large's 38mm case classifies it as a unisex model, and its contemporary styling gives the watch universal appeal. The brand notes that the size is popular with women who prefer the bold look and with men who favor understatement.

The case's rounded lines not only embrace the wearer's wrist comfortably, but they also elegantly frame the watch's discreet dial, which mixes hour-markers and Arabic numerals.

Along with several quartz models, an automatic Vara Large is offered in a rose-gold case with white dial and on a brown alligator strap with deployante buckle.

Fiamma Ferragamo is also credited with making her father's Gancino logo design instantly recognizable as the company's signature, which is found on everything from handbags to cuff links. The brand transforms the distinctive Gancino symbol into shapely cases to create the Gancino Fancy collection.

Most models in this collection are fitted with wide, calf-leather Logomania straps available in a selection of colors but, for a fun twist, the delicately curved Gancino case also can be integrated neatly into a whimsical satin strap: its multicolor design features Salvatore Ferragamo's vintage TOES motif, a vivid reminder of the company's rich couture heritage.

In fact, the entire Gancino Fancy collection epitomizes Salvatore Ferragamo's style and the brand values these particular timepieces as fantastic examples of the company's past emerging in contemporary design.

Each quartz-powered Gancino Fancy, like all of Salvatore Ferragamo's timepieces, is fluent in the language of fashion and adept at Old World ways of craftsmanship, offering a harmonic convergence of Italian style and Swiss precision.

ABOVE
The Gancino Fancy collection offers a selection of decorated straps.

FACING PAGE
LEFT   The Vara Large case recalls the buckle that Fiamma Ferragamo first used in 1978 to create the Vara shoe. Equipped with an automatic ETA movement, the 38mm rose-gold case appeals to both men and women.

RIGHT   This Vara Large balances dark and light tones in a version that combines a stainless steel case with a black dial and alligator strap.

CALIBRE 1887: MEASURE OF EXCELLENCE

On the occasion of its 150th anniversary and only a few weeks after commercializing the Monaco V4, TAG Heuer launches a new chronograph, produced and assembled in-house at its Swiss production sites in Cornol (Jura) and La Chaux-de-Fonds (Neuchâtel).

Based on an existing platform developed and patented since 1999 by SII (Seiko Instruments Inc.) of which TAG Heuer has acquired the intellectual property usage rights, Calibre 1887 was completely industrialized by the TAG Heuer Research and Development Team. The team also significantly re-developed some of its key components to match the new high-end Swiss assortment and increase its precision and reliability. The project has already generated 45 new production and assembly jobs.

Accurately measuring time is a complicated undertaking, and the Swiss watchmaking industry has been the standard bearer of excellence in the field since the 16th century. Even more difficult, however, is dividing time, precisely, into the smallest possible fractions by means of a chronograph function—a chrono-metric mechanism that accurately measures elapsed time. A more recent innovation, dating only from the 19th century, the chronograph is justly considered a most complex watchmaking complication in terms of construction and components. Once again, the Swiss are the unrivalled masters of its manufacture—and since 1860, TAG Heuer has been its pioneering virtuoso.

The world leader in avant-garde sports watches and chronographs market, TAG Heuer innovates more than any other watch brand. Refusing to rest on its laurels, it has again and again pushed back the limits of chronograph functionality and precision. Today, in this fiercely competitive industry, TAG Heuer—the only watch brand to master 1/10th and 1/100th of a second precision in a mechanical automatic chronograph movement—continues its committed drive towards manufacturing excellence.

A mix of time-honored artisanal craftsmanship with high-tech automation and spaceage materials allows TAG Heuer to create incredibly innovative products.

The movement is assembled in a new dust-free workshop built in 2008 when the company expanded its La Chaux-de-Fonds main site by 30%, adding a fourth building to its facility. TAG Heuer took inspiration from other high-tech sectors to develop a revolutionary semi-automated line on which each movement is individually traced by high-performance software.

After a visit to a station, the movement is automatically sent to the next relevant station, but humans are always in complete control. The fluid organization in two "U" cells—a modernization of classic Taylorism—optimizes the production process, and the mix of time-honored artisanal craftsmanship with high-tech automation and space age materials allows for the creation of incredibly innovative products. Assembly is just-in-time flexible and can be easily adapted to other tasks, quickly switching to the assembly of a different watch movement without having to make major modifications to the line. Once again, the state-of-the art equipment comes from the very best Swiss machine specialist.

However, TAG Heuer does not want to manufacture all its movements, and will continue to buy movements from top Swiss suppliers like Zenith, Dubois-Dépraz and ETA. The Calibre 1887 will equip only a small proportion of TAG Heuer's production. In tandem, by developing prestigious and rare movements in-house, such as the 2009 belt-driven mechanical V4, TAG Heuer stays true to its unique brand DNA—innovation, avant-garde, excellence, performance, and human achievement.

FACING PAGE
Reverse side of Calibre 1887.

THIS PAGE
TAG Heuer workshop.

TAG HEUER MONACO V4:
PIONEERING SWISS WATCHMAKING HISTORY

The world leader in luxury sport watches and chronographs since 1860, TAG Heuer maintains this preeminence by constantly reinventing itself, and, in the process, changing the world of watchmaking—revolutionizing what watches and chronographs can do, how they work, and the way they look.

In 2004, the company unveiled the Monaco V4 concept watch, the world's first watch with belt drives, linear mass and ball bearings. On the eve of its 150th anniversary, TAG Heuer has achieved the unbelievable, unveiling to the world what many industry insiders said would never see the light of day: The Monaco V4 in commercial production. Double-patented and 100% TAG Heuer-made, Monaco V4

outdoes its own legacy. A bold technical masterwork unlike any watch ever seen or imagined, it both exemplifies luxury Swiss watchmaking tradition at its finest, and completely turns that heritage upside down and inside out.

Until the V4, all modern mechanical movements, regardless of their complications, were generally based on "classic" watchmaking components, most of which date back to the 18th and 19th centuries. The principal components of this traditional system are: an energy reserve, by means of one or several springs; a transmission, using gears; and a regulatory function, usually organized around a recoil escapement.

TRANSMISSION

Gear transmission and automatic rewinding: the V4 team set these aside and started from scratch. The result is a complete paradigm shift, two worldwide patents, and a completely new generation of mechanical movements. In a world first, TAG Heuer's award-winning team of watch masters and engineers replaced the pinions and wheels of the traditional mechanical movement with a belt-driven transmission: a high-yield relay of five notched micro drive-belts whose tensions are controlled by two turnbuckles.

The transmission belts in polyether block amide have a 0.07mm section, about the same size as a single human hair, and are ten times smaller than any belt ever manufactured. Unlike a traditional caliber, this modular synchronous drive belt system requires no extra gears to send motion from one point to another. More efficient—minimizing vibrations, optimizing movement—and much easier to maintain, it allows power to be transmitted wherever it is required, allowing for more complications with no obstacles. Standout features include a dark blue alligator strap and stylish silver and blue dial with red hands. The new, fashion-forward animation on the chronograph dial is completely in line with the family's iconic heritage.

FACING PAGE
Monaco V4's caseback.

THIS PAGE
Monaco V4.

TAG HEUER:
PIONEERING DESIGN FOR 150 YEARS

TAG Heuer timepieces epitomize prestige and performance, brilliantly fusing technology with design. The world leader in luxury sports watches and chronographs since 1860, TAG Heuer has always focused on the "look" of its watches. Since the beginning, it has been a pioneer in watch design, even if the term "design" was not always used.

The brand is a repeat winner of every major watch design award there is, including five Red Dots, one DFA, two IF Design, one Chicago Athenaeum Good Design, one China's Most Successful Design Award, and two Design Watch of the Year Prizes at the Grand Prix d'Horlogerie de Genève.

This leading-edge design focus can also be seen in TAG Heuer boutiques and in its BaselWorld booth, SKIN. The most avant-garde booth ever built for the prestigious watch fair, SKIN won the Silver Award in EXHIBITOR Magazine's 23rd Annual Exhibit Design Awards competition in 2009.

Now, to celebrate and pay homage to 150 years of pioneering design, TAG Heuer is reissuing one of its most iconic creations of all time: the Silverstone chronograph.

SILVERSTONE:
A SIGNATURE CHRONOGRAPH OF F1

Originally launched in 1974, the Silverstone chronograph gets its name from the famous racetrack of the same name. An hour's drive west of London, between Northampton and Oxford, Silverstone is best known as the home of the British Grand Prix, which it first hosted in 1948. On May 13th, 1950, the opening race of the first-ever FIA Formula One World Championship started at Silverstone.

Since then, the Silverstone Race Track has provided 43 Formula One British Grand Prix starts and it became the "home" Grand Prix for McLaren with 12 wins in 35 years.

The racetrack has a special place in TAG Heuer's heart because many of its racing ambassadors and F1 team partners scored career-making victories on it. Silverstone's racetrack has pushed the best to achieve their best, including: Emmanuel de Graffenried, the very first ambassador, in 1949; Juan Manuel Fangio in 1956; Jo Siffert in 1968; Alain Prost in 1985 and 1989; Ayrton Senna in 1988; David Coulthard in 1999 and 2000; Mika Hakkinen in 2001; and Lewis Hamilton with Vodafone McLaren Mercedes Benz in 2008.

The top drivers of the 1970s admired the Silverstone chronograph for its distinctive name, unique shape and avant-garde look—and the buzz they generated helped make it a style icon of the period. TAG Heuer was Ferrari's timekeeper throughout that decade, but it was also partnered with McLaren, BRM and Surtees-Ford, and every driver from these teams wore a TAG Heuer watch. In 1974, the year the Silverstone chronograph was launched, Clay Regazzoni and Emerson Fittipaldi became TAG Heuer ambassadors. The two legendary drivers chose the chronograph as personal lucky charms. Fittipaldi won his second F1 World Championship that year, driving for McLaren while Regazzoni won the Silverstone GP in 1979.

FACING PAGE
The 2010 Silverstone reedition.

THIS PAGE
TOP
Lewis Hamilton, Vodafone McLaren Mercedes Formula One driver.

BOTTOM
Clay Regazzoni and his Silverstone.

From a small workshop in the Swiss Jura mountains, TAG Heuer has transformed into a watchmaking legend. Recognized throughout the world for its luxury sports watches and pioneering work in chronographs, TAG Heuer watches epitomize prestige and performance, brilliantly fusing technology with design. TAG Heuer has revolutionized 150 years of watchmaking history through a constant pursuit of excellence and innovation, maintaining a strong link between the company of today and the people who have shaped its history. From heroes of the past to the stars of the future, TAG Heuer's ambassadors read like a Who's Who of modern history: Edouard Heuer and Steve McQueen, Ayrton Senna and Leonardo DiCaprio, Lewis Hamilton and Shah Rukh Khan, Tiger Woods and Maria Sharapova. Together they all share a strong determination to achieve their ultimate goals, pushing the limits of what is possible through hard work and mental strength. We cannot know what the future holds, but we do know that if TAG Heuer continues to look forward, the brand will be the one who shapes it.

Jack Heuer in the TAG Heuer 360 Museum.

CHRONOLOGY

1860
The TAG Heuer watchmaking company is founded in Saint-Imier, Switzerland, by Edouard Heuer.

1886
TAG Heuer invents the famous "oscillating pinion" for mechanical chronographs.

1911
TAG Heuer presents the first watch for automotive instrument panels, featuring a trip-duration indicator.

1916
TAG Heuer tests the Micrograph, the first stopwatch measuring time with an accuracy of 1/100th of a second.

1933
The Autavia: the first chronograph dashboard for both automobiles and aviation.

1964
First Carrera automatic chronograph with a manual-winding movement.

1971-1979
TAG Heuer becomes the official timekeeper of the Scuderia Ferrari.

1985
TAG Heuer becomes McLaren partner, one of the longest successful partnerships ever.

1986
Launch of the TAG Heuer Formula 1 in stainless steel and fiberglass. Driver Alain Prost emphasizes the house's return in Formula One racing by winning the World Championship.

1987
TAG Heuer Link collection is created, which will become an icon

1992-2003
TAG Heuer is appointed official timekeeper of the Formula One World Championship.

1998
TAG Heuer collection is enriched with a new edition of the Monaco, the square chronograph worn by actor Steve McQueen in the 1971 movie *Le Mans*.

2004-2006
TAG Heuer becomes official timekeeper and chronograph of the Indy Racing League (IRL).

2006
TAG Heuer Carrera Calibre 360 chronograph: the first-ever mechanical chronograph accurate to 1/100th of a second, wins the Grand Prix d'Horlogerie de Genève in the Sports category.

2007
TAG Heuer launches the Grand CARRERA premium collection, inspired by motor racing and GT cars.

2008
TAG Heuer wins the Grand Prix de Genève with its Grand Carrera Calibre 36 RS Caliper Chronograph.

2009
Leonardo DiCaprio and TAG Heuer join forces to protect the environment through the NRDC (Natural Resources Defense Council) and Green Cross International. The contract signed by DiCaprio and TAG Heuer is unique and the royalties it produces, as well as several million dollars pledged by DiCaprio, will support the work of the NRDC and Green Cross International.

2010
TAG Heuer celebrates 150 years of Swiss watchmaking history.

GRAND CARRERA CALIBRE 6 RS   REF. WAV511B.FC6230

Movement: mechanical automatic-winding TAG Heuer Calibre 6 RS; COSC certified; Rotating System.
Functions: hours, minutes, seconds; date.
Case: fine-brushed steel case with curved faceted polished horns; Ø 40.2mm, thickness: 11.8mm; double antireflective, curved sapphire crystal; oversized screw-in crown; double sapphire caseback sealed with six screws; water resistant to 100 meters.

Dial: silver; opaline central area and external spiral effect area; rotating small second system decorated with Côtes de Genève and diamond-polished facets; hand-applied curved faceted indexes with double finishing; hand-applied TAG Heuer logo; polished hands with polished facets; luminescent markers on hands.
Indications: date at 3; permanent second at 6.
Strap: brown alligator strap; solid steel folding clasp with safety pushbuttons and applied TAG Heuer logo.
Also available: black or brown dial; on black alligator strap or a three-row multi-faceted steel bracelet with solid steel folding clasp with safety pushbuttons and applied TAG Heuer logo.

GRAND CARRERA CALIBRE 8 RS GRANDE DATE GMT   REF. WAV5113.FC6231

Movement: mechanical automatic-winding TAG Heuer Calibre 8 RS; COSC-certified; Rotating System (RS).
Functions: hours, minutes, seconds; grande date; second time zone.
Case: fine-brushed steel case with curved faceted polished horns; Ø 42.5mm, thickness: 13.0mm; double antireflective, curved sapphire crystal; oversize screw-in crown; double sapphire caseback sealed with six screws; water resistant to 100 meters.

Dial: brown dial with opaline central area and external spiral effect area; Rotating GMT System (second time zone) decorated with Côtes de Genève and diamond-polished facets; hand-applied grande date window; hand-applied curved faceted indexes with double finishing; hand-applied TAG Heuer logo; polished hands with polished facets; luminescent markers on hands.
Indications: grande date at 12; Rotating GMT System (second time zone) at 6.
Strap: brown alligator strap; solid steel folding clasp with safety pushbuttons and applied TAG Heuer logo.
Also available: silver or black dial; on black alligator strap or three-row multi-faceted steel bracelet.

GRAND CARRERA CALIBRE 17 RS2 CHRONOGRAPH TI2   REF. CAV518B.FC6237

Movement: mechanical automatic-winding TAG Heuer Calibre 17 RS; COSC-certified; two Rotating Systems (RS). **Functions:** hours, minutes, seconds; chronograph; date. **Case:** sand-blasted black grade-2 titanium case with curved horns; Ø 43mm, thickness: 14.83mm; sand-blasted black grade-2 titanium bezel with Tachymetre scale; black grade-2 titanium oversize screw-in massive pushbuttons; oversized black grade-2 titanium screw-in crown; double antireflective curved sapphire crystal; black grade-2 titanium caseback sealed with six screws;

smoked double sapphire caseback; water resistant to 100 meters. **Dial:** black dial with opaline central area and external spiral effect area; two Rotating Systems with black-gold coating decorated with Côtes de Genève and diamond-polished facets; hand-applied curved faceted indexes with double finishing and black-gold coating; hand-applied TAG Heuer logo with black-gold coating; polished hands with polished facets and black-gold coating; luminescent markers on hour and minute hands; hand-applied date window with black-gold coating. **Indications:** permanent second at 3; chronograph minute at 9; date at 6. **Strap:** high-tech soft-touch black alligator strap with red stitching and lining; solid titanium folding clasp with safety pushbuttons and applied TAG Heuer logo.

GRAND CARRERA CALIBRE 17 RS CHRONOGRAPH   REF. CAV511A.BA0902

Movement: mechanical automatic-winding TAG Heuer Calibre 17 RS; COSC-certified; two Rotating Systems (RS).
Functions: hours, minutes, seconds; chronograph; date.
Case: fine-brushed steel case with curved faceted polished horns; Ø 43mm, thickness: 14.83mm; screw-in pushbuttons; fine-brushed and polished bezel with tachymeter scale; double antireflective, curved sapphire crystal; oversized screw-in crown; double sapphire caseback sealed with six screws; water resistant to 100 meters.
Dial: black dial with opaline central area and external spiral effect area; two Rotating Systems decorated with Côtes de Genève and diamond-polished facets; hand-applied curved faceted indexes with double finishing; hand-applied TAG Heuer logo; polished hands with polished facets; luminescent markers on hands; hand-applied date window.
Indications: permanent second at 3; chronograph minute at 9; date at 6.
Bracelet: three-row multi-faceted steel bracelet: alternated polished and fine-brushed central row and fine-brushed lateral rows with polished edges; solid steel folding clasp with safety pushbuttons and applied TAG Heuer logo.
Also available: silver dial with black or brown alligator strap.

GRAND CARRERA CALIBRE 36 RS2 CALIPER CHRONOGRAPH TI2   REF. CAV5185.FT6020

Movement: mechanical automatic-winding TAG Heuer Calibre 36 RS; COSC-certified; two Rotating Systems (RS). **Functions:** hours, minutes, linear permanent second; chronograph; date. **Case:** black grade-2 titanium case with curved faceted polished horns; Ø 43mm, thickness: 15.50mm; black grade-2 titanium fine-brushed with polished facets pushbuttons; black grade-2 titanium fine-brushed and polished bezel with tachymeter scale; double antireflective, curved sapphire crystal; oversized black grade-2 titanium screw-in crown with red line; oversized black grade-2 titanium crown with redline at 10 allowing to use the Caliper Rotating Scale; smoked double sapphire caseback; black grade-2 titanium caseback sealed by 6 screws; water resistant to 100 meters. **Dial:** black dial; two Rotating Systems decorated with Côtes de Genève and diamond-polished facets; linear second at 9; hand-applied curved faceted indexes with double finishing; hand-applied TAG Heuer logo; polished hands with polished facets; luminescent markers on hour and minute hands; hand-applied date window at 4:30; Caliper Rotating Scale magnifying the reading of 1/10th of a second driven by the crown at 10. **Indications:** the chronograph minutes at 3 and the chronograph hours at 6; linear permanent second at 9; date at 4:30. **Strap:** black rubber strap with black grade-2 titanium end piece and grade-2 titanium folding clasp with safety pushbuttons and applied TAG Heuer logo. **Also available:** high-tech soft-touch black alligator strap with red stitching and lining.

TAG HEUER FORMULA 1 GRANDE DATE CHRONOGRAPH FULL BLACK   REF. CAH1012.FT6026

Movement: quartz chronograph.
Functions: hours, minutes, seconds; chronograph; small second.
Case: black titanium carbide coated case; Ø 44mm, thickness: 12.5mm; scratch-resistant titanium carbide coated unidirectional turning bezel with raised fine-brushed figures; scratch-resistant sapphire crystal; scratch-resistant titanium carbide coated Easy Grip screw-in crown with raised fine-brushed TAG Heuer logo; scratch-resistant titanium carbide coated stainless steel safety crown and pushbuttons; circular steel fine-brushed screwed caseback with special checked decoration; TAG Heuer engraving on the side of the case; water resistant to 200 meters.
Dial: black dial; hand-applied indexes; polished finished hands with polished facets; colored TAG Heuer logo; red second hands; luminescent markers on hands and indexes.
Indications: small second at 3; twin-hand semi-circular chronograph minutes counter at 9; 1/10th-of-a-second counter at 6 during the 30 first minutes then hour counter; grande date window at 12.
Strap: rubber strap with steel folding clasp

TAG HEUER FORMULA 1 LADY STEEL AND CERAMIC AND DIAMONDS   REF. WAH1213.BA0861

Movement: quartz.
Functions: hours, minutes, seconds; date.
Case: polished stainless steel case; Ø 37mm, thickness: 9.85mm; polished fixed ceramic & steel bezel with 60 Wesselton diamonds: 60 diamonds with Ø 1.10mm, total 0.35 carat; sapphire crystal; polished stainless steel bumpers protecting the crown at 9 (with TAG Heuer branding engraved) and at 3; polished screw-in crown; circular fine-brushed screw fitting caseback; water resistant to 200 meters.
Dial: white; hand-applied indexes and arabic figure at 12; luminescent markers on faceted minute and hour hands and above indexes; Monochrome TAG Heuer logo.
Indications: date at 3.
Bracelet: three-row alternate steel & ceramic (color assorted to dial) bracelet with NEW solid steel butterfly folding clasp and safety pushbuttons.
Also available: black dial and ceramic, color assorted to dial.

TAG HEUER FORMULA 1 LADY STEEL AND CERAMIC   REF. WAH1210.BA0859

Movement: quartz.
Functions: hours, minutes, seconds; date.
Case: polished fixed stainless steel & ceramic bezel; Ø 37mm, thickness: 9.85mm; polished stainless steel case; polished stainless steel bumpers protecting the crown at 9 (with TAG Heuer branding engraved) and at 3; polished screw-in crown; sapphire crystal; circular fine brushed screw fitting caseback water resistance to 200 meters.
Dial: black; Hand-applied indexes and arabic figure at 12; luminescent markers on faceted minute and hour hands and above indexes; Monochrome TAG Heuer logo.
Indications: date at 3.
Bracelet: three-row alternate steel & ceramic (color assorted to dial) bracelet with solid steel butterfly folding clasp and safety pushbuttons
Also available: white dial and ceramic, color assorted to dial.

TAG HEUER FORMULA 1 INDY 500 GRANDE DATE CHRONOGRAPH   REF. CAH101B.BA0860

Movement: quartz chronograph.
Functions: hours, minutes, seconds; chronograph.
Case: stainless steel case; Ø 44mm, thickness: 12.10mm; polished steel fixed bezel with tachymeter scale and INDY 500 writenning; scratch-resistant sapphire crystal; polished steel Easy Grip screw-in crown with raised fine-brushed TAG Heuer logo; polished stainless steel safety crown and pushbuttons; circular fine-brushed screwed caseback with special checked decoration; red INDY 500 engraving on the side of the case; water resistant to 200 meters.
Dial: silver dial with perlage; hand-applied indexes; polished finished hands with polished facets; luminescent markers on hands and indexes; colored INDY 500 logo; colored TAG Heuer logo.
Indications: small second at 3; twin-hand semicircular chronograph minutes counter at 9; 1/10th-of-a-second counter at 6 during the 30 first minutes then hour counter; grande date window at 12.
Bracelet: NEW three-row fine-brushed steel bracelet with double safety clasp and diving extension system.
Also available: black gold dial with perlage.

CARRERA LADY CALIBRE 5 DIAMOND DIAL & DIAMOND BEZEL   REF. WV2212.FC6264

Movement: mechanical automatic-winding TAG Heuer Calibre 5.
Functions: hours, minutes, seconds; date.
Case: polished steel case; Ø 36mm, thickness: 12.5mm; polished steel case set with 28 Top Wesselton diamonds (12 diamonds with Ø 1.30mm (0.11 ct), 16 diamonds with Ø 1.10mm (0.09 ct): total 0.20 carat); fixed bezel set with 32 Top Wesselton diamonds (24 diamonds with Ø 1.50mm (0.34 carat), 4 diamonds with Ø 1.30mm (0.03 ct), 4 diamonds with Ø 0.80mm (0.01 ct): total 0.38 carat); polished crown; Scratch-resistant sapphire crystal with antireflective treatment; scratch-resistant sapphire caseback; water resistant to 50 meters.
Dial: white mother-of-pearl; diamond dial with spiral effect in exterior zone; 13 Top Wesselton diamonds (13 Top Wesselton diamonds with Ø 0.90mm: total 0.048 carat); hand-applied polished indexes; polish-finished hands with luminescent markers; polished & protruded TAG Heuer logo.
Indications: date at 4:30.
Strap: white alligator strap; Solid steel folding clasp with safety pushbuttons.
Also available: five-row polished steel bracelet.

CARRERA LADY DIAMOND DIAL   REF. WV1417.BA0793

Movement: quartz.
Functions: hours, minutes, seconds; date.
Case: polished steel case; Ø 27mm, thickness: 9.07mm; polished steel fixed bezel; polished crown; scratch-resistant sapphire crystal; polished steel caseback, water resistant to 50 meters.
Dial: pink mother-of-pearl; diamond dial with spiral effect in exterior zone; 13 Top Wesselton diamonds (12 diamonds with Ø 1.20mm, 1 diamond with Ø 1.1mm: total 0.0981 carat); polish-finished hands with luminescent markers; polished & protruded TAG Heuer logo.
Indications: date at 3.
Bracelet: five-row alternate fine-brushed and polished steel bracelet with solid steel folding clasp and safety pushbuttons.
Also available: white mother-of-pearl diamond dial and black diamond dial.

CARRERA CALIBRE 16 DAY-DATE CHRONOGRAPH   REF. CV2A11.FC6235

Movement: mechanical automatic-winding TAG Heuer Calibre 16 Day-Date.
Functions: hours, minutes, seconds; day-date; chronograph with three counters.
Case: massive steel case with polished finishing; Ø 43mm, thickness: 16.3mm; polished steel fixed bezel with tachymeter scale; polished enlarged crown and push-buttons; scratch-resistant domed sapphire crystal with double-sided antireflective treatment; scratch-resistant sapphire caseback; water resistant to 100 meters.
Dial: silver; hand-applied numerals; polished finished hour and minute hands with luminescent markers; polished finished second hand and hour and minute counters' hands with red at the extremity; silver-ringed hour and minute counters; monochrome TAG Heuer logo; large day-date window at 3.
Indications: day-date at 3; chronograph hour at 6, running second at 9, minute counter at 12, center seconds.
Strap: black alligator strap with polished steel folding clasp with safety pushbuttons.
Also available: five-row alternate fine-brushed and polished steel bracelet and solid steel folding clasp with safety pushbuttons, black and brown dial.

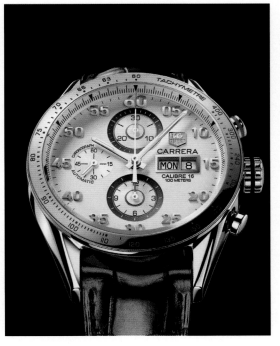

CARRERA CALIBRE 16 RACING CHRONOGRAPH   REF. CV2014.FT6014

Movement: mechanical automatic-winding TAG Heuer Calibre 16.
Functions: hours, minutes, seconds; date; chronograph with three counters.
Case: polished steel; Ø 41mm, thickness: 15.3mm; black tachymeter scale on an aluminum fixed bezel; scratch-resistant sapphire crystal; scratch-resistant sapphire caseback; water resistant to 100 meters.
Dial: black; sunray-effect center; spiral-effect outer band; hand-applied faceted indexes; polished finished hour and minute hands with luminescent markers; red central chronograph hand; silver-ringed counters (chronograph hours & minutes); monochrome TAG Heuer logo.
Indications: date at 3; chronograph: hour at 6 with red hand, small second at 9, minute counter at 12, center seconds.
Strap: thick black perforated rubber strap with embossed TAG Heuer and polished steel folding clasp with safety pushbuttons.
Also available: five-row alternate fine-brushed and polished steel bracelet and solid steel folding clasp with safety pushbuttons.

CARRERA CALIBRE S LAPTIMER   REF. CV7A10.FT6012

Movement: TAG Heuer Calibre S Laptimer - Electro-mechanical Chronograph, invented, patented, developed and manufactured by TAG Heuer. **Functions:** hours, minutes, seconds; perpetual Retrograde Calendar until 2099; time & chronograph display using central hour, minute, second hands; flyback chronograph with 1/100th-of-a-second accuracy; lap timer function with direct access to best lap time. **Case:** polished stainless steel case; Ø 43mm, thickness: 13.55mm; polished pushbutton crown with black varnish on the face and side; fixed black aluminium bezel with tachymeter scale; scratch-resistant sapphire crystal; screw-in caseback; water resistant to 100 meters. **Dial:** black; spiral effect; three hand-applied semi-circular counters, hand applied indexes; polished finished hour, minute and semi-circular counters' hands (Hour and semi-circular counters' hands with red at the extremity) luminescent markers on hands and indexes; red second hand; hand applied TAG Heuer logo. **Indications:** at 12, lap counter with Chrono mode indicator at 9:30; Best Lap mode indicator at 2:30; 1/10th-of-a-second retrograde counter at 4:30; 1/100th-of-a-second retrograde counter at 7:30.
Strap: black perforated rubber strap with embossed TAG Heuer and polished steel folding clasp with safety pushbuttons.
Also available: five-row fine-brushed and polished steel bracelet and fine-brushed steel folding clasp with safety pushbuttons; silver dial.

SILVERSTONE CALIBRE 11 CHRONOGRAPH   REF. CAM2110.FC6258

Movement: TAG Heuer Calibre 11- Electro-mechanical Automatic Chronograph-oscillating weight with Côte de Genève finishing and red vintage HEUER logo. **Functions:** hours, minutes, seconds; date; chronograph. **Case:** square-shaped case in polished stainless steel; Ø 42mm, thickness: 13.98mm; polished fine-shaped crown at 9 with vintage HEUER logo on the face and grooves around the side for easy grip; rounded polished chronograph pushbuttons at 2 and 4; scratch-resistant sapphire crystal; caseback fixed with screws: fine-brushed stainless steel base with polished edge; round sapphire crystal in the middle allowing direct view on the movement; water resistant to 50 meters. **Dial:** original blue; two square-shaped subcounters indexes and numbers with running second counter at 3 and chronograph minute counter at 9; white hands; white luminescent markers on hour and minute hands and indexes; monochrome vintage HEUER logo and SILVERSTONE lettering at 12; date window at 6 outlined by a white frame. **Indications:** running second counter at 3; chronograph minute at 9; date at 6.
Strap: blue perforated alligator strap and stainless steel folding clasp with vintage HEUER logo on the face and safety pushbuttons.
Also available: brown dial on brown alligator strap.
Note: limited edition of 3,000 pieces.

MONACO V4   REF. WAW2170.FC6261

Movement: exclusive TAG Heuer mechanical automatic-winding movement; belt-driven transmission; two pairs of barrels in series, set in parallel and linked by belts; tungstene ingot linear mass.
Functions: hours, minutes, seconds.
Case: polished platinum 950 case; Ø 39mm, thickness: 17.10mm; curved scratch-resistant sapphire crystal with antireflective double-sided treatment; polished white gold crown; sapphire caseback in 3 sections; water resistant to 50 meters.
Dial: seven silver fine-brushed bridges with haute horlogerie hand-finishings; escapement and belt-driven transmission visible from the front; hand-applied faceted indexes; faceted fine-brushed blue minute and hour hands with luminescent markers, blue small second hand; engraved blue TAG Heuer logo.
Indications: small seconds at 4.
Strap: blue alligator strap with hand-sewn blue stitching; folding buckle with safety pushbuttons in platinum 950.
Note: limited edition of 150 pieces.

MONACO LS CALIBRE 12 CHRONOGRAPH   REF. CAL2110.BA0781

Movement: mechanical automatic-winding TAG Heuer Calibre 12; linear second.
Functions: hours, minutes, seconds; date; chronograph with two counters.
Case: fine-brushed and polished stainless steel case; Ø 40.5mm, thickness: 16.50mm; curved scratch-resistant sapphire crystal; polished crown with red line; polished and fine-brushed steel pushbuttons; water resistant to 100 meters.
Dial: black dial with technical fine-brushed bridges; hand-applied faceted indexes with luminescent markers; faceted polished minute and hour hands, with luminescent markers; rhodium second hand with a touch of red; monochrome TAG Heuer logo.

Indications: chronograph minutes at 9 and chronograph hours at 6; big angled window date opening with black disc at 12.
Bracelet: steel bracelet; folding buckle with safety pushbuttons and a micro-adjustment cutting wheel.
Also available: black alligator strap; folding buckle with safety pushbuttons and TAG Heuer logo.

MONACO CALIBRE 12 RACING CHRONOGRAPH   REF. CAW2114.FT6021

Movement: mechanical automatic-winding TAG Heuer Calibre 12
Functions: hours, minutes, seconds; date; chronograph with two counters.
Case: fine-brushed and polished steel case; Ø 39mm, thickness: 14.20mm; curved sapphire crystal glass; water resistant to 100 meters.
Dial: black dial; hand-applied faceted indexes; faceted polished red and rhodium-plated minute and hours hands with luminescent markers, red second hand; monochrome TAG Heuer logo.

Indications: two subcounters with red hands; small seconds at 3 and chronograph minute at 9; date at 6.
Strap: rubber strap; folding buckle with safety pushbuttons.
Also available: black alligator strap, folding buckle with safety pushbuttons.

MONACO WATCH LADY GRANDE DATE BROWN GALUCHAT REF. WAW1316.FC6245

Movement: quartz.
Functions: hours, minutes, small seconds; grande date.
Case: polished steel case set with 26 Top Wesselton diamonds on horizontal facets (Ø 2.0, total 0.78 ct); 37x36mm, thickness: 11.85mm; antireflective double-sided treatment on the curved scratch-resistant sapphire crystal glass; water resistant to 100 meters.

Dial: brown dial with sunray effect and vertical snail in the middle, 13 Top Wesselton diamonds (Ø 1.1mm, total 0.081 carats); hand-applied faceted indexes; luminescent markers on diamond-shaped hands; monochrome TAG Heuer logo.
Indications: small seconds at 6, grande date at 12.
Strap: brown Galuchat strap; folding buckle with safety pushbuttons.
Also available: brown python strap, folding buckle with safety pushbuttons.

LINK CALIBRE 7 ADVANCED GMT MAGNETIC BEZEL   REF. WJ2010.BA0591

Movement: mechanical automatic-winding TAG Heuer Calibre 7 Advanced GMT, patented magnetic bezel system driving inner 24-city GMT disc.
Functions: hours, minutes, seconds; GMT; date.
Case: fine-brushed stainless steel case, Ø 42mm, thickness: 12.60mm; polished stainless steel rotating bezel with a 24-hour scale; hidden button at 10 to reset the GMT function; screw-in polished steel crown; antireflective double-sided treatment on the curved scratch-resistant sapphire crystal; sapphire crystal caseback; water resistant to 200 meters.

Dial: black dial with spiral effect in exterior zone; hand-applied curved and faceted indexes; faceted polished rhodium-plated minute and hour hands; luminescent markers on minute, hour and GMT hands; hand-applied monochrome TAG Heuer logo.
Indications: angled date window at 3.
Bracelet: fine-brushed stainless steel; solid steel folding clasp with safety pushbuttons.

LINK GRANDE DATE TIGER WOODS LIMITED EDITION   REF. WJF1010.BA0592

Movement: grande date quartz.
Functions: hours, minutes, seconds; grande date.
Case: fine-brushed stainless steel case; polished stainless steel fixed bezel; Ø 42mm, thickness: 12.45mm; screw-in polished steel crown; curved scratch-resistant sapphire crystal with antireflective double-sided treatment; caseback with Tiger Woods and Limited Edition number engraving; water resistant to 200 meters.
Dial: black dial with vertical-line texture; hand-applied curved and faceted indexes; luminescent markers on polished rhodium-plated minute and hour hands; hand-applied monochrome TAG Heuer logo.
Indications: red burgundy Tiger Woods lettering in the black small seconds counter with spiral effect; grande date at 12.
Bracelet: fine-brushed stainless steel bracelet; solid steel folding clasp with safety pushbuttons.

LINK CALIBRE 5 DAY DATE   REF. WJF2011.BA0592

Movement: mechanical automatic-winding TAG Heuer Calibre 5.
Functions: hours, minutes, seconds; date, day.
Case: fine-brushed stainless steel case; Ø 42mm, thickness: 13.05mm; polished stainless steel fixed bezel; curved scratch-resistant sapphire crystal with antireflective double-sided treatment; water resistant to 200 meters.
Dial: silver dial with vertical-line texture; hand-applied curved and faceted indexes; faceted, polished rhodium-plated minute and hour hands; luminescent markers on minute and hour hands; hand-applied TAG Heuer logo.
Indications: hand-applied date window at 6, day window at 12, both diamonded and angled.
Bracelet: fine-brushed stainless steel bracelet; solid steel folding clasp with safety pushbuttons.
Also available: black dial.

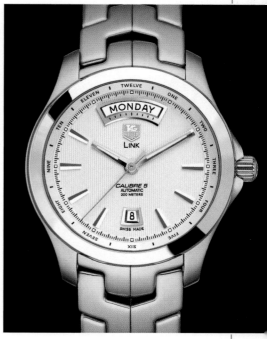

LINK CALIBRE 16 CHRONOGRAPH DAY DATE   REF. CJF211A.BA0594

Movement: mechanical automatic-winding chronograph TAG Heuer Calibre 16.
Functions: hours, minutes, seconds; date, day; chronograph.
Case: fine-brushed stainless steel case; polished fixed bezel with black tachymetre scale; Ø 42mm, thickness: 15.60mm; screw-in polished steel crown; curved scratch-resistant sapphire crystal with antireflective double-sided treatment; screw fitting caseback in sapphire crystal; water resistant to 200 meters.
Dial: black, exterior zone with spiral effect; hand-applied curved and faceted indexes; luminescent markers on minute and hour hands and on the flange; faceted polished rhodium-plated minute and hour hands; rhodium circles on the three counters; hand-applied monochrome TAG Heuer logo.
Indications: three counters, hour at 6, 30-minute counter at 12, oversized small seconds at 9; day-date at 3.
Bracelet: fine-brushed stainless steel bracelet, solid steel folding clasp with safety pushbuttons.
Also available: silver dial.

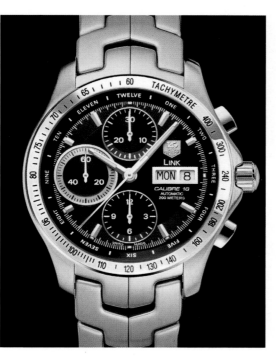

LINK CHRONOGRAPH LADY - JEWELLERY   REF.CJF1314.BA0580

Movement: quartz.
Functions: hours, minutes, seconds; date; chronograph with three counters.
Case: polished stainless steel case; Ø 33mm, thickness: 11mm; polished steel fixed bezel set with 56 Top Wesselton diamonds (Ø 1.5mm, 0.8 carat), screw-in polished steel crown; shaped polished stainless steel pushbuttons; curved scratch-resistant sapphire crystal; water resistant to 200 meters.
Dial: white mother-of-pearl dial set with 12 Top Wesselton diamonds (Ø 1.3mm, 0.114 carat); polished rhodium-plated faceted minute and hour hands; minute circle on the flange; monochrome TAG Heuer logo.
Indications: counters at 2, 6 and 10; date at 4:30.
Bracelet: polished stainless steel bracelet; double safety clasp with folding buckle.

373

AQUARACER GRANDE DATE QUARTZ ALUMINUM BEZEL CHRONOGRAPH   REF. CAN1010.BA0821

Movement: grande date quartz chronograph – 1/10th of a second
Functions: hours, minutes, seconds; date; chronograph with three counters
Case: fine-brushed steel with polished edges; Ø 43mm, thickness: 12.9mm; uni-directional turning bezel in fine-brushed steel with polished studs, a colored aluminum ring, easy grip grooves on the edge and a luminescent dot at 12; scratch-resistant sapphire crystal with antireflective treatment; polished screw-in crown and polished shaped pushbuttons; screw-in caseback with stamped diver decoration; water resistant to 300 meters.

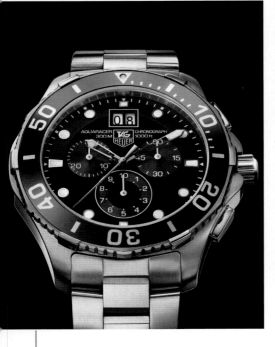

Dial: black dial; hand-applied polished indexes; polished skeleton hands; luminescent markers on minute and hour hands and indexes; polished rings on counters at 6; monochrome TAG Heuer logo;
Indications: spiral effect in all counters; minute at 9, small seconds at 3, dual-function counter at 6: 1/10th of a second during 30 minutes and then change to hour counter; grande date at 12.
Bracelet: three-row alternate fine-brushed steel bracelet; solid steel clasp, diving extension system and safety pushbuttons.
Also available: blue dial; rubber strap with folding buckle.

AQUARACER CALIBRE 5 ALUMINUM BEZEL WATCH   REF. WAN2111.BA0822

Movement: mechanical automatic-winding chronograph TAG Heuer Calibre 5.
Functions: hours, minutes, seconds; date.
Case: fine-brushed steel case; Ø 41mm, thickness: 11.6mm; unidirectional turning bezel in fine-brushed steel with polished studs, a colored aluminum ring, easy grip grooves on the edge and a luminescent dot at 12; scratch-resistant sapphire crystal with antireflective treatment inside; polished screw-in crown; screw-in caseback with stamped diver decoration; water resistant to 300 meters.

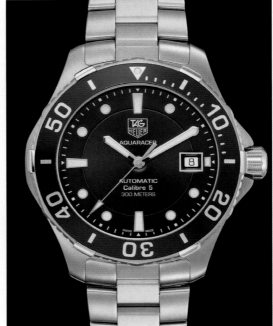

Dial: blue dial; hand-applied polished indexes; polished hands; luminescent markers on minute and hour hands and indexes; monochrome TAG Heuer logo.
Indications: date at 3.
Bracelet: three-row alternate fine-brushed steel bracelet, massive fine-brushed end-piece; double safety clasp, diving extension system.
Also available: black dial; rubber strap with folding buckle.

AQUARACER 500M CALIBRE 5 STEEL & GOLD   REF. WAJ2150.FT6015

Movement: mechanical automatic-winding TAG Heuer Calibre 5.
Functions: hours, minutes, seconds; date.
Case: fine-brushed steel case with fine brushed edges; Ø 43mm, thickness: 13.25mm; unidirectional turning bezel in fine-brushed massive gold (18K 5N) with polished rose-gold numerals, polished studs and a luminescent dot at 12; fine-brushed steel crown with black rubber coating on the face; scratch-resistant sapphire crystal with

antireflective treatment and sapphire caseback; automatic helium valve at 10; water resistant to 500 meters.
Dial: black with vertical streak effect; hand-applied indexes; black varnished hands; second hand with orange at the extremity; luminescent markers on hands and indexes; date window at 9 with a magnifying glass; hand-applied TAG Heuer logo.
Strap: black rubber strap with solid steel clasp, diving extension system and safety pushbuttons.
Also available: three-row fine-brushed steel bracelet with solid steel clasp, diving extension system and safety pushbuttons.

AQUARACER 500M CALIBRE 5   REF. WAJ2110.BA0870

Movement: mechanical automatic-winding TAG Heuer Calibre 5.
Functions: hours, minutes, seconds; date.
Case: fine-brushed steel case with fine-brushed edges; Ø 43mm, thickness: 13.45mm; unidirectional turning bezel in fine-brushed steel with a colored molded rubber coating, fine-brushed steel numerals and a luminescent dot at 12; fine-brushed steel crown with black rubber coating on the face; scratch-resistant sapphire crystal and sapphire caseback; automatic helium valve at 10; water resistant to 500 meters.
Dial: black with vertical streak effect; hand-applied indexes; polished finished hands; second hand with orange at the extremity; luminescent markers on hands and indexes; date window at 9 with a magnifying glass; hand-applied TAG Heuer logo.
Bracelet: three-row alternate fine-brushed steel bracelet with solid steel clasp, diving extension system and safety pushbuttons.
Also available: silver or blue dial; black rubber strap with solid steel clasp, diving extension system and safety pushbuttons.

AQUARACER CALIBRE 16 CHRONOGRAPH   REF. CAF2110.BA0809

Movement: mechanical automatic-winding TAG Heuer Calibre 16.
Functions: hours, minutes, seconds; date; chronograph with three counters.
Case: fine-brushed steel with polished edges; Ø 41mm, thickness: 14.9mm; unique dual bezel composed of fixed colored aluminum/steel ring and unidirectional turning bezel in fine-brushed steel with polished studs and minutes scale, engraved numerals with black varnish on the turning base, luminescent dot at 12; scratch-resistant sapphire crystal

with antireflective treatment; polished screw-in crown and polished shaped pushbuttons; screw-in caseback with stamped diver decoration; water resistant to 300 meters.
Dial: black dial with sunray effect; hand-applied indexes; polished hands; luminescent markers on hands and indexes; polished rings on counters at 6 and 12; monochrome TAG Heuer logo.
Indications: hours at 6, seconds at 9, minutes at 12; date window at 3.
Bracelet: three-row alternate polished and fine-brushed steel bracelet; double safety clasp, diving extension system and safety pushbuttons.
Also available: blue and silver dial with steel bracelet; silver dial for steel and gold version.

AQUARACER AUTOMATIC WATCH   REF. WAF2111.BA0806

Movement: automatic-winding TAG Heuer Calibre 5.
Functions: hours, minutes, seconds, date.
Case: fine-brushed steel case; Ø 39mm, thickness: 10.9mm; unidirectional turning bezel in polished steel with engraved numerals on the turning base and luminescent dot at 12; scratch-resistant sapphire crystal; screw-in caseback with stamped diver decoration; water resistant to 300 meters.
Dial: silver dial with Clous de Paris; hand-applied numerals and indexes; diamond-shaped hands with polished facets; luminescent markers on hands and indexes; monochrome TAG Heuer logo.
Indications: date at 3.
Bracelet: five-row alternate fine-brushed and polished steel bracelet with massive endpiece; double safety clasp and diving extension system.
Also available: black or blue dial.

AQUARACER LADY DIAMOND DIAL & DIAMOND BEZEL   REF. WAF1313.BA0819

Movement: quartz.
Functions: hours, minutes, seconds; date.
Case: fine-brushed steel with polished edges; Ø 32mm, thickness: 9.55mm; unidirectional turning bezel with polished steel base set with 42 Top Wesselton diamonds: 35 diamonds with Ø 1.5mm, 7 diamonds with Ø 1.4mm (total 0.567 carat); polished screw-in crown; scratch-resistant sapphire crystal; screw-in caseback with stamped diver decoration; water resistant to 300 meters.
Dial: white mother-of-pearl; hand-applied curved numeral at 12; 10 Top Wesselton diamonds (Ø 1.3mm, total 0.098 carat); polished finished hands with luminescent markers; polished & protruded TAG Heuer logo.
Indications: date at 3.
Bracelet: five-row alternate fine-brushed and polished steel bracelet; solid steel folding clasp and safety pushbuttons.

AQUARACER LADY DIAMOND DIAL & DIAMOND BEZEL STEEL & GOLD   REF. WAF1450.BB0825

Movement: quartz.
Functions: hours, minutes, seconds; date.
Case: fine-brushed steel with polished edges; Ø 27mm, thickness: 9mm; polished gold-plated (20 microns 18K 2N) unidirectional turning bezel set with 35 Top Wesselton diamonds (Ø 1.5mm, total 0.48 carat); polished gold-plated (20 microns 18K 2N) screw-in crown; scratch-resistant sapphire crystal; screw-in caseback with stamped diver decoration; water resistant to 300 meters.
Dial: white mother-of-pearl; hand-applied curved gold-plated numeral at 12; 10 Top Wesselton diamonds (Ø 1.2mm, total 0.07 carat); gold-plated hands with luminescent markers; monochrome TAG Heuer logo.
Indications: date at 3.
Bracelet: three-row fine-brushed steel and polished gold-plated (20 microns 18K 2N) bracelet, massive endpiece; solid steel clasp, diving extension system and safety pushbuttons.

ULYSSE NARDIN

SINCE 1846   LE LOCLE - SUISSE

When Rolf Schnyder acquired Ulysse Nardin in 1983, the company quickly raised its profile and collectors' eyebrows with the first piece in its Trilogy of Time, an acclaimed series of astronomical timepieces. More than 25 years later, Ulysse Nardin finds inspiration once again in the heavenly firmament for the Moonstruck, a watch that reflects the moon's various effects on the Earth.

Dr. Ludwig Oechslin, who was awarded the Special Jury Prize last year at the Grand Prix d'Horlogerie in Geneva, created the Moonstruck's complex UN-106 movement. His design offers an accurate depiction of the moon's phases, but unlike other lunar indicators, the Moonstruck goes a step further by simulating the moon and sun's relation to the Earth. The complication even allows one to surmise the current moonphase for any location on Earth.

The watch also indicates the influence of lunar and solar gravitation on the tides, showing their effects in relation to coastlines and oceans. In fact, the Moonstruck is the first watch in the world to indicate the gravitational influences of both the moon and sun. Adding another layer of functionality, the watch includes pushers that swiftly adjust the hour hand forward and backward to accommodate time-zone changes.

UN-106 is one of the latest movements designed and created exclusively in-house by Ulysse Nardin. Equipped with a cutting-edge silicon escapement and hairspring, the Moonstruck is a prime example of the company's dedication to the latest technology.

Moonstruck is the first watch in the world to indicate the gravitational influences of both the moon and sun.

Ulysse Nardin, led by the founder's son Paul-David Nardin, set the benchmark for mechanical marine chronometers in the late 1800s, starting a long tradition of acclaim, including eight Grand Prix wins between 1889 and 1964.

In the modern era, the company is earning raves for another complication: its perpetual calendar. Created by Oechslin, the GMT ± Perpetual holds three patents, one of which is for a system that synchronizes the hour and all calendar displays (date, day, month and year) via a single crown in either direction—even in the year 2100. According to the brand, GMT ± Perpetual is the only watch in the world with this capability.

Ulysse Nardin combines the strengths of its Marine and Perpetual Calendar collections in the Diver Perpetual Limited Edition, designed to complement active lifestyles on land and sea. Water resistant to nearly 200 meters, the titanium case includes a screw-down crown and a rotating bezel with orange highlights, which extend to the dial's indexes and hands. The Diver Perpetual Limited Edition is issued in 500 pieces.

Along with its mechanical innovations, Ulysse Nardin continues to pioneer the use of materials not traditionally associated with watchmaking. In recent times, the brand introduced an Executive Dual Time fitted with a ceramic bezel. The material is now carried to the caseside, where it appears on the patented plus/minus pushers used to adjust the second time zone.

With its breathtaking astronomical inventions and dedication to refining marine chronometers and perpetual calendars, Ulysse Nardin transforms science and imagination into the future of horology.

FACING PAGE
The moon and sun orbit independently around the Moonstruck's mother-of-pearl dial, accurately depicting their relationships to Earth. This limited edition includes 500 pieces in 18-karat red gold and 500 pieces in platinum.

THIS PAGE
TOP Ulysse Nardin brings the best elements of its Marine and Perpetual Calendar collections together in a single timepiece, the Diver Perpetual Limited Edition.

BOTTOM LEFT Pushers on the side of the Executive Dual Time's 43mm case make it quick and easy to adjust the second time zone.

BOTTOM RIGHT The GMT ± Perpetual's patented technology includes a system that synchronizes the calendar displays—date, day, month and

BLACK OCEAN
REF. 263-38LE-3

Movement: UN-26.
Case: black DLC-treated stainless steel; 42.7mm; turning bezel.
Strap: rubber/ceramic element.
Suggested price: $8,000
Note: limited edition of 1846 pieces.

BLACK SURF
REF. 266-37LE-3B

Movement: UN-26.
Case: 18K rose gold; 42.7mm; black rotating bezel; exhibition caseback.
Strap: rubber; black ceramic elements; ceramic deployant clasp.
Suggested price: $22,900
Note: limited edition of 500 pieces.
Also available: rubber and gold strap; bracelet.

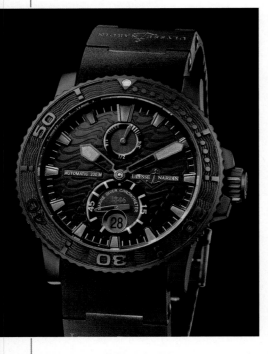

MAXI DIVER TITANIUM
REF. 263-90-3/92

Movement: UN-26.
Functions: power-reserve indicator; over-sized seconds hand.
Case: titanium and stainless steel; 45mm; exhibition caseback.
Suggested price: $9,400
Also available: various dial combinations; rubber/ceramic strap; bracelet.

MAXI DIVER TITANIUM
REF. 265-90-8M/91

Movement: UN-26.
Functions: power-reserve indicator; over-sized seconds hand.
Case: titanium and 18K rose gold; 45mm; exhibition caseback.
Suggested price: $18,900
Also available: various dial combinations; rubber/gold strap.

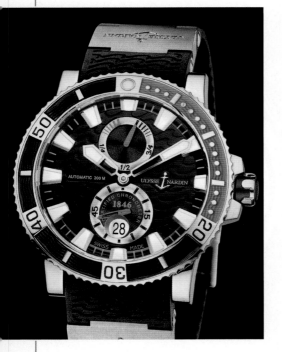

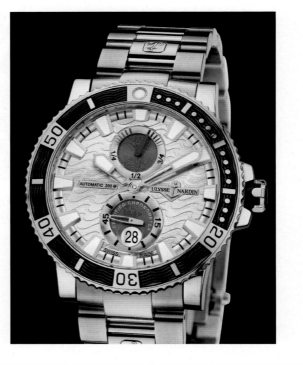

LADY DIVER
REF. 8103-101E-3C/10

Movement: UN-810.
Functions: date at 6.
Case: stainless steel; 40mm; exhibition caseback.
Dial: mother-of-pearl; diamond markers.
Suggested price: $10,500
Also available: 18K rose gold; various dial combinations; with diamond lugs.

LADY DIVER
REF. 8106-101E-3C/15

Movement: UN-810.
Functions: date at 6.
Case: 18K rose gold; 40mm; exhibition caseback.
Dial: diamond markers.
Suggested price: $24,400
Also available: stainless steel; various dial combinations; with diamond lugs.

CAPRICE
REF. 133-91AC-7C/691

Movement: UN-13.
Case: stainless steel; 34x35mm; diamond bezel; cabochon crown; exhibition caseback.
Dial: mother of pearl.
Suggested price: $19,300
Also available: 18K rose and white gold; various dial combinations; with or without diamond bezel; strap.

CAPRICE
REF. 136-91FC/06-02

Movement: UN-13; diamonds on rotor.
Case: 18K rose gold; 34x35mm; diamond case; cabochon crown; exhibition caseback.
Suggested price: $39,900
Also available: various dial combinations.

EXECUTIVE DUAL TIME REF. 243-00-3/42

Movement: UN-24.
Functions: second time zone on main dial with patented quickset; permanent home time in window at 9.
Case: stainless steel; 43mm; ceramic bezel and pushers; exhibition caseback.
Suggested price: $8,000
Also available: leather strap.

EXECUTIVE DUAL TIME REF. 246-00-3/42

Movement: UN-24.
Functions: second time zone on main dial with patented quickset; permanent home time in window at 9.
Case: 18K rose gold; 43mm; ceramic bezel and pushers; exhibition caseback.
Suggested price: $18,900
Also available: leather strap.

CLASSICO REF. 8150-111-2/E3

Movement: UN-815; chronometer certified.
Functions: date at 3.
Case: 18K white gold; 40mm; exhibition caseback.
Dial: enamel.
Suggested price: $15,900

CLASSICO REF. 8156-111-2/92

Movement: UN-815; chronometer certified.
Functions: date at 3.
Case: 18K rose gold; 40mm; exhibition caseback.
Suggested price: $11,900

ROYAL BLUE TOURBILLON REF. 799-90

Movement: UN-79; circular rack winding mechanism; sapphire bridges and main-plate.
Functions: flying tourbillon.
Case: platinum; 43mm.
Suggested price: upon request.
Note: limited edition of 99 pieces.
Also available: bracelet.

FREAK DIAMOND HEART REF. 029-80

Movement: UN-201; patented "Dual Ulysse" escapement in diamond.
Functions: carrousel-tourbillon; 7-day power reserve.
Case: platinum; 44.5mm.
Suggested price: $138,000
Note: limited edition of 99 pieces.

GMT ± PERPETUAL REF. 320-60/32

Movement: UN-32.
Functions: perpetual calendar adjustable backwards and forwards from a single crown; second time zone on main dial with patented quickset; permanent home time indicated by third hand.
Case: 18K white gold; 42mm.
Suggested price: $49,800
Note: limited edition of 60 pieces.
Also available: 18K rose gold; various dial combinations; bracelet.

SONATA CATHEDRAL DUAL TIME REF. 676-88/212

Movement: UN-67.
Functions: chiming 24-hour alarm with countdown indicator; dual time system with instant time-zone adjustor.
Case: 18K rose gold; 42mm.
Suggested price: $55,800
Also available: 18K white gold; bracelet.

For URWERK's chief watch-maker Felix Baumgartner and chief designer Martin Frei, the future is now. The third-generation watch-maker and visual artist launched URWERK in 1997, intent on redefining haute horology by harnessing the latest production techniques to transform nontraditional materials into otherworldly timekeeping sculptures.

Baumgartner stated in a recent published interview that the company is dedicated to developing and creating extreme complications in-house. "At URWERK, we are like a laboratory, always trying to work with the best tools, inventing complications that are definitely of our century, experimenting and pushing the boundaries."

The watches embody the duo's creative chemistry, a two-note harmony of art and technology that draws as much inspiration from their diverse backgrounds as from a shared vision of horology.

A constant for more than a decade, the rapport was already strong in 1997 when URWERK debuted at Basel with the UR-101. Its minimalist design was limited to an hour disc traversing a 90-degree arc beneath a clear sapphire crystal. It's no coincidence that URWERK refers to the orbiting hour as a satellite, an element partly inspired by Russia's historic Sputnik.

URWERK welcomed the UR-202 Turbine Automatic into its fold of elite designs in 2008. Continuing a tradition of innovation, it is the first watch in the world whose automatic winding rate is regulated by compressed air.

It achieves this with a pair of turbines on the back that are connected to the movement's rotor. Informed by the principles of fluid dynamics, the system uses air friction to cushion the winding system. At least part of the inspiration behind this design can be traced back centuries, when chiming clocks used air friction to regulate chiming speeds.

The UR-202's turbines can be seen whirling on the caseback beneath a pair of elongated sapphire crystals. A nearby three-way selector controls airflow, restricting it to increase air pressure and slow the rotor's spinning during bouts of vigorous activity.

The switch tailors the turbine's speed to compensate for three different levels of motion, from normal to extreme. The "Free" setting allows the turbines and rotor to spin uninhibited during periods of normal movement. The next position reduces the winding rate by about 35 percent for moderate activity. The final setting, used during physically demanding activities, blocks the turbines entirely.

URWERK's atelier makes
its home in Geneva, **a
city that truly runs on
clockwork.**

URWERK's bold look loudly proclaims the company's willingness to experiment with watchmaking convention.

The UR-202 could be considered Frei and Baumgartner's reinterpretation of the classic three-handed wristwatch. They replace the trio of hands with a rotating triskelion driven by URWERK's patented time-display system. It consists of three telescopic minute hands that take turns sweeping across the minute arc. Each minute hand extends out from one of three rotating blocks used to display the hours.

At the center of the display is a carousel; its angled surfaces are mirror-polished by a diamond cutter. The high-tech finish offers an introduction to URWERK's production resources, which includes computer numeric controlled (CNC) machinery capable of producing specialized parts accurately to one thousandth of a millimeter.

As a counterweight to the UR-202's futuristic elements, the watch includes a wink to tradition with the addition of moonphase and day/night indicators. Their semi-circle displays are tucked neatly at opposite ends of the watch's angled minute index.

URWERK's atelier makes its home in Geneva, a city that truly runs on clockwork. Its choice location in the horological universe provides the company with ready access to a network of talented artisans who specialize in everything from traditional engraving to cutting-edge nanotechnology. In their workshop, Baumgartner and Frei have assembled a skilled team of watchmakers, engineers and designers who share their passion for technologically advanced timepieces.

The UR-202 emerged from the atelier in 2008 and is now produced in four different case metals. Along with white- or red-gold models, the company also offers a platinum one dressed in a black coating by way of a process called plasma-enhanced chemical vapor deposition (PE-CVD). The final version is made from stainless steel treated with AlTiN, a mix of aluminum, titanium and nitride.

Today, more than 13 years after the independent Swiss firm began, URWERK has established an uncompromising personality, one that elegantly expresses its unconventional quintessence.

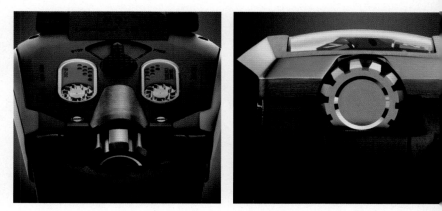

FACING PAGE
URWERK's patented revolving-satellite complication indicates the minutes with telescoping hands and hours with rotating blocks.

THIS PAGE
TOP   A look at the UR-202 movement outside of its case.

ABOVE LEFT   The back of the UR-202 features a pair of turbines that control the winding rotor's speed using air pressure. A three-way selector allows the automatic winding speed to be adjusted to match the user's level of physical activity.

ABOVE RIGHT   Positioned at 12:00 like in a pocket watch, the crown is fitted with rubber gaskets that make the UR-202 water resistant.

Vacheron Constantin completed its three-year-long tribute to the artistry of tribal masks at the Metropolitan Museum of Art in New York City last summer when the Geneva-based manufacture unveiled a complete set of its Métiers d'Art Les Masques, a collection of 12 timepieces featuring masks whose origins span more than two millennia and four continents.

Vacheron Constantin released 25 numbered Les Masques sets per year between 2007 and 2009, each of which contained four models with different handcrafted masks that re-created everything from a Chinese death mask to a face found on a fragment of a Mayan incense burner.

To create this limited edition, Vacheron Constantin enlisted the help of the Barbier-Mueller Museum, a nearby museum in Geneva that is home to one of the world's most extensive collections of primitive art. Jean Paul Barbier-Mueller, who founded the museum in 1977 to display his family's collection, loaned several masks to the brand so its craftspeople could accurately reproduce each mask down to the smallest detail.

To re-create the tiny faces, Vacheron Constantin first scanned each to make a three-dimensional rendering, which was then used to reproduce the original in precious metal. Next, the company's expert engravers set to work refining the details, using a chisel and, in some cases, chemistry to mimic centuries of aging without simply resorting to paint and brush.

The masks take center stage atop a Vacheron Constantin proprietary movement that displays the hour, minute, day and date on four rotating discs seen around the dial's perimeter. The mask rests atop a layer of tinted crystal that partially obscures the automatic movement below. Adding a final layer of creativity, each dial features a different poem by Michel Butor, whose words are inscribed in gold through a process called vacuum metallization.

Jean-Marc Vacheron made his first pocket watch in 1755, launching a proud tradition that continues centuries later at Vacheron Constantin.

With the Patrimony Contemporaine pocket watch, the company burnishes that legacy with a modern successor that evokes Victorian dandyism—a cultural benchmark for pocket watches. It filters the bygone era's ingenuity and elegance through a prism of 21st-century modernity to form an elegant anachronism that seeks to put time back in one's hands, both physically and figuratively.

Platinum was chosen for the 43mm case, the company says, for its purity, durable beauty, glowing patina, and density. The Patrimony Contemporaine pocket watch is limited to just 50 pieces, and Vacheron Constantin presents each pocket watch in a gray lacquered box accompanied by a watch cord and protective pouch, both made of soft calfskin. Upon request, the company will also create a matching platinum chain. Walking stick sold separately.

Vacheron Constantin introduced the Patrimony Tradition-nelle line three years ago, introducing a range of models that demonstrate its horological mastery, particularly its attention to aesthetics, a quality that has defined Geneva watchmaking for generations.

While each member of the collection is distinguished by its individual functions, they all share a number of classic details expressed with a modern sensibility, such as knurling around the clear caseback, silver dials, trapezoid hour-markers and dauphine hands.

Within the Patrimony Traditionnelle Perpetual Calendar Chronograph's 43mm pink-gold case resides the Vacheron Constantin 1141, a column-wheel chronograph. Beloved by aficionados for its peerless construction, the movement has appeared in a number of the company's best-known chronographs.

The silvered opaline dial displays the functions in a legible arrangement with a pair of chronograph counters lined up horizontally above a snailed subsidiary dial at 6:00 for the date and moonphase. The moon's waxing and waning is visible through an opening that reveals a hand-engraved gold plate rotating below the dial. A trio of windows for the days of the week, month and leap year are positioned unobtrusively on the upper half of the dial, near the company's signature gold Maltese cross.

Vacheron Constantin introduced its first wristwatches in 1889, debuting a tonneau-shaped case in 1912. Nearly a century later, the watchmaker welcomes the Malte Moon Phase Power Reserve, a worthy heir to that historic past.

Its curved outline (39x49mm) allows ample space for a silvered gold dial to be used as a canvas by gifted artisans who express their creative dexterity through a dynamic combination of finishes. Clous de Paris guilloché fills a circular field at the top of the dial, where a thin hand shows how much power is left on an arc-shaped indicator. On a small seconds display below, satin brushing is used for the background.

Where Vacheron Constantin pays tribute to tradition with the Malte, it revels in the unconventional with the Historiques American 1921, a cushion-shaped timepiece that features both the dial and the crown shifted to the 1:00 position.

The Historiques American 1921's design, a tribute to the style of the Roaring Twenties, was named Watch of the Year last fall in Geneva. It is Vacheron Constantin's second win in three years; the first was in 2007 for the Patrimony Contemporary Retrograde Date and Day. During his acceptance speech, Vacheron Constantin CEO Juan-Carlos Torres noted that the jury's decision rewarded and honored the excellence of the company's watchmaking tradition. "It also acknowledges," he said, "the technical performance and aesthetic elegance of our company, values that have been consistently handed down from one generation to the next for over 250 years."

QUAI DE L'ILE DATE SELF-WINDING
REF. 86050/000D-9343

Movement: mechanical self-winding Vacheron Constantin Caliber 2460QH; 43-hour power reserve; 27 jewels; 28,800 vph; hallmarked with the Geneva Seal.
Functions: hours, minutes, central seconds; date disc with optimal legibility (numerals engraved and inked on the sapphire dial) and ruthenium-coated with a white mark.
Case: palladium; Ø 41mm; screw-down back with sapphire crystal; water resistant to 30 meters (100 feet).

Dial: sapphire crystal (galvanic growth of nickel, metallization, and laser engraving with or without inking) and security transparent film (intaglio printing, security inks and micro-printing); numerals 3, 6, 9 and 12 are in galvanic growth of nickel; other numerals are engraved and inked in black or white.
Strap: black or brown hand-stitched, saddle-finished, square-scaled, high-shine alligator leather; triple-blade palladium folding clasp, polished half Maltese cross.
Note: delivered with a second strap in black or brown vulcarbonized rubber.
Suggested price: $30,000
Also available: in 18K pink gold or titanium.

QUAI DE L'ILE DATE SELF-WINDING
REF. 86050/000R-9342

Movement: mechanical self-winding Vacheron Constantin Caliber 2460QH; 43-hour power reserve; 27 jewels; 28,800 vph; hallmarked with the Geneva Seal.
Functions: hours, minutes, central seconds; date disc with optimal legibility (numerals engraved and inked on the sapphire dial) and ruthenium-coated with a black mark.
Case: 18K pink gold; Ø 41mm; screw-down back with sapphire crystal; water resistant to 30 meters (100 feet).

Dial: sapphire crystal (galvanic growth of nickel, metallization, and laser engraving with or without inking) and security transparent film (intaglio printing, security inks and micro-printing); numerals 3, 6, 9 and 12 are in galvanic growth of nickel; other numerals are engraved and inked in black or white.
Strap: black or brown hand-stitched, saddle-finished, square-scaled, high-shine alligator leather; triple-blade palladium folding clasp, polished half Maltese cross.
Note: delivered with a second strap in black or brown vulcarbonized rubber.
Suggested price: $31,500
Also available: in palladium or titanium.

QUAI DE L'ILE DAY-DATE AND POWER RESERVE SELF-WINDING
REF. 85050/000R-9340

Movement: mechanical self-winding Vacheron Constantin Caliber 2475SC; 43-hour power reserve; 27 jewels; 28,800 vph; hallmarked with the Geneva Seal.
Functions: hours, minutes, seconds; date and day indicated by hands; power reserve.
Case: 18K pink gold; Ø 41mm; screw-down back with sapphire crystal; water resistant to 30 meters (100 feet).
Dial: sapphire crystal (galvanic growth of nickel, metallization, and laser engraving with or without inking) and security transparent film (intaglio printing, security inks and micro-printing); numerals 3, 6, 9 and 12 are in galvanic growth of nickel; other numerals are engraved and inked in black or white.

Strap: black or brown hand-stitched, saddle-finished, square-scaled, high-shine alligator leather; triple-blade palladium folding clasp, polished half Maltese cross.
Note: delivered with a second strap in black or brown vulcarbonized rubber.
Suggested price: $41,300
Also available: in palladium or titanium.

OVERSEAS CHRONOGRAPH
REF. 49150/000R-9338

Movement: mechanical self-winding Vacheron Constantin Caliber 1137; 37 jewels; 21,600 vph; 40-hour power reserve; anti-magnetic protection.
Functions: hours, minutes, running seconds at 6; 30-minute and 12-hour totalizers at 3 and at 9, respectively; center chronograph seconds; chronograph mechanism to 1/6 of a second; date calendar shown in twin oversized dial apertures at 12.
Case: 18K pink gold; Ø 42mm; solid back stamped with "Overseas" medallion and secured with screws; water resistant to 150 meters (500 feet).

Dial: anthracite; 12 applied 18K pink-gold hour-markers with white luminescent strip.
Strap: hand-stitched alligator leather; pink-gold buckle.
Note: delivered with a second strap in dark brown vulcarbonized rubber.
Suggested price: $33,800
Also available: on 18K pink-gold bracelet.

OVERSEAS CHRONOGRAPH — REF. 49150/000W-9501

Movement: mechanical self-winding Vacheron Constantin Caliber 1137; 40-hour power reserve; 21,600 vph; 37 jewels; antimagnetic protection.
Functions: hours, minutes and seconds in center; column-wheel chronograph; 12-hour and 30-minute counters; large date at 12.
Case: stainless steel, titanium bezel; solid caseback stamped with "Overseas" medallion and secured with screws; water resistant to 150 meters.
Dial: slate gray, circular satin-finishing; painted exterior minute-track; finely snailed counters with diamond-polished filets; 12 applied hour-markers in 18K white gold with white luminescent strip.
Strap: dark gray hand-stitched alligator leather.
Note: delivered with a second strap in black rubber.
Suggested price: $16,200

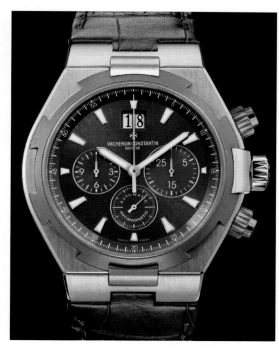

OVERSEAS AUTOMATIC — REF. 47040/000W-9500

Movement: mechanical self-winding Vacheron Constantin Caliber 1226; 40-hour power reserve; 28,800 vph; 36 jewels; antimagnetic protection.
Functions: hours, minutes and seconds in center; date window between 4 and 5.
Case: stainless steel; titanium bezel; solid caseback stamped with "Overseas" medallion and secured with screws; water resistant to 150 meters.
Dial: slate gray; circular satin-finishing; painted exterior minute-track; eight applied hour-markers in 18K white gold with white luminescent strip; four Arabic numerals in 18K white gold with black nickel finish.
Strap: dark gray hand-stitched alligator leather.
Note: delivered with a second strap in black rubber.
Suggested price: $9,900

HISTORIQUES AMERICAN 1921 — REF. 82035/000R-9359

Movement: mechanical manual-winding Vacheron Constantin Caliber 4400; approx. 65-hour power reserve; Ø 28mm, thickness: 2.8mm; 21 rubies; 28,800 vph; hallmarked with the Geneva Seal.
Functions: hours, minutes, off-center small seconds.
Case: 18K 5N pink gold; Ø 40mm; off-center crown; convex sapphire crystal with antireflective coating; transparent sapphire crystal caseback with screws; water resistant to 30 meters (100 feet).
Dial: sand-blasted finishing; painted Arabic numerals and minute track; hands in black oxidized 18K gold.
Strap: brown hand-stitched, saddle-finished, square-scaled alligator leather; 18K 5N pink-gold buckle with polished half Maltese cross.
Suggested price: $24,900

HISTORIQUE ULTRA-FINE 1955 — REF. 33155/000R-9588

Movement: mechanical manual-winding Vacheron Constantin Caliber 1003; more than 30-hour power reserve; thinnest in the world at just 1.64mm thick; 18 jewels; 18,000 vph; hallmarked with the Geneva Seal.
Functions: hours, minutes.
Case: 18K 4N pink gold; Ø 36mm, thickness: 4.1mm; water resistant to 30 meters.
Dial: silvered opaline; mirror-polished 18K gold Maltese Cross and indexes.
Strap: black hand-stitched, saddle-finished, square-scaled alligator leather.
Suggested retail price: $22,900

PATRIMONY TRADITIONNELLE CHRONOGRAPH PERPETUAL CALENDAR   REF. 47292/000R-9392

Movement: mechanical manual-winding Vacheron Constantin Caliber 1141; 21 jewels; 18,000 vph; 48-hour power reserve.
Functions: hours, minutes, small seconds at 9; column-wheel chronograph; 30-minute counter at 3; center chronograph hand; perpetual calendar and precision moonphase at 6.
Case: 18K pink gold; Ø 43mm; sapphire crystal with antireflective coating on the inside; transparent sapphire crystal caseback with screws; water resistant to 30 meters.
Dial: silvered opaline; finely snailed counter; black painted minute track.
Strap: brown hand-stitched, saddle-finished, square-scaled alligator leather.
Suggested price: $98,500

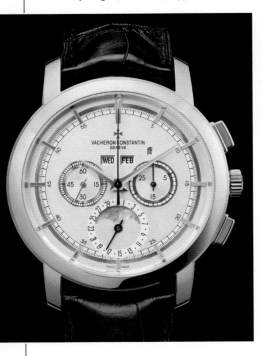

PATRIMONY TRADITIONNELLE CHRONOGRAPH   REF. 47192/000R-9352

Movement: mechanical manual-winding Vacheron Constantin Caliber 1141; 45-hour power reserve; 18,000 vph; 21 jewels.
Functions: hours, minutes, small seconds at 9; column-wheel chronograph; 30-minute counter at 3; center chronograph hand.
Case: 18K 5N pink gold; Ø 42mm; sapphire with antireflective coating on the inside; transparent sapphire crystal caseback with screws; water resistant to 30 meters.
Dial: silvered opaline; finely snailed counters at 3 and 9; black painted minute-track.
Strap: brown hand-stitched, saddle-finished, square-scaled alligator leather.
Suggested price: $39,000

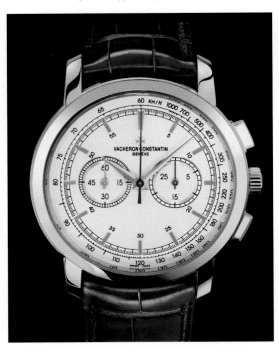

PATRIMONY TRADITIONNELLE AUTOMATIC   REF. 87172/000G-9301

Movement: mechanical automatic-winding Vacheron Constantin Caliber 2455; jewels; 11'''1/5; Ø 25.6mm, thickness: 3.6mm; 40-hour power reserve; 27 jewels; balance with 28,800 vph; decorated with circular-graining and Côtes de Genève patterns; beveled; hallmarked with the Geneva Seal.
Functions: hours, minutes, small seconds at 9; date at 3.
Case: 18K white-gold two-piece case; Ø 38mm, thickness: 8.1mm; polished finish; antireflective curved sapphire crystal; white-gold crown; screw-on back with knurled profile, displaying the movement through a sapphire crystal; water resistant to 3atm.
Dial: very light opaline silvered, finely grained; subdial decorated with circular beads; second and minute rings as black railway track on a dark silvered background; white-gold logo and bâton markers; white-gold dauphine hands.
Strap: black hand-stitched alligator leather; white-gold clasp.
Suggested price: $20,500
Also available: in pink gold.

PATRIMONY CONTEMPORAINE BI-RETROGRADE   REF. 86020/000R-9239

Movement: mechanical automatic-winding Vacheron Constantin Caliber 2460 R31 R7; 43-hour power reserve; 27 jewels; 28,800 vph; guilloché pink-gold rotor; hallmarked with the Geneva Seal.
Functions: hours, minutes; retrograde day and date.
Case: 18K pink-gold three-piece case ; Ø 42.5mm, thickness: 10.3mm; flared, polished finish; curved sapphire crystal; two correctors on the middle, for the date between 12 and 1; for the day between 9 and 10; pink-gold crown; snap-on back displaying the movement through a sapphire crystal; water resistant to 3atm.
Dial: silvered; grained; curved; applied pink-gold pointed and bâton markers and logo; minute track with hollowed pink cabochons; pink-gold bâton hands.
Indications: minute at 2; hour at 10; sliding disc, day of the week and fan-shaped date with retrograde hands in burnished gold at 6 and 12.
Strap: alligator leather; pink-gold double fold-over clasp.
Suggested price: $34,500
Also available: in white gold.

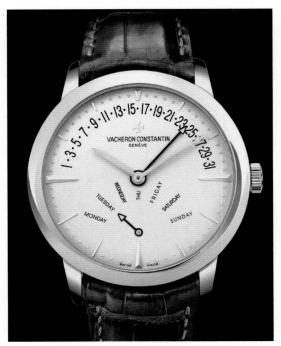

PATRIMONY CONTEMPORAINE AUTOMATIC   REF. 85180/000R-9248

Movement: mechanical automatic-winding Vacheron Constantin Caliber 2450; 49-hour power reserve; 27 jewels; 28,800 vph; guilloché 22K pink-gold rotor; hallmarked with the Geneva Seal.
Functions: hours, minutes, seconds; date at 6.
Case: 18K pink-gold three-piece case; Ø 40mm, thickness: 8.5mm; flared, polished finish; curved sapphire crystal; pink-gold crown; snap-on back displaying the movement through a sapphire crystal; water resistant to 3atm.
Dial: silvered, grained; applied pink-gold pointed and bâton markers; hollowed minute track with a gilded cabochon; pink-gold curved index hands.
Strap: alligator leather; pink-gold clasp.
Suggested price: $19,100
Also available: in white or yellow gold.

PATRIMONY CONTEMPORAINE   REF. 81180/00P-9332

Movement: mechanical manual-winding Vacheron Constantin Caliber 1400; 40-hour power reserve; 20 jewels; 28,800 vph; hallmarked with the Geneva Seal.
Functions: hours, minutes.
Case: 950 platinum; Ø 40mm; water resistant to 30 meters (100 feet).
Dial: light opaline silvered; grained; with a slightly curved perimeter; applied white-gold pointed and bâton markers; minute track with a white-gold cabochon; white-gold index hands.
Strap: black hand-stitched alligator leather; 950 platinum clasp.
Suggested price: $19,100
Also available: in pink, white or yellow gold.

MALTE MOON PHASE AND POWER RESERVE   REF. 83080/000G-9408

Movement: mechanical manual-winding Vacheron Constantin Caliber 1410; 40-hour power reserve; 22 jewels; 28,800 vph; hallmarked with the Geneva Seal.
Functions: hours, minutes, small seconds at 6; precision moonphase; power reserve.
Case: 18K white gold; 39x49mm; tonneau shaped; water resistant to 30 meters.
Dial: silvered "Clous de Paris" hand-guilloché interior zone; vertical satin-finished exterior zone; applied Maltese cross in 18K white gold.
Strap: brown or black hand-stitched, saddle-finished, square-scaled alligator leather.
Suggested price: $34,500
Also available: in 5N pink gold.

MALTE TONNEAU CHRONOGRAPH   REF. 49180/000G-9360

Movement: mechanical self-winding Vacheron Constantin Caliber 1137; 37 jewels; 21,600 vph; 40-hour power reserve.
Functions: hours, minutes, running seconds at 6; center chronograph seconds; chronograph mechanism to 1/6 of a second; 30-minute and 12-hour totalizers at 3 and at 9, respectively; date calendar shown in twin oversized dial apertures at 12.
Case: 18K white gold; 40x50mm; water resistant to 30 meters (100 feet).
Dial: guilloché "Clous de Paris" interior zone; vertical satin-finished exterior zone.
Strap: hand-stitched alligator leather; white-gold buckle.
Suggested price: $38,300
Also available: in 18K pink gold.

VALENTINO
TIMELESS

Valentino enjoys worldwide recognition as one of the most consistently creative houses worldwide, offering a wide range of luxury products from haute couture and prêt-à-porter to an extensive accessories collection that includes bags, shoes, small leather goods, belts, eyewear, watches and perfumes.

Valentino Timeless timepieces—product of TIMEX GROUP LUXURY DIVISION—are singular in their design and functions, a reflection of both the incomparable spirit of the Valentino brand as well as the prestige of a Swiss-made product. Each piece has the indelible stamp of the Italian fashion label and a fresh interpretation of iconic house symbols, as witnessed with the Rose models.

Traditionally, the rose has graced a wide range of Valentino's luxurious products. Whether embroidered on sculptured pumps or personified in eye-catching accessories, the flower always projects feminine elegance. That same spirit is present in all Rose watches from the Valentino Timeless collection.

The first is a voluptuous red Rose. Its crocodile strap attaches to a 36mm stainless steel case outlined with more than half a carat of round, red rubies. For a more intense effect, even the lugs are covered with these precious gems.

The sophistication continues onto the dial, where rose petals are first crafted in stainless steel and then set with 114 scintillating black diamonds that weigh nearly half a carat. The dark stones stand out against the light-gray shimmer of the watch's mother-of-pearl dial.

The side of the case is textured, giving the Rose a multidimensional look that is both attractive to the eye and sensuous to the touch. A faceted crown adds a final flourish that complements the watch's diamond decoration.

Among the remarkable range of Rose watches, Valentino Timeless presents a stunning all-black model. The bezel of its round, gleaming PVD-coated case and the dial's floral design are both drawn with black diamonds, bestowing more than a carat of dark preciousness.

Another Rose version presents an ion-plated case and matte dial, both in black, which contrast with sparkling white diamonds on the bezel, lugs and dial. The black dial appears in two other models without the diamond bezel: one in stainless steel and one plated in rose gold.

Finally, the Valentino Timeless collection offers two all-white models in stainless steel. Both feature white mother-of-pearl dials, one with a diamond-set bezel and the other without. The final Rose pairs a white mother-of-pearl dial with a rose gold-plated case.

Equipped with a reliable quartz movement, each model represents simple elegance.

THIS PAGE

LEFT   Coated in black PVD, the case and dial of this dark Rose features 186 black diamonds. The case houses a Swiss-made quartz movement and is water resistant to 30 meters (98 feet).

RIGHT   The white mother-of-pearl dial and case of this Rose display more than a carat of white brilliant diamonds.

FACING PAGE

This Rose's bezel and lugs are decorated with 72 rubies and 114 black diamonds to create the dial's floral design. The 36mm stainless steel case is secured with a red crocodile strap.

Valentino's legendary, timeless icons are reinterpreted within its watch designs.

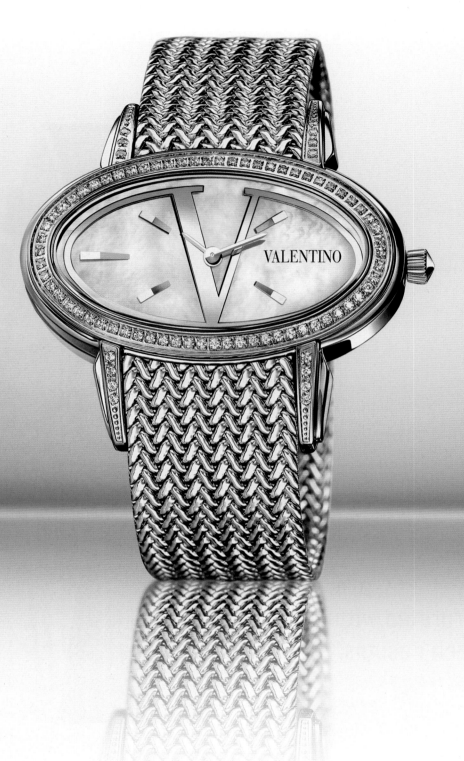

The icons of Valentino's tradition are reinterpreted within the watch designs throughout the collection. They emerge to reflect the originality and beauty of the Maison's legendary ability to combine luxurious fashions with femininity.

The connection to Valentino is writ large on the Signature watch's dial, where the "V" logo dominates. Made of stainless steel, the letter's diagonal stems branch out, following the case's oval shape to create a partial outline around the white, mother-of-pearl dial.

The bold symbol is contained within the glittery confines of the Signature's diamond-set bezel. Precious round brilliants spill from the bezel onto the lugs to complete the exclusive design.

Sumptuous scintillation continues with Signature's bracelet, which is made of stainless steel knitted together like a shimmering cloth of metal. The band wraps around the wrist and is secured by a clasp that disappears when closed, creating a seamless connection.

The Seduction Plissé personifies Valentino's signature bow with the oval case playing the part of the knotted middle and a metal-mesh bracelet serving as a loop of fabric. The bracelet's unique texture creates a plissé (pleated) finish, giving the model its memorable visage.

Mirror-polished stainless steel is used for the case, its delicate convex shape designed to fit the wrist comfortably. The bright sheen of the 36x26mm oval stands out against the darkly tinted guilloché dial.

The Plissé version is the latest addition to the Seduction family, which is once again based on the graphic lines of an iconic Valentino bow and now features a lizard-skin strap available in a range of fashionable color choices: lilac, blue, brown and black.

From the colorful Rose to the textured Seduction Plissé, each model epitomizes the perfect union of Valentino's renowned fashion statements and Swiss-made performance.

FACING PAGE
The Valentino logo looms large across the Signature's mother-of-pearl dial, which is framed by a diamond-set bezel.

THIS PAGE
LEFT A blue lizard strap complements the Seduction's 36x26mm stainless steel case with a glamorous look suitable for casual or formal occasions.

RIGHT The mesh stainless steel bracelet that secures the Seduction Plissé echoes the sumptuous fabric used for Valentino's haute couture creations.

VERSACE

Vertime SA is the Swiss-based company responsible for the manufacture and worldwide distribution of Versace watches and jewelry, and **Gianni Versace SpA is one of the leading international fashion design houses, a symbol of Italian luxury worldwide.** It designs, manufactures, distributes, and retails fashion and lifestyle products, including Atelier, prêt-à-porter, accessories, eyewear, fragrances, and home furnishings, all bearing the distinctive Medusa logo.

Versace timepieces are alluring and provocatively strong in character; they epitomize the maison's finest traditions and its history in watchmaking.

The latest models revolve around several themed collections that are characterized by an original approach to the communication of time, which they interpret through a combination of Swiss technology and avant-garde design. Says Paolo Marai, CEO of Vertime, "Our intention with these timepieces is to continue to promote Versace's values, which are dedicated to pure quality in shape, form and materials."

The collections for women are an exclusive expression of how classic style can be re-imagined in a truly glamorous way. These watches have been created by skillfully blending allure and function, tradition and modernity. These are women's timepieces conceived as true items of jewelry, and they are remarkable for their perfectly balanced execution. A mosaic in dazzling shades of gold, a harmonious combination of different aspects of design: from the pure lines of the product to the wonders of the Swiss-made mechanisms.

The Eon is not only a top-quality timepiece, but a true jewel. With its soft colors and elevated styling, it symbolizes the intriguing contrast between cool sensuality and elegant femininity.

Its round case, crafted in rose-gold-plated stainless steel, encloses a white mother-of-pearl dial with diamonds on the indexes. The outer rotating ring is decorated with a Clous de Paris pattern on one side, and engraved with the Versace logo on the other. The rose-gold-plated metal sphere bracelet adds a romantic and stylish appeal to the watch, also available in an extra luxurious version with diamonds set in the case and a smooth satin strap.

The Lady Acron, for instance, possesses an unmistakable personality. The timepiece, designed to clothe the feminine wrist with consummate elegance, features a polished round case in either stainless steel or rose gold, perfectly teamed with a strap of alligator skin with a deployant clasp. Lady Acron is also available in a truly opulent and desirable jeweled version, sprayed with circles of glittering diamond dust on the dial.

There are masculine lines in an ongoing dialogue between classic elements, high-tech solutions, and ambitious performance. Revolutionary mechanisms make their appearance in the men's collection, which represents a special alliance between the design flair of Versace and the top watchmaker's expertise. This combination creates the unique style and quality of Versace watches.

Perhaps the most iconic of all Versace timepieces, the DV One, unites form and function. The new GMT edition provides further evidence that the Maison is now one of the ultimate names in the field of Switzerland's top watchmakers. This timepiece, available in a choice of black or white, features an automatic movement and displays hours, minutes and seconds.

LEFT   Lady Acron.

RIGHT   Eon.

In 2009, Versace opened its second boutique in the world, dedicated entirely to the Maison's fine jewelry and watches in Dubai, UAE. The Versace Fine Jewellery flagship signals a new global retail strategy to open more Versace Fine Jewellery boutiques in the near future. Within its precious collections, this Versace Fine Jewellery boutique also offers an exclusive Versace Vintage Jewellery collection.

LEFT V-Master.

RIGHT DV One GMT.

A red hand with a triangular tip indicates the secondary time zone representing the GMT function on the main dial, which is protected by non-reflective mineral crystal. The case is 41mm and crafted in glossy scratch-resistant ceramic. The unmistakable Greek key motif is engraved on the top ring. It is water resistant to 5atm and features a black or white scratchproof ceramic bracelet.

The V-Master, a watch intended for the most discerning collectors, exhibits all the classic qualities of a high-end timepiece. It is an ultra contemporary watch that combines design elegance with the sporting impact of a triple-action chronograph: moonphase aperture at 6:00, 24-hour panel at 9:00 and day/month calendar at 12:00. The complexity of the movement is suggested by the date indicator that runs around the complete edge of the dial. The steel case encloses a black and white oval dial textured with an attractive lozenge pattern that perfectly sets off the pink-gold-plated Arabic numerals and details, while the crown is adorned with the Greek key motif. The strap in alligator skin is fastened with a deployant clasp. The water resistance of the chronograph is guaranteed to 5atm.

All Versace timepieces are carefully made to exacting standards in Switzerland.

VERSACE HIGHLIGHTS

In 1978, The Gianni Versace company is launched with a women's collection in Milan. Versace quickly becomes one of the most revered international design houses and a symbol for Italian luxury. In addition to clothing, the Versace Group soon ventures into the design and manufacture of other fashion goods.

In 1989, Versace's first watch collection, Atelier, is launched.

In 1996, Gianni Versace and Franck Muller work together to create a limited edition of watches. The line is designed by Versace and crafted and produced by Muller.

In 1997, Donatella Versace succeeds her brother as head of design for the Versace Group and is named Creative Director for the Masion.

In 1998, the Versace Group creates Versace SA that is devoted to the brand's luxury watch and jewelry segment in order to garner wider, more focused distribution.

In 2004, Versace and Timex Group, a leader in watchmaking with more than 150 years of experience, begin a licensing agreement together with the creation of Vertime SA. Based strategically in Switzerland, Vertime SA specializes in the production and worldwide distribution of Versace Precious Items—the realm of Versace luxury watches and jewelry.

DV-ONE GMT   REF. 02WCS1D001 SC01

Movement: Swiss automatic ETA 2893-2 GMT.
Functions: hours, minutes, seconds; date; GMT.
Case: stainless steel; Ø 41mm; white ceramic top ring with Greca pattern.
Dial: white enamel; center GMT indication; stainless steel indexes.
Bracelet: white ceramic; butterfly buckle.

DV-ONE COSC   REF. 16CCT9D008 SC09

Movement: Swiss automatic chronograph ETA 2894.2; COSC certified.
Functions: hours, minutes, seconds; date; chronograph.
Case: black scratchproof ceramic; Ø 43.5mm; stainless steel IP black details; stainless steel IP black/ matte black ceramic top ring with tachymeter scale.
Dial: matte black; center guilloché finishing; stainless steel indexes and hands (titanium color) with black SuperLumiNova.

Bracelet: matte black scratchproof ceramic and stainless steel IP black polish-finished insert; butterfly buckle.

V-MASTER COMPLICATIONS   REF. 20A99D001 S282

Movement: Swiss automatic chronograph ETA 7751 Valjoux.
Functions: chronograph; date; day, month; moonphase; 24 hours.
Case: stainless steel; 51x42.39mm.
Dial: matte white; Arabic numerals; rose-gold-plated finishing; center lozenge texture; blue hands.
Strap: dark blue or black genuine alligator leather; stainless steel folding clasp.

V-MASTER   REF. 20A380D008 S009

Movement: Swiss automatic ETA 2824-2.
Functions: hours, minutes, seconds; date at 3.
Case: rose gold; 51x42.39mm.
Dial: matte black; rose-gold indexes and Arabic numerals; center lozenge texture; Medusa head at 12.
Strap: black alligator-patterned calf leather; stainless steel and rose-gold folding clasp.

EON
REF. 79Q80SD498S080

Movement: Swiss quartz ISA K62-132.
Functions: hours, minutes.
Case: Ø 33.6mm; Clous de Paris decoration; one rotating rose-gold ring with Clous de Paris decoration on one side and engraved Versace logo on the other.
Dial: white mother-of-pearl dial; four white diamond indexes, average 0.011 carat.
Bracelet: rose gold; small spheres; jewelry buckle.

EON
REF. 80Q81SD498S002

Movement: Swiss quartz ISA K62-132.
Functions: hours, minutes.
Case: Ø 39mm; 40 white diamonds, average 0.3 carat; two rotating rose-gold rings: middle ring with Greca emblem on one side and engraved Versace logo on the other, outer ring with Clous de Paris decoration on one side and Greca emblem on the other.
Dial: white mother-of-pearl dial; four white diamond indexes, average 0.011 carat.
Strap: ivory technical satin strap; rose-gold folding clasp.

EON
REF. 79Q99SD498S099

Movement: Swiss quartz ISA K62-132.
Functions: hours, minutes.
Case: Ø 33.6mm; Clous de Paris decoration; one stainless steel rotating ring with Clous de Paris decoration on one side and engraved Versace logo on the other.
Dial: white mother-of-pearl dial; four white diamond indexes, average 0.011 carat.
Bracelet: stainless steel; small spheres; jewelry buckle.

EON
REF. 79Q91SD498S009

Movement: Swiss quartz ISA K62-132.
Functions: hours, minutes.
Case: Ø 33.6mm; 40 white diamonds, average 0.3 carat; one stainless steel rotating ring with Clous de Paris decoration on one side and engraved Versace logo on the other.
Dial: white mother-of-pearl dial; four white diamond indexes, average 0.011 carat.
Strap: black technical satin strap; stainless steel folding clasp.

ACRON POWER RESERVE — REF. 18A99D497 S497

Movement: Swiss automatic La Joux-Perret 3513; 42-hour power reserve.
Functions: hours, minutes, seconds; power-reserve indicator at 6; big date at 12.
Case: stainless steel; Ø 43mm; top ring with engraved indexes.
Dial: brown; stainless steel indexes.
Strap: chocolate brown strap; folding clasp.

ACRON — REF. 17A99D002 S099

Movement: Swiss automatic ETA 2824.
Functions: hours, minutes, seconds; date at 3.
Case: stainless steel; Ø 43mm; top ring with engraved Versace logo and indexes.
Dial: white; stainless steel indexes and details.
Bracelet: stainless steel; butterfly buckle.

LADY ACRON — REF. 78Q01SD98F S111

Movement: Swiss quartz ETA 956.032.
Functions: hours, minutes.
Case: 18K rose gold; Ø 33mm; top ring with 36 white diamonds, average 0.084 carat.
Dial: white mother-of-pearl; two lines of n°81 white diamonds, average 0.22 carat; rose diamond dust.

Strap: pink genuine alligator leather; 18K rose-gold clasp.

LADY ACRON — REF. 78Q70SD498 S001

Movement: Swiss quartz ETA 956.032.
Functions: hours, minutes.
Case: yellow-gold-plated 10 mic; Ø33mm; top ring with applied indexes.
Dial: white mother-of-pearl; 20 white diamond indexes, average 0.054 carat.
Strap: white alligator-patterned calf leather; yellow-gold-plated folding clasp.

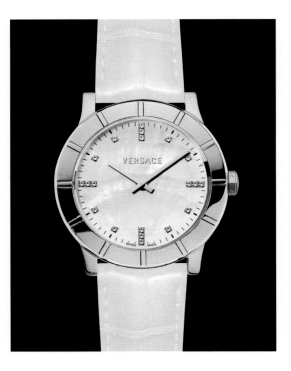

REVE CHRONO — REF. 68C99SD009 S099

Movement: Swiss quartz chronograph ETA 251.471.
Functions: hours, minutes, seconds; date; chronograph.
Case: stainless steel; Ø 40mm; top ring with engraved Versace logo; pushers with blue crystal cabochon.
Dial: matte black; six diamonds, average 0.03 carat.
Bracelet: stainless steel; butterfly buckle.

REVE — REF. 68Q99SD498 S099

Movement: Swiss quartz RONDA 785.
Functions: hours, minutes, seconds; date.
Case: stainless steel; Ø 35mm; top ring with engraved Versace logo.
Dial: white mother-of-pearl; eight diamonds, average 0.04 carat.
Bracelet: stainless steel; butterfly buckle.

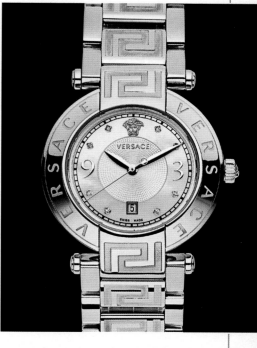

REVE CHRONO — REF. 68C70SD009 S009

Movement: Swiss quartz chronograph ETA 251.471.
Functions: hours, minutes, seconds; date; chronograph.
Case: yellow-gold-plated 10 mic; Ø 40mm; pushers with blue crystal cabochon.
Dial: matte black; six diamonds, average 0.03 carat; and gold-plated finishing.
Strap: black cocco-patterned calf leather; butterfly buckle.

REVE — REF. 68Q71SD498 S001

Movement: Swiss quartz RONDA 785.
Functions: hours, minutes, seconds; date.
Case: yellow-gold-plated 10 mic; Ø 35mm; 102 white diamonds, average 0.53 carat.
Dial: white mother-of-pearl; eight diamonds, average 0.04 carat.
Strap: white genuine python; butterfly buckle.

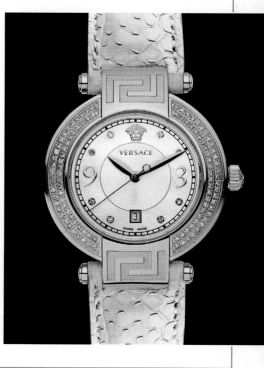

VINCENT BÉRARD

Acclaimed watch restorer turned watchmaker, Vincent Bérard captured collectors' interest in 2005 with an exquisite set of coach clocks based on the four seasons. A year later, Bérard's company joined with the Timex Group and began preparations for a new workshop.

Those plans were brought to life last fall when Vincent Bérard opened its new watchmaking workshop in a renovated farmhouse tucked among the hills and valleys that surround La Chaux-de-Fonds, Switzerland. The 300-year-old building retains much of its rustic charm in a nod to the 18th-century watchmakers who helped establish the Neuchâtel region as the center of the watchmaking industry.

Once inside, however, the aesthetic veil drops to reveal a thoroughly modern facility where the young company develops, decorates and assembles its watches by hand. This expansion allows the brand to boost its annual production to 100 timepieces, ensuring its reputation for both quality and exclusivity.

The idea of transforming a quaint farmhouse into a state-of-the-art center for watchmaking is emblematic of Bérard's creative process, which dictates that function must follow form. "When I create a form, the mechanical aspect has to follow it; the watch movement has to yield to my constraints, reinvent itself afresh to fit the form," he explains.

An example of this concept is the company's signature watch-case, which was inspired by the shape of a column Bérard saw at the Strasbourg Cathedral. "Creating is imagining that a mountain torrent, a Gothic figure, and a watch movement have something to say to each other," he says.

During the celebration to christen its new workshop, Vincent Bérard unveiled the Luvorene 2 and Talismane, two additions to its Fuseau de l'Infini (Spindle of Infinity) collection.

Luvorene 2 expands, quite literally, on the Luvorene introduced in 2008. This larger version (45mm) retains the case's shape, which is round and domed with a bulge on the side where the crown typically resides. The latest interpretation also keeps the movement's distinctive spindle-shaped bridges. That motif is referenced throughout the design, repeated by the hands, indexes and crown.

Transparency is the key to the Luvorene 2, which uses a clear sapphire crystal dial to highlight the visual and mechanical poetry being written beneath. The dial provides a view of the gears, levers and wheels as they interact, controlling the small seconds, moonphase and day-of-the-week indicators. The transparent design also offers an intriguing look at the oscillating balance, cradled neatly in the niche formed by a bowed section of the case.

Vincent Bérard opens two windows on the Luvorene 2's caseback: one for a 10-day power-reserve indicator and another for a "dorsal" small seconds display. When opened, the hinged caseback uncovers the exclusive VB 441 movement and the extensive hand finishing used to decorate its plate and five spindle-shaped bridges.

THIS PAGE
CEO Herbert Gautschi and founder Vincent Bérard.

FACING PAGE
LEFT   This black version of the Luvorene 2 features a 45mm red-gold case with a bump at 3:00 to accommodate the movement's balance.

RIGHT   Windows on the caseback showcase a 10-day power-reserve indicator and "dorsal" small seconds.

Transparency is the key to the Luvorene 2, as it highlights the watch's visual and mechanical poetry.

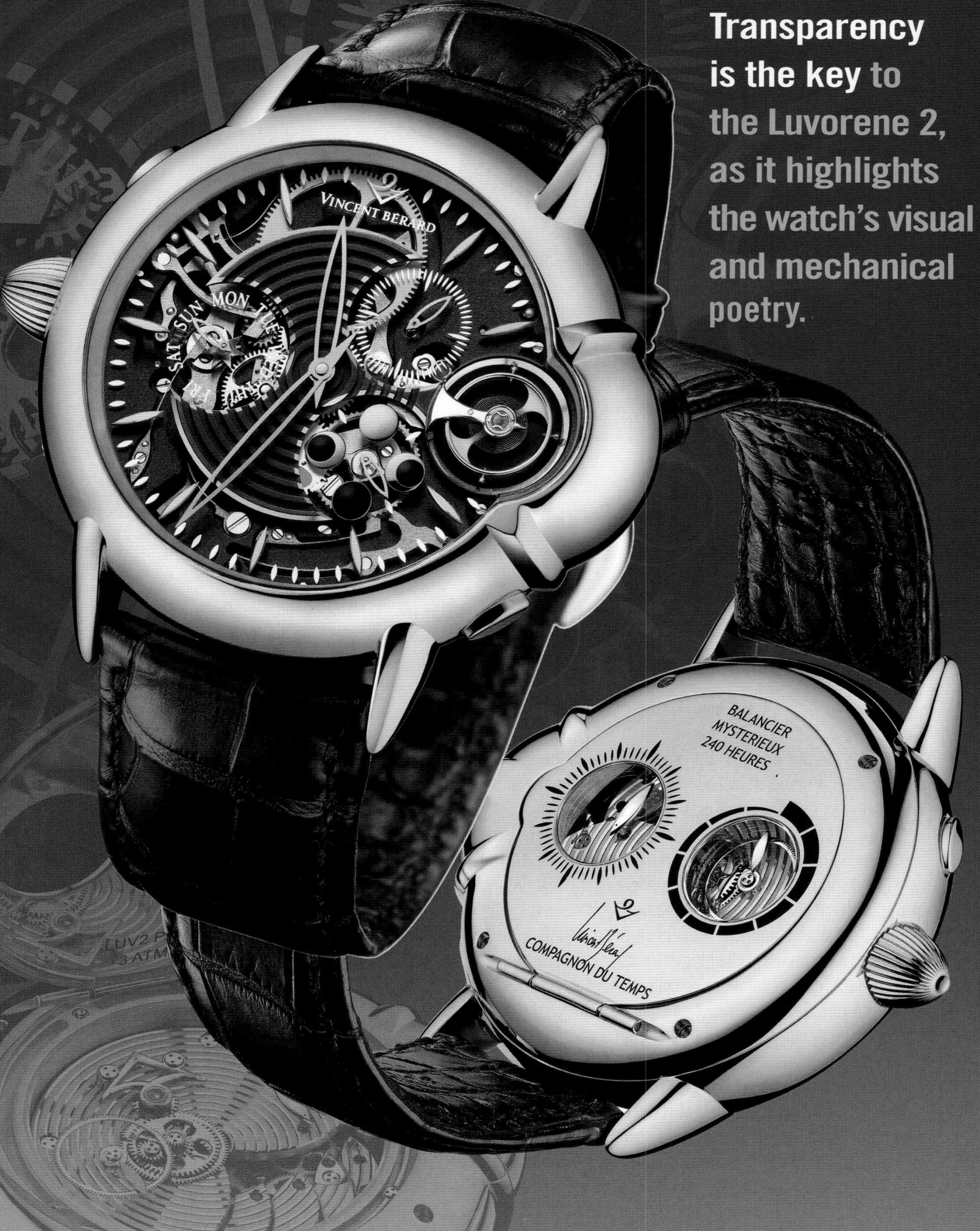
VINCENT BERARD
SAT SUN MON TUE
BALANCIER
MYSTERIEUX
240 HEURES
COMPAGNON DU TEMPS

ABOVE Vincent Bérard offers a 45mm platinum version of the Talismane in a limited edition of eight pieces.

RIGHT Each Talismane pocket watch reflects the spirit of a different season from within a 42mm, colored gold case that is covered with matching lacquer and decorated with precious gems.

Vincent Bérard revisits the seasonal cycle personified by the quartet of coach clocks it unveiled in 2004 for its new Talismane, a luxurious pocket watch intended—as its name suggests—as a lucky charm.

The company will create two versions of the Talismane. The first is an eight-piece limited edition in platinum that could be the Luvorene 2's strapless twin. Its 45mm case features the same elegant details, including the triskelion at the center of the dial, whose three arms embrace the subdials. The triskelion's "gauze"-patterned guilloché repeats on the movement's spindle-shaped bridges, which can be seen when the hinged caseback is raised.

The second Talismane is a collection of four one-of-a-kind pieces, each decorated to reflect a different season. To achieve the effect, each 42mm case is crafted in green, yellow, red or white gold and finished with matching lacquer. Precious stones—emeralds, rubies, yellow and blue sapphires—embellish the appropriate cases and are used for the hour-markers.

The visual homage to Mother Nature continues onto the dial where Vincent Bérard places a gold seasonal symbol atop the balance mechanism. On the opposite side, the movement conjures the appropriate seasonal theme with lacquered and engraved bridges. These meticulous artistic flourishes skillfully demonstrate the company's dedication to the high art of decoration.

Making a bold play for feminine attention, Vincent Bérard flirted with haute couture style with the 2008 introduction of its Luvorene 1 Quatre Saisons, four models for women who appreciate timeless fashion and mechanical beauty.

Like the aforementioned Talismane, this rendering of the Luvorene encompasses four season-inspired models made with colored gold and precious gems. They part company stylistically, however, with the case design. The Luvorene 1 Quatre Saisons trades lacquer and gems for stylized lugs modeled after a crocodile's tooth. Each set is fitted with hand-sewn straps made from sumptuous silk velvet on the outside and black crocodile leather on the inside.

Like the shifting seasons, Vincent Bérard continues to evolve as the brand passes from one stage to the next, carried into the future by the opening of its new workshop and the introduction of its latest inspirations.

The Luvorene 1 Quatre Saisons series includes four models: Spring in green gold with emeralds; Summer in yellow gold with yellow sapphires; Winter in white gold with blue sapphires; and Fall in red gold with rubies. Each comes on a complementing silk velvet strap.

ZANNETTI
HANDMADE WATCHES

The Italian flair for style and sophistication is legendary. **Riccardo Zannetti, the man behind the Zannetti brand, utilizes this sixth sense to the utmost in designing the brand's memorable timepieces.** Constantly going beyond surface qualities, Zannetti watches operate at an astounding technical level—hardly surprising, considering the team that creates each one with painstaking precision.

The Zannetti workshop swarms with a diverse team of watchmakers, engravers, case makers, goldsmiths, jewel setters, chisellers, miniaturists, designers, dial makers, mechanics and engineers, each bringing his or her own distinct skill set to the table. It is this unique mélange that makes each Zannetti watch a mixture of ancient techniques and modern technologies.

The Italian brand recently introduced two new construction techniques, putting the lie to the theory that only the giants of the horological industry perform extensive research and experimentation. The first technique might be called "the new black," as it blackens the movement with a PECVD treatment (plasma-enhanced chemical vapor deposition). The treatment integrates a layer of plasma into the substrate of the metal itself (not just on the surface), which enhances the metal's technical properties as well as adding a striking aesthetic effect. Fittingly, this cutting-edge technique has come to grace the Full Black version of the Racing Edition model in the Time of Drivers collection.

Zannetti blends the most advanced horological techniques with the strictest ideals of quality and originality.

The Full Black version retains the racing-inspired features of the classic collection, but incorporates the PECVD coating, protecting the steel from corrosion and wear.

The brand's other new construction technique is a throwback to a nearly lost art: champlevé enameling. The technique is labor-intensive: the artisan traces a design onto a metal plate, then scoops out the areas within the lines, allowing the enamel to fill the hollows. The artisan then fires the enameled piece as many times as is necessary to achieve the final effect, which seems to glow from within. Zannetti has breathed new life into this time-honored technique with the Champlevé Limited Edition series within the Regent collection. Dials that depict a stylized regatta theme or rising sun allow the option of customer participation; a watch lover can select both the design and the colors of his or her next purchase.

Not just a watchmaking master, Riccardo Zannetti is an intuitive designer and a true artist, passionate about his work as artists are about their creations. Blending the most advanced horological techniques with the strictest ideals of quality and originality, Zannetti focuses on exclusive mechanisms and historical traditions. The meticulous custom work extends not only to the case and dial, but also the smallest details of the hands and movement. The technical and aesthetic refinement of the timepiece is reflected even in post-production; each watch is numbered and registered.

FACING PAGE
Models in Zannetti's Racing Edition feature a cutting-edge metal plasma processing, known as the PECVD (plasma-enhanced chemical vapor deposition). The black finishing creates a striking visual effect, but also imbues the metal with exceptional hardness, with a low coefficient of friction, anti-printing protection and biocompatibility.

THIS PAGE
TOP RIGHT   The Regent Regatta, part of Zannetti's Champlevé Limited Edition, is available with different colors of enamel on the dial.

BOTTOM RIGHT   The Regent Rising Sun, available with different colors on the dial, is created with the time-honored tradition of champlevé enameling.

5-MINUTE REPEATER   REF. REPRA189331

Movement: 5-minute repeater; mechanical automatic-winding; Swiss made; Zannetti re-elaborated; totally skeletonized and hand engraved.

Functions: complicated 5-minute repetition ringing mechanism activated at any moment via a pushpiece and marking hours and its divisions by ringing.

Case: 18K pink-gold three-piece case; new case with redesigned handles; engraved totally by hand; Ø 44mm, thickness: 15mm; hand-personalized pressured closed crown; gold octagonal, engraved pusher at 8 for repeater; antireflective sapphire crystal; pink-gold caseback fixed by four pink-gold screws and with central sapphire crystal opening; water resistant to 2atm.

Dial: skeletonized; completely hand-made pink-gold dart-style hands.

Strap: hand-sewn Louisiana alligator leather; hand-engraved 18K pink-gold ardillon buckle.

Note: the Repeater is created exclusively in compliance with the demands and requests of the client, personalized in every single detail.

IMPERO GLADIATORE CHRONOGRAPH   REF. GLRV115.01

Movement: mechanical automatic-winding Valjoux 7750 caliber; rotor hand-engraved with a Greek-column pattern.

Functions: hours, minutes, small seconds; date at 3; three-counter chronograph: hours at 6, small seconds at 9, minutes at 12.

Case: white-gold three-piece case; Ø 44mm, thickness: 14mm; entirely hand-engraved; antireflective flat sapphire crystal; secret logo; white-gold hexagonal crown and pushers; sapphire crystal exhibition caseback fastened by eight screws, with hand-engraved laurel crown and individual number; water resistant to 3atm.

Dial: white mother-of-pearl dial with blue enameled, geometrical decorations; brushed white-gold flange with engraved quotation "Veni, vidi, vici"; applied pink-gold frames and markers; luminescent, black enameled leaf-style hands.

Strap: crocodile leather; hand-engraved white-gold fold-over clasp.

Also available: with engraved bezel; in palladium-plated 9K white gold with smooth or engraved bezel.

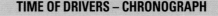

SQUELETTE XL STEEL   REF. SQFA.116.237

Movement: mechanical automatic-winding 2892A2 ETA caliber; Swiss made; personalized for Zannetti; movement and rotor totally skeletonized and hand engraved.

Functions: hours, minutes, seconds.

Case: steel three-piece case; Ø 41mm, thickness: 9.5mm; jointed central attachment; bezel with hand-engraved Arabic numerals; antireflective flat sapphire crystal with engraved logo; hand-personalized screw-down crown; back fastened by five screws, numbered, displaying the movement through a sapphire crystal; water resistant to 3atm.

Dial: hand-engraved white-gold flange; four round applied markers; blue PVD treatment; leaf-style blue steel hands with SuperLumiNova.

Strap: hand-sewn Louisiana alligator leather; Zannetti-personalized steel folding clasp.

Also available: 18K pink-gold three-piece case (inset), with rodiumed movement.

TIME OF DRIVERS – CHRONOGRAPH   REF. TODAV511.337

Movement: automatic-winding chronograph; 7750 Valjoux caliber; Swiss made; Zannetti re-elaborated.

Functions: hours, minutes, seconds; date at 3; three-counter chronograph: hours at 6, small seconds at 9, minutes at 12.

Case: stainless steel three-piece case; Ø 42.5mm, thickness 15.3mm; bezel with hand-engraved and enameled index numbers; hand-personalized pressured closed crown; curved antireflective sapphire crystal with engraved logo; stainless steel caseback fixed by four screws, with central sapphire crystal opening; water resistant to 3atm.

Dial: double-layer natural mother-of-pearl; numerals in bombe applied enamel; leaf-style hands with Super-LumiNova.

Strap: hand-stitched Louisiana alligator leather; and polished steel folding clasp with safety pushbuttons and engraved Zannetti logo.

Also available: white or yellow mother-of-pearl dial.

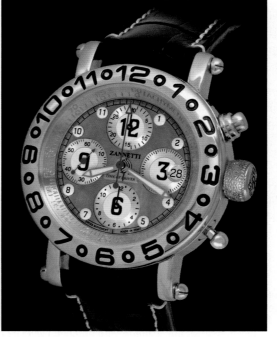

TIME OF DRIVERS–LIMITED EDITION "LUZZAGO - GIULIETTA SPIDER"   REF. TODAV20337AG

Movement: automatic-winding chronograph; 7750 Valjoux caliber; Swiss made; Zannetti re-elaborated.
Functions: hours, minutes, seconds; Pilotís edition steel two-counter chronograph: hours at 6, minutes at 12; date at 3.
Case: stainless steel three-piece case; Ø 42.5mm, thickness: 15.3mm; bezel with hand-engraved index numbers; hand-personalized pressured closed crown; curved antireflective sapphire crystal engraved with logo; stainless steel caseback fixed by four screws, central sapphire crystal opening; water resistant to 3atm.
Dial: totally hand engraved; XL leaf-style hands with SuperLumiNova.
Strap: hand-stitched Louisiana alligator leather; polished steel folding clasp with safety push-buttons and engraved Zannetti logo.
Available dials: Porsche (inset), Jaguar, Fangio, or traditional double-layer full black, blue or argenté.

REGENT TREE ORGY   REF. RTOAD160337

Movement: automatic winding ETA 2834 caliber with day-date; Swiss made; Zannetti re-elaborated; rhodium and perlage plate; Côtes de Géneve; blue steel screws.
Case: steel three-piece case; Ø 42mm, thickness: 10mm; hand-personalized pressured closed crown; antireflective sapphire crystal; stainless steel caseback with decentralized sapphire crystal opening and fixed with five screws; water resistant to 5atm.
Dial: silver colored; translucent colored nuances; hand engraved; yellow-gold-plated alpha hands.
Strap: hand-sewn Louisiana alligator leather; Zannetti-personalized steel deployant buckle.
Note: limited edition of 500 pieces.
Also available: Brain Orgy (inset); Bonsai Orgy.

REGENT FULL SKY   REF. SAA.118.11.137

Movement: automatic-winding ETA; Swiss made; Zannetti re-elaborated; rhodium and perlage plate; Côtes de Géneve; blue steel screws.
Case: stainless steel three-piece case; Ø 42mm, thickness: 10mm; hand-personalized pressured closed crown; sapphire antireflective crystal and engraved logo; stainless steel caseback with decentralized sapphire crystal opening and fixed with five screws; water resistant to 5atm.
Dial: natural mammoth bone; hand-enameled full-sky motif; yellow-gold-plated alpha hands with SuperLumiNova.
Strap: hand-sewn Louisiana alligator leather; Zannetti-personalized stainless steel deployant buckle.
Also available: Rosa Ventorum model (inset).

ZSPORT TITANIUM   REF. ZTV11710037

Movement: automatic-winding chronograph 7750 Valjoux caliber; Swiss made; Zannetti re-elaborated; rhodium and perlage plate; Côtes de Genève.
Functions: two-counter chronograph: hours at 6, minutes at 12; center seconds; date at 3.
Case: titanium three-piece case; sand-blasted finish; 45x44mm, thickness: 145mm; eight pink-gold screws, four on the top of the lugs and four on the sides; titanium and pink-gold screw-down crown, hand personalized; antireflective sapphire crystal; titanium caseback fixed with four screws; water resistant to 10atm.
Dial: multi-layered structure; four screws; printed Arabic numerals.
Strap: hand-sewn Louisiana alligator leather; Zannetti-personalized stainless steel deployant buckle.
Available dials: black or argenté.

ZENITH

SWISS WATCH MANUFACTURE

SINCE 1865

The quintessential expression of that fusion of engineering and art can be seen in the Zero Gravity Tourbillon, a movement whose tourbillon mechanism is secured by a gyroscopic cage, a miniature adaptation of the systems used to stabilize marine chronometers on boats. A wonder to behold, its graceful actions serve a higher purpose than simple vanity by keeping the escapement horizontal and practically eliminating rate fluctuations caused by gravity.

Making all this possible is Zenith's El Primero 8801, a movement with more than 300 parts, roughly half of which are dedicated to the gyroscopic cage. Two years after the caliber debuted in its Defy case, Zenith welcomes the movement into the Academy, its flagship collection dedicated to haute horology.

The hour/minute display abuts a slightly larger opening for the Zero G mechanism, forming a figure eight on the guilloché dial. The symbol, the company says, is something of a good luck charm. The dial also includes a small seconds display positioned diagonally across from the offset crown at 2:00.

Available in white or rose gold, the Academy Zero Gravity Tourbillon's case features a transparent caseback for an unobstructed view of the self-winding movement.

Zenith perpetuates its tradition of aesthetic and mechanical harmony with a new generation of time-pieces **that draw upon the 145-year-old watchmaker's unquenchable passion for precision.**

ABOVE   Jean-Frédéric Dufour was named Zenith's CEO in 2009.

RIGHT   The Zero Gravity Tourbillon movement is now available in Zenith's Academy case, which measures 45mm in diameter and features the crown positioned at 2:00. First introduced in 2008, the El Primero 8801 movement features a gyroscopic cage that keeps the balance horizontal, ensuring better precision than other tourbillons and gyrotourbillons.

Zenith delivers designs that epitomize the meaning of its name.

Rewinding from the futuristic to the historic, Zenith commemorates the 1969 launch of the original El Primero, which remains the only high-frequency mechanical automatic chronograph movement in the world.

The watchmaker features an updated version of the original caliber in a modernized version of the New Vintage 69 case. Its distinctive lines frame a black dial that include three chronograph counters, a date window and a tachymetric scale.

The watchmaker revisits a modern classic with a pair of introductions to the ChronoMaster Open, an award-winning collection characterized by an opening on the dial that provides a detailed view of the escapement.

The first is the ChronoMaster Open Grande Date Sun and Moonphase, its trademark dial aperture mirrored by a second opening—covered by sapphire crystal—that reveals the date display's rotating discs and the hand-finished decoration adorning the movement plate below. The guilloché dial also plays host to a moon- and sunphase display.

The second ChronoMaster model is the Lady Moonphase. Its diamond-set case proffers nearly five carats of sparking evidence to confirm Zenith's skill as master of haute jewelry. To complement the precious design, the watchmakers equipped the case with a column-wheel chronograph that includes day, date, month and moonphase indicators.

With all of its latest inventions, Zenith delivers designs that epitomize the meaning of its name.

TOP   The New Vintage 69 pays tribute to Zenith's legendary El Primero movement, an invention that remains the world's only high-frequency mechanical automatic chronograph.

BOTTOM LEFT   The opening on the left side of the ChronoMaster Open's guilloché dial reveals the El Primero 4047's balance as it vibrates an extraordinary 36,000 times an hour.

BOTTOM RIGHT   More than 500 diamonds decorate the ChronoMaster Lady Moonphase's white-gold case, which includes two pushers to control the column-wheel chronograph.

413

NEW VINTAGE 1969 BLACK DIAL

Movement: El Primero 469 automatic column-wheel chronograph; 50-hour power reserve; 31 jewels; 36,000 vph; 278 components; metal oscillating weight decorated with Côtes de Genève.
Function: hours, minutes; small seconds at 9; date at 4:30; chronograph: central seconds hand, 30-minute counter at 3, 12-hour counter at 6, tachometric scale.
Case: stainless steel; Ø 40mm; curved sapphire crystal with antireflective treatment on both sides; transparent sapphire caseback; water resistant to 5atm.
Dial: glossy black; white counters; hand-mounted applied indexes in rhodium with SuperLumiNova; black sanded hands with white SuperLumiNova SLN C1.
Strap: black alligator; stainless steel tongue buckle.
Note: exclusive, limited and numbered edition of 500 pieces.

CHRONOMASTER OPEN GRANDE DATE EL PRIMERO XXT

Movement: El Primero 4039 automatic chronograph; 50-hour power reserve; 41 jewels; 36,000 vph; 331 components.
Function: hours, minutes; small seconds at 9; chronograph: central seconds hand, 30-minute center at 3; patented three-disc system for grand date at 2.
Case: stainless steel; Ø 45mm; ZENITH pushbuttons and crown; curved sapphire crystal with antireflective treatment on both sides; transparent sapphire caseback; water resistant to 3atm.
Dial: silver; soleille guilloché; hand-mounted applied indexes and numerals; integrated TR90 plates; ruthenium hands; rose-gold power-reserve hand.
Strap: handmade black alligator leather lined with silky Alzavel calfskin; stainless steel ChronoMaster triple-folding buckle with ZENITH Star on cap.
Also available: stainless steel with black dial; rose gold with silver dial; T-version case: 40mm.

CHRONOMASTER LADY MOONPHASE WHITE GOLD PAVE

Movement: El Primero 410 automatic; 50-hour power reserve; 31 jewels; 36,000 vph; 357 components; 22K gold oscillating weight with Grain d'Orge guilloché.
Functions: hours, minutes; small seconds at 9; triple calendar (day, date, month) via windows; chronograph: central seconds hand, 30-minute counter at 3, 12-hour counter at 6.
Case: 18K white gold; Ø 37.5mm; horns and bezel set with 533 round Top Wesselton diamonds (4.88 carats) pure to IF—VVS; curved sapphire crystal with antireflective treatment on both sides; transparent sapphire crystal caseback; water resistant to 3atm.
Dial: white mother-of-pearl; Grain d'Orge guilloché; beveled and decorated calendar windows; hand-mounted indexes and numerals; 18K gold Roman numerals; faceted 18K gold hands.
Strap: handmade white crocodile leather lined with silky Alzavel calfskin; 18K white-gold triple-folding buckle.
Also available: rose-gold case.

CHRONOMASTER OPEN GRANDE DATE SUN AND MOONPHASE

Movement: Open El Primero 4047 automatic column-wheel chronograph; 50-hour power reserve; 41 jewels; 36,000 vph; 332 components; 22K rose-gold oscillating weight with Grain d'Orge pattern.
Functions: hours, minutes; small seconds at 9; three-disc grand date at 2; sun and moonphase indicator at 6; chronograph: central seconds hand, 30-minute counter at 3; sapphire moonphase-disc with gold moon.
Case: 18K rose gold; Ø 45mm; curved sapphire crystal with antireflective treatment on both sides; transparent sapphire crystal caseback; water resistant to 3atm.
Dial: silver; Grain d'Orge guilloché; integrated TR90 segments over the calendar discs; opening at 10 revealing heart of 4047 caliber; hand-mounted applied 18K rose-gold indexes and Roman numeral markers; faceted 18K rose-gold hands.
Strap: handmade black crocodile leather lined with silky Alzavel calfskin; 18K rose-gold triple-folding buckle.
Also available: stainless steel; black dial.

CLASS ELITE MOONPHASE

Movement: Elite 691 automatic; 50-hour power reserve; 27 jewels; 28,800 vph; 228 components; 22K gold oscillating weight with Grain d'Orge guilloché.
Functions: hours, minutes; small seconds at 9; two-disc grand date indicator at 2; moonphase display at 6; stop second mechanism.
Case: 18K rose gold; Ø 40mm; curved sapphire crystal with antireflective treatment on both sides; transparent sapphire caseback; water resistant to 3atm.
Dial: silver; Clou de Paris guilloché; hand-mounted applied indexes and numerals in 18K gold; beveled and decorated date window; faceted 18K rose-gold hands.
Strap: handmade black crocodile leather lined with silky Alzavel calfskin; 18K rose-gold tongue buckle.
Also available: stainless steel case; plain dial and black-nickel-coated numerals and indexes.

CLASS EL PRIMERO MULTICITY TITANE

Movement: Open El Primero 4037 automatic; 351 components; 43 jewels; 36,000 vph; metal oscillating weight with Grain d'Orge guilloché.
Functions: hours, minutes; small seconds at 9; three-disc grand date at 2; 24 time-zone system with day/night indicator; chronograph: central seconds hand, 30-minute counter at 3.
Case: Ti 2 black titanium; Ø 46mm; curved sapphire crystal with antireflective treatment on both sides; transparent sapphire crystal caseback; water resistant to 5atm.
Dial: silver; Grain d'Orge guilloché; open dial revealing the heart of the El Primero; hand-mounted rhodium indexes and numerals; faceted ruthenium hands.
Strap: handmade integrated gray alligator leather; red stitching lined with silky Alzavel calfskin; Ti 2 black titanium triple-folding buckle.

ACADEMY ZERO GRAVITY TOURBILLON

Movement: El Primero 8801 automatic; 50-hour power reserve; 43 jewels; 36,000 vph; 160 components; unique gyroscopic system that ensures perfect horizontal positioning of the regulating organ.
Function: hours and minutes at 11; small seconds at 7:30; self-regulating module Zero-G Tourbillon at 5.
Case: 18K gold; Ø 45mm; unique crown positioning at 2; four antireflective sapphire crystals; 18K gold caseback with two curved sapphire crystals that cover the Zero-G module and caliber; water resistant to 3atm.
Dial: black; Grain d'Orge guilloché; wave guilloché on the small seconds counter; applied 18K gold numerals and indexes; faceted 18K gold hands.
Strap: black crocodile leather lined with silky Alzavel calfskin; 18K gold triple-folding buckle.
Note: individually numbered edition.
Also available: silver dial.

CALIBER 135

Movement: Elite 689 automatic; COSC certified; 50-hour power reserve; 31 jewels; 28,800 vph; 146 components; 22K gold oscillating weight with Côtes de Genève guilloché.
Function: hours, minutes; small seconds at 6.
Case: 18K rose gold; Ø 40mm; curved sapphire crystal with antireflective treatment on both sides; transparent sapphire crystal caseback; water resistant to 3atm.
Dial: brown; sunray; hand-mounted 18K gold indexes; faceted 18K rose-gold hands.
Strap: handmade brown crocodile leather lined with silky Alzavel calfskin; 18K rose-gold tongue buckle.
Note: exclusive, limited and numbered edition of 100 pieces.

Brand Directory

A. LANGE & SÖHNE
Altenberger Strasse 15
01768 Glashütte
Germany
Tel: 49 35053 440
USA: 310 205 5555

ALAIN SILBERSTEIN
200 Boulevard Saint-Germain
75007 Paris, France
USA: 310 205 5555

ALPINA
8 Chemin de la Galaise
1228 Plan-les-Ouates, Geneva
Switzerland
Tel: 41 22 860 87 40
USA: 877 619 2824

AUDEMARS PIGUET
1348 Le Brassus, Switzerland
Tel: 41 21 845 14 00
USA: 212 688 6644

B.R.M
2 Impasse de l'Aubette
ZAC des Aulnaies
95420 Magny-en-Vexin, France
Tel: 33 1 61 02 00 25
USA: 214 231 0144

BELL & ROSS
350 Rue Saint Honoré
75001 Paris, France
Tel: 33 1 42 86 61 27
USA: 203 604 6840

BERTOLUCCI
Route des Acacias 43
1211 Geneva 26, Switzerland
Tel: 41 22 756 95 00
USA: 212 204 0580

BLANCPAIN
Le Rocher 12
1348 Le Brassus
Switzerland
Tel: 41 21 796 36 36
USA: 201 271 1400

BOUCHERON
20 Rue de la Paix
75002 Paris, France
Tel: 33 1 42 44 42 44
USA: 866 983 3747

BOVET FLEURIER SA
9 Rue Ami-Lévrier
1211 Geneva 1
Switzerland
Tel: 41 22 731 46 38
USA: 305 502 9001

BREGUET
1344 L'Abbaye
Switzerland
Tel: 41 21 841 90 90
USA: 866 458 7488

CARL F. BUCHERER
1805 South Metro Parkway
Dayton, OH 45459, USA
Tel: 800 395 4306

CARTIER SA
Boulevard James-Fazy 8
1201 Geneva, Switzerland
Tel: 41 22 721 24 00
USA: 212 355 6444

CHANEL
25 Place du Marché St. Honoré
75001 Paris, France
Tel: 33 1 55 35 50 00
USA: 212 688 5055

CHOPARD
Rue de Veyrot 8
1217 Meyrin-Geneva 2
Switzerland
Tel: 41 22 719 31 91
USA: 212 821 0300

CLERC
Rue de Lausanne 37A
1201 Geneva, Switzerland
Tel: 41 22 716 25 50
USA: 212 397 1662

CONCORD
MGI Luxury Group SA
Rue de Nidau 35
2501 Bienne, Switzerland
Tel: 41 32 329 34 00
USA: 800 547 4073

CORUM SA
Rue du petit Château 1
2301 La Chaux-de-Fonds
Switzerland
Tel: 41 32 967 06 70
USA: 949 788 6200

CUERVO Y SOBRINOS
Via Cantonale 54
6825 Capolago
Switzerland
Tel: 41 91 921 27 73
USA: 561 330 0088

DE GRISOGONO
176 bis Route de St. Julien
1228 Plan-les-Ouates
Switzerland
Tel: 41 22 817 81 00
USA: 212 439 4240

DIOR HORLOGERIE
44 Rue François 1er
75008 Paris, France
Tel: 33 1 40 73 54 44
USA: 866 675 2078

EBEL
MGI Luxury Group
113 Rue de la Paix
2300 La Chaux-de-Fonds
Switzerland
Tel: 41 32 912 31 23
USA: 800 920 3153

ETERNA
Schützengasse 46
2540 Grenchen
Switzerland
Tel: 41 32 654 72 11
USA: 212 308 1786

FRANC VILA
6 Grand Rue
1204 Geneva
Switzerland
Tel: 41 22 317 07 27
USA: 305 517 7427

FRÉDÉRIQUE CONSTANT SA
Chemin du Champ des Filles 32
1228 Plan-les-Ouates, Geneva
Switzerland
Tel: 41 22 860 04 40
USA: 877 619 2824

GREUBEL FORSEY
Eplatures-Grise 16
CP 670
2301 La Chaux-de-Fonds
Switzerland
Tel: 41 32 751 71 76
USA: 310 205 5555

GUY ELLIA
21 Rue de la Paix
75002 Paris, France
Tel: 33 1 53 30 25 25
USA: 212 888 0505

H. MOSER & CIE.
Rundbuckstrasse 10
8212 Neuhausen am Rheinfall
Switzerland
Tel: 41 52 674 00 50
USA: 561 330 0088

HERMÈS
55 East 59th Street
New York, NY 10022, USA
Tel: 212 759 7585

HUBLOT
Chemin de la Vuarpilliére 33
CP 2464
1260 Nyon 2, Switzerland
Tel: 41 22 990 90 00
USA: 800 536 0636

IWC
Baumgartenstrasse 15
8201 Schaffhausen
Switzerland
Tel: 41 52 635 62 37
USA: 212 891 2460

JACOB & CO.
Richelien 39
1290 Versoix
Switzerland
Tel: 41 22 775 33 33
USA: 212 888 2330

LEVIEV
31 Old Bond Street
London W1S4QH
United Kingdom
Tel: 44 20 7493 3333
USA: 212 763 5333

LONGINES
2610 Saint-Imier
Switzerland
Tel: 41 32 942 54 25
USA: 201 271 1400

LOUIS MOINET
Rue de Temple 1
CP 28
2072 Saint-Blaise, Switzerland
Tel: 41 32 753 68 14
USA: 919 521 5610

MCT
Rue du Coq d'Inde 24
2000 Neuchatel, Switzerland
Tel: 41 22 301 49 67
USA: 310 205 5555

MONTBLANC MONTRE
Hellgrundweg 100
22525 Hamburg, Germany
Tel: 49 40 84 001 0
USA: 908 508 2334

MOVADO
MGI Luxury Group SA
Rue de Nidau 35
2501 Bienne, Switzerland
Tel: 41 32 329 34 00
USA: 800 810 2311

PANERAI
Via Ludovico di Breme 44/45
20156 Milan, Italy
Tel: 39 02 363138
USA: 212 888 8788

PATEK PHILIPPE
Chemin du Pont du Centenaire 141
1228 Plan-les-Ouates
Switzerland
Tel: 41 22 884 20 20
USA: 212 218 1272

PIAGET
37 Chemin du Champ-des-Filles
1228 Plan-les-Ouates
Switzerland
Tel: 41 22 884 48 44
USA: 212 355 6444

PORSCHE DESIGN
Schützengasse 46
2540 Grenchen
Switzerland
Tel: 41 32 654 72 11
USA: 212 308 1786

RALPH LAUREN
8 Chemin de Blandonnet
1214 Vernier Geneva
Switzerland
Tel: 41 22 595 59 00
USA: 212 434 8000

RAYMOND WEIL SA
Avenue Eugène-Lance 36-38
1211 Geneva 26
Switzerland
Tel: 41 22 884 00 55
USA: 212 355 3350

RICHARD MILLE
11 rue du Jura
2345 Les Breuleux Jura
Switzerland
Tel: 41 32 959 43 53
USA: 310 205 5555

ROLEX
Rue François Dussaud 3-7
1211 Geneva 24
Switzerland
Tel: 41 22 302 22 00
USA: 212 758 7700

SALVATORE FERRAGAMO
Vertime SA
Via Cantonale-Galleria 1
6928 Manno, Switzerland
Tel: 41 91 610 87 00
USA: 203 523 7249

TAG HEUER
Louis-Joseph Chevrolet 6A
2300 La Chaux-de-Fonds
Switzerland
Tel: 41 32 919 80 00
USA: 973 467 1890

ULYSSE NARDIN
3 Rue du Jardin
2400 Le Locle
Switzerland
Tel: 41 32 930 74 00
USA: 561 988 8600

URWERK
34 rue des Noirettes
1227 Carouge-Geneva
Switzerland
Tel: 41 21 900 20 25
USA: 310 205 5555

VACHERON CONSTANTIN
Rue des Moulins 1
1204 Geneva, Switzerland
Tel: 41 22 930 20 02
USA: 212 713 0707

VALENTINO
Vertime SA
Via Cantonale-Galleria 1
6928 Manno, Switzerland
Tel: 41 91 610 87 00
USA: 203 523 7263

VERSACE
Vertime SA
Via Cantonale-Galleria 1
6928 Manno, Switzerland
Tel: 41 91 610 87 00
USA: 203 523 7263

VINCENT BÉRARD
Boulevard des Endroits 24
2300 La Chaux-de-Fonds
Switzerland
Tel: 41 32 926 16 46
USA: 310 205 5555

ZANNETTI
Via Monte d'Oro 19
00186 Rome, Italy
Tel: 39 06 68 192 566

ZENITH
2400 Le Locle
Switzerland
Tel: 41 32 930 62 62
USA: 973 467 1890